D1544499

WORKING VERSE IN VICTORIAN SCOTLAND

Working Verse in Victorian Scotland

Poetry, Press, Community

KIRSTIE BLAIR

OXFORD
UNIVERSITY PRESS

OXFORD
UNIVERSITY PRESS

Great Clarendon Street, Oxford, OX2 6DP,
United Kingdom

Oxford University Press is a department of the University of Oxford.
It furthers the University's objective of excellence in research, scholarship,
and education by publishing worldwide. Oxford is a registered trade mark of
Oxford University Press in the UK and in certain other countries

First Edition published in 2019

Impression: 1

Published in the United States of America by Oxford University Press
198 Madison Avenue, New York, NY 10016, United States of America

British Library Cataloguing in Publication Data
Data available

Library of Congress Control Number: 2019931474

ISBN 978–0–19–884379–5

Printed and bound by
CPI Group (UK) Ltd, Croydon, CR0 4YY

Acknowledgements

The research for this book was generously supported by various funders. Initial scoping research into the Dundee press was funded by the Carnegie Trust, with a Curran Fellowship from the Research Society for Victorian Periodicals enabling investigation into local newspapers and archives across Scotland. A Leverhulme Trust Research Fellowship funded the completion of the research and time to write. I am extremely grateful to these funding bodies for their assistance. I also owe a great deal to helpful librarians and archivists, particularly the staff of the National Library of Scotland, the Mitchell Library in Glasgow, Dundee Central Library, and libraries and local history centres in Hamilton, Airdrie, Ayr, Linlithgow, Stirling, and Dumfries.

Moving into Scottish studies was intimidating, but far less so because of the support and encouragement of colleagues in the field at Stirling, Glasgow, and Strathclyde, particularly Scott Hames, David Goldie, Eleanor Bell, and many others. Working with Gerry Carruthers, Catriona MacDonald, Michael Shaw, and Honor Rieley on the 'People's Voice' project, a Carnegie Collaborative Grant investigating Scottish political poetry and song, gave new dimensions to my research and constantly informed the content and arguments of this book. Likewise, working with PhD students Lauren Weiss, Erin Farley, and Elizabeth Adams has deepened my understanding of Victorian Scotland and British working-class culture. The staff and committee members of the Association of Scottish Literary Studies (ASLS), which published the companion anthology to this book, *The Poets of the People's Journal*, have also been unfailingly helpful and welcoming. Thanks are also due to the members of the public who have listened to me talk about 'their' local poets on various occasions in the last few years, and who have contacted me with family stories and information. Their interest has helped to foster mine.

In the wider context of Victorian studies, I have again benefited from the advice and collegiality of colleagues and friends in Victorian poetry studies and beyond. These are too many to name, but I owe especial debts to Alison Chapman, Linda Hughes, Florence Boos, Charles LaPorte, Meredith Martin, Joshua King, and especially Jason Rudy, who shared material from his own new monograph and generously commented on a chapter of this study. Dale Townshend and Mike Sanders also read draft chapters and offered very helpful feedback. During the final stages of writing, I worked on a new project and grant application with Mike and Oliver Betts: their enthusiasm and our many conversations about working-class literature and culture were inspiring.

The collegiality of staff in English, History, Languages and Media studies at Stirling and Strathclyde has helped to keep me inspired by research, and the friendship and support of Rachel Smith, Bryony Randall, Elizabeth Anderson, Karen Boyle, Katie Halsey, and many other fellow academics in Glasgow and further afield, has been unfailingly helpful. Fergus and Elsa Creasy have been more important than anyone in ensuring that I took enough time away from work, and Corinna and Philip Creasy, Mary Blair, and Bonnie Soroke were always there to help care for them. Above all, none of this research could have been carried out without Matthew Creasy.

NOTE ON REFERENCES

The hard copy, microfilm or bound volumes of newspapers consulted for this study were not always paginated, or, when collected into volumes, had been repaginated. Where a page number is not given for a newspaper article or poem, this is because it would only be relevant if the reader consulted exactly the same issue I used. In such cases I have left out page numbers to avoid confusion.

Contents

Introduction

In 1883, W. C. Sturoc, a self-made lawyer, politician, Scottish emigrant, and the 'Bard of Sunapee', New Hampshire, sat down to write a letter to his friends in his childhood home, Arbroath, a historic town on the north-east coast of Scotland. In it, he enclosed a poem on Arbroath, deliberately composed on the same day and hour that J. M. McBain was delivering a lecture on 'Arbroath Poets and Their Songs' in the town, sponsored by the Arbroath Literary Club. It opened:

> However our footsteps may wander,
> Or distant the lands that we roam,
> That weather-beat pile, standing yonder,
> Still beckons us back to our home.[1]

'Although I would like to be as cosmopolitan as any one', Sturoc wrote,

> I cannot but confess that I have considerable interest and pride in Mr McBain's intelligent efforts to establish for old Aberbrothock a claim to be regarded as the home and birthplace of poets and poetry, and perhaps to have given rise to a few singable songs.[2]

Sturoc's letter and poem, with a recommended air for singing his verses, were published alongside the lecture, which appeared as a booklet and was also reprinted in a local newspaper, the *Arbroath Guide*. They were accompanied by the Chairman's thanks to McBain, which described the evening as 'a historical occasion'. 'All over the globe', he continued, 'wherever the "Guide" circulated, the report of this meeting would be read with interest by true sons of St Tammas'.[3] Descriptions of worthy nineteenth-century poets in the lecture include George C. Smart, railway clerk (published as 'T. N. D.' in the Dundee press); Thomas Watson, weaver and house-painter (poems widespread across the Glasgow and British press, in ' "Howitt's Journal", "Tait's Magazine", "Cassell's Paper", the "Glasgow Citizen" and other periodicals'; John Christie, who worked in a sawmill (published in the local press as 'Thomas Kydd'); and two poets who appear briefly later in this book, David Carnegie and G. W. Donald.[4]

---

[1] 'Aberbrothock's Historic Old Walls' (Air: 'Auld Scotia, the Gem of the Ocean'), in J. McBain, Arbroath Poets and Their Songs: A Lecture, Delivered in the Public Hall, Arbroath, on 6 March 1883, under the Auspices of the Arbroath Literary Club (Arbroath: T. Buncle, n.d. [1883]), p.56.

[2] McBain, p.55.

[3] Reported in McBain, p.52. 'St Tammas' is a nickname for Arbroath, from the Abbey of St Thomas.

[4] Ibid., pp.16, 28, 40.

All these writers, including Sturoc, were thought worthy of commemoration, celebration and anthologizing in the 1880s and into the early twentieth century. None have been discussed since. The reason, we might think, is obvious: if their poetry is all of the standard of Sturoc's opening stanza, it is not worth remembering, since it is banal, clichéd, and utterly conventional. As this book argues, however, there is no meaningful relationship between twenty-first century standards of 'good' poetry (as upheld, for instance, by academics, reviewers, editors of literary magazines), and Victorian popular poetics. Sturoc is not attempting to write an innovative, original, mould-breaking, or 'authentic' poem, one that will reward close readers with ever-new insights into the interaction of language and form.[5] He is consciously demonstrating his ability to conform to generic norms by producing a poem that follows conventions, conventions his readers will recognize. He is also, of course, writing verses that are intended to be sung, and that, in listing an 'Air' (as do many of the poems cited in this book), expect that a reader will hear the words to the familiar music of a known tune. Conventionality in form and content does not mean that these verses are devoid of affective power. The affect of 'Aberbrothock's Historic Old Walls' rests on shared cultural norms, shared language, shared sentiment, and a shared understanding of what a poem produced by an emigrant writer for this kind of occasion ought to look like. Many of the poems discussed here are similarly conventional, though I do also seek to show that poets can have more complex and sophisticated engagements with these conventions.

Working Verse in Victorian Scotland strongly relates to two important recent studies: Michael C. Cohen's *The Social Lives of Poems in Nineteenth-Century America*, and Jason Rudy's *Imagined Homelands: British Poetry in the Colonies*. Cohen similarly notes that a 'large majority of nineteenth-century poems seem unable to hold up to the rigors' of close reading, 'the careful analysis of formal, complex uses of language', and suggests a need to find 'alternative ways of making meaning' from poetry.[6] As he observes:

> People could use poems in ways that may now seem strange and to ends that may now seem naïve, but the repertoire of uses made poetry central to public culture—or, to put the point more strongly, it made poetry constitutive of public culture.[7]

Rudy, focusing on colonial poetry, argues that its dismissal as 'verse' ignores its ubiquity and its importance as a 'fundamentally political' genre in framing ideas of homeland, belonging, and place. Emigrant writers like Sturoc, he argues 'carried

---

[5] Authenticity is a loaded concept, especially in considering working-class writers. For an important brief discussion, see Jacques Rancière, *Proletarian Nights: The Workers' Dream in Nineteenth-Century France*, trans. John Drury, intro. Donald Reid (London: Verso, 2012 (first published 1989)), p.x. I agree in this study with Stuart Hall's comment, in his seminal essay 'Notes on Deconstructing "the Popular"' that 'There is no separate, autonomous, "authentic" layer of working-class culture to be found'. In Raphael Samuel, ed. *People's History and Socialist Theory* (London: Routledge, 1981), pp.227–41, 229.

[6] Michael C. Cohen, *The Social Lives of Poems in Nineteenth-Century America* (Philadelphia, PA: University of Pennsylvania Press, 2015), p.7.

[7] Ibid., p.186.

poetry within them, in their hearts, their minds, and their blood'.[8] As in both these studies, I am concerned here with the *work*—in terms of efforts to achieve particular ends—that poems did in public spaces. Sturoc's poem and McBain's lecture are excellent examples of this. Why does a successful lawyer, who had educated himself against the odds and escaped difficult economic circumstances in Scotland, sit down in his sixties to write about and post a poem to his hometown, thousands of miles away? Why did he first *start* writing poetry, as a young working man in the Scotland of the 1840s? What is at stake in an American Scottish emigrant representing himself as part of a community of 'local' Scottish poets, and in Sturoc's use (and rejection) of 'cosmopolitan' as a category?[9] Why *are* there so many poets in Arbroath, and is this exceptional or not? Why does it matter to contemporaries that these poets are described and recorded in print? What did the town's Literary Society do, and who belonged to it? Why would local newspapers devote so much space to a lecture on poetry? Why did so many Victorian newspapers and periodicals publish poems by writers like Sturoc, Smart, and Watson, and how did these men choose where to send their poems?

This one instance raises large questions of nationality and belonging, and on the roles of Victorian print culture and associational culture—from local to global—in fostering these. Above all, it raises questions about the place and purpose of poetry, questions which ripple out from the 'public hall' in Arbroath to North-East Scotland, the rest of Scotland, on throughout Britain, and, as Rudy has shown, to the English-speaking colonies and communities around the Victorian world. This book, in part, sets out to answer these questions, even while it continually raises new ones. In British Victorian studies, and especially within Scottish studies, the kind of poetry I examine here was profoundly neglected for most of the twentieth and into the twenty-first century, and has only recently attracted renewed scholarly attention.[10] We have often failed to recognize, as this book demonstrates, both how important and influential this culture of local poetic production was, as a

---

[8] Jason Rudy, *Imagined Homelands: British Poetry in the Colonies* (Baltimore, MD: Johns Hopkins University Press, 2017), pp.2, 10, and *passim*.

[9] Sturoc is the only poet in this study who described himself as cosmopolitan. As a term, 'cosmopolitan' has received considerable critical attention: for an example, see the special issue of *Victorian Literature and Culture* 38 (2010) on 'Victorian Cosmopolitanisms', ed. Tanya Agathocleous and Jason R. Rudy.

[10] Besides those works already cited, many recent publications in Victorian poetry include a reassessment of non-canonical poets and poems, and consider the work of poetry within communities and in popular publication venues, especially periodicals. Of particular significance to my work for this book are Mike Sanders, *The Poetry of Chartism: Aesthetics, Politics, History* (Cambridge: Cambridge University Press, 2009); F. E. Gray's *Christian and Lyric Tradition in Victorian Women's Poetry* (London: Routledge, 2010), for its study of popular devotional poetics (and Gray's recent study of poetry and journalism, cited in Chapter 1); Fabienne Moine's *Women Poets in the Victorian Era: Cultural Practices and Nature Poetry* (London: Routledge, 2015), for her similar consideration of neglected popular poems by genre; Alison Chapman's *Networking the Nation: British and American Women's Poetry and Italy, 1840–1870* (Oxford: Oxford University Press, 2015), for its investigation of how poetic networks and communities operate; and Kirsten Harris's *Walt Whitman and British Socialism: The Love of Comrades* (New York: Routledge, 2016), for its focus on the significance of poetry to late-century socialism.

major component of 'Victorian literature' and in the everyday lives of writers and readers; and how relevant it might be to our twenty-first-century concerns. George C. Smart of Arbroath, for example, is almost certainly the author of 'The Night Signalman', a poem about the exhausting labour of watching the signal wires and a resulting fatal train accident, which reflects on the unsustainable and unhealthy relationship between unsleeping new technologies and the human body, issues discussed further in Chapter 4.[11] Thomas Watson of Arbroath wrote 'The Superseded Man', published in 1851 in the *Glasgow Citizen*, which focuses on workers out of employment due to technological advances and on the failure of the rich (and the state) to recognize and support them:

> Tell me now, ye men of iron,
> To this evil deaf or blind,
> What avails your vaunted progress
> To the wretch you leave behind?[12]

Resorting to begging for backbreaking work as a navvy, the 'superseded man' sees the contractor 'shake his head and smile', 'For he has his choice of thousands/From prolific Sister Isle'; in the form of Irish Catholics. 'Belated' and 'bewildered' by his situation, he blames both new industries and cheap, readily available immigrant labour for his plight. Watson's argument is that working-class men who feel left behind by progress and doomed to poverty require our understanding and sympathy, not simply from charitable impulses, but because they are politically dangerous to the status quo. Smart's point is that treating workers like machines will have a direct impact on the well-being of all classes in society. And Sturoc's point is that in a networked world where new technologies enable almost instantaneous communication, a writer over a thousand miles from 'home' will still be intimately aware of, and connected to, events in his former community, even if he is no longer physically present. If we are seeking poems which will speak to students in the twenty-first-century classroom, or to contemporary audiences outside higher education, the immediacy of works like these should not be ignored.

Recognizing the inherent interest of these poems for us in historical and political terms, and recovering the specific contexts to which they spoke, however, should not mean forgetting that these writers deliberately chose poetry as a medium. As I discuss throughout this book, there are cultural, social, political, personal, formal, and indeed practical reasons why writers like Smart and Watson produced poems rather than prose. 'Poetry' is, of course, a loaded term, because of its use as a category of value by the gatekeepers of culture in the nineteenth century, and because it is implicitly separated, in our current usage, from 'song'. This separation is very seldom evident in Victorian popular verse culture. Whether a set of verses appear in print with a stated tune or not, they are almost always *both* a 'poem' and a 'song',

---

[11] T. N. D., 'The Night Signalman', *People's Friend*, 5 May 1875. Reprinted in *The Poets of the People's Journal: Newspaper Poetry in Victorian Scotland* (Glasgow: ASLS, 2016), pp.194–6. At the time of editing this anthology I had not identified 'T. N. D., Dundee' with George Smart of Arbroath.

[12] T. Watson, Arbroath, 'The Superseded Man', *Glasgow Citizen*, 25 January 1851, p.1. Reprinted in Thomas Watson, *The Rhymer's Family* (Arbroath: Kennedy & Ramsay, 1851), p.29.

since any piece of verse could be, and usually was, set to an old or new tune. As Cohen argues, '*in the nineteenth-century, poetry is not a genre*' (his italics), in that 'poetry' is considered as an abstraction, usually separate from the ways in which poems and songs operate in varying contexts.[13] In this book, 'verse culture' is a more accurate description of the various kinds of text that I examine, and the description I would prefer. But given the historical freight that these terms carry, to use 'verse' throughout rather than 'poetry', might imply an assessment of literary worth: here, I interpret 'poetry' in the most capacious sense, in terms of all written texts in verse, including texts presented as 'song', while also investigating its use as an abstract category in the particular contexts I examine. Likewise, while recognizing that many of the writers cited in this study would have hesitated to claim the weighty title of 'poet', a poet in this book is defined as anyone who writes a poem. Pierre Bourdieu's suggestion that a 'work of art is an object which exists as such only by virtue of the (collective) belief which knows and acknowledges it as a work of art' is important in relation to the poetry I consider, since the question as to whether a poem like Sturoc's is 'a work of art' or even 'poetry' is relational: it depends on the collective.[14] The Arbroath Literary Society thought it was. The fellows of an Oxford college in 1883 might have disagreed. Since we—where by 'we' I mean scholars of Victorian literature and culture—have more often than not taken the views of Oxford, Cambridge, London, and the literary worlds associated with them as representative, I will argue here that it is time to consider the opinions of Arbroath.

The 'social conditions of the production of a set of objects socially constituted as works of *art*, i.e. the conditions of production of the field of social agents (e.g. museums, galleries, academies, etc.)', in Bourdieu's phrasing, were in many respects the same in 1880s London as at the peripheries, the margins.[15] But in other respects they were different. One of these differences relates, in this book, to the conditions of the production of poetry in Scotland and by Scots, at home and abroad. As I discuss in the opening of Chapter 1, Scottish Victorian commentators tended to claim that these were distinctive, in that Scotland offered superior social conditions for particular poetic cultures to flourish; especially that of 'peasant', labouring-class, or working-class poetry. It was not that Scottish poetry—other than in its use of Scots or Gaelic—was necessarily different in form and content from English poetry, this argument runs, it was that more of it was produced and appreciated by 'the people', as opposed to members of elite or privileged society. What was distinctive about Scottish poetry, then, was the overlap between 'Scottish poetry' and 'working-class poetry'. This is an argument that I support in this book, to some extent. There is absolutely no doubt that Victorian Scotland had an extraordinarily rich and diverse culture of poetry written by working men and women. Yet emerging research suggests that there were also rich and diverse cultures of local

---

[13] Cohen, p.13.

[14] Pierre Bourdieu, *The Field of Cultural Production*, ed. and intro by Randal Johnson (Cambridge: Polity Press, 1993), p.35.

[15] Ibid., p.37.

poetry in locations around the English-speaking world.[16] This book uses Scotland as a particular model for the kinds of work done by poetry and poetics, but its conclusions should be read as transferable. The forms and formations, habits and patterns discussed here are applicable—with due attention to differences as well as similarities—to other cultures at the 'periphery', whether in Northern England, India, South Africa, or New Hampshire.

I set out here to offer a substantial intervention, within the broad field of Victorian studies, in four intersecting areas: popular poetic cultures centred on locality; newspaper history and culture (discussed further in Chapter 1); working-class poetry; and Scottish literature in the Victorian period. This last means that this study is also a significant intervention in Scottish studies, with clear revisionary aims. To take this aspect of my arguments first, Victorian Scottish literature has attracted very little critical attention until recently, with the majority of publications in Scottish literary studies, from the eighteenth century to the twenty-first, centred on the Romantic period or on the early twentieth-century Scottish Renaissance and beyond. There are only two full-length monographs on Scottish Victorian literature, both concentrating on fiction and prose: William Donaldson's seminal *Popular Literature in Victorian Scotland* and Andrew Nash's revisionary study *Kailyard and Literature*.[17] Scottish Victorian writers, including some poets (Robert Louis Stevenson, W. E. Aytoun, the 'spasmodic' poet Alexander Smith, Ellen Johnston, John Davidson, James Thomson) have received some attention as individuals or as part of broader trends in Victorian literature or poetics. A focus on individual writers of distinction, however, and on writers who often operated partly or primarily outside Scotland, has obscured the sense of a distinctive Scottish verse culture. Rather than surveying all Scottish poets of this period, I focus on Scottish *popular* poetics, and largely on poets who remained in, and operated via, local Scottish contexts.

Throughout the twentieth century and into the twenty-first, critical views of Victorian Scottish literature, and especially Scottish popular poetry, tended to be resoundingly negative. Hugh MacDiarmid's highly self-interested condemnation of Scottish Victorian poetics as consisting of 'the mindless vulgarities of parochial poetasters', or 'dreadful examples of the excesses of self-parody into which imitative post-Burnsianism has been forced under conditions of progressive Anglicisation'—a condemnation which is in large part based on distaste for working-class writers and readers—has, quite remarkably, frequently been treated as a statement of fact.[18] Critics have tended to follow his lead in condemning popular Scottish Victorian writers for failing to live up to an imagined ideal of Scottish national literature and thus, in Alan Riach's words, 'couthily submitting to the status quo: Anglocentric

---

[16] As selective examples, see Rudy's Imagined Homelands, cited above, and Mary Ellis Gibson's *Indian Angles: English Verse in Colonial India from Jones to Tagore* (Ohio, OH: Ohio University Press, 2011).

[17] Donaldson, *Popular Literature in Victorian Scotland: Language, Fiction and the Press* (Aberdeen: Aberdeen University Press, 1986). Andrew Nash, *Kailyard and Literature* (Amsterdam: Rodopi, 2007).

[18] Hugh MacDiarmid, *Contemporary Scottish Studies*, ed. Alan Riach (Manchester: Carcanet, 2005), pp.42, 49. These essays were originally published as polemical articles between 1925 and 1927.

hegemony, explicitly in politics, implicitly in culture'.[19] Duncan Glen notes that the Victorian period 'has been seen as the nadir of Scottish poetry', backing this up with his comment that Scots poets in this period were 'utterly provincial—of the kailyard—and of low ambition'.[20] Roderick Watson suggests that Victorian Scottish poetry 'seems to have completely lost its way' and describes it as in a 'desperate plight'.[21] Douglas Gifford, while acknowledging the value and import- ance of several working-class poets of this era, comments:

> It is true that there was a cultural dearth in the 1840s and '50s, and that there was then a risk that Scottish writing, as a literature examining Scottish issues in an indigenous and mature way, could have disappeared, leaving the field to romanticism and senti- mentalization—an external distortion and internal escapism which certainly continued to flourish . . . [T]here is no denying that a huge amount of literary production in the century was tainted with distortion or avoidance of the real social and political condi- tions and issues, from Highland clearance and ghastly urbanization to imperial expan- sion and home politics.[22]

As recently as 2012, Michael Fry described the Victorian period in Scotland as a 'ghastly literary phase', and felt justified in asking, 'What, precisely was it, then, that failed in the Scottish literature of the Victorian era?'[23]

As will become clear, my research into Scottish popular poetry sharply contra- dicts this narrative of failure, impotence, and a lack of ambition. Most of the materials featured in this book have never been read by scholars of Scottish literature. Gifford and Hazel Hynd, writing on the nineteenth century, comment on 'the need for modern literary historians to explore neglected sources of local poetry, especially the work of the many self-taught "autodidact" poets who remained within their localities and wrote for their local newspapers', and William Findlay also observes that 'the extent and nature of the poetry published in the same popu- lar medium' (the newspaper press), 'has still to be examined. Also awaiting thor- ough investigation are the many small books of locally published local poetry'.[24] But these suggestions—from 1988 and 2002—were not acted on until now. (This daunting research is, of course, made much more feasible by the existence of the internet and by searchable newspaper and periodical databases.) It is not surprising that previous critics generally reached such negative conclusions on 'local' Scottish Victorian poetry, based on reading a limited selection available by known poets and in Victorian anthologies. Studying the newspaper poetry columns, and other

---

[19] Riach, 'Introduction' to Contemporary Scottish Studies, p.xxiii.
[20] Duncan Glen, *The Poetry of the Scots: An Introduction and Bibliographical Guide to Poetry in Gaelic, Scots, Latin and English* (Edinburgh: Edinburgh University Press, 1991), pp.xxx, xxxi.
[21] Roderick Watson, *The Literature of Scotland: The Middle Ages to the Nineteenth Century*, 2nd edn (Houndmills: Palgrave, 2007), p.296.
[22] Douglas Gifford, 'Scottish Literature in the Victorian and Edwardian Era', in Douglas Gifford, Sarah Dunnigan and Alan MacGillivray, eds., *Scottish Literature in English and Scots* (Edinburgh: Edinburgh University Press, 2002), pp.321–32, 321.
[23] Michael Fry, *A New Race of Men: Scotland 1815–1914* (Edinburgh: Birlinn, 2013), pp.364, 369.
[24] Gifford and Hynd, 'James Young Geddes, John Davidson and Scottish Poetry', in Gifford, Dunnigan and MacGillivray, pp.349–78, 349. William Findlay, 'Reclaiming Local Literature: William Thom and Janet Hamilton', in Gifford, ed. *The History of Scottish Literature, vol III: Nineteenth Century*, (Aberdeen: Aberdeen University Press, 1988), pp.353–73, 354.

neglected and ephemeral sources for poetry publication, gives a very different picture, far more akin in its depth and breadth, to that found by Donaldson in his investigation of newspaper prose and popular fiction. What I argue here is that Scottish poets are indeed often imitative, parochial, provincial, romantic, sentimental, and escapist. These are not flaws. They are strategic positions adopted on cultural and political, as well as personal, grounds; positions which we need to understand and re-assess. *Working Verse in Victorian Scotland* thus forms part of recent and ongoing efforts to re-evaluate Victorian Scottish culture beyond concerns about 'Anglocentric hegemony', recognizing both that this is an over-simplification of the complicated 'unionist nationalism' of Victorian Scotland, and that it is problematic to judge Scottish Victorian literature in terms set up by twentieth-century commentators seeking an explicitly nationalist vision of Scottish literature and Scotland.[25]

Reassessments of Victorian Scotland have begun to make these arguments.[26] They should also seem familiar to scholars of Victorian studies, since considerable scholarly efforts have been made (especially in relation to women's writing) to perform these re-evaluations of romantic and sentimental literature. Studies such as Kathryn Ledbetter's *British Victorian Women's Periodicals*, to take only one example, take a similar line to this monograph in arguing that women's periodical poetry was the location for 'traditional sentiments now considered embarrassingly simplistic to some critics', but which were 'influential and value-laden' and are worth recovering.[27] The same is true for working-class literature. In some ways similar to the narrative constructed about Scottish literature, Victorian working-class writers have sometimes been seen as dubious conformists to the generally conservative norms of established literary cultures, adopting 'Parnassian' attitudes, and failing to describe the harsh realities of the world around them in favour of conventional sentimentalized tropes. Martha Vicinus, in her foundational study of English working-class writers, argued that many of their poems were not adequately 'attuned to working-class life':

> These poets did not offer insight into their urban and industrial communities, but gave instead idealizations of Nature, Poesy and Love. Nor did they look to their own experiences...rather, they wrote about emotions they had learned in books. The moral clichés that dot their works were embraced along with everything else that seemed to be a part of the richer cultural world they longed to enter, for they were certain its values were the highest.[28]

[25] On nationalism in Victorian Scotland, see Graeme Morton, *Unionist Nationalism: Governing Urban Scotland, 1830–1860* (East Linton: Tuckwell Press, 1999).

[26] See, for example, *Scotland and the 19th Century World*, ed. Gerard Carruthers, David Goldie and Alastair Renfrew (Amsterdam: Brill, 2012), especially Gifford's 'Preparing for Renaissance: Revaluing Nineteenth-Century Scottish Literature', which is much more positive on the connections between the Victorian period and the Scottish Renaissance than Gifford's earlier assessments. Michael Shaw's 'Transculturation and Historicisation: New Directions for the Study of Scottish Literature c.1840–1914', *Literature Compass* 13 (2016), 501–10, provides a very helpful overview of new directions in this field. See also his *The Fin-de-Siècle Scottish Revival: Romance, Decadence and Celtic Identity* (Edinburgh: Edinburgh University Press, 2020).

[27] Kathryn Ledbetter, *British Victorian Women's Periodicals: Beauty, Civilization and Poetry* (Houndmills: Palgrave, 2009), pp.9, xii.

[28] Martha Vicinus, *The Industrial Muse: A Study of Nineteenth-Century British Working-Class Literature* (London: Croom Helm, 1974), p.144.

The focus, evident in Vicinus and other critics, and also evident in the very influential 1990 Scottish working-class anthology by Tom Leonard, *Radical Renfrew*, was on recovering a radical working-class tradition which emphasized, in terms of content, the politics of labour, and, in terms of form, drew on older song and broadside traditions. As more recent work, especially by Michael Sanders on Chartist poetics, has shown, however, poems on 'Nature, Poesy and Love' can equally be political poems, supplying a different kind of insight into working-class 'urban and industrial communities'.[29]

I define 'working-class' in this study in terms of precariousness, following Jacques Rancière's identification of the 'travailleur precaire' and Emma Griffin's helpful definition of the working classes as 'those who had no income other than that which they earned, those working as manual labourers, and those sufficiently close to the margins of a comfortable existence that a stint of ill health or unemployment posed serious difficulties'. As she notes, this can include a range of circumstances, from 'the reasonably comfortable' to 'the desperately poor'.[30] Unstable economic circumstances and limited access to formal education characterized most of the known authors discussed here. As in studies by Sanders and a number of other scholars of working-class readers and writers, I am engaged with the question of why such men and women devoted considerable time and effort to writing (and reading) poetry, and the work that they wished poetry to do for them. I agree with Rancière that efforts to acquire culture, to find time 'to discuss, write, compose verses, or develop philosophies', are acts of resistance for those usually excluded from cultural participation:

> For the workers of the 1830s, the question was not to demand the impossible, but to realize it themselves, to take back the time that was refused them by educating their perceptions and their thought in order to free themselves in the very exercise of everyday work, or by winning from nightly rest the time to discuss, write, compose verses, or develop philosophies. These gains in time and freedom were not marginal phenomena or diversions in relation to the construction of the workers' movement and its great objectives. They were the revolution, both discreet and radical, that made these possible, the work by which men and women wrenched themselves out of an identity formed by domination and asserted themselves as inhabitants with full rights of a common world, capable of all the refinement or all the asceticism that had previously been reserved for those classes relieved of the daily cares of work and bread.[31]

This provides a means to read the literature produced by such workers, literature which often models itself on established literary norms, not as a betrayal of class values or a turn towards inauthenticity, but as an act of assimilation, defining 'assimilation' in Michel de Certeau's terms, less as 'becoming similar to' than 'making something similar to what one is, making it one's own, appropriating or

---

[29] See Tom Leonard, *Radical Renfrew* (Edinburgh: Polygon, 1990) and Sanders, *The Poetry of Chartism* (Cambridge: Cambridge University Press, 2009) *passim*.

[30] Emma Griffin , *Liberty's Dawn: A People's History of the Industrial Revolution* (New Haven, CT: Yale University Press, 2013), p.64.

[31] Rancière, p.ix.

reappropriating it'.[32] This is what I attempt to show in, for instance, Chapter 3's discussion of pastoral poetics as used by working-class Scottish writers, or Chapter 5's discussion of how working-class poets playfully appropriated the standards for 'good' and 'bad' poetry set by newspaper editors.

In Scotland of the mid-late Victorian period—my key period of interest—there is also a specific and contemporary political edge to this work of acquiring and deploying cultural literacy, because, I argue, it has a direct relationship to the cause of Reform. From the radical 1820s to the success of the 1832 Reform Act, to the 1867 Reform Act, 1872 Education Act and 1884 Reform Act, Scotland had been broadly pro-Reform and Liberal in politics across all classes. The period I study sees the incorporation of radical and Chartist plans into liberal and reformist principles, and equally witnesses a gradual blending of radically inclined publications (the unstamped newspaper press, for instance) and the Romantic, highly politicized poetics of the 1780s to the 1820s, into the new popular press and new forms of popular literature. I use 'incorporation' and 'blending' here rather than 'decline' or 'shift' because, as Tom Devine and Eugenio Biagini have argued, there was 'a remarkable thread of continuity' between 1820s radicalism and later Victorian movements. Working-class liberalism 'was not the fruit of the ideological success of bourgeois ideas during the mid-Victorian decades, but rather the continuation of older and genuinely popular plebeian traditions', and the reformist 'frame of mind' emerges from these traditions, and is visible in literature as well as other discourses.[33] Intellectual and moral improvement, whether self-improvement (e.g. in private reading) or, just as often, mutual improvement (in associations, clubs or societies both formal and informal), was central to this frame of mind. As Jonathan Rose comments in his seminal study of workers and their intellectual engagements, '[t]he founders of the Labour party and other self-educated radicals realized that no disenfranchised people could be emancipated unless they created an autonomous intellectual life'.[34]

Looking back from the 1880s, Alexander Mitchell, historian of social and political movements in Dalkeith, Midlothian, argued that 'the intellectual activity now manifested throughout the empire' might be attributed to 'the excitement connected with the passing of the Reform Bill' (in 1832), and that 'the higher tone of the national mind resulting from political activity' had led to local improvements, including the establishment of a library and reading room in Dalkeith and

---

[32] Michel de Certeau, 'Reading as Poaching', in *The Practice of Everyday Life (1984)*. Reprinted in *The History of Reading*, ed. Shafquat Towheed, Rosalind Crone and Katie Halsey (New York: Routledge, 2011), pp.130–9, 131. See also Hall on 'reform and transformation' rather than 'struggle and resistance' as key to popular culture (p.228).

[33] T. M. Devine, *The Scottish Nation, 1700–2000* (London: Allen Lane, 1999), p.280. Eugenio F. Biagini, *Liberty, Retrenchment and Reform: Popular Liberalism in the Age of Gladstone, 1860–1880* (Cambridge: Cambridge University Press, 1992), pp.6, 17.

[34] Jonathan Rose, *The Intellectual Life of the British Working Classes*, 2nd edn (New Haven, CT: Yale University Press, 2010), p.7.

the expansion of the town's local press.[35] Of course, like most such commentators, he was biased, since he was heavily involved in social and municipal reform and served on the committees of the societies he discusses. Nonetheless, this link between cultural literacy and political gains for working men and women appears to have been widely felt, and is evident in virtually every poem and publication venue consulted for this book. William Donaldson, an ardent pro-Reform shoemaker poet from Keith, Moray, summed up the general attitude towards improvement in 'An Anthem for the Age':

> Those wha wish to be progressin'
>   Shouldna work without an aim;
> We maun get our mental lesson
>   If we would our birthright claim.[36]

The last two lines form the refrain. 'Birthright' refers specifically here to the second Reform Act of 1867. The association of poetry, more than any genre, with cultural capital and intellectual ability meant that the ability to write a poem that fell within the 'horizon of expectations' for Victorian popular poetry, and the ability to vote, were intimately linked.[37] This connection drew force from John Stuart Mill's influential argument, in his *Considerations on Representative Government*, that suffrage should be conditional on voters demonstrating basic literacy and mathematical knowledge, and that votes should also be weighted so that those who could show 'superiority of mental qualities' would have a greater say in the affairs of the country, since 'the opinion, the judgment, of the higher moral or intellectual being, is worth more than that of the inferior'. Though Mill conceded that a better system of national education would have to underpin this, he also argued that his plan was not necessarily discriminatory in class terms, since it would 'be open to the poorest individual in the community to claim its privileges, if he can prove that, in spite of all difficulties and obstacles, he is, in point of intelligence, entitled to them'.[38] What better way to prove 'superiority of mental qualities' and the possession of 'higher moral or intellectual' thought and feeling than by writing a poem like Alexander Pope, Thomas Gray, Robert Burns, Walter Scott, or, as the century progressed, Alfred Tennyson and Henry Wadsworth Longfellow? Such imitative poetry by working men and women is very deliberate. Publicly demonstrating working-class mastery of the standards of 'high' culture, as they were well aware, could have political as well as cultural benefits.

---

[35] Alexander Mitchell, *Political and Social Movements in Dalkeith, from 1831–1882* (Printed for private circulation, 1882), p.23. This material first appeared in the Dalkeith Herald, a newspaper founded in the 1860s to promote reform.

[36] William Donaldson, *The Queen Martyr, and Other Poems* (Elgin: J. McGillivray and Son, 1867), p.131.

[37] 'Horizon of expectations' is a term drawn from Hans Robert Jauss, 'Literary History as a Challenge to Literary Theory', trans. Elizabeth Benzinger, *New Literary History* 2.1 (1970), 7–37.

[38] J. S. Mill, 'Considerations on Representative Government', in Mark Philip and Frederick Rosen, eds., *On Liberty, Utilitarianism and Other Essays* (Oxford: Oxford University Press, 2015), pp.181–408, 297, 291, 294. Liberal Scottish newspapers cited Mill's opinions favourably in the run-up to the Second Reform Bill of 1867.

Most of the poems cited in this study imagined a 'local' readership and present themselves as highly invested in local concerns. Fiona Stafford's major study, *Local Attachments*, highlights the importance of Romantic poetics in re-valuing the concept of the local:

> The period now known as 'Romantic' constitutes a defining moment in literary history, when local detail ceased to be regarded as transient, irrelevant or restrictive, and began to seem essential to art with any aspiration to permanence. The debates of this revolutionary age also prompted passionate justifications of poetry's vital role in modern society, which in turn transformed the work of the local poet into a task of national and universal proportions.[39]

Stafford's argument for the significance of local detail, and its presence in poets whose work was a major influence on working-class authors, specifically Robert Burns and William Wordsworth, is crucial in understanding how important 'local attachments' were to Victorian poets. When she argues in relation to her selected authors, however, that they 'were not "local" in the sense of having meaning only for those living in the areas in which they were set, but represented a kind of art whose truthfulness was universally recognizable', then her study differs from mine.[40] I am interested in local poets who, while often paying lip service to Romantic ideals of poetic genius and the vital task of poetry, had no expectations of permanence or 'universal' significance for their writings. How could they, when these writings usually appeared in publication venues defined by their transience and anonymity, such as broadsides, pamphlets, and newspapers? The poems I discuss here market localism very differently to those Stafford considers: narrowing rather than widening their scope by referencing details that would only be known to local readers in a particular historical moment, or indeed using language in ways only fully comprehensible to readers from their region. They advertise their provinciality as a virtue through intimate relationships with particular places and the people who live in them. Thomas Watson, a gardener in Lasswade, Midlothian (not to be confused with Thomas Watson of Arbroath), for instance, published a dialogue with Lasswade herself, who intervenes in the affairs of 'her poet' when she thinks he has been letting her down by going out drinking:

> "Take care!" said I, "What do ye mean?
> Lasswade, you're surely saucy,
> Your poet has na farther been
> Than just out seein' his lassie."[41]

This is a joke about the appropriate behaviour for the town's poet—drinking is bad, since most newspapers and authorities support temperance, courting is good, as it is a staple poetic topic as well as appropriate behaviour for a young man—and

---

[39] Fiona Stafford, *Local Attachments: The Province of Poetry* (Oxford: Oxford University Press, 2010), p.30.

[40] Ibid., p.21.

[41] Thomas Watson, 'Lasswade Chronicles', in *A Collection of Poems* (Edinburgh: Printed for the Author, 1835), p.78. Watson identifies his profession on the title page.

about the pride and anxious interest taken by Scottish towns in 'their' poets. Watson's poem advertises a sense of community ownership and possession that is strikingly different to, for instance, Wordsworth's relationship to the inhabitants of Grasmere. Poets like Watson, I argue, inserted themselves in an imagined community of writers and readers that consisted of residents of a particular location, and explicitly engaged in the 'manufacture of local identity'.[42] But this community, we should note, is exclusive rather than inclusive, since it tends to be implicitly white, heterosexual, Protestant (usually Presbyterian) and Scottish-born—characteristics not necessarily shared by everyone in a Scottish village in the 1830s, even before the waves of immigration from Catholic Ireland and elsewhere.

This sense of localism, so strongly evident in the verse cultures I examine here, is further complicated because poems like 'Lasswade Chronicles' potentially speak to an extensive international diaspora of readers who still consider themselves to be locals. In *Blackwood's* of 1822, Christopher North comments that if his colleague writes about some Glasgow experiences, London readers will say, in derogatory terms, that 'it is *local*', and then adds, 'Our ambition is, that our wit shall be local all over the world'.[43] 'Local all over the world' is an excellent description of the operations of Scottish provincial verse, since its tendency to circulate in newspapers and periodicals and as song lyrics meant that it did often end up more influential in, say, New Zealand, than in London, and might have a temporally longer and geographically wider afterlife than the writer anticipated.[44] Although my investigation of Scottish working-class poetry in English and Scots may also seem to invite the '*local*' accusation from scholars, the literature studied here had a surprisingly global reach.

In the course of researching *Working Verse*, I realized that what had initially seemed like a relatively narrow topic instead involved an extremely large, complex and often untapped archive. For every one poem cited here, I have located ten others on a similar theme; for every poet whose work is mentioned, there are ten others whose life and works would richly repay more study; for every newspaper cited, ten more also had a poetry column with its own distinctive flavour. Early in my research I considered writing a book on *all* Scottish poetry in this period, and I expected to cover every region in Scotland. But as I realized the richness of the resources contained in a single local library, or in the poetry columns of one local newspaper, it became evident both that this was not feasible in the confines of one

---

[42] This phrase is from Catriona M. M. Macdonald's helpful assessment of local identities and literary cultures in Paisley, 'The Vanduaria of Ptolemy: Place and the Past', in Dauvit Brown, R. J. Finlay and Michael Lynch, eds., *Image and Identity: The Making and Re-Making of Scotland Through the Ages* (Edinburgh: John Donald, 1998), pp.177–94. 'Imagined community' is drawn from Benedict Anderson's still-helpful *Imagined Communities: Reflections on the Origins and Spread of Nationalism*, rev. edn (London: Verso, 2006 (first published 1983)).

[43] *Blackwood's Edinburgh Magazine*, April 1822. Reprinted in John Wilson et al., *Noctes Ambrosianae*, with memoirs and notes by R. Shelton Mackenzie, vol I: 1819–1824 (New York: Redfield, 1859), p.172.

[44] For one example of the international circulation of Scottish popular verse, see my case study, '"The Drunkard's Raggit Wean": Broadside Culture and the Politics of Temperance Verse', *Cahiers Victoriens et Édouardiens* 84 (Autumn 2016), 20 paras.

book, and that the most significant argument emerging from this material concerned working-class writers. Scotland had many known poets, and many more forgotten poets, who were critics, academics, ministers, doctors, lawyers, businessmen, schoolteachers, and members of well-off families. Yet they did not always participate in the cultures that I discuss here in the same way, nor were they part of the enormously influential discourse, discussed in Chapter 1, on Scotland's unique identity as a home for working-class poets.[45] I also reluctantly concluded that I was not qualified to assess poetry in Gaelic. Fortunately, in contrast to most Victorian poetry in Scots and English from Scotland, Gaelic poetry and song from this period has already been recognized and recovered through excellent scholarship.[46]

In terms of geographical scope, this book draws on poems, poets and newspaper poetry columns from Aberdeenshire, Angus (Forfarshire), Ayrshire, Banffshire, Clackmannanshire, Dumfries & Galloway, East Lothian, Fife, Inverness-shire, Lanarkshire, Midlothian, Moray and Nairnshire, Perthshire, Renfrewshire, Stirlingshire, West Lothian, and several other counties. This is very far from comprehensive, however, and few of these areas are discussed in adequate depth. There are substantial regions—the Borders, Ayrshire, Fife—which feature here but could easily have had a much greater presence in this study. Other regions, especially the Highlands and Islands, deserve a separate book which would consider whether geography, history, and linguistic difference does or does not result in an affinity with the conclusions reached here. My decision to use the Dundee-based *People's Journal* as a major primary source (my 2016 edited anthology of poems from the *People's Journal* is a companion to this monograph), to concentrate on a particular Glasgow-centred archive in Chapter 2, and to include a chapter on industrialism and poetry, does mean that Dundee, Glasgow, and Lanarkshire, the most heavily industrialized cities and region in Scotland, feature more substantially than other areas. This is a justifiable focus, I would argue, given that both cities were very active centres for working-class self-improvement, and hubs for the newspaper industry.

Newspapers are an outstanding source for locating hitherto unknown poems and poets in a working-class tradition, and I chose to focus on them to the exclusion of other periodicals and magazines, judging, as Chapter 1 notes, that Victorian periodical poetry, and indeed Victorian periodical culture, is better-known by scholars in the field than the poetic culture associated with the provincial press. Reading newspaper poetry columns is highly time-consuming. Given that it is rarely viable to search for poems by a named author or with a known title, there is no way to investigate these columns other than physically studying every page, whether in a digitized, microfilm, or hard copy newspaper, for the white space and

---

[45] All Scottish poets, of course, might appropriate the personae or voice of a working-class speaker, especially when writing in Scots and in the tradition of Burns. Though most of the poets I identify as 'working-class' in this study do give an account of their background as workers, anonymous and pseudonymous poems are identified as part of 'working-class poetry' if they overtly present themselves as such. The authenticity or otherwise of the writer is less important than the way in which the poem situates itself within the contexts I discuss.

[46] See especially Donald E. Meek, *Tuath Is Tighearna/Tenants and Landlords: An Anthology of Gaelic Poetry of Social and Political Protest from the Clearances to the Land Agitation (1800–1890)* (Edinburgh: Scottish Gaelic Texts Society, 1995).

irregular lines that signify 'poem'. I make no claims that my reading of newspapers is in any way comprehensive, though in extensive research, I have found nothing that contradicts the general arguments of this book. I sampled as many available newspapers from the regions above as possible, and where poetry seemed to be a key feature, followed up by reading selections of 5 to 10 years in depth. To enable comparison across newspapers in a rough time frame, I concentrated particularly on the crucial years after the repeal of the Stamp and Paper Acts, the late 1850s through to the 1870s, though the wider scope of this study incorporates a longer 'Victorian' era, from the 1830s to early 1900s.

The most obvious omission in this book is the lack of any specific discussion of Scottish working-class women writers. This is a conscious choice. Faced with a mass of material, most of it unknown to scholarship, I have chosen to focus as much as possible on poems that have not already been discussed, and to use genre rather than gender as the overarching category. (I also wished to reserve discussion of some important poems by Scottish working-class women for another forthcoming publication).[47] It is, moreover, difficult to identify the gender of many authors, especially those who chose to publish anonymously or pseudonymously, with any certainty. Scholarship on Scottish Victorian working-class women writers has already benefited enormously from the work of recovery carried out by Catherine Kerrigan, Florence Boos, and others.[48] Working-class women poets from Victorian Scotland have been anthologized, and they have received positive critical attention in both published works and unpublished theses. Of particular note is the wealth of criticism on Ellen Johnston, the 'Factory Girl' and on Janet Hamilton, plus the recent critical revival of Glasgow poet Marion Bernstein.[49] Readers are strongly advised to supplement my discussion here with these works.

---

[47] Blair, 'Dialect, Region, Class, Work', in Linda Hughes, ed., *The Cambridge Companion to Victorian Women's Poetry* (Cambridge: Cambridge University Press, 2019, 129–44). I have also previously discussed Janet Hamilton in ' "He Sings Alone": Hybrid Forms and the Victorian Working-Class Poet', *Victorian Literature and Culture* 37 (2009), 523–41.

[48] Catherine Kerrigan's *An Anthology of Scottish Women Poets* (Edinburgh: Edinburgh University Press, 1991) contains a substantial selection of Victorian women writers. Florence Boos, ed. *Working-Class Women Poets in Victorian Britain: An Anthology* (Peterborough, ON: Broadview, 2008) includes a number of Scottish poets.

[49] Johnston has received more critical attention than any other writer in this book. Important studies include H. Gustav Klaus, *Factory Girl: Ellen Johnston and Working-Class Poetry in Victorian Scotland* (Frankfurt: Peter Lang, 1998); Boos, 'The "Queen" of the "Far-Famed Penny Post": The "Factory Girl Poet" and Her Audience', *Women's Writing* 10 (2003): 503–26 and Judith Rosen, 'Class and Poetic Communities: The Works of Ellen Johnston, the "Factory Girl" ', *Victorian Poetry* 39 (2001), 207–27. On Hamilton, see Boos, ' "Nurs'd up among the scenes I have describ'd": Poetry of Working-Class Victorian Women', in Christine Krueger, ed., *The Functions of Victorian Culture at the Present Time* (Athens, OH: Ohio University Press, 2002), pp.137–56; Boos, 'Janet Hamilton: Working-Class Memoirist and Commentator', in Glenda Norquay, ed., *The Edinburgh Companion to Scottish Women's Writing* (Edinburgh: Edinburgh University Press, 2012), pp.63–74; and Kaye Kossick, ' "And aft Thy Dear Doric aside I Hae Flung, to Busk oot My Sang wi' the Prood Southron Tongue": The Antiphonal Muse in Janet Hamilton's Poetics', in John Goodridge and Bridget Keegan, eds., *A History of British Working-Class Literature* (Cambridge: Cambridge University Press, 2017), pp.208–25. Bernstein's poems have recently been anthologized, in Marion Bernstein, *A Song of Glasgow Town: The Collected Poems of Marion Bernstein*, ed. Edward H. Cohen, Anne R. Fertig and Linda Fleming (Glasgow: ASLS, 2013); see also Cohen and Fertig, 'Marion Bernstein and the Glasgow Weekly Mail in the 1870s', *Victorian Periodicals Review* 49 (2016), 9–27.

Women poets are included in each chapter as contributors to the genres I discuss. They do, however, appear less often due to the additional barriers they faced in entering performed and occasional verse cultures and forming connections that assisted publication. Though there were undoubtedly women songwriters, for instance, it would have been difficult and dangerous for a woman to pursue the career of a street performer, who recited verse and sold broadsides in public, or a tramping poet, who sold broadsides and songsters door to door. Beyond the street, 'occasional' poems were performed and produced in social spaces dominated by men, such as taverns, and in dinners, club and society meetings. Lauren Weiss's recent investigation of Victorian 'literary' societies suggests that it was not until late in the century that most societies, many of which had substantial working-class member-ship, opened their doors to women members.[50] Outside formal societies, many Scottish towns or workplaces had groups of like-minded men who met to discuss poetry. I have found no mention of women participants. Newspapers often pub-lished fictional 'conversation' pieces (modeled on periodical exchanges), in which characters in a social setting, such as a barber's shop, a newspaper office, or a Christmas party, discuss local poets and poetry. No female characters feature in any of these. Poetry is by no means exclusively a male pursuit—many working-class Scottish women published poems in the newspapers, and some attained a level of local fame as a poet—but the social networks that were so vital in assisting work-ing-class poets to publication and recognition were near-exclusively male. Overall, and unsurprisingly given the likely domestic commitments of many women, there are far fewer newspaper poems or surviving published and unpublished works by identifiable women than there are by men.

Women also faced particular gendered and generic expectations centred on the contested figure of the 'poetess', meaning that poems signed with a female name (in many cases, possibly a pseudonym) are more likely to situate themselves as poems on courtship, love, romance, and elegy (especially elegies for children). In terms of the genres I discuss here, poems by women are included, alongside similar poems by men, in Chapters 3 and 4. The most interesting absences are in Chapters 2 and 5. Women did write comic and satiric verse (Jane Duthie of Montrose is a strong example of a comic newspaper poet), but the particular culture of 'bad' verse examined in Chapter 5 had no known female participants, unless we include Susannah Hawkins of Dumfries, who sold her verse door to door throughout her region, but who was active over two decades before this culture appears in the newspapers. Most significantly, Scottish working-class women poets do not feature strongly in a genre where their works might be expected, and in which women poets had made numerous canonical contributions: nursery verse. The Scottish nursery verse tradition that I identify in Chapter 2 is especially important in that male poets were celebrated for their contributions to it, particularly for contributions in which they appropriated a mother's voice. As I suggest in this chapter, this is

---

[50] Lauren Weiss, *The Literary Clubs and Societies of Glasgow in the Long Nineteenth Century.* Unpublished PhD thesis, University of Stirling, 2017.

part of a re-valuation of working-class masculinity, parenthood, and domestic life in politicized terms. What working mothers thought about this genre and the male poets who participated in it, however, has not been recorded.

Chapter 1 of this book provides an introduction to, and overview of, occasional verse and performed verse, and considers the functions of newspaper poetry columns. Its broad remit underpins the detailed studies in the later chapters, and sets up the arguments about the work done by Scottish working-class poetry which re-occur in these. Chapter 2 supplies the first case study, of the social networks and relationships of patronage which shaped the very successful series of *Whistle-Binkie* anthologies. Tracing a path from the radical 1820s into a more 'Victorian' poetic mode, this chapter argues that, while the influence of older traditions of song, ballad, and Romantic-era poetics remains, there is a distinctive change in Scottish working-class poetry from the 1830s to the 1840s onwards, and that *Whistle-Binkie*—often excoriated by critics, and seldom taken seriously—is both a response to, and partly responsible for, this change. In the long concluding section of Chapter 2, I turn to nursery verse, another genre fostered by *Whistle-Binkie* and common throughout the Scottish press. Chapter 3 moves to reconsider pastoral poetics, and the nostalgic and sentimental modes associated with depictions of Scotland's natural beauty. I argue that working-class pastoral, resituated in its newspaper contexts, made a crucial contribution to political and environmental debates about land use and ownership, debates which also fed into pro and anti-emigration rhetoric. In Chapter 4, I move from nature to industry, examining how poets dealt with the newly industrialized Scotland and found poetic modes in which to represent labour and industry. With particular attention to miners and railway poets, and including a case study of miner-poet David Wingate, I suggest their differing ways of writing as workers and about the kinds of labour that were rapidly changing in the Victorian period. Railway and engine poets, I argue, were also adept at using the formal and rhythmic qualities of poetry to represent the vexed relationship between human and machine.

Chapter 5 turns to 'bad' poetry. It uses the critical mode of the 'To Correspondents' columns to suggest that newspapers, while genuinely attempting to assist readers in becoming writers, also made capital from aspiring writers' failure. Anxiety about the quality of poems produced by Scottish workers went hand-in-hand with the celebration, noted in Chapter 1 and throughout, of the quantity of such poems. As I argue in Chapter 5, however, the attempt by newspaper critics and editors to separate good poetry from bad became complicated when 'bad' poetry became popular in its own right, and especially when pseudo-bad poets became minor newspaper celebrities. Besides William McGonagall, the obvious candidate, I focus here on Alexander Burgess, or 'Poute'.

While each chapter includes a range of poems from the 1830s to the 1890s, closing with McGonagall takes the book up to the turn of the century. In a very brief afterword, I note the intensity of the effort to collect and preserve popular Scottish poetry, from the 1880s to the 1930s, just at the point when it was dismissed and to some extent superseded by the Scottish 'Renaissance' and new attitudes towards what poetry might do for Scotland and Scottish nationalism. The cultures I examine here do not disappear, but they unquestionably dwindle in significance. The vitality, the fervour, the ambition of local Scottish poets in the Victorian period, the ubiquity of these poems in the social life of Scotland, and the shared sense that poems were doing important work in society and politics, would never again reach the heights it achieved in the Victorian provincial press.

1

The Work of Verse

Throughout the Victorian period, critics, editors, and authors repeatedly and confidently asserted that Scotland had untold numbers of local poets. Famously, *Blackwood's Edinburgh Magazine* suggested of Paisley in 1858, that 'there are more poets living and breathing in this little town than in the whole of England, from the south bank of the Tweed on to Cornwall'.[1] 'We believe that, on average, there are half a dozen poets in every Scottish parish', Charles Mackay observed in 1868.[2] By the 1880s, this was a standard line. '[I]n more recent times every parish has had its poet—almost every village its native bard', as one reviewer noted.[3] 'Hardly a parish on the Border, or north of it, but used to possess its poet', George Eyre-Todd recalled in 1890, with H. Gilzean Reid agreeing, in the same year, that 'Every district [in Scotland] has its group of "Bards", some of whom are known only within their own parish, others to a more extended circuit.'[4] The reasons for this abundance of poets, most commentators concurred, lay in the combination of Scotland's superior educational system, dissenting religious and political beliefs, national pride, natural beauties, plus the impact of a long-standing song and ballad tradition and the particular influence of Robert Burns.[5]

Not only did Scotland have more poets, according to this widely disseminated claim, she could also boast that the majority of her nineteenth-century poets, from Burns onwards, had 'sprung from the lower orders'.[6] 'Scotland has more reason to be proud of her peasant Poets than any other country in the world', the *British Minstrel* asserted in its first issue. Samuel Smiles, the most influential writer of the period on self-improvement, suggested that 'With the exception of Scott and Wilson, nearly all the poets of Scotland have been men of humble birth, who have written their songs and lyrics for persons of their own class.'[7] His biography of

---

[1] 'Rambles Round Glasgow', *Blackwood's Edinburgh Magazine* 83 (10 April 1858), 467–83, p.480. This is a review of Hugh MacDonald's *Rambles Round Glasgow* (see Chapter 3).

[2] Charles Mackay, 'Minor Poetry', *The London Review* 17 (17 October 1868), 457–9, 457.

[3] 'Modern Scottish Poetry', *Golden Hours* (August 1884), 510–12, p.510.

[4] George Eyre-Todd, 'A Cobbler-Artist', *The National Review* 16 (September 1890), 105–12, 105. H. Gilzean Reid, 'Unaccredited Heroes', *Gentleman's Magazine* 269 (October 1890), 384–96, 394.

[5] Though Walter Scott is revered in nineteenth-century criticism, his poetry is not accorded the same level of influence. Excepting the lines on national feeling from The Last Minstrel, I have found little direct reference to Scott's poems, compared to constant allusions to Burns in the genres discussed here, though this might have been different if I had concentrated on historical poetry and balladry.

[6] 'Apollodorus' [George Gilfillan], 'The Modern Scottish Minstrel', *The Critic* 16 (2 March 1857), 101–4, 104. This is a review of Charles Rogers' *The Modern Scottish Minstrel*.

[7] 'On the Poetical Character of the Scottish Peasantry', *British Minstrel* 1 (January 1843), 290–1, p.290. The author claims to be citing *Blackwood's*. Samuel Smiles, 'The Story of Robert Nicoll's Life', *Good Words* 16 (December 1875), 313–18, p.317.

poet, bookseller, and radical newspaper editor Robert Nicoll added a poetic case study to his stirring exemplars of Scottish engineers and inventors. In an 1853 preface to the poems of Walter Watson (herd-boy, weaver, soldier, and factory worker), newspaperman and working-class poet Hugh MacDonald described Scotland's 'lyrical productions' as the 'threads of gold' that linked society together, noting that although 'bards of low and high degree' have contributed to these productions:

> It is to individuals of humble origin and condition, however, that we are indebted for by far the larger and most valuable proportion. In other lands, the lyre has been comparatively seldom touched by the lowly and illiterate.

In contrast, 'there are few districts, towns, or even villages of Scotland, which cannot boast their own minstrels'.[8] Henry Shanks, 'The Blind Poet of the Deans', lecturing to the Bathgate Mechanics' Institute on 'The Peasant Poets of Scotland', described Scotland's position as 'The Peasant Poetic Queen of Nations' at length, stating that:

> It makes one's heart swell with patriotic pride to think that out of a population so numerically inferior to many of the other civilized nations of the world, she has in her People Poets, but more especially in the number and quality of her Peasant Poets, excelled them all; and in view of this important fact it is impossible to resist the temptation to give vent to a mental hurrah... These are a permanent and glorious inheritance, upon which the Scottish poets of the future may draw without stint or hindrance, as on a mine of inexhaustible wealth.[9]

Shanks argues that it is only in assessing the 'peasant and artisan' poetry of a nation that its true 'moral force and mental activity' can be measured, just as a sample from the bottom of a water tank will be more representative 'than one drawn from the top only.'[10] For Shanks—who himself contributed significantly to the literary culture of Bathgate by founding its 'Under the Beeches' literary society, requiring members to 'be able to write an original stanza on any subject' in order to join— for MacDonald, and for most other Victorian critics surveying the field of Scottish poetry, it was *quantity* rather than quality that mattered.[11] Shanks particularly mentioned the January 1881 circular of Glasgow's new Mitchell Library, which stated that it had collected the writings of 1395 Scottish poets.[12]

Most of these sources are, of course, highly partisan, and claims about Scotland's peasant poets tend to be made by those who had a vested interest in promoting Scotland, poetry, or both. As I note in the Introduction, similar poetic cultures not

---

[8] Preface to Walter Watson, *Poems and Songs, Chiefly in the Scottish Dialect* (Glasgow: David Robertson, 1853), pp.vi–vii. A handwritten note in the NLS edition identifies its author as MacDonald, who was part of the committee that sponsored this collection.

[9] Henry Shanks, *The Peasant Poets of Scotland and Musings Under the Beeches, with Memoir and Portrait of the Author* (Bathgate: Laurence Gilbertson, 1881), pp.167, 166. Shanks was born in 1829 and worked in trade and as a farmer until the early 1860s, when increasing blindness meant that he had to try to make a living from his writings.

[10] Ibid., p.167.

[11] 'Bathgate – "Under the Beeches"', *West Lothian Courier*, 24 January 1874, p.2.

[12] Shanks, p.161.

only existed elsewhere in Britain, but throughout the Anglophone world in the Victorian period. Attempts to promote the notion that Scotland had more working-class poets than any other country were highly successful, however, in that editors and anthologizers amassed a body of evidence to this effect, which other regions or nations did not produce to the same degree.[13] This chapter maps—very partially—some of the operations of verse culture in Victorian Scotland, but without wishing to suggest that these were materially different to the ways in which poetry might be set to work in Britain and beyond. What I do want to argue, however, is that the tenacity of belief in Scotland as the 'Peasant Poetic Queen of Nations' makes Scottish poetry a valuable test case for the ways in which local and provincial working-class verse cultures were valued and utilized for social, cultural, and political ends.

As the Mitchell Library collection and D. H. Edwards's fourteen-volume anthology *Modern Scottish Poets* indicate, national poetic honours rested on numerical superiority rather than aesthetic excellence. Assessors of Scotland's literary scene in this period were perfectly well aware that the poets they promoted would never live up to the towering figures of Burns and Walter Scott, not to mention James Hogg or Robert Tannahill. Edwards, beginning his twenty-year mission to preserve the minor poets of Scotland in his biography of Alexander Laing, *The Poetry of Scottish Rural Life* (1874), noted that contemporary poets were like 'farthing candles' compared to 'sunbeams', when measured against past excellence, yet we should not forget that 'the one possesses the properties of light as much as the other, and that they differ only in intensity'.[14] Alan Reid, another late-century editor, agreed: perhaps with Edwards' analogy in mind, he wrote of Scotland's peasant poets that, 'No one of us condemns the feeble flicker of a *cruisie* because it is not a sun.'[15] In the absence of stronger illumination, Reid implies, humble lights are still of use; they provide some (intellectual) light for households that have no other. Aesthetic skill, originality, and innovation—signs of what Edwards calls 'intensity' in poetics—were not essential criteria in assessing why poetry mattered, particularly when that poetry was produced by working-class writers. *All* poetry was a symptom of cultural literacy, indicative of hard work and a drive to improvement, a signal of what Matthew Arnold would influentially figure as 'sweetness and light'.[16] As such, the more poets Scotland possessed, the better.

The claim that 'No nation under the sun has produced so many bards as Caledonia' was repeated so often in volume prefaces, in reviews, and in biographical and autobiographical accounts of Scotland's working-class poets, that it became a

---

[13] The compilers of the Nottingham Trent Labouring-Class Poets Database note that 'well over half' of the entries relate to poets who are 'Scottish by birth or acculturation', and that this reflects the 'higher valuation given to labouring class poets in Scotland' and the consequent preservation of records ('Introduction – Statistical Notes'). See https://lcpoets.wordpress.com/introtobibliography/ (consulted 18 September 2018).

[14] D. H. Edwards, *The Poetry of Scottish Rural Life or A Sketch of the Life and Writings of Alexander Laing* (Brechin: D. H. Edwards, 1874), p.5.

[15] Alan Reid, *The Bards of Angus and the Mearns* (Paisley: J. & R. Parlane, 1897), p.xx.

[16] Arnold, *Culture and Anarchy*, ed. Jane Garnett (Oxford: Oxford University Press, 2006), p.26 and *passim*.

cliché.[17] Not surprisingly, the more cosmopolitan Scottish literati of Edinburgh, London, and beyond were deeply sceptical about such claims, and especially about the worth of these literary productions. 'It is somewhat too much the fashion to pat Scotch literature on the back', Robert Louis Stevenson wrote in an ironic review of James Grant Wilson's *The Poets and Poetry of Scotland* and its claims for Scottish poetic superiority.[18] One 1890 reviewer in the *Scots Observer*, edited by Stevenson's friend W. E. Henley from Edinburgh, was scathing about the efforts of Edwards and other late-century anthologizers, mocking the idea of preserving poets from the ' "Poet's Corner" in the various local newspapers in Scotland' and drily noting that Edwards' poets 'all write with equal industry and badness': 'as poets the pity is not that some are dead but that any are living'.[19] Such exasperated comments are understandable attempts to counter the cohesion of a narrative that extolled Scotland's poetic glories and in effect rated the act of producing poetry more highly than the quality of the poems produced. They also show that Edwards' perception that he was adding value to his modern Scottish poets by representing them through their most standard sentimental, humorous, religious, and domestic verse, consciously leaving out poems on more disturbing political or social themes and underplaying radical sympathies wherever possible, was a serious misstep. Yet even in 1890, the *Scots Observer* review is so scathing because the reviewer, at that time, was countering a very powerful discourse. In every local newspaper, every periodical, in the associational culture of Scots across the British Empire and the colonies, the sense of Scotland's working-class poets as her glory was remarkably persistent and highly influential.

Efforts to promote Scotland as a nation of people's poets had the self-perpetuating effect of encouraging working men and women to try their hand at poetry, and ensuring that poetry retained a very high cultural status in Scotland throughout the Victorian period. Scottish working-class autobiographies and biographies of workers from the nineteenth century, irrespective of the author's profession, include standard episodes where he (or, more rarely, she) begins to write verse. In common with the wider tradition of the 'improving' autobiography, most also dwell on poetry reading and writing as a social and communal pursuit, whether in terms of workplace culture, as in William Thom's reminiscences of discussing and singing Byron, Scott, Thomas Moore, and Tannahill in his Aberdeen weaving factory, or through friendships between individuals.[20] In John Younger's Borders village,

---

[17]　D. H. Edwards, *One Hundred Modern Scottish Poets* (Brechin: D. H. Edwards, 1880), p.ii.

[18]　Robert Louis Stevenson, 'The Poets and Poetry of Scotland', *The Academy*, 197 (February 1876), 138–9, p.138.

[19]　'The Lives of the Poetasters', *Scots Observer*, 3 (8 February 1890), 332–3, 332. For a discussion of Henley and the Observer's take on poetry see Linda K. Hughes, 'Periodical Poetry, Editorial Policy, and W. E. Henley's Scots and National Observer', *Victorian Periodicals Review* 49 (2016), 202–27.

[20]　William Thom, *Rhymes and Recollections of a Handloom Weaver*, ed. W. Skinner (Paisley: Alexander Gardner, 1880), p.viii. Jonathan Rose comments that British working-class autobiographers 'wrote at length about their reading', but does not discuss whether they also described their writing (2010, p.2). Stephen Colclough notes that working-class autobiographers frequently include scenes of friendship amongst book-lovers, though he warns (as does David Vincent) that tropes of literary self-improvement in working-class autobiography are not representative or unproblematic. Stephen Colclough, *Consuming Texts: Readers and Reading Communities, 1695–1870* (Houndmills: Palgrave,

Younger (a shoemaker) started writing verse himself after befriending a poetical blacksmith's apprentice; hearing about a 'real' poet in the area, farmworker Andrew Scott, Younger dropped everything and rushed to see this luminary, 'out I sallied, and flew like a meteor over a mile of ground to Whinfield, dropt into the farmer's kitchen, and found Andrew Scott, my friend to be, sitting on a form seat, tailing his old grey coat, which had got very poetically out at the elbows'.[21] While this was a come-down for Younger's romantic vision of a poet as one whose 'soul soared above the thick dross of common thought', it proved a valuable introduction to the lively social world of local poets.[22] Peter Taylor, an engineer in Paisley, started writing comic and satirical verse for his workmates in his teens. His poetic efforts, his autobiography suggests, were not separate from his successful career as inventor and entrepreneur, but were part of the same ambitious drive towards self-betterment. In his moves around Scotland, Taylor always made an effort to meet the poets in the area (Marion Aird in Ayrshire, for instance), whose work he was familiar with from the Glasgow press.[23] Substantial sections of Hugh Miller's autobiography, *My Schools and Schoolmasters*, perhaps the most famous working-class autobiography of the period, are concerned not with Miller's developing geological interests but with his efforts in 'enormously bad verse', spurred by a friendship with a 'literary cabinetmaker' and poet in the neighbourhood, and by access to his collection of poetry books.[24]

In 1856, in the Glasgow *Commonwealth*'s competition for working-class autobiographers, seven out of the nine prize-winning autobiographies published in the year after the competition describe the author writing poetry at one period in their lives.[25] While two of the autobiographies helped to launch the careers of men later well-known in their communities as poets, miner David Wingate and tailor James Nicholson, it is more important to note how writers with no intention of being 'a poet' (such as an anonymous weaver and a shoemaker) included discussion of poetry reading and composition as indicative of aspiration in a hard working life. These literary inclinations were also evidently valued by the judges of the autobiographical prize. In Scottish working-class autobiography and biography, fondly recollecting a love of poetry is such a standard trope, that when William Jolly wrote a biography of John Duncan, weaver and self-taught botanist, he felt

2007), pp.155, 149; David Vincent, *Bread, Knowledge and Freedom: A Study of Nineteenth-Century Working-Class Autobiography* (London: Methuen, 1981).

[21] John Younger, *Autobiography of John Younger, Shoemaker, St Boswell's* (Kelson: J and J. H. Rutherford, 1881), pp.120, 180–1.

[22] Ibid., p.181.

[23] Peter Taylor, *The Autobiography of Peter Taylor* (Paisley: Alexander Gardner, 1903), p.115 and *passim*.

[24] Hugh Miller, *My Schools and Schoolmasters, or The Story of My Education* (Edinburgh: Johnstone and Hunter, 1854), pp.79–80, 48.

[25] 'Narrative of a Miner', *The Commonwealth*, 25 October 1856, p.4; 'The Autobiography of a Journeyman Shoemaker', 22 November 1856, p.3; 'The Life of a Journeyman Baker' (Part II), 20 December 1856, p.3; 'Adventures of an Author', 3 January 1857, p.3; 'The Life of Jacob Holkinson, Tailor and Poet', 31 January 1857, p.3; 'The Life of a Letterpress Printer', 7 February 1857, p.3; 'Life of a Handloom Weaver', 5 April 1857, p.3. See Chapter 4 for further discussion of Wingate and this competition.

obliged to insert a lengthy apology for his subject's failure to write or read Scottish verse, describing this as a 'defect' in his constitution, and assuring the reader that although Duncan 'purchased few books of poetry...it is certain that he was not wanting in appreciation of the poetical aspects of nature'.[26]

For these writers, and many others, an emphasis on poetic effort shows the author's broad commitment to literacy and self-improvement, as well as a desire to represent themselves as contributors to Scotland's literary and cultural traditions. Becoming known as a poet also brought with it cultural capital and an enhanced reputation—in local, regional, national, and in some cases international circles— plus the potential to turn this into actual capital. Verse-writing, as we shall see, was a marketable as well as highly respected skill. Poets always represented themselves as writing from choice, but the evidence suggests that they often wrote 'with an eye to the main chance', as a review observed of Dumfries poetry saleswoman, Susannah Hawkins.[27] Although only the rare few managed to use a talent for poetry to escape a life of manual labour (and often grinding poverty), and no working-class Scottish poet in this period succeeded in making a living solely from their poems, the patronage and attention attracted by verse production might have tangible benefits. Three of the best-known Scottish working-class poets of the period, Alexander Smith, James Smith, and Alexander Anderson, were given posts at the University of Edinburgh and Edinburgh Mechanics' Institute, effectively as a sine-cure to lift them out of poverty and enable them to write more, but these cases were exceptional. More usually, poets might expect to bring in small additions to the family income from sales, impress employers and patrons with a view to pro-motion or a change of career, or simply earn a free drink.

As a marketable skill that was not dependent on physical strength and health or on the possession of a steady job—and that was open to both men and women— poetry could potentially supply a minimal income for those who could no longer engage in manual labour due to illness, disability, or old age, or were suffering from the effects of unemployment. Sarah Parker, who published in the Ayrshire and national press (including the Chartist *Northern Star*) as 'The Irish Girl', supported herself and her unemployed husband through his door to door sales of her poems, and Elizabeth Campbell of Lochee similarly provided for her family by selling her poems after her husband became too ill to work.[28] Peter Still of Aberdeenshire, 'The Buchan Bard', was deaf, lame, and suffered for years from other illnesses that destroyed his ability to work as a farm labourer; thanks to his poetry, he received financial support from King's College, Aberdeen, and after his death enough funds were raised to send his son (also a poet) to school and university.[29] Some Scottish

---

[26] William Jolly, *The Life of John Duncan, Scotch Weaver and Botanist* (London: Kegan Paul, 1883), p.489. Jolly's biographical account first appeared in *Good Words*.

[27] 'Miss Susannah Hawkins', *Dumfries and Galloway Courier*, 27 February 1849, p.3. Hawkins was a well-known personality in her local area and famed more as a 'bad' poet than a good.

[28] On Parker, see D. H. Edwards, *Modern Scottish Poets* (Brechin: D. H. Edwards, 1881), III, p.282. On Campbell, see 'Another Self-Taught Minstrel', *People's Journal*, 3 April 1875, p.2.

[29] See Still's autobiography in the preface to *The Cottar's Sunday, and Other Poems, Chiefly in the Scottish Dialect* (Aberdeen: George and Robert King, 1845).

poets, with the help of patrons, also managed to gain limited support from the Royal Literary Fund or a civil list pension.[30]

If nothing else, getting a poem published brought with it the satisfaction of achievement, of demonstrating ability in the arena of culture and being recognized for skills beyond those required for labour. It also, as later chapters show more fully, enabled poets to enter into new social networks and feel part of a communal enterprise. Moreover, depending on the poem's content and genre, it might further any number of causes dear to the writer, including social, political, religious, and environmental causes. Some arguments, poets clearly felt, would attract more attention if couched in verse. This applies both to subgenres such as the huge mass of electoral and Reform poems and songs produced in Scotland, and to works like farmer Colin Macpherson's *The Farmer's Friend: The Errors in the Present Method of Rearing and Breeding Cattle Exposed* (1878), which advises readers how to treat and purchase healthy cattle in the form of Scots poetic dialogues.[31] Advocating a case in a striking and memorable way was more important than any other factor, and trumped authorial reputation for the many poets who wrote anonymously or under unidentifiable pseudonyms.

Autobiographies, biographies, published letters and articles, volume prefaces, and published poems—all key sources for working-class poets discussing their poetry—are, of course, highly mediated forms, relating to a selected minority of working people. What they tell us about the pleasures and choices involved in writing and reading poetry in Victorian Scotland is important, but does not indicate how or whether poetry mattered to the majority of men and women working in Scotland in this period. What is clear, however, is that verse culture, whether sung, spoken, heard or read, was indisputably part of their everyday life. Poetry and song were inescapable, whether in the streets, in the local printer or bookseller's shop, in dedicated new shops like the 'Poet's Box' of Glasgow and Dundee, on advertising hoardings, in pubs, theatres, music-halls and domestic social settings, and most of all in prominent positions in the local press. What this chapter focuses on, then, is *where* and *how* verse cultures featured in Victorian Scotland, in terms of performance and print culture, and hence on the kinds of work that poetry could do. The first section considers the function of poetry in performance, with an emphasis on speech rather than song, and particularly concentrates on poetry that might be deemed 'occasional' (responding to current incidents or events), or improvisational, in that it is composed, or at least presented as if composed, as a rapid response to events. The second turns to the newspaper press, and its emphasis on shaping readerly communities through the poetry column, while continuing

---

[30] For example, Alexander McLagan, plumber and then clerk, and a *Whistle-Binkie* contributor, received £30 a year from a civil list pension. Francis Jeffrey was one of his patrons. See James Grant Wilson, *The Poets and Poetry of Scotland: From the Earliest to the Present Time*, 4 vols (London: Blackie & Son, n.d.), vol IV, p.341.

[31] Colin Macpherson, *The Farmer's Friend: The Errors in the Present Method of Rearing and Breeding Cattle Exposed* (n.p.: published for the author, 1878). On the functions of Scottish political poetry in this period see the essays for 'The People's Voice' project, https://thepeoplesvoice.glasgow.ac.uk/essays/ (consulted 29 September 2018) and the *Scottish Literary Review* (2018) on 'Scottish Political Poetry and Song'.

the discussion of poetry and locality and the crucial significance of the 'local' bard in Scotland's cultural imagination.

Brian Maidment argued, in his influential anthology *The Poorhouse Fugitives*, that 'the idea of bardic community remained strongly embedded in nineteenth-century industrial towns, even when those towns expanded into vast cities':

> The poet was seen to possess a widely recognized skill or talent. He was accordingly encouraged to develop that skill as a social duty with the support of the community, and in return offered his poetic output to the community on the agreed social occasions for poetry.[32]

It is this sense of verse culture as providing a *service*, one that includes but goes beyond entertainment, that comes through in the culture of performed and occasional verse. As Maidment's argument, focused on industrial Manchester, suggests, Victorian working verse cultures also show us how the concept of the local bard survived, indeed flourished, in the shift from rural to industrial communities (a shift explored in more detail in Chapters 3 and 4). Poetry also negotiated changes in print culture, as oral and traditional forms, such as street ballads, intersected with the expansion of the provincial press. Newspapers, as suggested below, very strongly supported bardic community and local poetry, and they assisted these communities to become virtual, to expand over geographic space and over the time of serial reading. Scotland's bardic communities could contract to the size of a bookshop, a printer's shop, a temperance hotel, or they could expand to the size of a nation and far beyond.

STREET, STAGE, SOCIETY: THE PLACE OF OCCASIONAL VERSE

In April 1846, the *Dumfries and Galloway Courier* published the following anecdote:

> A young man, genteelly dressed, but at the same time way-worn looking, if not exhausted, called at the shop of Mr Halliday, printer and publisher, and, after a brief pause, said—'I will write a poem on any subject you please.' Someone in the shop, friend or customer, replied, 'O! by all means; write on the exclusion of goats and asses from the Dock Show Yard.' On hearing this, the poet laureate of the persecuted bestial nodded assent, and found his way out of the premises as quietly as he found it in. Next morning, however, he reappeared, manuscript in hand, which, agreeably to compact, he handed to the printer.[33]

On further inquiry from Halliday, it turned out that the man was homeless and had spent the previous night sleeping rough, 'It now appears that, after daylight dawned, the manuscript was penciled on the crown of a hat, turned upside down, in lieu of a table.' The printer offered a meal, the poem 'was printed and sold well,

---

[32] Brian Maidment, ed., *The Poorhouse Fugitives: Self-Taught Poets and Poetry in Victorian Britain* (Manchester: Carcanet, 1987), p.324.

[33] 'Romantic, Yet True', *Dumfries and Galloway Courier*, 13 April 1846, p.3.

all things considered', and the itinerant poet was able to move on from Dumfries with 'a little money available for sustenance, the repair of a pair of boots and other needfuls'. In a denouement more typical of the popular novel, we are told that it later emerged that the poet was a gentleman escapee from a lunatic asylum.

As an indication of how poetry worked in provincial Scottish culture, this is a revealing anecdote. Local printers would print poems to order if they thought there was a chance of a decent return, especially if they dealt with a topical event. An agricultural show and its regulations, although suggested sardonically as a poetic topic, is precisely the kind of locally and immediately relevant theme that offered potential for humorous or satirical verse, and a show or fair was a good venue for the sale of broadside verse due to the influx of a larger audience into the town. Any reasonably decent Victorian poet, if he or she was flexible or desperate enough to write on any topic, could plausibly survive on occasional verse: Manchester working-class poet John Critchley Prince, for instance, tells an anecdote of finding himself destitute and composing a poem in a tavern, 'amid the riot and noise of a number of coal-heavers and others', on paper bought with his last cash from the sale of his waistcoat, in a desperate bid to write something he could sell to stave off imminent starvation.[34] James Macfarlan, a Glasgow poet who continually resisted the efforts of well-meaning patrons to help him out of alcoholism and poverty, used to write in the 'taproom', taking his poems to a local printer, hawking them 'for what he could procure', and then returning to drink the profits.[35] Such transactions are a vital part of working-class verse culture, though they tend to be occluded because this kind of poetry, written to order and for material gain, contradicted the popular perception of the inspired poet writing for pleasure, and was thus less likely to be preserved by poets (or their later biographers and editors) and transmitted in volume form: much of this kind of verse has not survived.

What the *Dumfries Courier* anecdote also indicates is the tendency of newspapers to report on and publish instances of itinerant and 'occasional' verse. Occasional verse includes poems written *for* a particular occasion—to be read or sung at a meeting, a dinner, a funeral, or wedding—which, as discussed below, often appear to have been solicited or actively commissioned by the parties involved. Then there are poems *about* an occasion, which seek to capitalize upon listeners' interest in an event (like the Dumfries Show), but are not authorized by anyone connected to it, which may deal with national or international events as well as local, and which would generally be performed in public spaces. Occasional verse can relate to a recurring occasion as well as a one-off event. For example, throughout the century every Scottish newspaper seems to have published a Christmas appeal for tips from the newsboys (the young boys who sold newspapers in the street) or delivery boys, which took the form of a single sheet of verse, as in 'The News Boy's Carol to the Subscribers of the Edinburgh Weekly Journal' (1824), or 'The Deliverers'

---

[34] John Critchley Prince, *Hours With the Muses* (Manchester, 1841), p.xx.
[35] Charles Rogers, *A Century of Scottish Life* (Edinburgh: William P. Nimmo, 1871), p.224.

New Year Address to Readers of the North British Advertiser' (1831).[36] These serve as advertising verse for the newspapers as well as appeals for charity:

> This day's *North British Advertiser* now,
> Wi' its Deliverers, mak' their annual bow
> To you, kind readers, calling your attention
> To sundry facks and items, not to mention
> That, by the guidness o' our Messrs Gray,
> The paper's gratis – not a rap to pay.[37]

This 1868 instance is a good example of verse that is deliberately written with Scots slang and misspelling ('facks') because the supposed speaker is a working-class boy. Occasional verse is usually characterized by such spontaneity, by a relationship with spoken rather than 'literary' English and Scots, by relatively simple or crude forms, and a general lack of pretension to aesthetic value. Where such verse was published outwith the newspaper columns, it generally appeared in broadside form—that is, printed on one side of a sheet of paper—just as Halliday would have printed the Show Yard poem in the *Dumfries and Galloway Courier* anecdote.

Broadside and pamphlet verse, verse that might be characterized as consciously ephemeral, was produced for a very wide variety of occasions and purposes, ranging from ballads about gory murders and executions sung in the streets (a form with a very long history) to, for example, the broadside containing Dundee poet James Easson's 'The Blind Girl' and the unsigned poem 'The Blind Mother', published with the note:

> A gift to the Members and Friends of the Dundee Wesleyan Band of Hope from James Scrymgeour their Secretary, presented on the occasion of a lecture delivered by him on 'The Blind' in the Wesleyan Chapel, Tally Street, on the Evening of Tuesday the 3rd March 1863.[38]

Any single sheet of verse, printed on one side, is still a broadside. The difference between Scrymgeour's respectable poems and a scurrilous song lies in degree (presentation, quality of paper, and production values), rather than in kind. A note such as the above, identifying the occasion for which the verses were printed, does not indicate that the circulation of these poems was restricted to the specified lecture. This sheet might well have been distributed and sold more widely in Dundee, moving beyond its particular occasion to become a message about how temperance advocacy, charity for the disabled, Christianity, and literary culture operated together in the town; as well as, rather more cynically, an advertisement for Scrymgeour's generosity and ability as a public speaker.

---

[36] Pasted into James Maidment's Scrap Book (contains newspaper cuttings and ephemera 1825–1873). NLS Special Collections S. 276.c. Examples were also preserved by A. C. Lamb, e.g., 'The Printer Boy's New Year's Address to the Readers of the Northern Warder' (1853–1859) (Dundee Central Library, A. C. Lamb Collection).

[37] 'New Year's Address of the Deliverers of the North British Advertiser, to the Readers of that Paper' (1868). James Maidment's Scrap Book.

[38] A. C. Lamb collection, Dundee Central Library.

Broadside verse has a long history, and studies of the genre tend to concentrate on earlier periods than the nineteenth century.[39] While in the early decades of the century, as the biographer of broadside author and publisher James Catnach observes, 'the whole of the United Kingdom was overrun with chapmen, ballad singers, and itinerants of every grade and description', the presence of these itinerants on the street faded during the Victorian period, as broadsides 'gradually declined in popularity' and the popular press, established printshops such as the Poet's Box, and the music hall, took over as the primary venues and vendors for popular song and verse.[40] Forfarshire farmer-poet John Wilson, in a poem published in 1875 on street musician 'Blind Jock', who specialized in 'sellin' sangs or verses', noted in a footnote that 'Street musicians are held to be a nuisance at present, but about 1842 and previously they were rather liked and encouraged by the public', suggesting that this shift had occurred in his lifetime (he was born in 1793).[41] Nonetheless, street verse and broadside culture certainly survived well into the late Victorian period, and tramping poets, 'who hawk terribly bad sets of verses from door to door', were still in existence when Hugh MacDiarmid wrote his essay on William McGonagall, in 1936.[42]

In Scotland, editors and critics made a concerted effort to preserve the memories, and in some cases the verse, of well-known street singers like Hawkie of Glasgow, whose autobiography (suitably bowdlerized) was recorded and published by bookseller David Robertson and edited by his friend John Strathesk. Performers like Hawkie were best known for their own verse and patter, usually impromptu, that was 'chaunted' on the street, and they carried on the traditional function of relaying news of local, national, and international events to an audience of listeners. They also produced verse for special occasions. Hawkie, for example, recalled publishing 'twelve pages of six-line poetry' for a 'Crispin' procession in Edinburgh (Crispin was the patron saint of shoemakers, and their annual celebration always included broadsides on 'King Crispin'). Despite Hawkie's best efforts in persuading the printer not to identify himself on the broadside, he still found, an hour after starting to sell, that his verses had been plagiarized, and that others were 'crying' them at a discount.[43]

Many of the poets featured in this study either wrote verses with the intent of broadside publication, or found their verses republished in broadside form. Broadside republication was particularly important in repurposing poetry as popular song,

---

[39] For a good overview of the field of broadside scholarship, and an emphasis on the relative lack of research into nineteenth-century broadsides, see Steve Roud, 'Introduction', in David Atkinson and Steve Roud, eds., *Street Ballads in Nineteenth-Century Britain, Ireland and North America: The Interface Between Print and Oral Traditions* (Farnham: Ashgate, 2014), pp.1–17.

[40] Charles Hindley, *The Life and Times of James Catnach, Late of Seven Dials, Ballad Monger* (London: Seven Dials Press, 1970 (first published 1878)), p.35; Martha Vicinus, *Broadsides of the Industrial North* (Newcastle upon Tyne: Frank Graham, 1975), p.9.

[41] John Wilson, *Samples of Common Sense in Verse by A Forfarshire Farmer* (Brechin: Black & Johnston, 1875), pp.142–3. Wilson was an early *Whistle-Binkie* contributor as well as local newspaper poet.

[42] Hugh MacDiarmid, *Scottish Eccentrics*, ed. Alan Riach (Manchester: Carcanet, 1993), p.66.

[43] John Strathesk, ed., *Hawkie: The Autobiography of a Gangrel* (Glasgow: David Robertson, 1888), ch. 13. James Maidment's Scrap Book contains several examples of broadsides on the St Crispin's Day procession.

by suggesting a traditional tune for a set of verses or simply extracting part of a longer poem to construct song lyrics; this is as true in the period for works such as Tennyson's 'Come into the Garden, Maud' as it is for local Scottish verse. While most broadsides were anonymous and reprinted from a wide variety of sources, some writers and performers became well-known enough that their works were later collected. John Milne of Glenlivat, born in 1792 and operating as a poet from the 1820s into the mid-Victorian period, is a good example. His songs and poems were published posthumously, edited from the *Aberdeen Free Press* office, and he was remembered with affection in letters, poems and an obituary in the *People's Journal* on his death in 1870.[44] Milne was trained as a shoemaker, but when some 1826 verses that he had written on the local excisemen were taken up by 'the general herd of ballad singers, who were themselves destitute of the rhyming faculty', and were reprinted and sold 'in every town in Scotland', he was inspired to begin a new career as a ballad writer and seller himself, 'As long as he was able to "crawl", John missed no opportunity of attending feeing markets [the hiring fair for labourers] and other gatherings, and there he drove a roaring trade in ballad literature.'[45] Like most street performers of verse, his performance fell 'somewhere between "singing and saying"', and was more humorous than pathetic; he also specialized in election verse for Liberal candidates and in poems warning farm labourers about hard masters. Alexander Mitchell recalled that 'If there was a disagreement at any farm, they sent Johnnie particulars, and he would compose verses and sell them at the feeing market'.[46] Though none of these poems by Milne survive, this culture of conveying specific, local warnings via occasional broadside verse was evidently widespread. John Taylor, a navvy and labourer, republished a poem in his collection about lodgings near Banchory, Aberdeenshire:

> Now all brother navvies who, passing this way,
> May look out for lodgings on some future day,
> I tell you take warning, I bid ye beware, –
> Oh! risk not your life in the Hammerman Square.[47]

Taylor's invocation to a set of listeners, 'Now all brother navvies', is a typical broadside opening phrase, designating a particular audience. Like Milne's lost feeing fair poems, this shows the immediacy and relevance of some occasional verse, and its function in offering advice as from one worker to another, particularly advice that might contradict the representations of those with more money and power (employers, landladies, owners of 'model' lodgings).

---

[44] See 'The Late John Milne of Glenlivat', *People's Journal*, 25 November 1871, p.2.

[45] John Milne, *Selections from the Songs and Poems of the Late John Milne of Glenlivat* (Aberdeen: Free Press Office, 1871), p.xi; 'The Late John Milne of Glenlivat', p.2.

[46] A. Mitchell, *Recollections of a Lifetime* (Edinburgh, 1911), cited in Ian A. Olson, 'Bothy Ballads and Song', in John Beech, Owen Hand, Fiona MacDonald, Mark A. Mulhern and Jeremy Weston, eds., *Oral Literature and Performance Culture*, vol X of Scottish Life and Society: A Compendium of Scottish Ethnology, 14 vols (Edinburgh: John Donald, 2007), pp.322–59, 340n.

[47] John Taylor, 'The Model Lodgings and Landladies of Hammerman Square: A True Story in Rhyme for Navvies', in *Poems, Chiefly on Themes of Scottish Interest*, intro. by W. Lindsay Alexander (Edinburgh: Andrew Stevenson, 1875), p.37.

The author of the introductory biography to Milne's *Selections* states that Milne printed and sold around three hundred poems, but 'some of these were confessedly not his own composition; and in other cases the repetition, not only of idea, but of phraseology in separate pieces, rendered it inadvisable to extend the bulk of this volume.'[48] The examples that were preserved of Milne's verse, then, are carefully curated, and it is likely that the verse he performed was far more personal, scurrilous, and political than the samples chosen by editors. These include 'A New Song in Favour of Her Most Gracious Majesty Queen Victoria':

> Our Queen can rove on Scots mountains,
>   And view the grouse, deer, and the roe,
> Or pass through woods and by fountains –
>   She never will meet with a foe.
>
> She can tread upon dark Lochnagar,
>   Like Byron, that brave English bard;
> Or go from Tweedside to Braemar
>   Without having any Life Guard.
>
> Our Queen is so loved by the Scots,
>   If she's inclined to go
> From Maidenkirk to John o' Groats,
>   She never will meet with a foe.[49]

'Lochnagar', as I discuss in Chapter 3, was one of Byron's best-known works, in part because it was so widely reprinted as a broadside; it is a poem Milne's listeners would have known as a popular song. Formally, Milne's verse has the repetition of lines and phrases typical of spoken broadside verse, it is metrically uneven, and it verges on comic in shaping content to fit rhyme, as in 'bard' and 'Life Guard'. His repetition of the assurance that Victoria 'never will meet with a foe' may be a conscious reference to current affairs (if, for instance, this broadside related to her early visit of 1842, shortly after an assassination attempt in London) or alternatively, might seem like protesting too much given his supportive recollection of the Jacobite cause on the next page ('Scots loved Charlie most dearly') and his desire that the Queen 'every oppression withdraw,/And all our great taxes make less.'[50] Even Victoria's free roving through the countryside might seem suspect, if we consider ongoing local disputes between workers and the 'foes' of factor and gamekeeper, who prevented walkers from moving freely through the Highlands. Whether Milne performed this to his typical audience of farm labourers as straightforward patriotic verse or otherwise is hard to tell, as it would depend on the tone of his interpretation.

In common with many broadside sellers or tramping poets, Milne was not known as a skilled singer, and his verse is part of a contemporary spoken word culture rather than primarily related to street song. This spoken broadside verse was often formally characterized by couplets, as in Milne's anti-Catholic poem, almost certainly about the 'Papal Aggression' of 1851 (when Cardinal Wiseman

---

[48] Milne, p.xix.   [49] Ibid., p.62.   [50] Ibid., p.63.

was appointed by the Pope as a new British cardinal), which rehearses a popular history of Roman Catholic oppression:

> If any did the Romish Church forsake
> They burned were to death just at the stake,
> The Pope oft laid the Romish Church foundation
> By fire and sword in many a nation;
> And it was known for certain, as a fact,
> That many thousands suffered on the rack.
> The boots and thumbkins were in fashion then,
> May Scotchmen never see such days again,
> It oft did put our forefathers to a stand,
> When the Pope bore rule in Scotland,
> But though Popery in England far advance
> It will not in Scotland have the same chance.[51]

Doubtful rhymes (fact/rack), varying line lengths, unnatural emphases caused by the way in which the stress falls ('ScotLAND'), and an interest in blood and violence, are also strong markers of performed broadside verse. The definite end-rhymes are one of few characteristics that mark this as verse, and in spoken performance would likely have been emphasized while the remainder of each line was more conversational; differing line lengths would be reconciled by the timing of the spoken line. What seem, in print, like amateurish attempts at a regular poetic form, would have been counteracted in performance, and contemporary auditors and readers seeing this verse on the printed page would naturally have recognized its roots in the oral.

By mid-century, as Paul Maloney has studied in detail, music hall was starting to dominate Scottish popular culture and theatre.[52] While the very common use of poetry in popular 'national' dramas, such as the ever-expanding and updated versions of *Rob Roy*, lies outside the scope of this study, it is important to note that audiences from around mid-century were used to hearing spoken verse, not simply song, in theatrical entertainments of all kinds.[53] A number of poets discussed in this monograph were stage performers, perhaps most strikingly in the many entertainments sponsored by temperance societies. W. P. Crawford of Glasgow, in an epistle poem to tailor-poet James Nicholson (who also published a botanical work as 'Father Fernie'), recalls Nicholson's local fame as a performer for the Glasgow temperance cause:

> At Temp'rance gala or soiree,
> When young folk's hearts danc'd wild wi' glee,
> The wale o' treats was then tae see

---

[51] Milne, 'The Pope of Rome', p.97.

[52] Paul Maloney, *Scotland and the Music Hall, 1850–1914* (Manchester: Manchester University Press, 2003).

[53] For a highly valuable study of Scottish popular theatre, see Alisdair Cameron and Adrienne Scullion, eds., *Scottish Popular Theatre and Entertainment* (Glasgow: Glasgow University Library Studies, 1996).

> And hear blythe Faither Fernie.
> His stories an' poetic lore
> Aye kept the house a' in a roar[54]

Many of the poems in Nicholson's published collections were performance scripts, presented 'at social gatherings in and around Glasgow'. Poetic dialogues such as 'Wee Tibbie and Her Bib', which opened with the drunken father (Nicholson) facing his little daughter (Miss M. Sharpe) 'standing dressed in her regalia' as a child member of the Good Templars, and closed with the father pledging himself to temperance, record these performances.[55] The rise of new forms of popular entertainment also enabled poets and songwriters like James Houston, whose day job was as an engineer, to move gradually into full-time careers as a performer. Starting as a participant in occasional verse culture, by writing songs and poems for the 'annual festivals and excursions' of the Vulcan Foundry in Glasgow, Houston eventually became a leading music-hall performer and comedian in Scotland.[56] The 'Songs and Sketches' included in his memoir show him as a politicized poet addressing fellow-workers, as in 'The Engineers and the Short-Time Movement':

> The masters they have shut their hearts,
>   And drawn their purse-strings tightly;
> They say to starve us till we yield
>   Would only serve us rightly[57]

yet also as a comic performer, recounting local incidents in his own life, such as a visit to Dunoon:

> Dunoon has long been famous as a favourite resort
> For invalids and tourists in quest of health and sport –
> In sunny shores and shady bowers where lovers gently roam,
> Its gardens and neat cottages, churches, and sea-side home.[58]

As in most tourist broadside verse celebrating holiday destinations or particular locations, the description here is effectively interchangeable with any similar location, and is designed to flatter the inhabitants, to whom the author is marketing his verse. Houston's verse was probably printed and sold in broadside form as well as performed, though he does not confirm this in his memoirs. That he included a substantial selection of poems, however, shows that he wanted to be remembered not just as a performer, but as one of Scotland's poets and lyricists, capable of adapting genre and form for different audiences and venues.

---

[54] W. P. Crawford, 'Epistle to "Faither Fernie"', *Poets of the People's Journal*, p.209. Nicholson is discussed further in Chapter 2.

[55] James Nicholson, *Wee Tibbie's Garland, and Other Poems* (Glasgow: James McGeachy, 1873), p.22.

[56] James, Houston, *Autobiography of Mr James Houston, Scotch Comedian* (Glasgow and Edinburgh: John Menzies, 1889), p.19. On Houston, see Bill Findlay, 'Scots Language and Popular Entertainment in Victorian Scotland: The Case of James Houston', in Alisdair Cameron and Adrienne Scullion, eds., *Scottish Popular Theatre and Entertainment* (Glasgow: Glasgow University Library Studies, 1996), pp.15–38.

[57] Houston, p.132.   [58] Houston, p.92.

Milne and Houston managed to turn their skills in producing and marketing verse into careers, where the ability to write and perform became their primary (though not always very reliable) source of income. They were, in effect, professionals, who expected to profit by their verse. The difference between their careers shows us how the cultures of verse performance shifted during the century. Milne, trained in an artisanal profession (shoemaking) that brought with it a measure of independence, was part of an older tradition of street performers, who worked outdoors and at rural gatherings, and travelled the country with their pack of broadsides. Houston, born in 1828, when Milne's career was already underway, worked in a large firm in an industrial city, and made a career in new Victorian entertainment venues catering largely for city workers; he had greater mobility (he lived for a time in Australia, and performed across Britain) and was part of a more professionalized network of Scottish entertainers. Although broadside verse and street performers did survive throughout the Victorian period, the difference between these two writers shows the culture of verse performance moving off the streets, and becoming part of modern entertainment culture.

Writers who managed to turn a skill for writing occasional verse into a career were rare. It is when we turn to the culture of amateur occasional verse that the scale of its importance in Victorian verse culture, and its prevalence as a recognized part of the daily life of communities, becomes apparent. The reason why most volumes of verse by Scottish working-class poets contain multiple elegies, for example, is because these were written for and about members of the poets' communities in an immediate, and almost certainly invited, response. Lanarkshire stonemason William McHutchison's 'Lines, on the Death of Archibald Wark, Calderbank, who Died 29th January, 1875, aged three years – deeply regretted', were printed in the newspaper with the note '*Written by request*'.[59] That McHutchison was in demand as an elegy-writer in his locality is suggested by the inclusion of more elegies, such as 'Lines on the Death of Alexander Paterson' and 'Lines on the Death of Janet Anderson Lang, aged eleven months, who died 17 December 1857, on board the "Merchant Prince," while going to Australia with her parents' in his published collection, though it is only the newspaper note that shows us that these were most likely also commissioned.[60] Mitchelson Porteous, a printer in Maybole, Ayrshire, who was at the centre of a network of local Ayrshire poets, supplied elegies for local people over several decades: 'To the Memory of Mr Thomas Orr, Merchant, Maybole', 'In Memory of the Late John Campbell, MD, Maybole', 'To Miss B, on the Sudden Death of Her Husband', or the more sardonic, 'Epitaph for Allan, A Noisy Whig'.[61] He also wrote series of birthday poems for friends in the area, as well as pamphlet verse for local celebrations.[62] A. C. Lamb, proprietor of

---

[59] *West Lothian Courier*, 3 April 1875, p.3.

[60] William McHutchison Poems (n.p., n.d. [Airdrie, 1868]), pp.141, 146.

[61] Mitchelson Porteous, *Odd Time: A Selection of Original Varieties* (Maybole: printed for the author, 1842), p.89; Mitchelson Porteous, *Carrickiana* (Maybole: printed for the author, n.d.), pp.23, 92, 21.

[62] *Carrickiana* contains four odes 'To Mr William Hannay on his Birth Day', written between 1850 and 1859 (pp.64–72).

Lamb's Temperance Hotel in Dundee, who had a magpie-like tendency to keep every piece of verse he found, preserved numerous poems published on single sheets with black borders, evidently designed to be handed out at funerals. It is probable that all the elegies that working-class poets collected for their volumes were first distributed in this ephemeral form, after which they might, like McHutchison's elegy, be reprinted in the local newspaper press, serving as obituaries. This particular culture of local elegy-writing was, of course, not exclusive to Scotland: the most famous nineteenth-century example of a fictional local elegist is Mark Twain's Emmeline Granger in *Huckleberry Finn*, a respectable if rather morbid young lady in provincial America, whose bad poems are famously satirized.[63] It does show, however, the part that a local Victorian poet was expected to play in preserving memories for their community, and indicates the common three-stage process for commissioned poems—from a single sheet, to a newspaper poetry column, to a published volume.

Most collections of Scottish working-class verse from this period include various poems subtitled with the occasion for which they were written, and on which they were delivered. Newspapers published multiple instances of the subgenre that we might call associational verse, poems written for a specific audience at a meeting, event, dinner, or other social occasion. The annual January celebration of Burns's birthday at Burns Society or other meetings was by far the single most popular 'occasion' for poetry (many collections contain multiple Burns anniversary poems, with poets obliged to compose a new one year after year). But almost every meeting featured a poem. These are not exclusively the province of working-class poets— occasions attended by middle- or upper-class audiences also included poems, composed by poets from all backgrounds—nor is occasional poetry a Victorian invention. *Blackwood's* 'Noctes Ambrosianae' includes a number of fictionalized social gatherings in the 1820s at which the assembled company will recite or sing specially composed verse: for example, songs celebrating salmon on a fishing expedition, including one by James Hogg, the Ettrick Shepherd.[64] Studying this subgenre does, however, show how common it was for local working-class authors to compose verses, either to be sung or read, to meet the requirements of different audiences at social events.

To take a political example, radical poet John Mitchell (of Aberdeen, as opposed to the earlier Paisley poet John Mitchell), who left shoemaking to become a bookseller, newsagent, and editor dedicated to Chartism and temperance, republished a 'Hymn, Written for, and Sung at, a Meeting of the Aberdeen Working-Men's Association, to celebrate the Presentation of the National Petition' in his 1840 collection. It falls into the genre of the Chartist hymn, in which religion and politics are intertwined to express faith in God's support of the Chartist cause: 'A nation's

---

[63] Mark Twain, *The Adventures of Huckleberry Finn*, ed. John Seelye and Guy Cardwell (Harmondsworth: Penguin, 2009), pp.114–16.
[64] 'Song of the Salmon', in John Wilson et al., *Noctes Ambrosianae*, with Memoirs and Notes by R. Shelton Mackenzie, vol I: 1819–1824 (New York: Redfield, 1859), pp.22–3.

cry, O! do thou hear;/Increase our hope, dispel our fear'.[65] In contrast to this political exhortation, however, much associational verse was straightforwardly celebratory. It might praise the cause of the meeting, for instance the 'north country salmon', as in another original fishing song by Robert Smith 'written for the occasion' of the annual salmon dinner in the Royal Hotel, Aberdeen.[66] It might also celebrate the achievements of the assembled company. Farmer-poet Laurence Drysdale, who specialized in occasional verse for 'ploughing matches' and 'shows of the agricultural society, for which he was poet laureate' produced a 'Song' for an agricultural club dinner:

> For the raising of large turnips, and curing hay so sweet,
> And for draining of our land, we do it so complete,
> With the best of materials, such as wood, stone, and tiles,
> And the av'rage draned for premiums is fully thirty miles.[67]

This has the ring of broadside verse, in its couplets, strong end-rhymes, and uneven rhythms. Drysdale speaks to the collective, improving identity of his agricultural society. Associational verse can also laud the person honoured by the meeting or dinner: the *Dundee Advertiser* reported a tenants' dinner to welcome home Lord Hallyburton at which 'Mr David Ritchie, farmer, Greenbarns, here rose and volunteered to read an address to His Lordship which he had put into rhyme… Mr Ritchie then went up to His Lordship, and handed him the MS of the piece, shaking hands with him over the table.'[68] Verse also seemed an appropriate medium for proffering thanks, as in Walter Watson's 'Langsyne', which the editors of his collection published with a detailed note preserving its provenance:

> The following verses were recited by the author at a Concert of Vocal Music, given in a 'big barn' at Avenuehead, near Moodiesburn, on the first of April, 1850, by several musical friends, for the purpose of endeavouring to raise a few pounds for his benefit.[69]

Or it could praise a company and its products, as in Glasgow engineer poet Alexander Murdoch's eulogy to Singer's sewing machine, 'It shines within the rich man's hall, and cheers the poor man's hearth,/The tiniest yet mightiest invention on the earth', in verses 'sung at the Annual Soiree of the Singer Manufacturing Company's Workers in the City Hall, Glasgow, 23rd February, 1877'.[70]

'Associational' poets were in demand by their community. A Robert Ramsay, for instance, delivered verses within six months of 1883 at the Bathgate Chemical Works Annual Dinner and two different Bathgate temperance society events,

---

[65] John Mitchell, *Poems, Radical Rhymes, Tales etc* (Aberdeen: Published by the Author, 1840), pp.37–8. On Chartist hymns, see Sanders, ' "God is our Guide! Our Cause is Just!": The National Chartist Hymn Book and Chartist Hymnody', *Victorian Studies* 54 (2012), 679–705.

[66] 'The Salmon Dinner', *Aberdeen Herald*, 2 February 1850, p.19.

[67] Reprinted in James Beveridge, ed., *The Poets of Clackmannanshire* (Glasgow: John S. Wilson, 1885), pp.118, 126.

[68] 'Dinner to Lord J. F. G. Hallyburton at Coupar Angus', *Dundee Advertiser*, 21 October 1859, p.3.

[69] Watson, p.59.

[70] Alexander G. Murdoch, *Rhymes and Lyrics* (Kilmarnock: James McKie, Glasgow: Alexander G. Murdoch, 1879), p.92.

for the Good Templars and the Blue Ribbon Army. His Chemical Works poem, as reprinted in the *West Lothian Courier*, is over fifty lines of comic verse, referencing workers and masters present at the dinner, and in broad Scots:

> I dinna ken ye a', but there's a chiel'
> I tak' for Mr Scott, frae Addieweel.
> An' there's the man wha kens the perfe't cure,
> A' mends oor broken banes, Dr Langmuir.
> But for that birkie there, I'm in a fix,
> I trow he's Moritz, though, wha mak's the bricks;
> A' real guid men: we ocht to feel richt prood.
> What say ye chaps? dae ye no, think we should?
> We wha frae week to week ha'e claes sae oily,
> This nicht are dinin' wi' a worthy Bailie.[71]

Ramsay's verse presents itself as spontaneous speech, as he looks around the assembled company and addresses individuals seemingly at random, yet, of course, the rhymes—like the clever rhyme on fix/Moritz/bricks—show the care he has put into this composition (and, incidentally, celebrate a presumably European worker in this firm). The fact that the newspaper could reprint the entire poem also suggests it was supplied to the press as a written manuscript, as we might presume is the case with all such reprinted associational verse. In lines like 'What say ye chaps?' Ramsay invites audience participation, through applause or cheers. The poem thanks and honours the worthies present, from the perspective of a worker with 'claes sae oily', a perspective also shown by Ramsay's choice to deliver this in Scots. The verse is designed to celebrate good relations between workmen and dignitaries, but it simultaneously highlights the distance between them and the rarity of such occasions. Ramsay delivered it when called up for a song, to the 'surprise and astonishment' of the company, who were 'electrified' by his recitation. In contrast, and showing the versatility of associational poets, his Blue Ribbon Army poem was a tragic tale, in standard English, of a boy's fall into alcoholism, 'listened to with rapt attention' by its audience. Little is known of Ramsay outside these references.[72]

All such examples show how original verse, recited or sung, reinforced a sense of shared community and pride in the reason for the meeting: workplace and professional pride, pride in shared skills and pursuits, or pride in shared political or regional identity. That *verse*, rather than a prose speech, was deemed an important part of these meetings was due both to the pleasure in listening to, or singing, a piece with clearly marked rhythm and rhyme; and to the high status of poetry in Victorian culture. Any society and any meeting wanted to show that they could call upon a member or participant to produce a poem, because this was a sign of collective cultural literacy. In the case of a tenant farmer presenting his poem to the laird, or a worker reciting his verses in front of the masters, such purpose is particularly marked, as it blurs the class distinction between cultured and

---

[71] 'Bathgate Chemical Works Annual Dinner', *West Lothian Courier*, 11 February 1882, p.2.
[72] *West Lothian Courier*, 24 June 1882, p.2 and 'The Blue Ribbon Army in Bathgate', 16 September 1882, p.2.

uncultured, consciously highlighting the literary talents of working-class participants in these occasions.

Satire was another established mode for performed occasional and associational poems, particularly satire of employers. Few such poems have survived, probably because poets judged them either too obscure or too scurrilous for general readers and for reprinting. Editor and literary man James Hedderwick, for instance, recalled a *Scotsman* office event, for which 'One of the staff had prepared some off-hand rhymes for the occasion, in which the various heads of departments were hit off in a ludicrous fashion.'[73] Taylor, the ambitious Paisley engineer who wrote poems in his spare time, recalled his horror on realizing that the manager and foreman of his firm had come to a social evening for the firm's debating society, for which Taylor had composed a poem satirizing the management (presumably like Ramsay's Bathgate poem, only less polite), filled with references to 'kent folk': 'Here was I with a piece which took me 25 minutes to deliver, and the rhyme was impossible to alter, and the boys were gasping for it.'[74] That this was a twenty-five minute performance shows how long some of these social pieces could be, and the effort that went into composing them. After the performance, Taylor's manager asked for a copy of the manuscript, but on reflection he burned it rather than hand it over, and managed to keep his job. The semi-fictional hero of James Myles's *Chapters in the Life of a Dundee Factory Boy* (1850) was less fortunate:

> I must premise that at this early age I had a knack of writing verses and satirical lampoons on the passing events of our locality…Well, as it might be expected, my master was too good a target to shoot at to escape my young shafts. I accordingly penned a rather respectable parody on 'Rob Roryson's Bonnet', in which the weak and prominent points of Mr Dobson's character were rather ludicrously and painfully exposed. The song got abroad…The author was discovered and ordered to quit the premises.[75]

Alexander Gordon, a factory clerk and poet in Aberdeen in the 1830s, was also dismissed from his position after 'a piece from his pen appeared in a scurrilous sheet', and had to become a soldier.[76] While satirical verse was a traditional genre in which to lampoon local worthies and officials, producing it could be dangerous. Even when circulating satires anonymously or pseudonymously (Gordon published as 'The Planter') rather than performing them to an audience in person, authors were not safe. More than one nineteenth-century court case centred on libel prosecutions in relation to verse satire, for example 'The South Leith Libel Case' of 1855, in which the case hinged on whether a scurrilous poem about church

---

[73] James Hedderwick, *Backward Glances or Some Personal Recollections* (William Blackwood & Sons: Edinburgh and London, 1891), p.80.

[74] Taylor, p.70.

[75] Unsigned [James Myles], *Chapters in the Life of a Dundee Factory Boy* (Dundee: James Myles, 1850), p.75. Myles was a well-known Dundee artisan who, by the 1840s, ran a bookshop and newsagency. Chapters first appeared in the Northern Warder in 1850. See Christopher Whatley, 'Altering Images of the Industrial City: The Case of James Myles, the "Factory Boy" and Mid-Victorian Dundee', in Louise Miskell, Christopher A. Whatley and Bob Harris, eds., *Victorian Dundee: Images and Realities* (East Linton: Tuckwell Press, 2000), pp.70–95.

[76] See William Walker, ed., *The Bards of Bon-Accord, 1375–1860* (Aberdeen: Edmond & Spark, 1887), p.617.

office-bearers had been authored by the minister, Mr Duff, or by a disaffected tile manufacturer, Adam Brown Todd, who circulated the verses as an act of revenge, knowing they would be attributed to Duff.[77]

In the 'Barber's Shop' column in the 1859 Dundee *Weekly News*, which purports to show a group of working-class characters—including a poetically inclined weaver, Treddle, gossiping about the news of the day (a conceit following the more famous conversational pieces in *Blackwood's*)—the character Sandy Swab, recounting what happened at a Dundee Harbour Board dinner the previous night, tells his friends that the post-dinner entertainment included an 'original song':

TREDDLE – A ha! wha wad expectit that – pity ye didna bring it away, Sandy; was it in the real Byronical style?

SWAB – A kind o' that wi' a cross o' the street ballant style in it. I just mind twa verse o't.

RASPER – Sing them, Sandy, we're all contention.

SWAB – Ah but I couldna mind the tune, it was a real pecooliar metre.

TREDDLE – Never mind the gas question, gies the sang.

SWAB – Weel, I suppose I'll try it to the tune o' 'Johnnie Grumlie' –

He then sings the two verses, of which the second runs:

> The Harbour board's a model board,
> And now a hint I'd throw out –
> That twice, instead of once a year.
> They'd give us their annual blow-out.[78]

'Shade of blind Hughie!', Treddle cries, 'and have we come to this?'. 'Hadn't we better ask Tennyson to resign?' adds the barber, Rasper. From the start of the conversation, the collective are ironic about the inevitability of an 'original song' appearing at such a dinner, and about the likely quality of this occasional verse. They view it as a dubious 'cross' between high poetic culture, represented by Byron and Tennyson, and street verse and 'ballants', represented by Blind Hughie, a famous street singer of Dundee. This particular stanza is amusing because the crudeness of asking for a second dinner, and the slang of 'blow-out', contrast with the expectation that verse recited at a function like this will celebrate the function and thank its sponsors. The listeners, here, show a sophisticated understanding of the relation of occasional verse to the verse cultures of established poetry and of the public street. While this song is probably (though not necessarily) invented in order to mock the Dundee Harbour Board dinner, readers would have recognized its similarity to works like those by Laurence Drysdale, because they would themselves have heard them, or indeed produced them.

---

[77] See 'The South Leith Libel Case', *Paisley Herald and Renfrewshire Advertiser*, 11 August 1855, p.1.

[78] *Weekly News*, 1 October 1859, p.2. 'John Grumlie' was a comic song about a man who tried to do his wife's household jobs for a day, and failed miserably. See *Lyric Gems of Scotland, with Music* (Glasgow: David Jack, 1856), p.54. The author/s of the 'Barber-Shop' column are unknown.

What this moment of community shows us is the shared bank of musical knowledge that working men are assumed to possess—immediately able to pick a new tune, known to all of them, to fit a given verse—and the presumption that original sung or spoken verse, albeit poorly executed, will be part of a formal occasion. It also shows us that an imagined listener *remembered* what he had heard, even if only 'twa verse' rather than the verses in entirety. Such productions, occupying a hybrid position between oral and written verse cultures, and between published poetry by established writers and street broadsides, circulate through differing kinds of public space and in differing print formats throughout the period. They show us that original poetry, not simply the quotations from established poets so common in Victorian public speech, was valued and judged as part of public discourse, and that its composition and performance were viewed as useful social skills for an aspirational worker.

SHAPING COMMUNITIES: NEWSPAPER POETRY AND THE CONSTRUCTION OF THE LOCAL POET

Locating the historical moment for which a poem was written, especially in the case of occasional verse, would be virtually impossible without the actions of local newspapers in printing and reprinting poems. Newspaper poetry is at the heart of this study, and, as I and other scholars have argued elsewhere, is central to any study of working-class poetics.[79] While this is also true to some extent of the eighteenth century, it is the dramatic expansion of the provincial and popular press after the abolition of stamp and paper duties, changing the newspaper 'from being an item few could afford to an item few could afford to be without', which enabled the rise of newspaper verse.[80] As William Donaldson notes:

> The new press aimed itself, typically, at the upper working-class—the decent respectable working men and women with a little disposable cash in their pockets and their white-collar cousins in the rapidly expanding lower middle class.[81]

---

[79] Kirstie Blair, 'The Newspaper Press and the Victorian Working-Class Poet', in John Goodridge and Bridget Keegan, eds., *A History of British Working-Class Literature* (Cambridge: Cambridge University Press, 2017), pp.264–80. See also Sanders' discussion of the Northern Star in The Poetry of Chartism, Cohen and Fertig on Bernstein in the Weekly Mail, and Rosen on Johnston in the Penny Post. On the significance of newspaper poetry more broadly, see Natalie Houston, 'Newspaper Poems: Material Texts in the Public Sphere', *Victorian Studies* 50 (2008), 233–42; Andrew Hobbs, 'Five Million Poems, or the Local Press as Poetry Publisher, 1800–1900', *Victorian Periodicals Review* 45 (2012), 488–92; Andrew Hobbs and Clare Januszewski, 'How Local Papers Came to Dominate Victorian Poetry Publishing', *Victorian Poetry* 52 (2014), 65–87; and F. Elizabeth Gray, 'Journalism and Poetry in the Nineteenth Century', *Journalism Studies* 18 (2017), 807–25. Hughes on Henley, cited in FN19, also focuses on poetry in a specific newspaper.

[80] Matthew Rubery, *The Novelty of Newspapers: Victorian Fiction After the Invention of the News* (Oxford: Oxford University Press, 2009), p.4.

[81] Donaldson, Popular Literature, p.3. On the extent and nature of the newspaper press in early Victorian Scotland, see the seminal study by R. M. W. Cowan, *The Newspaper in Scotland: A Study of its First Expansion, 1815–1860* (Glasgow: George Outram, 1946). For an important new study of the Victorian provincial press and its readers in England, see Andrew Hobbs, *A Fleet Street in Every Town: The Provincial Press in England, 1855–1900* (Open Book Publishers, 2018).

It was these aspirational readers who provided the content for the 'Poets' Corner'. The newspaper as primary publication venue profoundly shapes the content, style, and form of Victorian working-class verse, and the particularly rapid growth of new provincial newspapers in Scotland (combined with Scotland's higher rates of literacy amongst working people and relatively lower costs of newspapers) is a direct cause of the ubiquity of Scottish working-class poets. Although the press was not solely responsible for inspiring these would-be poets, it was the leading agent in promoting the notion that poetry was endemic to Scotland, and consciously helped to create the culture it purported to describe. Indeed, the majority of published volumes by Scottish working-class poets were either printed directly by a newspaper office, or by the same press and printer that also published the local paper. While it would be an impossible task to trace the original publication venue of every poem cited in this monograph, it is a near certainty that most, if not all, were first published in a newspaper, and many were reprinted in multiple newspapers, at home and abroad.[82] Put simply, the verse cultures described here would for the most part neither have existed nor been preserved without the provincial press.

The focus on newspapers rather than periodicals here does not, of course, counter the significance of periodicals and magazines in publishing Victorian poetry. As recent criticism has shown, poetry was an integral part of periodical culture.[83] While the specific presence of working-class poets in leading periodicals has not been studied extensively, the poets discussed in this volume certainly aspired to feature in *Blackwood's Edinburgh Magazine*, *Chambers's Journal*, *Good Words*, *Household Words* and a host of other leading periodicals, not least because they offered payment for poems, while newspapers did not. William Shelley (aka William Fisher) of Aberdeen, who led a varied career as a hawker, labourer, engraver, and clerk, and who published across the Scottish press as 'S. Sherif' and 'Flaxdresser', had his greatest success when *Good Words* paid several guineas for 'Among the Field Flowers', while Macfarlan's biographer notes the 'liberal recompense' he received when his poems were accepted by *Household Words*.[84] Periodicals run by writers known to be sympathetic to working-class literature, culture, or politics, such as *Howitt's Journal*, *Ben Brierley's Journal* and *Eliza Cook's Journal*, were also vital. John Cassell's *The Working Man's Friend* was especially significant for several Scottish poets: Janet Hamilton published here, and Nicholson recalled seeing the launch of

---

[82] On the practice of reprinting and copyright law in America and Britain, the best study is Meredith McGill, *American Literature and the Culture of Reprinting, 1834–1853* (Philadephia, PA: University of Pennsylvania Press, 2003).

[83] For example, see Ledbetter (2009) and Harris (2016) (see Introduction) and the essays in a recent special issue of Victorian Poetry (2014), on 'Victorian Periodical Poetry', ed. Alison Chapman and Caley Ehnes. Chapman's 'Database of Victorian Periodical Poetry' is an important online resource for identifying the range of poems published in periodicals, http://web.uvic.ca/~vicpoet/showpageimage-2/database-of-victorian-periodical-poetry/ (consulted 18 September 2018). Linda K. Hughes provides a significant new overview in 'Poetry', in Andrew King, Alexis Easley and John Morton, eds., *The Routledge Handbook to Nineteenth-Century British Periodicals and Newspapers*, ed. (London: Routledge, 2016), pp.124–37).

[84] Walker, p.574. James Macfarlan, *The Poetical Works of James Macfarlan*, Intro. and Memoir, Colin Rae-Brown (Glasgow: Robert Forrester, 1882), p.vi.

Cassell's periodical as a 'golden opportunity for working men'.[85] In the establishment of the *People's Journal* in Dundee, which arguably did more to encourage working-class Scottish poets than any other newspaper, its owner, John Leng, may have seen Cassell's earlier venture as a model.

As a generalization, nationally known periodicals primarily aimed at a middle-class readership were far less likely than newspapers to publish and identify work-ing-class poets, unless they were doing so to make a case for exceptionalism, as in the relationship between David Wingate and *Blackwood's*, discussed in Chapter 4. Trades journals did provide another major venue for poetry by working writers, and, as David Finkelstein's new research into printers' journals has shown, there is significant crossover between the Scottish poets who published in the local press, and those who sent their work to periodicals aimed at other readers in the same profession.[86] The same is true of Chartist and socialist newspapers, as well as other national newspapers and magazines dedicated to specific political causes. For Scotland, the most important of these is probably Glasgow's *Chartist Circular*, whose attitude towards poetry and literary culture has already been examined by Michael Sanders.[87] Both poems and poetry criticism by working men and women also appeared in the published and manuscript magazines of Scottish mutual improvement and literary societies. As Lauren Weiss's recent research into these little-known sources has shown, they indicate that nineteenth-century societies (often primarily composed of artisan workers), enjoyed imitating the format and style of periodicals, and took these as a model for improving their writing, editorial, and critical skills. Though such magazines were not unique to Scotland, Weiss's investigation tentatively suggests that this culture of self-created or independently printed society magazines, usually circulated privately amongst a small group of readers, may have been especially prevalent in Scotland or amongst Scottish com-munities in England and beyond.[88]

Further research into British periodical culture in the period will undoubtedly uncover new information about the operation of working-class poetic networks. For every poet studied in this book, however, all other publication venues paled beside the importance of the local newspaper press, which offered immediacy, convenience and cheapness (local poets could even hand-deliver to the newspaper office, as William McGonagall did with Dundee's *Weekly News*), a less daunting

[85] James Nicholson, *Kilwuddie and Other Poems*, intro. Alexander Macleod (Glasgow: Scottish Temperance League, 1863), p.18. This is extracted from Nicholson's entry in the Glasgow Commonwealth competition, discussed below.

[86] David Finkelstein, *Movable Types: Roving Creative Printers of the Victorian World* (Oxford: Oxford University Press, 2018). In chapter 3, Finkelstein discusses printer poets and notes that he has identified over 400 poems in print trade periodicals from 1840–70 (p.124).

[87] Michael Sanders, 'Courtly Lays or Democratic Songs? The Politics of Poetic Citation in Chartist Literary Criticism', in Kirstie Blair and Mina Gorji, eds., *Class and the Canon: Constructing Labouring-Class Poetry and Poetics, 1750–1900* (Houndmills: Palgrave Macmillan, 2013), pp.156–73.

[88] See Lauren Weiss, 'The Manuscript Magazines of the Wellpark Free Church Young Men's Literary Society, Glasgow: A Case Study', in Paul Raphael Rooney and Anna Gasperini, eds., *Media and Print Culture Consumption in Nineteenth-Century Britain: The Victorian Reading Experience* (Basingstoke: Palgrave Macmillan, 2016), pp.53–73.

standard of competition, and the knowledge that the poet's local community, including family, friends and workmates, would see the poem in print. The rise of the British provincial press, as David Vincent noted, 'constituted at once a nursery and a shop window for new literary talent' and made getting into print 'much the easiest stage in the journey' to becoming an 'author'.[89] Prefaces, memoirs and real and fictional autobiographies amply attest to the 'exquisite, the thrilling pleasure' of getting a poem into The Poet's Corner.[90] James Ferguson, Perthshire millworker, labourer, and surfaceman, who published extensively in the *People's Journal* and *Friend* as 'Nisbet Noble', reported that when he saw his first poem in the newspaper 'Earth seemed too small for me. I needed wings.'[91] Glasgow poet John Young's preface to *Poems and Lyrics* comments that during a stint in the poorhouse he sent one of his poems, 'Nancy Whiskey', to a Glasgow newspaper, 'and was at once made the happiest of my long-faced compeers by having "Nancy" accepted, and seeing my name in print for the first time'.[92] 'I dispatched the following poem to the *Juteport Express*', writes the anonymous author of *The History of a Village Shopkeeper* of a fictional (Dundee) newspaper, 'my first attempt to jingle my thoughts in rhyme. To my great delight it was inserted.'[93] One of the pseudonymous winners of the Glasgow *Commonwealth*'s competition for working-class autobiography, shoemaker poet and would-be journalist 'Stirrup', recalled his first appearance in the *Inverness Courier*:

> Oh, my feelings! who can depict them. Editors little know the anxiety of their new fledged correspondents waiting to see the fate of their efforts. I was no longer the little unknown boy that I was an hour ago; now my name was known, printed, and circulated. I was an author.[94]

Such accounts are so common that they become another recurring trope in Scottish working-class autobiography, albeit one occasionally treated with cynicism, as in shoemaker Thomas Denham's recollection of first appearing in the *Aberdeen Journal* and *Herald*, 'There was pride at first in being in print, but the silly feeling rolled away before the stern realities attendant on poverty!'[95]

Andrew Hobbs, one of few scholars to study the presence of poetry in the provincial press, has shown that the Northern press published substantial numbers of poems, and it was unusual for any Victorian newspaper to print no poetry whatsoever.[96] As writers such as Joseph Tatlow, a railway clerk who moved from England to work in Glasgow in the early 1870s, suggested, however, it was not simply the existence

---

[89] Vincent, *Literacy and Popular Culture: England 1750–1914* (Cambridge: Cambridge University Press, 1989), p.214.

[90] Alexander Murdoch, cited in Blair (2016), p.xiv.   [91] Edwards, 1880, p.147.

[92] John Young, *Poems and Lyrics* (Glasgow: George Gallie, 1868), p.v.

[93] (*The History of a Village Shopkeeper* (Edinburgh: John Menzies, 1876), p.75).

[94] Stirrup, 'The Autobiography of a Journeyman Shoemaker', Part II, *Commonwealth*, 29 November 1856, p.3.

[95] Thomas Denham, *Poems and Snatches of Prose* (London: Smith, Elder, 1845), p.i.

[96] See Andrew Hobbs, works cited in FN 79 and 81, and Reading the Local Paper: Social and Cultural Functions of the Press in Preston, Lancashire, 1855–1900. Unpublished PhD thesis, University of Central Lancashire, 2010.

of the cheap popular press, but specifically *Scottish* print culture that encouraged working men to try their hand at getting poems into print:

> It was not until I lived in Scotland, where poetical taste and business talent thrive side by side…that I became courageous, and ventured to avow my dear delight. It was there that I sought, with some success, publication in various papers and magazines of my attempts at versification, for versification it was that so possessed my fancy.[97]

Tatlow's perception of Scottish print culture as more welcoming to poetry written by a railway employee might indicate how successfully editors and reviewers, including those cited at the start of this chapter, had promoted the perception of Scotland as supportive of working-class authors. Scottish (and British) newspapers published two kinds of poetry: 'original' and reprinted, with 'original' usually implying that the newspaper was the first, and consciously selected, publication venue. The most frequently reprinted poets were, not surprisingly, the global poetic celebrities of their day, Alfred Tennyson and Henry Wadsworth Longfellow, with a definite bias towards Longfellow and his inspirational verse. The 'canon' of Scottish newspaper poets was, however, less focused on poets with strong literary reputations in Britain (writers such as Arnold, Robert Browning, Arthur Hugh Clough, Dante Gabriel Rossetti, Christina Rossetti and A. C. Swinburne appear very seldom), and more likely to include popular periodical poets who either had direct links to Scotland, or were in some way involved with working-class self-improvement, such as Eliza Cook, Gerald Massey, Frances Browne, or Charles Mackay. Newspapers also regularly reprinted anonymous and pseudonymous poetry from other Scottish, British, Irish, American, and occasionally Australian, New Zealand, or South African papers.

My focus here is on the 'Original' poetry, explicitly or implicitly 'written for this paper'. Scottish editors liked to claim that they were drowning in poetry submissions. The Dundee *People's Journal*, which from its 1858 foundation strongly encouraged the submission of poems, letters and articles by working-class readers, repeatedly published notes asking for a moratorium: 'We have promised the insertion of as many poems as we can publish for some weeks to come, and must request our correspondents to keep their productions by them until they see we are running short again', 'Poetical contributions are setting in on us in such overwhelming numbers, that we could easily fill half our available space with very respectable verse.'[98] In 1861, the *Journal* editor lamented the quantities of MS poems in the office and announced he was burning them in an editorial 'slaughter of the innocents'; delighted readers responded with Scots and English letters and poems bewailing his decision, 'My brithers o' rhyme,/ This has been a sad time'.[99] In the *Glasgow Citizen*'s satirical 'A Glance into the Sanctum', a 'constant reader'

---

[97] Joseph Tatlow, *Fifty Years of Railway Life* (London: The Railway Gazette, 1920), p.6.
[98] 'To Our Poetical Correspondents', *People's Journal*, 9 July 1859, p.2; and 'To Correspondents', *People's Journal*, 24 December 1859, p.2.
[99] From a parody of the tragic song 'The Bonnie House o' Airlie', in 'Miserable Comforters', *People's Journal*, 16 February 1861, p.2. See also 'The Murder of the Innocents', *People's Journal*, 19 January 1861, p.2 and 26 January 1861, p.2.

arrives in the editor's office and is astonished to see the 'humplock o' papers' ('humplock' is a heap or mound) written in 'sic a variety o' han's' on the editor's desk:

> *Editor* – The merest trifle, I assure ye, sir, to what we have occasionally to encounter . . . What you see before you, sir, are contributions to the Poet's Corner.
>
> *Constant Reader* (holding up his hands) – Gude preserve us a'! what a doonricht wastry o' paper! Weel, wha wad hae thocht that. In an age that's stigmateezed wi' being the reverse o' poetical, there were sae mony fules! For my part, I'm thankfu' that I was never sae far left to mysel' as to perpetrate either sang or sonnet.[100]

The purpose of the dialogue is for the literary-minded editor, whose English suggests a high level of education, to convince the prosaic, elderly and down-to-earth Scots reader that there is value in writing poetry. The editor argues that he personally knows many of the 'poetising brotherhood' who are 'far above the average in regard to intelligence, industry and moral worth', and that he supports their efforts in poetry because in supplying aspirations beyond their everyday labour, it improves them as labourers as well as individuals, 'The best pair of shoes that ever I had were fabricated synchronously with a lyric of no ordinary merit.' While he fails to convince the Constant Reader, the expectation is that the wider (and younger) readership will agree that supporting Scotland's working poets is the right stance for a forward-looking Glasgow paper. The more an editor comically lamented the mountains of poetry received, the more it encouraged an idea of poetry composition as open to all, as well as reinforcing the impression of that paper as friendly towards working-class poets.

All Victorian Scottish newspapers published poetry now and then, and many published at least one poem a week. But not all newspapers showed the same commitment to supporting original verse. It was far more common to have a regular poetry column in weekly (especially Saturday) papers than in daily, perhaps because a paper for weekend reading was expected to contain a higher ratio of entertainment to news. Virginia Berridge has convincingly argued, moreover, that weekend papers had a particularly large working-class readership, and were direct inheritors of a cultural tradition linked to 'the political radicalism of the unstamped and the Chartist papers' which encouraged lively involvement from readers: poetry columns, though she does not mention these, are a sign of such involvement.[101] It was also more common for original poems by local writers to feature when a paper was explicitly courting a (new) local readership. The *Invergordon Times*, for example, was relatively uninterested in poetry until after its March 1862 announcement that the price was dropping to a penny and the paper would henceforth be 'published entirely in Invergordon, rather than being made up half in London . . . The County of Ross will thus have a newspaper made up wholly within itself.'[102] This new

---

[100] 'A Glance into the Sanctum', *Glasgow Citizen*, 2 October 1852, p.1.

[101] Virginia Berridge, 'Popular Sunday Papers and Mid-Victorian Society', in George Boyce, James Curran and Pauline Wingate, eds., *Newspaper History, from the Seventeenth Century to the Present Day* (London: Constable, 1978), pp.247–64, 249, 251.

[102] 'Special Announcement', *Invergordon Times*, 5 March 1862, p.4.

46 *Working Verse in Victorian Scotland*

commitment to locality was shown by the poem published on the same page as this announcement, 'The Rose of Invergordon' (signed Philander, Heather-Bank Cottage), and by the 'Poetry' column which began appearing in April 1862. Supporting local writers, and publishing writing on local themes, demonstrated a paper's commitment to its core community of readers and their interests. Inspiring readers to see themselves and members of their community as potential *contributors* to the local press, as well as passive consumers of it, was potentially vital in creating readers' loyalty and sense of investment in 'their' newspaper. In addition, newspapers showed their engagement with regional and national literary culture through reviews, by publishing series of articles devoted to contemporary or historical poetry and song, and by sponsoring local authors through publishing, advertising, and collecting subscriptions for their volumes. As I have discussed elsewhere, and as featured in Chapter 5, editors from mid-century onwards also often ran 'Notices to Correspondents' columns which included substantial numbers of responses to poems submitted for editorial judgement, usually with extracts from or even entire poems.[103]

It is not surprising that so many Scottish editors included poems alongside the news. Firstly, they often tended to support the publication of poetry simply because they were aspiring or published poets themselves, with a personal interest in supporting poetry publication. A very substantial number of newspaper editors and staff in Victorian Scotland wrote poetry on the side, 'verses for love, and leaders for bread', as editor James Hedderwick put it, listing Mackay, William Motherwell, Robert Nicoll, and George Outram as examples, and even arguing that if Burns had lived into the Victorian period, he would have worked for the press.[104] Many newspapermen got their first start in the job through submissions to the poetry column. William Forsyth, who worked for the *Aberdeen Herald* and *Inverness Courier*, began by sending his poems to the *Herald*'s poets' corner: 'His writings in the *Herald* drew on him the attention of Mr Carruthers of Inverness, no mean judge of literary ability, and towards the end of 1842 that gentleman gave Mr Forsyth a post on "the Courier."'[105] William Latto, one of the most influential figures in Scottish popular culture through his editorial work on the *People's Journal* and his writings as 'Tammas Bodkin', started his career in the poetry columns of the Fife press. Hugh MacDonald, cited above and discussed in Chapter 3, was a block-printer who began by publishing poems in the *Chartist Circular* and then the *Glasgow Citizen* as 'Caleb'; he became sub-editor of the *Citizen*, and a key supporter of its poets, then editor of the *Glasgow Times* and *Morning Journal*. In Dumfries, William McDowall, author of engaging radical, Chartist and proto-environmentalist poems in *The Man of the Woods*, became editor of the *Dumfries and Galloway Standard* in 1846 after stints at the *Scottish Herald* and Belfast's *Banner of Ulster*. Thomas Aird, editor of the Conservative-leaning *Dumfries Herald* from 1835, was also a poet,

---

[103] See Kirstie Blair, '"Let the Nightingales Alone": Correspondence Columns and the Making of the Working-Class Poet', *Victorian Periodicals Review* 47 (2014), 188–207.

[104] Hedderwick, pp.172, 171.

[105] William Forsyth, *Selections from the Writings of the Late William Forsyth, with Memoir and Notes* (Aberdeen: L. Smith and Son, 1882), p.vi.

'His own verses appeared in the paper, and he gave encouragement to others in their literary efforts.'[106] Such figures at the helm encouraged local writers to see 'their' papers as sympathetic to poetic submissions.

Secondly, poetry supplied a way to burnish cultural credentials with minimal effort or expenditure. Newspapers were not expected to pay poets for their copy (publication was presented as conferring a favour on amateur authors), both original and reprinted verse was in ample supply, and it was a convenient filler. An editor could keep suitable poems on hand and simply insert one that fitted the left-over space in a column. Dundee and Alyth poet James Young Geddes, in 'A Proposal, Addressed to the Poetical Contributors of the Dundee "Evening Telegraph"', joked about this practice, suggesting that newspaper poets form a union dedicated to supplying editors with the right length of poem on demand:

> should there be a stress
> For want of news – if anything retards
> A telegram – if there should be a mess
> Concerning space – instead of fuming on it,
> We could be ready with a song or sonnet.[107]

Geddes' poem satirically comments on the unremunerated labour that poets supply to the press; hence the half-joking need for unionization. Though verse was useful filler, readers did enjoy it, as many response poems, letters, and memoirs indicate. 'I recollect spending many happy minutes, when a young man, in perusing the contents of the poets' corner', William Lindsay (Aberdeen shoemaker, political activist, and newspaper agent) recalled:

> Much that appeared there was more than mere versifying. Portraitures of country life as spent in hill and dale were often very effective, while love-making in its constancy and inconstancy was dealt with in a way that gave pleasure and enjoyment to large numbers of young folk. Heroism, patriotism and political reform had their poetic representatives, who did ample justice to these subjects.[108]

Working-class poets like James Hogg of Lanarkshire (born 1839, and working as a pit-head labourer in the 1880s), reported that they were encouraged to make their own attempts by reading the poetry columns: 'When about twenty years of age he began to read the *Hamilton Advertiser*, and soon not only became a lover of "The Poet's Corner" but also occasionally composed short poems and songs.'[109] Material practices indicating a desire to preserve newspaper verse also provide evidence of the extent to which readers engaged with the poetry columns. Weaver-poet Jamie Gow's workshop in Dundee was decorated with poems cut from newspapers:

> The wall at the back of his loom, the two front posts, and the swords of his lay were covered in poems cut from 'The Chartist Circular', 'The True Scotsman', 'The Northern

---

[106] William McDowall, *The Man of the Woods, and Other Poems* (Dumfries: J. McKinnell, 1844). Julia Muir Watt, *Dumfries and Galloway: A Literary Guide* (Dumfries: Dumfries and Galloway Libraries, 2000), pp.98–9, 102.

[107] James Y. Geddes, *The New Jerusalem and Other Verses* (Dundee: James P. Mathew, 1879), p.64.

[108] William Lindsay, *Some Notes: Personal and Public* (Aberdeen: W. W. Lindsay, 1898), pp.310–11.

[109] Edwards, *Modern Scottish Poets, IX* (Brechin: D. H. Edwards, 1886), p.163.

Star', the local and other newspapers. His favourite pieces…were pasted, as gems above all others, the one on his lay and the other on the wall behind him.[110]

Many, such as John Taylor or William Tennant of Gartmore (probably related to brother-poets Robert and George Tennant from that area), kept a scrapbook of poems drawn from the local press.[111] These scrapbooks—and the spaces where poems have been cut out, not uncommon in surviving hard-copy newspapers— show readers' interest in *rereading* newspaper verse, and the function of newspaper poetry columns in supplying self-directed anthologies, especially important for readers who could rarely afford to buy volumes of verse. Tennant's scrapbook even imitates a common division in Scottish poetry volumes of the period by separat- ing his choices into 'poems' (at the front) and 'songs' (at the back). That Scottish newspaper readers may have had such scrapbooks or their equivalent to hand (as well as their tendency to learn poems and song by heart) is suggested by their extra- ordinary ability to identify plagiarized verse in the press, even if the plagiarized poem had appeared more than a decade ago in a different paper.[112]

Publishing original poetry by working-class authors was, moreover, a politicized choice. As I argue in the Introduction, championing political Reform and cham- pioning the poets of the people were not separate but strongly interrelated causes. In general, the more Liberal or Radical a mid-Victorian provincial newspaper was in its political loyalties, the more likely it was to support working-class literary endeavour via the extensive publication of, and commentary on, working-class poetry. As Martin Hewitt notes, the repeal of the 'taxes on knowledge' 'did, at least in the short term, shift the balance of newspaper politics fairly decisively towards Liberalism', meaning that the press across Britain became more Liberal in outlook.[113] Scotland had Tory newspapers, of course, which also published poems, but the popular newspapers that loom largest in this study—such as the Dundee *People's Journal* and *Weekly News*, the Glasgow *Penny Post*, *Citizen* and *Commonwealth*, the *Aberdeen Herald*, or the Hamilton, Bathgate and Airdrie papers—all heavily sup- ported Liberal MPs and causes, the extension of the franchise, and the rights of workers as opposed to landowners and masters. They also all supported causes which were seen as improving (temperance, for instance), and their championing of writing by working men and women was explicitly linked to this. The reason why large sectors of the *Scottish* provincial press were particularly dedicated to the inclusion of poems by working men and women in their columns, then, was not simply because of a national investment in cultural identity, in seeing Scotland as a land of poets, but also because of an investment in Scotland's political identity, as reformist, liberal, and progressive.

---

[110] 'History of James Gow, the Weaver Poet', *People's Journal*, 10 June 1872, p.2.

[111] John Taylor recalled that he 'began to keep a scrap-book for poems' while working as a stable boy in the 1850s (p.11). William Tennant's Book, a newspaper poetry scrapbook, is held in the local studies collection of Airdrie Library.

[112] For example, on 15 January 1870, the *People's Journal* commented that several correspondents had identified a Christmas prize poem as plagiarized from Cassell's Illustrated Family Paper of 1858.

[113] (Martin Hewitt, *The Dawn of the Cheap Press in Victorian Britain: The End of the 'Taxes on Knowledge', 1849–1869* (London: Bloomsbury, 2014), p.124).

By far the most prominent topics for original poetry published in the Victorian newspaper press are nature, love and courtship, death and mourning, and nostalgic recollections or portrayals of home and childhood. Although, as Chapter 3 of this study argues most forcibly, these genres can serve particular ends in the newspaper press—and in Scotland—that they do not necessarily serve elsewhere in Victorian poetic culture, these topics would likely be the same, and the poems very similar, across the English-language press. There might, however, be a significant difference in *language* between a poem on a common topic published in the London papers or the Scottish press. One of the crucial aspects of the rise of poetry in the Scottish provincial press is that it promotes the use of Scots, and indeed of regional dialect variations within Scots. As Donaldson has argued most trenchantly in relation to Scots prose, 'the second half of the nineteenth century is not a period of decay, but of resurgence, renewal, and growth almost without precedent', and this is in large part due to the rise of provincial newspapers:

> There arose in Scotland during these years a number of distinct local prose traditions based on the speech idioms of specific communities whose distinguishing features were represented orthographically. The movement was intimately bound up with the development of the local press. Papers tended to sell within homogenous speech communities where vernacular usage was the central feature of local identity and they often adopted the local form of Scots in their role as representatives of the people.[114]

The kind of Scots used in Victorian poetry has not been viewed positively by twentieth- and twenty-first-century critics. Yet while an in-depth examination of distinct variations in regional Scots poems is beyond the scope of this monograph, even a cursory consideration of the poems cited here strongly suggests that Donaldson's claims hold equally true for poetry as for prose.

Poets evidently saw vernacular Scots as a means to highlight their role as representatives of a local community. Porteous, for example, produced a pamphlet poem, 'Rejoicings at Maybole on the 10th of March 1863, in Honour of the Marriage of HRH the Prince of Wales, to Alexandra, Princess Royal of Denmark'. This is one of hundreds of celebratory poems on the Royal Wedding of 1863, including Tennyson's laureate poem on the occasion, yet what makes it stand out is Porteous' decision to write in Scots. His area (Carrick), he notes, can boast of a claim to royalty through Robert Bruce, 'Ye can look bouky, straught your back/ Gar Bruce's glory ring', and on Maybole's celebrations, he writes:

> Nae wonder Minnibole is skeigh,
> An' sets her bells to jow;
> An' gars, to warm her toddy-skreigh,
> A muckle bonfire low.[115]

'Bouky', in the Dictionary of the Scottish Language as 'boukie', is a relatively unusual adjective meaning imposing or affluent: 'skeigh' (high-spirited, excited), 'jow' (toll), 'skreigh' (whisky) and 'low' (light) are also all dialect terms whose

---

[114] William Donaldson, *Popular Literature in Victorian Scotland*, pp.71, 53 and *passim*.
[115] Porteous, *Carrickiana*, pp.1, 3.

meanings, though partially evident from context, seem unlikely to be instantly familiar to readers without Scots. Using Scots to write a 'laureate' poem is a means of emphasizing Porteous' position as a local laureate. It also shows Scotland's stake in British affairs. It might be over-reading to suggest that Porteous' references to Bruce, and in the next verse, to William Wallace, somewhat counter the sense of unquestioned loyalty to English royalty, given how common these references are in Scottish verse, but the poem's linguistic choices do emphasize Scotland's distinctiveness, in the midst of this universal British rejoicing. This one example, out of thousands, serves to show that the uses of Scots can be complex, and very often politicized, as is also evident in many of the Scots poems cited in the following chapters.

Whether poets *spoke* the Scots they wrote, or whether poetic Scots was a literary construction with a lessening relationship to speech, has been a contentious question. What evidence there is suggests that the poets discussed here often were Scots speakers, and that those who acquired education made a deliberate choice to retain Scots in their everyday speech: Rogers notes that MacDonald, for instance, 'insisted on using the native Doric'.[116] Northern papers, such as the *Oban Times*, also used their columns to support contemporary Gaelic poetry. Between 1868 and 1870 the balance of English to Gaelic verse in the *Oban Times* shifted towards Gaelic (though often accompanied by translations), with one reader writing that:

> Hundreds of the readers of your excellent paper must, like myself, be much pleased with the attention you bestow on contributors in Gaelic Poetry: and not the less delighted with the very able translations from that language into English verse that have from time to time appeared in your columns.[117]

Supporting Gaelic verse is part of a newspaper's commitment to its region, though it could also, especially in the last decades of the century, signal a political commitment to Highland causes.[118] I have not located any Gaelic poems in the southern or central Scottish press: given the wide geographical circulation of Scottish newspapers, Gaelic speakers in larger Scottish cities would have been able to subscribe to, and, if they wished, write for, the newspapers of 'their' region.

Though many newspaper poetry columns responded to current events primarily, for instance, by publishing a poem titled 'Spring' in April, newspaper reading nonetheless shows that Scottish Victorian poetry is far more politically and socially aware, attuned to, and ready to comment on current affairs, than has necessarily been recognized from studies of collected or anthologized poems. Evidence suggests that poets who made it to volume publication, like Glasgow's Marion Bernstein, may have deliberately chosen to exclude some of their more political newspaper verse.[119] Moreover, since most nineteenth-, twentieth- and twenty-first-century anthologies of working-class poetry, or indeed of Victorian poetry, group poems by author,

---

[116] Rogers, p.223.
[117] 'Altera Mercus', Letter to editor, with translation, *Oban Times*, 31 July 1869, p.2.
[118] For an example of a newspaper using Gaelic poems in this way, see *The Highlander*.
[119] Cohen, Fertig and Fleming note that some of Bernstein's political poems on women's suffrage and strikes were not republished after their appearance in the *Glasgow Weekly Mail* (pp.239, 247).

unsigned and pseudonymous newspaper verse, which was often *more* inclined towards politics and protest than verse by named authors, has been neglected. A representative newspaper protest poem, one of many hundreds of potential examples, is 'The Coal Famine', published in January 1873 in the Ayrshire *Ardrossan and Saltcoats Herald*:

I

Coal, nor wood, nor peat:
　　Nothing to put in the grate:
And the East wind hurling along the street,
Dashing the window with rain and sleet,
And rifting through roofing and slate.

II

What are the bairns to do?
　　Their duds are old and thin:
And all day long, all the night through,
Shaking the soot from the smokeless flue,
　　The wind comes pouring in.

III

Hardly a cinder there.
　　Nothing but ashes grey:
I've burnt my chest and my mother's chair,
And O but the house looks cold and bare
　　With the relics of love away.[120]

The coal famine of late 1872 and early 1873—during which time coal tripled in price—was a major topic in the Scottish press and attracted numerous poems.[121] This unsigned poem is particularly effective in the contrast, in the first two stanzas, between the slowness of the first two lines and the active motions of the winter weather in the second two. Punctuation, repetition, and trochaic measure lengthen the line 'Coal, nor wood, nor peat:', while the present participles and use of two unstressed beats, doubled line length (ten syllables rather than five) and rhyme of 'street/sleet' emphasize speed and movement. Newspapers tended to publish poems that were seasonally appropriate, and this is no exception. Its 4 January publication date means that readers are experiencing the wintry weather described, and also emphasizes the contrast between the misery here and the cheer of the just-past New Year celebrations. The poem makes an appeal to Victorian sentimental domesticity, in its scene of suffering children and the desolate household. Readers of newspaper verse would have been especially familiar with the painful affect associated with having to burn 'my mother's chair' via Eliza Cook's 'The Old Arm-Chair', one of

---

[120] 'The Coal Famine', *Ardrossan and Saltcoats Herald*, 2 January 1863, p.3. 'Rifting' is probably a typesetter's error for 'drifting'.
[121] For another example, see 'Coals' by W. T. E., *People's Journal*, 22 March 1873. Reprinted in (Kirstie Blair, ed., *The Poets of the People's Journal: Newspaper Poetry in Victorian Scotland* (Glasgow: ASLS, 2016), p.117).

the most frequently reprinted popular poems of this period. In the final stanzas, the speaker's hopelessness turns to anger:

VI

They heed not how we dine,
　　They heed but wage and hire:
Master and man, they will let us pine,
Though there's plenty of coal to be dug from the mine,
God means for the poor man's fire.

VII

The great lord's iron heel,
　　The rich man's selfish pride,
They were hard to bear, but it's worse to feel
The poor man turning a heart of steel
　　To the poor folk at his side.

It is, of course, impossible to identify the status of the actual author of this poem, but the perspective presented here is that of the 'poor folk'. In popular opinion, the coal famine was caused both by the greed of the coalmasters, and their desire to raise prices, and the intransigence of miners in refusing to work longer hours to meet rising demand. It is therefore, as this poem despairingly concludes, a bitter topic because there is no comfort in working-class solidarity and sympathy. Given that the speaker of the poem is located in a domestic space and thinking about childcare and the provision of food ('For there's little to boil or bake'), s/he could be read as a working woman. 'They' and 'we' may be constructions more reliant on gender than class, in that both 'master and man' are leaving women and children to starve.

Typically of newspaper verse, 'The Coal Famine' seeks to arouse sympathy and indignation, supplementing impersonal editorials with a deeply personal perspective, and, for better-off readers of the newspaper, giving insight into the sufferings of the poor. It is also typical in that it discusses an issue immediately affecting the readers of the newspaper. Newspaper editors, critics and patrons fostered the view that Scottish poets, for both practical and moral reasons, should pursue locally relevant themes, and their poetry should primarily be realist and topical, drawn from their lives and surroundings. Anthony Anton, in the *People's Friend*, praised Janet Hamilton on the grounds that 'her own fireside is her study, and her own little village contains the inhabitant she must seek to elevate by her example and by her precept'.[122] Rev. George Gilfillan of Dundee, an indefatigable sponsor of, and patron to, Scottish working-class poets, repeatedly advised them to look to the local for their themes:

Let the poet who would wish to excite a new and permanent interest restrict his song to subjects with which he is familiar. Let him paint a puddle in flood which he has seen, rather than a Niagara which he has not seen. Let him write an ode on the Law,

[122] Anthony Anton, 'Pickings from the Prose and Poetry of Janet Hamilton', *People's Friend*, 14 June 1871, pp.374–5.

rather than a poem on Mont Blanc. Let him go down to the docks and describe the launch of a ship, rather than get into spasms of contorted weakness in striving to picture the birth of a sun.[123]

'Spasms' here refers specifically to the 'spasmodic school', a loose collective of 1850s poets, featuring Gilfillan's protégé Alexander Smith, whose works enjoyed a brief flare of success before criticism and satire extinguished them. Gilfillan's turn to the local is in part because he had been critiqued for admiring the bombastic, epic, and transcendental poetics of spasmodism.[124] Following Gilfillan's line, the *People's Friend* advised one aspiring poet, 'Old Clo':

> The piece is descriptive of twilight creeping over the fields and woods, and from your occupation of a ploughman it would have been thought that the description of the gloaming hour would have been from your own observation, yet the second line in the following verse tells at once that such is not the case, for whoever heard the nightingale in Forfarshire?[125]

Poets justifiably found this advice patronizing. 'Old Clo' responded indignantly in verse in a succeeding issue, noting the different standards applied to the uneducated poet and established writers:

> And hoo it could be wrang o' me (as by your note I fand)
> To speak aboot the nightingale, I canna understand.
> Though Shakespeare, England's greatest bard, to many a land has ta'en us,
> And laid some o' his grandest scenes in Egypt, Rome, and Venice,
> Are we to think he was at Troy, and there shook hands with Hector?[126]

Despite such trenchant defence—which also serves to show 'Old Clo''s knowledge of Shakespeare's works—the preference of editors for works written 'from your own observation' ensured that poets marketed local verse whether or not they were located in the place described. In between the publication of this criticism and response, indeed, Old Clo had amply met editorial requirements in his poem on a homely pendulum clock, 'Auld Granny's Wag-at-the-Wa".[127] This does not necessarily mean that poets *only* pursued poems about Scottish domestic interests. Poems on international political and social themes, such as emigrant poems, political poems on European nationalism and its revered heroes, Kossuth and Garibaldi, or poems on British politics, in support of Gladstone, liberalism, and Reform, were prominent in the press. But these were, of course, still seen as realist poems about events happening in and to Scotland, given that all these leaders toured parts of Scotland and expressed vested, reciprocal interests in her land and people.

---

[123] (Preface to James Easson, *Select Miscellany of Poetical Pieces* (Dundee: Park, Sinclair & Co, 1856), p.vii).

[124] Mark A. Weinstein, *W. E. Aytoun and the Spasmodic Controversy* (New Haven, CT: Yale University Press, 1968) remains an important study of the background to spasmodism. On Gilfillan as supporter and patron to Dundee's working-class poets, see Aileen Black, *Gilfillan of Dundee 1813–1878: Interpreting Religion and Culture in Victorian Scotland* (Dundee: Dundee University Press, 2006).

[125] 'To Correspondents', *People's Friend*, 17 April 1872, p.256.

[126] 'To Correspondents', *People's Friend*, 22 May 1872, p.336.

[127] *People's Friend*, 1 May 1872, p.279.

Newspaper poems did not simply relate to communities of Scottish readers by reflecting news and topics of interest to them. They also modelled social and literary interactions. Newspaper poetry columns provided a serial and synchronous reading experience, because they were a vital venue for *response* and *correspondence* poems, in which ongoing relationships between poets, readers and editors were publicly staged. Poetry columns were interactive, both in the form and mode of their critical response to poetry, as discussed further in Chapter 5, and in the playful and strategic responses of poets to each other's work. In the *Elgin and Morayshire Courier* of 1865, for instance, 'La Teste' (William Hay Leith Tester), a well-known newspaper poet across eastern and central Scotland, wrote a comic 'Epitaph' for a fellow poet in the town, 'Cutler Jamie' (James Murdoch), recalling their nights drinking together. Jamie was a well-known street character in Elgin, but readers outside the town might have wondered if the obituary was genuine—until they read Cutler Jamie's response, 'Elegy on the Late La Teste', one week later.[128] These poems are not simply an entertaining exchange: they satirize the elegiac tendency of the poetry columns, and in particular their tendency to commemorate local 'worthies', including the town's poets, usually glossing over the poverty and drunkenness which these poems (albeit humorously) take as their focus.

John (Jack) Pettigrew, who usually published as 'R.H.P.' and was a jobbing gardener and occasional labourer in Parkhead Forge, in Glasgow's East End, provides another good example. He was determined to make his mark on the poetry columns, and one of his strategies was to involve editors in offering him advice by staging a competition with a fellow poet. The *Hamilton Advertiser* noted in February 1864 that:

> W. B. and R. H. P., Parkhead, – send us an effusion each this week, accompanied by the modest request, 'we would be very much obliged if you would tell us who is the best poet.'... Really, rhymers, we think you are about a par... Persevere.[129]

This was disappointing: Pettigrew probably hoped that the editor would publish both poems and invite readers to join him in judging them. He did persevere, however—R. H. P.'s poems were critiqued by the editor in the correspondents' columns of the *Advertiser* in April 1864, and in October 1864 the editor published a fuller critique, congratulating R. H. P. on 'the manner in which you have improved yourself already'. Despite regular mentions, however, he did not get a full poem into the poetry column in the paper until October 1866. Meanwhile, he was trying his hand in other venues, including the *People's Journal* and Glasgow's *Penny Post*.

'W. B.' may or may not have been David Willox, a Parkhead weaver who rose to become a city councillor in Glasgow, and who published poems in the local newspapers 'before he could read and write'. He recalled of his friendship with Pettigrew:

---

[128] La Teste, 'Epitaph on the Late Cutler Jamie', *Elgin and Morayshire Courier*, 28 July 1865; Cutler Jamie, 'Elegy on the Late La Teste', *Elgin and Morayshire Courier*, 4 August 1865. Murdoch also published extensively in Elgin's second newspaper, the Elgin Courant, in the 1860s. La Teste was an early correspondent of Johnston's in the *People's Journal*.

[129] 'Notices', *Hamilton Advertiser*, 20 February 1864, p.2.

We entered into what I may term a poetical conspiracy, that he should write a piece laudatory of his birthplace, Keppochhill, I think it was, under the name of McDuff, and I was to write a poetical criticism of it. This worked out well, and continued for a few weeks, indeed it drew others into the controversy, until the editor either saw through the game, or became tired of us washing our dirty linen through the medium of his paper.[130]

I have not located this newspaper exchange, but R. H. P. did publish a poem on Keppochhill in the *Penny Post* in 1865:

> Thou'rt sadly changed, my dear birthplace,
>   Since first I bid farewell to thee;
> Few of my comrades now I trace –
>   Some dead, and some have crossed the sea.
> And where honeysuckle did sweetly twine,
> Are dens of noxious grovelling swine.
>
> Methinks it is but yesterday
>   I joined the merry laughing bands,
> And pull'd blue bells and roses gay
>   Where now that huge iron foundry stands.[131]

As I note of this poem elsewhere, it is typical of the 'lost home' genre of newspaper verse, yet also contains trenchant reflections on emigration, on industrialization (Glasgow readers would probably have been able to see the exact foundry referenced here), and on temperance ('dens of swine' are pubs; as is true of many working-class poets, R. H. P.'s poetry espoused temperance even while Pettigrew became an alcoholic).[132] Such affecting recollections may be entirely sincere, but R. H. P.'s various negotiations in the press also suggest that they are part of a long-term strategy—a *collaborative* strategy, with either one or several different friends—to increase his visibility and his chances of publication.

Many volumes by working-class writers, such as the early twentieth-century collection of late Victorian and Edwardian poems by Isa Forrest, included exchange poems (probably originally from the *Banffshire Journal*, the publisher of her book) which are unclearly positioned in terms of authorship and authenticity. Forrest's volume includes four comic poems in a sequence, 'Lassie, Gin Ye Lo'd Me', by Redcastle; 'Reply to Redcastle'; 'A Confession', by Redcastle; and 'Reply to Redcastle's Confession' (the first is by a male speaker soliciting romance, the second by a woman promising it, in the third and fourth poems Redcastle and correspondent admit that they are both already married to others and their romantic overtures were false).[133] Was Forrest the respondent to Redcastle, reprinting his poems in her collection so that readers have both sides of the exchange? Or did Forrest write all four poems, setting up an entertaining fictional narrative for readers by composing

---

[130] David Willox, Memories of Parkhead (unpublished, written 1920), Mitchell Library.

[131] R. H. P., 'Address to Keppochhill', *Penny Post*, 26 December 1865, p.1.

[132] Blair, ' "Let the Nightingales Alone" ', pp.195–6, 198–9.

[133] Isabella Forrest, *Islaside Musings* (Banff: Banffshire Journal, 1926), pp. 72–5. Forrest's profession is not known, but she identifies herself as a working woman in her poems. Her great-granddaughter Katrina Giebels reports that Forrest grew up illegitimate and in poverty (private correspondence).

both sides of the story? Or, as with R. H. P. and La Teste, was Redcastle someone she knew in person, so that this exchange was staged and pre-planned? These questions are unanswerable, though what is clear is that many newspaper poems that present themselves as 'genuine' were carefully strategized to ensure publicity and reader interest, and that it was not unknown for both sides of an apparent correspondence to be carried on by the same author under different pseudonyms.

One of R. H. P.'s many correspondents in the *Penny Post* was Ellen Johnston, 'The Factory Girl'. No Scottish poet was more adept at marketing herself via newspaper relationships with other poets than Johnston, one of the best-known working-class women writers from this period, and, as noted in the Introduction, one of the most discussed by literary critics. The *Penny Post*, her leading champion, was a paper with a large working-class readership in Glasgow and surroundings. Walter Freer recalled it as a favoured choice for shared reading by workers:

> I see a picture of workmen meeting every evening round the thatched houses at Glasgow Cross, listening intently as one of them, better learned than the rest, reads the newspaper. The 'Penny Post', ardently Radical, was the favourite.[134]

Edited at this point by Alexander Campbell, the *Penny Post* was known for its support of poets. As Johnston's biographer, H. Gustav Klaus, notes, 'Under his editorship the poetry column of the *Penny Post* became a veritable forum of exchange for working-class writers.'[135] Johnston was already an experienced newspaper poet by the time she moved to Glasgow, but it was in this particular newspaper that she became a favoured participant in a circle of admiring exchanges between poets. Sometimes these took narrative form, as in the poems between Johnston and G. D. Russell, which appeared to tell of their doomed engagement, allegedly entered into just before Russell sailed to Queensland. Mostly, however, these poems were fannish exchanges, in which poets celebrated their mutual pleasure in each other's work. During 1866, it was a rare week that did not include either a poem by Johnston, or about her. In just six weeks, for instance, the following appeared:

3 March 1866 'To the Factory Girl, Dundee' by Peter McCall, George St, Ayr

24 March 1866 'Lines to the Factory Girl', by Edith

7 April 1866, 'The Factory Girl's Reply to Edith', by Ellen Johnston

28 April 1866, 'Glasgow, The Factory Girl' by H. Smith

5 May 1866, 'Lines to Mr H. Smith, Glasgow', by Ellen Johnston

12 May 1866, 'Lines to Miss Johnstone, the Factory Girl' by R. H. P.

19 May 1866, 'Edith's Reply to the Factory Girl'

26 May 1866, 'Lines to Mr Colin Steel, from his old schoolmate and companion, "The Factory Girl"', by Ellen Johnston

Readers were expected to remember and follow these exchanges across the weeks. The reason for this flurry of activity is explained by the need to increase subscriptions

---

134 Walter Freer, *My Life and Memories* (Glasgow: Civic Press, 1929), p.129.
135 Klaus, *Factory Girl: Ellen Johnston and Working-Class Poetry in Victorian Scotland* p.69.

for Johnston's volume, which the *Penny Post* had started advertising as forthcoming in January 1866, and was actively promoting throughout these months. In July the editor published a sardonic note about such adulatory poems: 'We think those whose sympathies have been awakened to poetic action should bestir themselves to evince the value of their sympathies by the number of subscribers they obtain for her poems.'[136]

Johnston's participation in this social network of newspaper poets has been examined by critics, but she is only exceptional in that it was more unusual for a young female poet to be prominent in a newspaper coterie than for a young male poet. One of the most notable features of all recurring poetry columns in the period is this tendency to attract clusters of poets who interact with each other via the press. Another of Johnston's 'sympathizers', for instance, was aspiring poet David H. Morrison, of Moffat and Caldervale, who worked in mining, in a paper mill, and then at Caldervale Printfield, where he became a night watchman. Morrison published poems in praise of Johnston in the *Penny Post*, as well as poems dedicated to 'The Ploughman's Wife' (who aimed to raise funds for a memorial to Robert Tannahill; the paper identified her as Jessie Rae Cairns) and to 'Edith', another of Johnston's poetic correspondents. His 1870 collection, published by the *Airdrie Advertiser* office, is a good example of the way in which an aspiring poet could shape their reputation through newspaper correspondence poems. Evidently proud of his circle of poetic acquaintance, Morrison incorporated poems from D. Thomson, Hillend (D. T.), from R. H. P., from 'Edith', and from Johnston, this last accompanied by a letter thanking him for his newspaper verses:

> My dear friend, I will reply to them next week, for I am too late this week. It is most likely they will appear in the *Penny Post*. Will you be so kind as to send me three copies of the paper your verses are in, as I would like to send them to my friends.[137]

Social exchanges, as this shows, operated around and beyond the poetry column. In William Tennant's scrapbook, he cut out Morrison's newspaper poem to Johnston, and hers to him, and pasted them beside each other so that their connection was evident, showing how readers valued and preserved these interactions.

Correspondence poems, especially when poets were known to live in the same area, followed a pattern of lavish praise of the addressee, lament for the author's own inadequacy as poet or friend, and a desire or direct request to meet in person. Morrison's poem to Thomson, another local poet, invites him to visit:

> If e'er you think it worth your while
> Tae paiddle wast for twa-three mile,
> I'll meet you wi' a hearty smile,
>   And ha'e a crack
> Aboot the poets o' our isle
>   At some dyke-back.

---

[136] *Penny Post*, 14 July 1866, p.4.
[137] David H. Morrison, *Poems and Songs* (Airdrie: Baird and Hamilton, 1870), pp.26–8, 56.

My puir auld coat, worn tae a rag,
That hings aboot me like a bag,
I'll tear him up and mak' a flag
          For our auld lum:
That you may see my colours wag
          Whene'er you come.[138]

Like many correspondence poems, this is heavily inspired by Burns's epistle poems to his fellow poets, known for their use of the habbie stanza. The purpose of meeting another local poet is to encounter someone with shared conversational interests and bolster a sense of belonging, hence Morrison's specific request that they discuss Scottish poetry. He suggests creating a signal, sacrificing something useful but marked by poverty (his ripped coat), to flag his poetic status. The coat here is an analogy to the poem—modest and unworthy of preservation, but suitable as a signal of kinship and shared interests. Morrison's poem is both humble, since this genre requires the author to praise the addressee's greater talents, and proud, since Morrison claims authorship with his signature: 'David Morrison, Watchman. Moffat'. Giving profession and location, as many newspaper poets do, is an invitation to direct correspondence, and also means that readers in that location can easily find the poet in person.

Morrison's collection additionally republishes a nice example of a fake response poem, from 'Longfellow'. When Longfellow was visiting England in 1868, and had travelled as far north as Carlisle, Morrison had published 'An Invitation to Henry Wadsworth Longfellow, esq, Poet', opening 'O come and see our Caledonian hills'. 'Longfellow' then replied in the press, in a clever parody of the famous hexameter of Longfellow's *Evangeline*:

This is the land of the bard, where the blossoming broom and the thistle –
Emblems of freedom – still wave in the low lying glens and the valleys.

The verses identify Morrison's location,

Obscure in the district of Moffat, that is situate south of the Lothians,
Where onward meandering slowly incessantly murmurs the Calder,
Dwells there a poet of note, who like to the Skalds and the Vikings,
Strikes on the deep-toned lyre[139]

The notion that one of the world's most famous poets would read the local Scottish press, and notice 'the humble bard of Caldervale', as Morrison styled himself, is a joke about the distance between a local working-class poetic circle and international poetic celebrity, which is as much at Longfellow's expense as Morrison's. Longfellow can be gleefully appropriated and rewritten, in lines that, amongst other things, are subtly critical of his failure to visit Scotland and appreciate his fans there, satirize the notion that Scotland's working-class poets are descendents of the Norse, and undo Longfellow's attempt to render the hexameter a form suitable for tragedy and

---

[138] 'To David Thomson, Hillend' by David Morrison, Watchman, Moffat, *Airdrie Advertiser*, 18 August 1866, p.2.
[139] Morrison, pp.48–9 and 84–5. I have not located these poems in the press, but William Tennant's scrapbook contains the Longfellow poem as a newspaper cutting.

epic. Morrison's inclusion of this poem in his volume suggests that he knew the author, or even that he was the author.

Poetically inclined working men had always formed social communities, in pubs, workshops, or other meeting spaces. But the poetry columns made these relationships public, as well as enabling communities that were not dependent on poets needing to meet in person, or necessarily on any relationship beyond the press. This included, as in the example of Johnston, enabling women poets to correspond with each other and with male poets, especially important since it was not until late in the period that women could participate more in the kinds of associational culture long patronized by Scottish men. Readers could identify these clusters and aspire to join them. Robert Fisher, in Dumfries, encouraged Alexander Doig (from Dundee, also living in Dumfries) into print by giving examples of working poets who exercised the 'doric lyre' in the style of Burns:

> And brither Murdoch tries it hard
>   Wi' a' his pith.
> And Anderson, and Young, and Ford,
>   And Jamie Smith.[140]

Alexander Murdoch, Alexander Anderson, Robert Ford, James Smith and either Thomas or John Young were all well-known enough that Fisher can assume readers will recognize them from their last name alone. Ford, Murdoch and Anderson knew each other personally and were part of a Glasgow-centric circle publishing in the *People's Friend*. Fisher was less known, however, and there is no evidence that he was part of this circle, effectively the working-class poetic elite by the late 1870s: in describing Murdoch as a 'brither' poet, he perhaps hopes to position himself as one of them, as well as displaying his knowledge of contemporary working poets.

Newspaper editors and writers wanted readers to see 'their' poets not simply as individual contributors but as a loyal collective, a real-life version of the semi-fictional social collective that *Blackwood's* had famously promoted in 'Noctes Ambrosianae'. The *Aberdeen Herald*, for example, highlighted this in its reports on 'Our Annual Trip', a day out in the country for *Herald* staff, characterized by the presence of the newspapers' poetic contributors. The 21 August 1858 account of this trip, opening with a poem by 'S. Sherif', also featured comments and poems by 'W. A.' (William Anderson), 'Benedick', who 'took his tuneful brethren...aside, and chimed to them the following beautiful lines' and, in absentia, 'Zelia':

> One of the Staff unpocketed a bundle of MS poetry, and read to them the following pleasant lines by sister, 'Zelia', the reading being accompanied by parenthetical lamentations that our present trip arrangements did not admit of 'fair contributors' forming part of the company.[141]

What this means, in the tongue in cheek reference to 'present trip arrangements', is that the day out centred on drinking. The *Aberdeen Herald* included this report

---

[140] Robert Fisher, '*Epistle to Alexander Doig, a Brother Bard*', *Poetical Sparks* (Dumfries: Robert Fisher, 1881), p.89.

[141] 'Our Annual Trip', *Aberdeen Herald*, 21 August 1858, p.5.

on a social occasion, as did other papers on their own parties or celebrations, because it gives readers the impression of a supportive (male) community centred on the paper, and driven by friendship and shared literary pursuits rather than economic concerns. In the conceit of 'Our Annual Trip', poetry is both enthusiastically and spontaneously produced as part of a communal enterprise, and read out from pre-prepared manuscripts. The poets themselves are minor celebrities: the annual trip reports are presented as giving readers insight into poets' personal interactions and behaviour, and they drop tantalizing hints about the real identities behind the pseudonyms.

The majority of Scottish newspaper verse was anonymous or pseudonymous, though the practice of identifying the place from which the poem had been sent doubtless enabled local readers to engage in detective work. Poets were known to operate under more than one pseudonym, and could adopt multiple personae which might redefine them in class, gender, or generic terms. For example, Robert Ford wrote comic verse as 'Matilda Lapstane', and serious verse under his own name; George Sproat contributed to the *Kirkcudbright Advertiser* 'and other local papers' as 'Venetia'; and John Fullerton published as 'Wild Rose', 'Alice Douglas', 'Robin Goodfellow' and 'Rob Gibb'.[142] There are fewer recorded examples of Scottish women poets choosing to use a male pseudonym, though it is highly likely that, given the greater policing of the themes and content of women's poetry, many women chose to publish only with their initials, or left their poems unsigned.

Once a poet had made his or her reputation in a newspaper column, he or she could venture on publishing a collection with some hope that the newspaper office would produce the volume, as well as advertising and reviewing it, and that either the newspaper would directly help to collect subscriptions, or their support would indirectly help in gaining a subscriber list, where such was necessary. Presumably because newspaper verse did not have the highest reputation for quality and longevity, however, very few poets acknowledge the newspaper in which their poems appeared. Some happily leave behind the pseudonym under which their newspaper poems were usually published, while others, like Johnston, 'The Factory Girl', Parker, 'The Irish Girl', Alexander Anderson, 'Surfaceman', or Adam Wilson of Dundee, 'The Factory Muse', feature it prominently. In these cases, pseudonyms help to market the published poems, whether to an ethnic group or a professional group. This was not always successful, of course: Johnston is a famous example of a poet well-known to readers, yet who could not turn her adoring readership in industrial Glasgow into subscribers.

Publication by subscription was almost certainly much easier for those who lived in a relatively small community, where subscribers knew each other and the poet. In one particularly trenchant example, Robert Sanderson, a weaver from West Linton,

---

[142] On Ford, see his biography in 'Humorous Scotch Readings by Robert Ford', *People's Friend*, 12 October 1881. On Sproat, see Malcolm McL Harper, *The Bards of Galloway: A Collection of Poems, Songs, Ballads, &c, by Natives of Galloway* (Thomas Fraser: Dalbeattie, 1889), p.247; John Fullerton, *Poems* (Peterhead: P. Scrogie, 1905), p.xi. This is a posthumous collection of Fullerton's 'Wild Rose' verse.

Peebleshire, divided the subscription list in his 1865 collection by location, so that interested readers could track the geographical spread of his reputation. It had certainly reached Edinburgh, less than twenty miles away: he was presumably proud to have twenty-two councillors from Edinburgh on the list, so they feature prominently, with profession and addresses.[143] But Glasgow, at over fifty miles away, was too far; it supplied only one subscriber. West Linton supplied 108. Usually, Sanderson only lists the profession of his subscribers if it shows his support from respectable middle- or upper-class men (ministers or teachers, for example). For his home town, however, he chose to show the extent of his support amongst tradesmen and artisans:

> William Morgan, draper,
> T. Thomson, baker.
> J. Alexander, grocer.
> H. Alexander, draper.
> R. Alexander, flesher.
> M. Ballantine, grocer.
> D. Paterson, innkeeper.
> R. Brown, baker.
> A. Wilson, saddler
> M. Rough, grocer.
> W. Burns, stationer.
> J. Bain, shoemaker.[144]

Listing subscribers by trade might be a means of thanking them by advertising their wares, or, more cynically, a ploy to attract subscribers; given the extent of this list, which West Linton tradesman would want to gain a reputation for *not* backing local poetic enterprise?

What newspaper poetry columns and occasional verse show us, far more so than published volumes, is the extent to which local working-class verse cultures were sophisticated and experimental in their manipulation of the expectations of editors, readers, and listeners, and invariably engaged in complex negotiations about the economic, political and aesthetic work of verse. Provincial newspaper poetry, in particular, is indicative of the ways in which Scottish verse cultures in this period presented themselves as public, transactional, and part of a felt communal effort and national enterprise. The vision of Scotland as a country filled with 'peasant' poets did not mean that named poets were writing verse for publication in poetry volumes, to be pored over by private readers. It meant that poetry played a very visible and public role in the field of culture and society; that no subject matter was inappropriate; and that there was no location in which a poem was out of place.

---

[143] Robert Sanderson, *Poems and Songs* (Edinburgh: Colston & Son, 1865), pp.67–8. Sanderson probably gained this support in Edinburgh through his patronage by well-known Edinburgh poet James Ballantine.

[144] Sanderson, p.71.

As Victorian critics and poets grappled with a sense of gloom about the prospects of poetry as a genre in the modern scientific and technological age, this popular poetics constructs a different narrative; a narrative that rests upon diffusion, growth, productivity, enterprise, and networking, and one in which poetry survives and flourishes at the grass-roots level.

2

Reforming the Social Circle

Nursery Verse, Poetic Community, and the Politics of *Whistle-Binkie*

Whistle-Binkie is the overarching title for a series of extremely popular Scottish poetry anthologies, including verse for spoken and sung performance as well as private reading. Produced in and published from Glasgow, these span the Victorian period, with the first issue in 1832 and the last in 1890. In this chapter, I narrow the focus to these collections and turn to the foundation of a specifically *Victorian* Scottish poetics—though with strong links back to the verse cultures of the late eighteenth and early nineteenth century—in the 1830s. It is especially important to revisit *Whistle-Binkie* because it would be difficult to overemphasize the opprobrium with which it has been regarded in the twentieth and partly the twenty-first century. Writers from the Scottish Renaissance onwards have taken these volumes as indicative of everything that was wrong with the literature of Victorian Scotland, 'mawkishly pathetic', resounding with 'the sentimentality into which Scots vernacular verse had sunk in the mid to late nineteenth century', showing 'the pawky sentimental level to which Scottish poetry had been reduced' and 'a sentimental, complacent and utterly trivialized notion of what poetry might be'. [1] As summed up by J. Derrick McClure, *Whistle-Binkie* is devoid of anything 'conducive to intellectual stimulation, let alone social or political unorthodoxy or subversion'. '[T]he *Whistle-Binkie* anthologies are monuments to unimaginative, unadventurous literary and artistic sterility', he concludes. [2] 'Whistle-Binkie must have thought it ruled the roost', Edwin Morgan wrote, in a highly influential essay:

> Victorian morality took strong root in Scotland, and these tightly packed, assiduously produced, biographically annotated, and constantly revised anthologies, in which you would be hard put to find a dozen really good poems, but which seemed so innocuously comic and sentimental, were carefully devised as instruments of social control. [3]

---

[1] Trevor Royle, 'Whistle-Binkie', in *The Mainstream Companion to Scottish Literature* (London: Random House, 2012), n.p.; Glen, p.85; Roderick Watson, *The Literature of Scotland: The Middle Ages to the Nineteenth Century* (Houndmills: Palgrave, 1984 (2nd edn 2007)), p.296.

[2] J. Derrick McClure, *Language, Poetry and Nationhood: Scots As a Poetic Language from 1878 to the Present* (East Linton: Tuckwell Press, 2000), p.27.

[3] Edwin Morgan, 'Scottish Poetry in the Nineteenth Century', in Douglas Gifford, ed., *The History of Scottish Literature, vol 3: Nineteenth Century* (Aberdeen: Aberdeen University Press, 1988), pp.337–52, 340.

Whether poems are 'really good' or otherwise depends, of course, on the definition of 'good', as I discuss in the Introduction. And while my assessment below demonstrates that *Whistle-Binkie* went considerably beyond comic and sentimental verse, I also argue, throughout this book, that there is indeed nothing 'innocuous' about these genres, though not necessarily for the reasons Morgan assumes. Even presuming *Whistle-Binkie* was wholly politically and socially conservative, and that the implicitly sinister aims Morgan imputes to it are true—and returning to the original sources does introduce considerable doubt about this—the evident success of these aims, as shown in the vast popularity of the series, would surely indicate the need to examine rather than dismiss it.

Critics of Scottish literature have shown a concerted tendency to use *Whistle-Binkie* as a straw man against which the occasional 'good' Victorian Scottish poet can be measured. Hence, Douglas Gifford concludes that 'such anthologies do not, however, represent fairly the achievement of many of the lost voices of Victorian Scotland' and Valentina Bold's important study of the autodidact tradition in Scotland situates poets like James Hogg as 'well placed to avoid the sometimes repellent and debilitating politeness of self-styled "educated" poets, from Wilson to the Whistlebinkie school'.[4] The later poets Bold considers, including James Young Geddes, David Wingate and Alexander Anderson (all featured in Chapter 4), are 'honourable exceptions' to this school.[5] Gerard Carruthers' 2009 introduction to Scottish literature comments:

> Standard critical narratives see the systemic, infantilized descent of Scots poetry in the nineteenth century exemplified by the hugely popular *Whistle Binkie* anthologies (1832–90), in which Scots is seen as the preserved area for sentimental, mawkish and comic observation (most notably, 'Wee Willie Winkie' by William Miller, 1810–72, features in one *Whistle Binkie* volume). More recently, though, critics have detected to some extent a more socially engaged, mature poetry in Scots in the nineteenth century, albeit by poets who have to be disinterred from the periodical press and forgotten pamphlets.[6]

This helpfully critiques the standard line, but once again it sets 'socially engaged, mature poetry' in opposition to *Whistle-Binkie*: the assumption in this statement is that 'Wee Willie Winkie', for instance, *is* sentimental and mawkish. It is notable that a more recent account, the introduction to *Scotland and the 19th Century World*, co-authored by Carruthers, is satirical about the tendency to read 'Wee Willie Winkie' as 'the poem which placed the Scottish vernacular tradition into a coma from which it would not wake until deep into the twentieth century' and suggests that *Whistle-Binkie* itself is 'not always as debilitatingly conservative as might first appear, providing a sometimes unexpected outlet for the potentially unsettling

---

[4] Gifford, Douglas, 'Scottish Literature in the Victorian and Edwardian Era', in Douglas Gifford, Sarah Dunnigan and Alan MacGillivray, eds., *Scottish Literature in English and Scots* (Edinburgh: Edinburgh University Press, 2002), p.332.

[5] Valentina Bold, *James Hogg: A Bard of Nature's Making* (Bern: Peter Lang, 2007), pp.23, 267.

[6] Gerard Carruthers, *Scottish Literature* (Edinburgh University Press, 2009: Edinburgh Critical Idiom), pp.58–9.

demotic voice'.[7] This is somewhat faint praise, however, and largely reliant on *Whistle-Binkie*'s one claim to fame, its publication of Burns's 'The Tree of Liberty'. It is fair to say that overall, and in the decided lack of any substantive critical assessment of the *Whistle-Binkie* series, a perception of it as a symptom of the weakness, decline and 'infantilism' of Scottish poetry post-Burns remains largely unchallenged.

This chapter builds on tentative efforts to reassess this series, and argues, moreover, that any serious consideration of British working-class verse cultures in the Victorian period ought to take *Whistle-Binkie* into consideration. Almost all the contributors to *Whistle-Binkie*, and its greatest champions, were working men. (One area in which it was unquestionably conservative was in its general exclusion of women poets). Not only did the series provide a very significant publishing venue and sense of communal enterprise for a group of working-class men, but the survival of correspondence, manuscripts, and proofs relating to Glasgow bookseller, publisher, and editor David Robertson's involvement with the series provides us with vital insight into the practices underlying the construction of Scottish working-class poetics and poetic communities in this period. *Whistle-Binkie* was fully integrated into the publication and performance contexts discussed in Chapter 1 in its relationships to newspaper verse, oral culture, occasional verse and broadsides. Robertson picked up lyrics from 'street orators' (like his friend William Cameron or 'Hawkie'), from the local newspaper press, and even in one instance from a friend who found a song 'not in the most literary place, a tobacconist', and republished them in the series.[8] John Carrick, the first editor, and Alexander Rodger, who took over after Carrick's early death, were newspaper editors and journalists as well as poetic contributors. Other well-known poets published in *Whistle-Binkie* who worked for the press included William Motherwell, editor of the *Glasgow Courier* from 1830 to his death in 1835, William Kennedy, former editor of the *Paisley Advertiser*, and Nicoll, who quadrupled the circulation of the radical *Leeds Times* in 1836.[9] The series also celebrated newspapermen such as James Scott of the *Greenock Advertiser* (who published several of the poets included in the series in the paper's poetry column and introduced them to Robertson) and Jamie

---

[7] Gerard Carruthers, David Goldie and Alistair Renfrew, eds., *Scotland and the 19th-Century World* (Amsterdam: Rodopi, 2012), pp.15, 19. Christopher Harvie similarly noted that while 'much of what the later generations said' about the collection is valid, some of its poems have 'a sharp, dry humour and a lively social awareness'. See Christopher Harvie, 'John Buchan and *The Northern Muse*: The Politics of an Anthology', in Barbara Korte, Ralf Schneider and Stefanie Lethbridge, eds., *Anthologies of British Poetry: Critical Perspectives from Literary and Cultural Studies* (Amsterdam: Rodopi, 2000), pp.211–22, 216.

[8] Robertson included a prose and verse piece about Hawkie and other 'Street Orators' in the Second Series, with a note that 'when a lad' he 'used to follow Hawkie about the street and pick up his oratory'. See *Whistle-Binkie; or, the Piper of the Party, Being a Collection of Songs for the Social Circle*, Chiefly Original. 2nd series (Glasgow: David Robertson, 1842), p.71. The poem found in the tobacconist was 'Adam Glen', Robertson comments that 'a note inserted in the first issue brought out by the editor of a Northern newspaper the author's name'. *Whistle-Binkie* (Glasgow: David Robertson, 1842), pp.59–60; editor's note in GUL Sp Coll copy.

[9] David Robertson, *Biographical Note on Robert Nicoll*, *Whistle-Binkie Fifth Series* (Glasgow: David Robertson, 1843), p.50.

McNab of the *Glasgow Herald*.[10] The radical newspaper editor James Hedderwick of the *Glasgow Citizen* also had connections to the *Whistle-Binkie* editors, as did many other leading figures in Glasgow's print culture.[11] And, of course, many of the poems published first in *Whistle-Binkie* then rapidly circulated through the newspaper poetry columns of Scotland, Ireland, England, and Wales.

The series had an equally strong two-way relationship with broadside and song culture. While *Whistle-Binkie* differs from earlier and later collections of Scottish song in emphasizing original compositions, it also gathered traditional and current street songs and republished lyrics from the late eighteenth and early nineteenth century that seemed in danger of being lost. Burns's 'The Tree of Liberty' is one key example, but the series also incorporates a number of other songs from the same period, including 'The Kail Brose o' Scotland', published with additional verses that Robertson suggests had been suppressed in the 1780s, and Susanna Blamire's 'The Loss of the Roebuck'.[12] Popular songs from *Whistle-Binkie* would rapidly be reprinted as broadsides and songsheets and continue to circulate, with or without authorial identification. James Ballantine's 'Castles in the Air', a Scots poem about a young boy gazing into the fire, is perhaps the best example. Borrowed by Robertson for the *Whistle-Binkie* spin-off *Songs for the Nursery* (1844), it rapidly appeared on broadsides in Scotland and further afield, yet, with music composed by Robert Adams, also became an extremely popular Victorian parlour song with international circulation. In 1859 Andrew McIlwraith, a working-class emigrant to Ontario, noted in his diary that he 'Got Castles in the Air copied and dispatched to Miss Goldie' (his future wife).[13] E. Lawrence Abel's bibliography of sheet music produced in the Southern U.S. during the confederacy years lists five copies of Ballantine's poem, and a copy survives published in Melbourne from the same period; numerous copies of 'Castles in the Air' were also included in songsters in Britain and beyond.[14]

'Castles in the Air' shows both the international reach of *Whistle-Binkie*, and the way in which its songs moved into the parlour and the concert-room. An anonymous song about the pleasures of drinking like 'Cripple Kirsty',

> Wha among us has na heard
> O weel-kent Cripple Kirsty?
> A porter met her on the street
> An' speert gin she was thirsty[15]

[10] Alexander Rodger, 'Jamie McNab', in *Whistle-Binkie* (Glasgow: David Robertson, 1842), p.24. This edition is the same as the 1839 Second Series, cited FN 11 below. Robertson's manuscript note on the proofs identifies and praises McNab. James Scott's friendship with Rodger is discussed in the note to Rodger's 'Behave yoursel' before folk', p.40.

[11] William Thom wrote to Robertson that Whistle-Binkie's connection with Hedderwick 'must be an agreeable one'. GUL Sp Coll MS Robertson 19/255 (undated).

[12] *Whistle-Binkie*, Second Series (Glasgow: David Robertson, 1839) pp.101, 35; Third Series (Glasgow: David Robertson, 1842), p.35.

[13] A. C. Holman and R. B. Kristofferson, eds., *More of a Man: Diaries of a Scottish Craftsman in Mid Nineteenth-Century North America* (Toronto: University of Toronto Press, 2013), p.195.

[14] E. L. Abel, *Confederate Sheet Music* (Jefferson NC: McFarland, 2004), p.37. See also 'Castles in the Air' (Melbourne: McCulloch and Stewart, 1859–61).

[15] *Whistle-Binkie: A Collection of Comic and Sentimental Songs* (Glasgow: David Robertson, 1832), p.65. A note on the poem indicates that it appeared in the Belfast Newsletter in August 1832.

in contrast, moved from print in the first edition of *Whistle-Binkie* into ballad and folksong. Published simply under the title 'A Parody', readers were expected to know that it was a parody of 'Maggie Lauder' and used the same tune. No record survives of where the editors found the lyrics of 'Cripple Kirsty' or who wrote it. 'Cripple Kirsty' was a well-known street character in Edinburgh in this period, but whether the song is about her, or she was named after the song, is unclear.[16] It was excluded from later editions of *Whistle-Binkie* (probably in respect to the rise of the temperance movement) and, in contrast to 'Castles in the Air', does not seem to have had an extensive afterlife in songsters and other anthologies. It survived in broadside form in the Victorian period, though, and in oral form, as it was recorded by song-collectors Gavin Greig and Hamish Henderson in Scotland and James Madison Carpenter in the United States in the early to mid-twentieth century.[17]

Whistle-Binkie's verse, as these examples show, is a key instance of how poems and songs circulated through the Victorian culture of reprinting, as lyrics moved in and out of the collections and resurfaced in different guises. This chapter does not primarily seek to defend such Whistlebinkian poems and songs by reassessing their literary merit. It is undeniably true that the majority of verse published in the First to Fourth series, my focus here, consists of light sentimental and comic songs; and it is also undeniable that a number of the songs, particularly those that deploy Highland and Irish dialect for comic effect, make uncomfortable reading today. It is, moreover, clear that as the series progresses from 1832 through Victoria's coronation in 1837 and into the 1840s, it becomes gradually more conservative and less overtly politicized in content, so that Morgan's notable characterization of it as 'an instrument of social control' holds at least partly true.[18]

Yet this, in itself, supplies an important narrative about the way in which verse cultures developed and changed in the early Victorian period. What I argue in the first section of this chapter is that *Whistle-Binkie* shows us Scottish poetry in transition. It is deeply ambiguous in its generic and ideological loyalties and in its uneasy position on social and political issues. Poised between the poetry of the street and the poetry of the drawing-room, between the radicalism of the 1780s to the 1830s and the consensus liberalism of the late 1830s and 1840s, the changes from first publication (1832) to the Fifth Series (1843) show us how Scottish working-class verse cultures became Victorian. In this, they followed wider trends. Richard Cronin's important study of English literature from 1824 to 1840 particularly identifies the 'transformation of revolutionary poetry into a poetry of citizenship' as characteristic of this period, and concludes that one possible generalization about literary trends in this period is the growing sense that 'Writing has its origin in a shared world, and achieves its proper end only when it is recovered by this

---

[16] See unpublished memoir by D. A. Small, cited in Ralph Lownie, ed., *Auld Reekie: An Edinburgh Anthology* (Edinburgh: Mainstream, 2004), n.p.

[17] 'Cripple Kirsty' is 6030 in the Roud Folksong Index. See http://www.vwml.org for information on the song's collection (consulted 18 September 2018).

[18] Morgan, p.340.

world'.[19] As I discuss in the second section of the chapter, for a series that gradually established a collective—the Whistlebinkians—and that attempted to market itself as part of the 'social circle', this holds remarkably true. Unpublished manuscript correspondence enables us to assess the relationships and transactions between editor and contributors that informed the construction of this collective, and to see how writers shared and developed a sense of the 'Whistlebinkians' as a fraternal society of working-class male writers with shared ambitions.

In 1843, after the Fifth Series, *Whistle-Binkie* expanded its remit and sought to make a profit from the Christmas gift market by advertising a new enterprise, 'Songs for the Nursery', to be issued 'early in Winter' and which would be eminently suitable for improving children's minds through 'elevated conception and feeling expressed in simple language'.[20] In the event, *Songs for the Nursery* was to prove the most influential publication of the *Whistle-Binkie* series through its development of 'nursery verse'. If 'infantilism' is one of the prime charges against the Whistlebinkians, their nursery verse collection must be the prime exhibit. The final, and longest, section of this chapter, taking the narrative up to the 1870s and the family oriented poems of the *People's Friend*, focuses specifically on *Songs for the Nursery* and the verse culture it inspired, arguing that the existence of a substantial number of poems for and about children by Scottish working-class poets is of crucial importance both for Scottish Victorian literature and, indeed, for children's literature in the Victorian period. Nursery verse has been more maligned or simply ignored than any other genre discussed in this monograph, in both Scottish studies and nineteenth-century studies.[21] We cannot, however, dismiss its enormous popularity with readers in Scotland and far beyond, nor should we, because giving due attention to this genre uncovers its fascinating intersections with political ideologies of domesticity and hotly contested debates, not simply about the position of working-class families and children in a changing society, but also about the use and survival of the Scots language.

Twentieth- and twenty-first-century critics, as the comments cited above suggest, have usually seen nothing remotely positive about *Whistle-Binkie's* extensive investment in Scots.[22] But this assessment is not based on any close consideration of what the Whistlebinkians were trying to do with the Scots language and why they thought it mattered. The Preface to *Songs for the Nursery* is one of the most trenchant defences of Scots as a 'poetic' language published in this period. Whether they succeeded or not, the poets and editors of *Whistle-Binkie* and the 'Nursery Songs' did not believe that they were contributing to the decline of the Scots language, or its codification as childish and cutesy. They believed that they were saving it. The intelligence and care that went into the Scots dialect used in many of these

---

[19] Richard Cronin, *Romantic Victorians: English Literature 1824–1840* (Houndmills: Palgrave, 2002), pp.248, 259.

[20] Back page advertisement, *Whistle-Binkie*, Fifth Series (Glasgow: David Robertson, 1843), n.p.

[21] See, for example, Donelle Ruwe's recent *British Children's Poetry in the Romantic Era* (Houndmills: Palgrave, 2014), in which she comments that 'nursery verse has long been held in low esteem' (p.12).

[22] See, for example, McClure's suggestion that *Whistle-Binkie* offered 'a domesticated Scots: the devitalized language of a people drained of confidence' (p.28).

poems, written in most cases by working-class Scots speakers, should not be underestimated, and letters and proof corrections between the editors and their friends show a deep engagement with the minutiae of local Scots speech and an effort to preserve its 'best' qualities, albeit that these were often defined in terms of vulgarity versus sophistication. While the songs of *Whistle-Binkie* are so varied in language, theme and content that it is hard to make an overarching argument about their uses of dialect, this is not true for *Songs for the Nursery*, in which there is a clear ideological intent behind the use of Scots and English, and in which the 'childishness' of Scots is simultaneously contested and supported. The third part of this chapter thus additionally explores the complicated history of Scots in the nursery, from the 1840s to the 1880s.

WHISTLE-BINKIE, REFORM POLITICS, AND THE RISE OF VICTORIAN CULTURE

Whistle-Binkie, as befitted its ambiguous position in early Victorian print culture, halfway between a cheap popular songster or chapbook and a bound volume of poetry, was not a stable text. Beginning as an unbound pocket-size collection, and succeeded by four more parts of increasing length, these were then collected or reissued at various points, so that different 'series' sometimes appeared in the same year. Poems were omitted, added, altered, or republished in the same format but with a different tune attached, as standard practice. Editions of *Whistle-Binkie* from the early 1840s onwards, however, do show a decided shift away from the more political, topical and controversial verse included in the original 1832 edition, and most likely in the original Second Series (no original of this appears to be extant), as opposed to the collected First and Second series, reissued later. Perhaps because the 1832 edition is so rare, it is later editions of *Whistle-Binkie* that appear to have guided critical opinion of its conservative sentimentality. But for contemporary readers in the 1830s and 1840s, *Whistle-Binkie* was inescapably a collection that emerged from 1820s radical culture and a product of Reform politics. As an early review in *Tait's Edinburgh Magazine* observed, its character resembled a 'patriot' 'chirruping over his cups' in the bar, and 'chanting... the praises of liberty and the triumph of Reform'.[23]

The first editor, John Carrick, had worked his way up from casual labour to running a pottery business, before turning to a literary and journalistic career. He was well-known as an enthusiast for Reform. Writing to Robertson in 1833, William Motherwell noted that the proprietors of a new Kilmarnock newspaper intended to espouse Reformist causes, and thus Carrick would be an ideal editorial appointment, 'they never could light upon a more energetic and uncompromising and at the same time prudent, sagacious and enlightened advocate of their principles than

---

[23] *Tait's Edinburgh Magazine*, vol II, no. VII (October 1832), p.125.

they will find in the person of Mr Carrick'.[24] The second editor and a primary contributor from the outset, Alexander 'Sandy' Rodger, was an even more striking advocate for Reform and radical politics. Trained as a weaver, in 1819 Rodger began to work for the radical Glasgow journal *The Spirit of the Union*, and when the editor was found guilty of sedition, Rodger was caught up in the repressions of spring 1820 and briefly imprisoned. According to Robertson, he amused himself in jail by 'singing, at the top of his lungs, his own political compositions'.[25] Rodger was a well-known and well-liked Glasgow political activist, journalist and satirist in prose and poetry, who had also published in 'some of the most noted London Radical periodicals, such as the Black Dwarf'.[26] At the point when he became involved with *Whistle-Binkie* he was working for the *Reformer's Gazette* and widely publishing his political poems, songs, and satires under various pseudonyms. In 1839, and again in 1842 and subsequent editions, Robertson's biographies of Rodger and Carrick appeared as a supplement to the collected First Series of *Whistle-Binkie*. As the readership of *Whistle-Binkie* expanded beyond a local Glasgow and Edinburgh market, Robertson thus ensured that new readers knew Rodger and Carrick as political men. And while Robertson himself disliked public speaking and was retiring in politics, he was also part of Glasgow's pro-Reform literati.[27]

Why, then, were these ardent reformers invested in a collection of 'comic and sentimental songs', as the original 1832 title deemed them, 'adapted either for "Bachelor's Hall" or "The Family Circle"'? Firstly, and most obviously, they spotted a gap in the market. By hedging his bets in the subtitle and promising songs suitable for two quite different social circles—male clubs and domestic parties—Carrick doubled the potential audience and attempted to appeal across gendered lines. His promise to exclude songs of 'an indelicate or immoral description' equally appeals across class lines.[28] He offers to supply original, cheap, high-quality popular song that is more respectable than that offered for sale from Hawkie and his contemporaries on the streets. Carrick's preface, the 'Dissertation on Whistle-Binkies', imagines a scenario in which two guests invited to provide entertainment at a party ('whistle-binkies') fail to show up, leaving the hostess embarrassed. 'It would be doing a service to a number of our female acquaintances, and perhaps to the public at the same time', Carrick writes, 'if we could manage to get up a sort of substitute for such saucy whistle-binkies'.[29] The volume, this suggests, is intended to privatize, indeed to domesticate, the performance of contemporary Scottish song, by supplying readers with new words to familiar tunes (the 1832 collection does not give suggested tunes, but all later versions do) and enabling them to sing

[24] MS Robertson 9. The letter is cited in part in Robertson's biography of Carrick, *Whistle-Binkie* (1842), p.xxii.

[25] *Whistle-Binkie* (1842), p.xxviii.

[26] Preface to Alexander Rodger, *Stray Leaves from the Portfolios of Alisander the Seer, Andrew Whaup and Humphrey Henpeckle* (Glasgow: Charles Rattray, 1842), p.vii.

[27] Radical journalist and editor Peter Mackenzie, for instance, places Robertson in the Tontine Coffee House with reformers in 1831, waiting to hear about the Bill, and lists him as a signatory to the petition for city-wide celebrations. *Reminiscences of Glasgow and the West of Scotland 2 vols* (Glasgow: John Tweed, 1866), vol II, p.243.

[28] *Whistle-Binkie* (1832), Preface, p.v.   [29] Ibid., p.v.

for themselves, individually or collectively. Carrick's preface, then, suggests a primary audience of respectable women readers, a readership also imagined through his opening poem and prose piece, 'Scottish Tea-Party'.[30]

Yet this is complicated by the inclusion of politicized and 'bachelors' hall' poems and the importance of *Whistle-Binkie* in an actual all-male social circle, as discussed below. And it is complicated further by the fact that throughout the original preface Carrick's tongue is firmly in his cheek, to the point that the reader suspects satire. Beneath the surface of his facetious 'Dissertation on Whistlebinkies' lurks a serious engagement with questions about language and about popular literature and its audiences. Robertson's manuscript note describes this preface as 'a sort of practical joke on the celebrated Mr Jamieson', referencing John Jamieson's *Etymological Dictionary of the Scots Language* (first published in 1808, and completed in 1825).[31] Carrick mocks elaborate academic research into common Scots terms in his pseudo-learned questioning of Jamieson's definition of a 'whistle-binkie' as:

> One who attends a penny wedding, but without paying any thing, and therefore has no right to take any share of the entertainment, a mere spectator, who is as it were left to sit on a bench by himself, and who, if he pleases, may whistle for his own amusement.[32]

In contesting this rather speculative definition, Carrick argues that Jamieson is mistaken and that the whistle-binkie, far from being a gatecrasher and an onlooker, is an invited entertainer who plays or sings in return for food and drink. As a sardonic footnote signalling *Whistle-Binkie*'s politics points out, this fair exchange sets him in opposition to 'many of the magnates of our own times' who 'look on it as an object of laudable ambition to be fed at the public expense'.[33] Questioning Jamieson's *Dictionary* in this way is not an apolitical act. Carrick's joking redefinition effectively rewrites Jamieson's lower-class scrounger from 'a mere spectator' to a key participant in the community, from onlooker to agent. He is implicitly able to do this, because, unlike Jamieson, he knows the popular context in which such terms are likely to be used. Jamieson's Preface makes it very clear that his imagined reader, who is interested in using the *Dictionary* to interpret 'ancient MSS', including the books in his 'old libraries', is far removed from the working classes; this reader's interest in Scots may stretch to the colloquial, but definitely does not encompass words 'such as belong to a still lower class, being mere corruptions, cant terms, and puerilities'.[34] What is important in *Whistle-Binkie*'s 'practical joke', then, is that the whistle-binkie and *Whistle-Binkie* belong to popular culture, with an authorship and readership who understand contemporary Scots—*Songs for the Nursery* does include a short Glossary, presumably for the benefit of child readers, but no other edition of *Whistle-Binkie* does—and for whom it is a living language, corruptions and all.

---

[30] *Whistle-Binkie*, Fourth Series, with Supplement (Glasgow: David Robertson, 1842), p.vii.
[31] Manuscript note, *Whistle-Binkie* 1842, p.v. GUL Sp Coll.
[32] John Jamieson, *An Etymological Dictionary of the Scottish Language, 2 vols* (Edinburgh: Edinburgh University Press, 1808), II, p.665. Consulted at 'Jamieson's Etymological Dictionary of the Scots Language Online', http://www.scotsdictionary.com, 18 September 2018.
[33] *Whistle-Binkie* (1832), p.vn.   [34] Jamieson, 'Preface', p.iii.

While the editorial and publishing team behind *Whistle-Binkie* were undoubtedly interested in repositioning Scottish song in emerging markets, then, their reformist bent also fed into a desire to display, for the benefit of readers of all classes, the continuing existence of a vibrant culture of Scottish song and verse created largely by working men. That Sandy Rodger the radical poet can—and frequently does—write song lyrics for *Whistle-Binkie* such as 'Lovely Maiden', opening

> Lovely maiden, art thou sleeping?
> Wake, and fly with me, my love
> While the moon is proudly sweeping
> Through the ether fields above[35]

is not a sign of an abandonment of radicalism. It is rather, as I argue in the Introduction and Chapter 1, an indication of cultural capital that helps to shore up the credibility of radicalism as a viable political position, adopted by educated and culturally literate men. The 1832 *Whistle-Binkie*, in which 'Lovely Maiden' immediately follows the unsigned Reform poem 'The Carter's Rant', made little attempt to disguise its general leaning towards the spirit of Reform. It incorporates several songs directly relating to the political unrest around the passing of the Reform Bill (finally passed as the Reform Act on 8 June 1832) including the anonymous 'The Tories in the Dumps', 'Away to the Tavern' and 'The Carter's Rant', plus Rodger's signed 'Highland Politicians'. Since 'The Tories in the Dumps' provides a satirical account of the Pitt Dinner of early June 1832—reported by the press as a last Tory hurrah before the passing of the Act—it dates the collection to a period shortly after the Act had been passed. 'The Carter's Rant' is presented as a song performed at the Carters' Reform Supper, drawing on Burns's 'A Man's a Man for a' that':

> Now should you gentry, ca'd 'the Lords'
> Throw out the Bill an a' that
> And boldly tell us to our face
> That *we're their slaves* an a' that,
> Shall we submit to a' that,
> Their saucy sneers an a' that?
> The death o' dogs befa' the rogues
> That wad succumb tae a' that.[36]

Enlisting Burns's support by reworking his poem, the speaker calls on a tradition of Scottish patriotism, appealing to Wallace and Bruce in threatening dire consequences if the Bill is not passed. 'Away to the Tavern' hints still more strongly at the possibilities of carrying Reform by physical force. The song in entirety runs:

> Away to the tavern, brave spirits!
> Thou mad-caps of revel and glee!
> And pledge to his virtues and merits,
> Who dare to be poor and be free.

---

[35] *Whistle-Binkie* (1832), p.59. [36] *Whistle-Binkie* (1832), p.58.

> Though ragged his jerkin and sorry,
>   And sallow the hue of his nose,
> He can quaff to 'love, freedom and glory'
>   And wash down the cobweb of woes.
>
> He can spurn at the great, as the jackass
>   That kick'd at the lion in pride
> He can pistol and pike too – let that pass
>   As things by the gods ratified.   (1832, p.106)

Readers, in these poems, observe working-class radicalism rather than being part of it: 'Away to the tavern' would read very differently if 'He' were 'We'. 'Away to the Tavern' is typical of several poems on current affairs in *Whistle-Binkie*, which are openly pro-Reform and supportive of working men, yet treat the topics of poverty and political agitation at a remove and in poems which are balanced between the comic and the serious. The comparison to Aesop's jackass and reference to 'mad-caps' are not complimentary, and the poem mocks the physical appearance of the drinkers. But while it does not ratify the potential use of 'pistol and pike', it does not condemn it either—indeed it might imply that violence *could* be ratified by higher powers. Rodger's 'Highland Politicians' is still more representative of this uneasy wavering between mocking and supporting working-class reformers, by presenting a serious conversation about the likely effects of Reform in faux-Highland dialect:

> An ne'er let lairds nor factors more
>   Pe do ta poor man's harm, man,
> Nor purn him's house apoon him's head,
>   An' trive him aff ta farm, man.[37]

Such dialect signals comic verse, since it mocks the Highlanders' provinciality, ignorance about the Reform Bill, and lack of education, but the poem makes a serious point about land rights and injustice, unusual in other comic 'Highland' poems. Of the Reform poems published in the 1832 *Whistle-Binkie*, only 'Highland Politicians' made it into any further editions, with a historical footnote added by Robertson stating that it was 'Written at the time when the whole country was pressing the government to have the Reform Bill passed'.[38] 'The Carter's Rant' and 'Away to the Tavern' were evidently judged either too political in general, or too tied to events of 1832, for republication.

The later editions of *Whistle-Binkie* do, however, continue to publish overtly political poems. Older republished poems such as John Robertson's 'The Toom Meal Pock' (empty oatmeal bag) stand out for their bitterness and deployment of Scots. The speaker suggests sending a starving weaver to confront the lords in London:

> Speak no ae word about Reform,
>   Nor petition Parliament,
> A wiser scheme I'll now propose
>   I'm sure ye'll gie consent; –

---

[37] *Whistle-Binkie* (1832), p.79.   [38] *Whistle-Binkie* (1842), p.79.

>   Send up a chield or twa like *him,*
>   As a sample of the flock,
>   Whose hollow cheeks will be sure proof
>   O' a hinging toom meal pock.[39]

The threat in this poem, moreover, is of an end to a union that is failing to benefit the poor:

>   Tell them ye're wearied o' the chain
>   That hauds the state thegither,
>   For Scotland wishes just to tak',
>   Gude nicht wi' ane anither.[40]

On the one hand, Robertson's footnote places this poem firmly in history, by noting that it relates to the condition of weavers in 1793. On the other, he emphasizes its continuing relevance by noting its currency in his own social circle as a song, 'Our worthy friend, Mr George Miller, Blantyre, sings it inimitably'.[41] It is increasingly typical of the later *Whistle-Binkie* series to insert editorial disclaimers about content when poems deal with working-class discontent, as in the note appended to 'The Tree of Liberty' after its attribution to Burns (no author was given on its first appearance in the Second Series), which appeases admirers of a more conservative Burns by suggesting that if Burns had lived to see the consequences of the French Revolution, he 'would doubtless have qualified many of the expressions'.[42] The editors sought to preserve and disseminate Scotland's tradition of radical verse, yet without openly assenting to its aims. It is also typical that an increasing number of poems about working men show them resisting the temptations of drink or crime: so in Rodger's 'I had a hat, I had nae mair', a drunk whose hat and head were smashed on a night out takes to 'drinking water'; or in David Webster's excellent 'Tak it, man, tak it', a miller resists the desperate temptation to steal some grain from the mill, 'Yet I see that it disna well suit,/ Honest men to begin to the thieving'.[43]

As the Reform and Chartist agitation in Glasgow of the 1830s settled into a broader cross-class liberal consensus supporting gradual Reform, the poems in *Whistle-Binkie* reflect this change.[44] They look forward to a positive and stable future, though it is worth noting that this future is premised on continued political Reform and the maintenance of those rights that have already been achieved. Hence in the unattributed song, 'Laugh and be thankfu', described by Robertson in his manuscript note as a 'most excellent social contentment speaking song', 'social contentment' relies on the preservation of 'liberty'; as the song observes,

---

[39] Ibid., p.64.

[40] Leonard includes 'The Toom Meal Pock' and 'Tak it Man, Tak it' (discussed below), in Radical Renfrew, pp.5, 94. His copies are drawn from other sources.

[41] *Whistle-Binkie* (1842), p.64.   [42] *Whistle-Binkie* (1839), p.101.

[43] *Whistle-Binkie* (1842), pp.17, 10.

[44] I. G. C. Hutchison comments that between the first and second Reform Acts (1832–1867) in Glasgow, 'the tenor of working-class radical politics was as a rule less hostile to middle-class liberalism, than was the case in many other parts of Britain'. See his 'Glasgow Working-Class Politics', in R. A. Cage, ed., *The Working Class in Glasgow, 1750–1914* (London: Croom Helm, 1987), pp.98–141, 104.

'May the enemies o' liberty ere long get a kick,/ They've aye gott'nt hitherto, and sae shall they yet'.[45] Even the loyalist poems celebrating Victoria's coronation make it clear that a successful reign depends on due consideration of the people's needs. Rodger's words to the tune of 'God Save the Queen' include the lines:

> Grant her an Alfred's zeal
> Still for the Commonweal,
> Her people's wounds to heal.[46]

John Paterson's 'Britain's Queen, Victoria', urges her to 'Let reform and knowledge march,/ Through perfection's glorious arch' and 'Equal rights and equal laws,/ Let the people all enjoy'.[47] Like many contributors, Paterson was a radically inclined weaver, 'At every election Paterson was a conspicuous person, ever lending his influence against the Conservative cause'.[48] The suggested tune to his poem, 'Rob Roy MacGregor, O' (a song which itself borrows an older tune from 'Duncan Gray'), evokes the lyrics of that song, which urges forgiveness of Rob Roy's transgressions, 'A' that's past, forget, forgie'.[49] Writers like Rodger, known for his bitter satire about George IV's visit to Edinburgh in 1822 ('Sawney, now, the king's come,/ Kneel, and kiss his gracious—') are prepared to forget and forgive, but only on the condition that the new Queen recognizes that the wounds of the past need to be healed, and is prepared to usher in a new age of popular politics.[50]

The manuscripts and proofs of *Whistle-Binkie*, including poems the editors rejected, show the extent to which Robertson and Rodger were aware of developing tastes in their audience which we might justifiably connect to 'Victorian' preoccupations: an emphasis on sentimentalized domesticity; a growing number of emigrant poems from abroad and immigrant poems from Ireland and the Highlands; an engagement with pastoral, seasonal poems about the Scottish countryside; an enjoyment of comic Scots poems, particularly about marital woes; an interest in temperance; and a lowered tolerance for risqué religious, sexual, and political satire. Several of these genres are discussed in Chapter 3. Poems which did not speak to these tastes, like Hawkie's 'The Monopoly Dandy', a satirical song about the attitude of rich to poor—'In our curricle we'll ride,/ And the sooty poor deride'—and a lament about the rise of 'Cotton Mills' and 'power looms', were, after careful consideration, rejected.[51] William Cross's 'The Grand Lady's Mither', a poem about a mother rejoicing that her daughter will marry a wealthy minister, caused problems for Rodger and Robertson because of its satirical references to clerical wealth. 'I am afraid some of the expressions in the original might give offence to certain sensitive minds', Rodger noted on the manuscript. Robertson suggested changes, such as substituting the words 'gude lad' for 'bright saunt', to remove the offence

---

[45] *Whistle-Binkie* (1842), p.34.   [46] Ibid., p.89.   [47] Ibid., p.107.
[48] William Harvey, ed. *The Harp of Stirlingshire* (Paisley: J. and R. Parlane, 1897), p.118.
[49] See Roud Folksong Index (V285) for examples of this song's circulation: http://www.vwml.org/roudnumber/V285.
[50] Rodger, *Stray Leaves*, p.15.
[51] Manuscript poem, 'Monopoly Dandy' [title altered by Robertson to 'Monopoly in the Land']. MS Robertson 17/60.

caused by using the religious term 'saint' sardonically, but ultimately noted that the poem was 'Not printed as the author would not permit the alterations'.[52] That Rodger, who had gleefully described clergy along with aristocrats in the 1820s as 'a vile, profligate, sinecure band,/ Devouring by wholesale the fat o' the land' and joked about ministers sleeping with whores, when they were not 'hanging and starving' the poor, objected to Cross's poem shows both that times had changed, and that the editors saw their role in *Whistle-Binkie* as to please rather than discomfit a mixed male and female audience.[53]

That audience, Robertson and Rodger envisage, would enjoy a standard song about spring, such as William Calder's 'Spirit of Love and Beauty', but would be less interested in the song about tailoring work that Calder sent with it, which was rejected.[54] Readers would be offended by jokes about religion—Thomas Latto's 'Woman's E'e' is turned down with a note 'Good but would give offence' because it contains a pun referencing the Garden of Eden—and by crude humour, so Latto's 'Ye're aye in the right, gudewife', in which a henpecked husband notes that he has a hole in his breeches in a place 'I dinna like to name', is also turned down.[55] Sometimes the editors resisted. William Fergusson's 'Jock' features a titular character, a miller's son, who is repeatedly reproved by 'the Laird's son' in successive verses for his drunkenness and uncouth behaviour at work, at the Fair, and after Church. Unusually, Jock is unrepentant, and the published poem concludes (in lines reworked by Robertson), 'Sae haud your whisht, whate'er ye think,/ And let me tak my wee drap drink'. The editors had no problem with Jock's rudeness to a member of the upper classes, but Robertson was clearly worried about the application of these lines to a readership likely to complain about his support for drinking. He inserted a paragraph-long defensive footnote to the poem aimed at temperance advocates, stating that *Whistle-Binkie* advocates 'moderate use' of alcohol, and that forcing people into total abstention threatens 'the Liberty of the subject'.[56]

What emerges from the proofs, as these examples show, is a sense of the editors constructing *Whistle-Binkie* to suit the tastes of a heterogeneous but presumptively respectable audience, sometimes against their own inclinations. And what also emerges is a clear sense of working-class poets selecting themes and genres because they know that they will suit these tastes. Excluding the newspaper and periodical press, *Whistle-Binkie* was the single most important publication venue of this period for Scottish working-class poets, and the best way that their songs could reach a wider middle-class audience. The significance of this anthology in promoting a particular vision of working-class literary culture, actively mediated by the editors, is vital to our understanding of the relationships between producers and consumers of Scottish poetry and song.

---

[52] See MS Robertson 17/68.

[53] See 'The Twa Weavers' and 'Black Coats, and Gravats Sae White', in Rodger, *Stray Leaves*, pp.3, 5. These poems were written in the 1820s.

[54] MS Robertson 18/116.   [55] MS Robertson 19/215 and 19/216.

[56] MS Robertson 18/124. 'Jock' was published, with footnote, in the Fourth Series, *Whistle-Binkie* (Glasgow: David Robertson, 1842), pp.23–5. However, it does not seem to have been republished in the late-century editions.

POETIC FRATERNITIES

Whistle-Binkie pre-empted, and in part inspired, the Victorian enthusiasm for anthologizing local Scottish poets, and celebrating the importance of working-class writers for Scottish national pride and identity by showcasing their most respectable verse. But what distinguishes it from contemporary and later songsters and anthologies, some of which had similar aims, is the survival of correspondence which shows the collaborative intent of editor and contributors in shaping the anthology, and the reasons—often directly material and financial—for their choices. Collective, social groups or clubs of male working-class writers were, of course, very common in this period throughout Britain: many *Whistle-Binkie* contributors, like William Thom, belonged to a circle of local poets who met regularly in a pub or workplace. But it is unusual to have first-hand evidence of the strategic and rhetorical moves that lay behind poetic friendships and relationships of patronage, as we have in the Robertson MSS collection. Robertson, himself the son of a farmer who had worked his way up from an apprentice bookseller, was a very active patron. In Glasgow, where he was known affectionately as 'The Facetious Bibliophile', Robertson's Trongate shop was 'the resort of most of our local celebrities', and 'a lounge for the entire literati of the city', and he himself was involved in wide and overlapping social circles of male clubs and coteries.[57] As *Whistle-Binkie*'s success moved it beyond a local audience of Glasgow and Edinburgh authors and readers, he expanded this patronage to a growing stable of writers across Scotland and into Northern England.

Robertson's editorial footnotes, both published and carefully handwritten into the proofs, emphasize the labouring background of the *Whistle-Binkie* authors in order to ensure that the anthology is presented, to contemporary and future readers, as a conscious product of working-class literary culture. David Webster is described, for instance, as 'an operative weaver in Paisley... deceased some years ago leaving a widow and family in very destitute circumstances'.[58] In a typical Whistlebinkian transaction, Robertson provided financial assistance, and Webster's wife returned him two songs for publication. Thomas Dick is also described by Robertson as 'a very humble weaver in Paisley'; Alexander McLaggan of Edinburgh is 'an operative' and former alcoholic ('at this time he is a member of a Temperance Society'); William Fergusson 'also belongs to the operative class' (he was a plumber); and Alexander Smart is another working man from Edinburgh (one of several in the printing trade who were contributors) who is commended as an example of 'good behaviour to his class'.[59] While Robertson notes these particular instances and supplies short biographies for poets who are dead and who might be unfamiliar to

---

[57] See John Strang, *Glasgow and its Clubs* (Glasgow: John Tweed, 1864), p.446 and James A. Kilpatrick, *Literary Landmarks of Glasgow* (Glasgow: Saint Mungo Press, 1893), p.206.

[58] Handwritten note by Robertson, in proofs of *Whistle-Binkie* (Glasgow: David Robertson, 1839), p.9. GUL Special Collections.

[59] *Whistle-Binkie* (1842), manuscript notes pp.33, 12, 6–7, 42–3. It is probable that these hand-written notes were originally intended to form the basis of future footnotes in the series.

readers, he would also have assumed that most readers knew that better-known contributors to *Whistle-Binkie*, like William Thom of Inverurie or James Ballantine of Edinburgh, were working men.

The social circle in which *Whistle-Binkie* was formed was therefore represented as reliant on friendship between men in more financially secure, professional positions, and those who were of 'the operative class' and whose income and status were precarious. These friendships were fostered through in-person meetings and correspondence and were based on the assumption of shared literary interests and aspirations. The collections are full of in-jokes and allusions to male associational culture, as in the song 'The Herring-Head Club', which Robertson notes in a manuscript comment was 'got up for the use of' a Glasgow club to which he belonged (1842, p.119), and they set up *Whistle-Binkie* as a product of such connections between men, at the centre of overlapping circles of relationships between working Scottish poets in different parts of the country (or indeed the world). Ballantine, one of the most prolific contributors and 'the publisher's dear and cherished friend' (1842, p.18) was particularly influential in extending *Whistle-Binkie*'s Edinburgh circle by finding and befriending new local writers, including Fergusson and McLaggan, and then recommending them to Robertson. Authors leveraged their friendships to join the Whistle-Binkie collective. When suggesting himself as a contributor, for instance, Smart notes in a letter to Robertson that he has been close to Alexander Laing, an existing contributor, for twenty years.[60] Thom, who joined the Whistlebinkians in the early 1840s, served as a conduit for recruiting his poetic circle from the North of Scotland, including John Imlah, Peter Still, and George Murray, asking their permission to send their works to Robertson for consideration: 'I shall try to make myself useful...I have procured the like freedom from Peter Still a copy of whose book I now enclose'.[61] The standard method of enlisting contributors, letters suggest, was for Robertson's friends and existing contributors to send him poems they thought might suit *Whistle-Binkie*. If Robertson approved, he would then approach the potential new contributor either himself or through an intermediary. So, in the case of Murray, Thom forwarded Robertson's comments on a poem and Murray then wrote to Robertson expressing how honoured he would be to join *Whistle-Binkie*, with all its 'delightful associations...not the least of which is that I first read it in London, Upper Canada'.[62]

By the 1840s, as the correspondence which Robertson preserved clearly shows, *Whistle-Binkie* was very well-known (well beyond Britain, as Murray's letter suggests) and would-be poets aspired to join its authorial community. Although we cannot take the comments in letters to Robertson at face value, given that their authors were well aware that Robertson could supply both publication and financial support, they are lavish in their admiration for *Whistle-Binkie* and repeatedly emphasize its novelty as a collection of poems by working writers. Thom wrote in November 1841 that he had received the six copies of *Whistle-Binkie* sent by

---

[60] Letter from Alex Smart, October 1842, MS Robertson 19/243.
[61] Letter from Thom, 20 April 1842, MS Robertson 18/155.
[62] Letter from Murray, July 1843, MS Robertson 19/218.

Robertson and distributed five 'amongst those who, I think, will one day add a feather to the "Piper's bonnet"' by becoming contributors:

> Your little Book presents to the timid and unassuming, the means of at once gratifying his selflove and pouring into many a sympathizing breast the yearning aspirations of his own – If, twenty years ago, when my mind was un-fretted, and full even unto bursting with all that was fanciful – if then such an opportunity – such encouragement – O how intensely would I have watched, how kindly cherished and eagerly cultivated the little Twig that my young hand stole from your Holy hill! – But such was the taste editorial of that day... many a verse of mine, prettier than aught I have written since, passed unheeded into recordless night, stifling hope in that way – and fairly throwing a wet Blanket at once on exertions and ambitions.[63]

This letter is a masterpiece of humble self-construction from Thom, revisiting his well-known past as a ruined weaver and widower, and portraying himself as the hard-working lone parent sustaining 'the quiet little Heaven that nightly closes round the Widowed hearth' and enjoying 'all of consolation that Heaven had left – the rearing of my little Family – and the sweet and guileless reverie of Song'.[64] Any working-class poet corresponding with a middle-class potential patron, particularly one known to have published biographical information on 'his' poets, would have written with one eye to possible publication of the letter, as well as the poem supplied ('My Heather Land'; Robertson accepted it). And the reasoning behind Thom's inclusion of this absolutely genuine sob story is also indicated by his enclosure of an advertising flyer for his weaving business, which Robertson would be able to publicize to acquaintances in Thom's region. Nonetheless, it is important that Thom characterizes *Whistle-Binkie* as offering innovative opportunities for working-class poets, and still more important that these are explicitly characterized in terms of the poetry of affect ('pouring into many a sympathetic breast'), of fancy, and of prettiness. *Whistle-Binkie* established an outlet for this sentimental poetics, often linked to femininity and established women poets such as Felicia Hemans or L. E. L., but in this particular context appropriated by male working-class poets; partly in order to reach an imagined audience of women readers, and partly to emphasize that these workers were men of feeling. As Isobel Armstrong has convincingly argued (specifically in reference to Tennyson), the development of a 'poetry of empathy' in the 1830s and 1840s can be associated with the 'desperate desire to produce a new account of communality which would transcend social division', a political and cultural aim very much aligned with *Whistle-Binkie*'s promotion of cross-class sympathy between and amongst writers and readers.[65]

Thom's renewed relationship with the Aberdeen press and the rapid spread of his reputation dated from early 1841, so Robertson had recruited him within a year of

---

[63] Letter from Thom, 9 November 1841, MS Robertson 18/156.   [64] Ibid.
[65] See Isobel Armstrong, *Victorian Poetry: Poetry, Poetics, Politics* (Oxford: Blackwell, 1999), pp.95, 110. On the poetry of the 1830s, see also Cronin.

his first appearance in the *Aberdeen Herald*, and probably sooner.[66] John Crawford of Alloa, a house-painter, was approached directly by Robertson via a poem published in the *Glasgow Courier*: 'I am proud of the notice you have taken of the verses which I sent to the Courier...I would never attempted [sic] a piece for Binkie and it was only because you requested it that I have sent the enclosed'.[67] Robertson sent Crawford gifts of his publications, including a Glossary of Scots— an interesting incentive to develop his Scots poetry—his biography of Motherwell, and a copy of the comic miscellany *The Laird of Logan*. Crawford's letters, far less polished than Thom's, and indicating a lower level of education in their lack of punctuation and calligraphy, seem genuinely overwhelmed by Robertson's attention: 'I am at a loss how to address you as your kindness has quite overpowered me and as I feel myself incapable of expressing my feelings I will not at this time trouble you with many words'. Crawford, like Thom, explicitly links his admiration for *Whistle-Binkie* to its support for working-class verse. Its 'brightest' gems:

> I am proud to think have dropt from the pens of working men – This is a kind of childish predilection but it always gives me pleasure to think that when ages shall have rolled away the descendants of those Scotsmen now peopling distant countries may not trace their descent to those who have trampled on the rights of the widow and orphan but to the lowly philanthropist who shared his mite with the needy and sung his own with their sorrows to rest –[68]

Besides indicating the likely political views of would-be contributors, and providing a fascinating vision of a diasporic community which will value its descent from working-class poets, this image of the poet as 'lowly' philanthropist and comforter suggests that Crawford perceives *Whistle-Binkie* as a product by and for the poor. As in Thom's letter, his imagined poet will find a sympathetic ear in the imagined readership, and thus soothe their sorrows, and his own, in a quintessential representation of the poetry of affect.

A further set of writers approached Robertson directly. As he appears to have preserved only letters from poets who did become contributors, it is impossible to tell how large this group was, but it is likely to have been substantial. 'I have taken the liberty of sending you my Guid coat o' blue', John Paterson writes, in 1843:

> I would be proud to see it in Whistle Binkie I have some langer pieces but they may perhaps be too long I would wish to know when you will publish another volume of Whistle-Binkie I would be glad to receive a line from you on these matters but it is perhaps too much for a stranger to ask yours John Paterson[69]

Paterson's manuscript poem also lacks punctuation. As was standard practice, the editors inserted it. Paterson's song was accepted, and an indication of its lasting

---

[66] The *Aberdeen Herald* published 'The Blind Boy's Pranks', by 'W. T., Inverury', on 2 January 1841 with a supportive note. It immediately attracted a response poem and led to further submissions. The first dated letter from Thom in MS Robertson is November 1841, but this was not their first correspondence.

[67] Letter from John Crawford, 4 December 1842, MS Robertson 19/173.

[68] Letter from Crawford, 1842, MS Robertson 19/172, and 19/175.

[69] Letter from John Paterson, 25 January 1843, MS Robertson 19/229.

currency is given by the indignant letters sent to the *People's Journal* when 'My Guid Coat o' Blue' was plagiarized in the *People's Journal Songster* in 1867: an Oliver Davie, Calender Worker, Hawkhill, for instance, wrote that he had recognized it immediately, 'I found myself crooning it at my work upwards of twenty years ago!'[70] To be accepted by Robertson meant not simply a chance to publish a song that might be sung by working men 'for nearly thirty years' or more, it also, as we have seen, meant entering an exclusive fraternity in which Robertson was the 'Respected Dad o' Whistle-Binkie'.[71] Writers were clearly proud of 'Our Book'.[72]

In the depressions of the 1840s, many of the Whistlebinkians admitted to financial hardship, at which point the material aspects of Robertson's patronage come strikingly into the foreground in the unpublished correspondence. While there is no evidence in the manuscripts that Robertson paid poets directly for their contributions, there is considerable evidence that he supplied free copies of books and provided financial and other forms of support to 'his' authors. 'You are right in your conjectures in regard to that universal complaint, want of employment', Smart wrote to Robertson, outlining his difficult situation in the Edinburgh printing trade, 'I feel greatly obliged and gratified my dear sir by the kind interest you take in my welfare, and by the offer of your influence in my behalf in procuring better employment'.[73] Latto, in Edinburgh, thanked Robertson for showing kindness to his shopkeeper brother in Glasgow, noting the problems that the retail trade was facing. Several writers were clear that their circumstances were such that they lacked the physical, mental and material resources for poetry composition without Robertson's intervention. Thom's shop in Inverury was struggling, and he could no longer make a living from weaving; he apologizes for neglecting the Muse, but 'in the stomach of this crisis, I would much rather (Forgive me!) see a douse, honest country woman at my shop door, with the world's want—of four pair o' blankets, than <u>Her</u> the airy hizey'.[74] If Robertson does not fund his writers, they imply, they cannot find time or resources to produce the copy he needed. 'Ye ken I was alyes unwilling to tell the publick of my poverty', William Cameron ('Hawkie') wrote. 'I have now thirty subjects new to the world but I have only completed thierten page of peaper as my dask is the bottom of a window and writes standing on the left foot'.[75]

Most remarkable are a selection of letters from George Donald, a former Glasgow radical, Chartist poet, and journalist whose family had left him due to his alcoholism and who, in the early 1840s, was producing copy for *Songs for the Nursery* while effectively homeless (he later gained employment with a radical newspaper in Glasgow, perhaps through Robertson's assistance). 'I write this on my

---

[70] See *People's Journal*, 9 February 1867, p.2.

[71] 'Knockimdhun', letter to *People's Journal*, 9 Feburary 1867, p.2. See poem by unidentified author to Robertson, opening with 'Respected Dad', MS Robertson 16/45.

[72] See letter from Thom to Robertson, 19 November 1842, 'I congratulate you and all my associates in song, on the widespreading fame that has followed Our Book I beg to own my obligations to the fraternity'. MS Robertson 19/257.

[73] MS Robertson 11. Manuscripts bound in this volume are unnumbered.

[74] 9 November 1841, MS Robertson 18/156.   [75] See MS Robertson 7/221.

knee', he noted in a near-illegible letter, thanking Robertson for the gift of some clothing: 'shoeless and shirtless I am starving I cannot write from the cold – I will call tonight at or about 7 – I will keep your trowsers till I get what will be in <u>keeping</u>'. His next letter observes:

> I thank you for what you gave me – it enabled me to break my fast – My thoughts at times are fearful…I dread the time is not far distant when I shall fall down in the streets – And I am ashamed to make my situation known[76]

Such accounts show the distance between the fantasies of loving family and contented domesticity constructed in *Whistle-Binkie* (*Songs for the Nursery* in particular) and in the wider poetic culture that encompassed it, and the actual situation of their authors. It is rare to have such insight into the relationships between editors and contributors to a collection of working-class verse, and these surviving letters strongly highlight the problems in such relationships. Robertson presents himself as the social equal, admirer, and champion of these poets; he supplies generous encouragement and material assistance, asked and unasked. But there is, of course, an unspoken price in the assumption that poets will supply him with suitable verses in return. Literally starving and without even a pair of trousers to his name, a radical political poet would write whatever he knew was immediately welcome to a local patron: in Donald's case, poems such as 'My Bairnies, You're All the Wide World to Me' or 'My Doggie'.[77]

Nowhere is it clearer than in these letters that Scottish working-class poets operated under constraints that later critics have not always taken into account; it is a sad irony that inclusion under the *Whistle-Binkie* brand name has assisted in the conscious forgetting of political poets like Donald in later centuries. Despite overt discussions of fraternity, the material difference in circumstances between Robertson and his contributors does, as these examples show, militate against a relationship of equality, in which they might have had power to shape the product they contributed to. Yet I do not wish to dismiss the verse that poets such as Donald did produce, simply because they produced it to order. Writing children's verse, as an alcoholic, homeless radical journalist on the streets of one of the world's most important industrial cities, is not an apolitical act. As I discuss below, indeed, such verse provides perhaps the most trenchant example of how Whistlebinkian poetics did not eschew earlier radical and reformist loyalties, but remained deeply allied to them.

NURSERY VERSE AND THE WORKING-CLASS FAMILY

One of the most important, and most neglected, aspects of *Whistle-Binkie*'s influence was its creation of Scottish nursery verse as a recognized and reputable genre for working-class poets. Many of the best-known and highly respected Scottish

---

[76] MS Robertson 11.
[77] 'My Bairnies' was seemingly not accepted for publication, 'My Doggie' is in *Songs for the Nursery*, p.69.

working-class poets of the period tried their hand at this genre. By the end of the century, it was established enough for the editor, working-class poet, and folklore collector Robert Ford to put together a substantial anthology of contemporary Scottish nursery verse, *Ballads of Bairnhood* (1892). As he noted in his preface:

> The *Whistlebinkians* were the first in Scotland, or perhaps in the world, to give united attention to the music of the nursery, and their various efforts will not soon be forgotten.[78]

Ironically, a few decades later, the nursery verse of the Whistlebinkians and their successors was only remembered negatively, as in MacDiarmid's discussion of William Soutar's children's verse:

> [T]he reality of the Scottish literary renaissance movement can hardly be better exemplified than just by the difference between these poems for Scots children and the previous sentimental trash designed for this purpose from the days of the *Whistle-Binkie* school to our own time.[79]

Such claims of difference are highly exaggerated. There is a great deal worth recovering in Scottish Victorian nursery verse, a genre that amply merits more detailed examination.[80] While critics rightly see Robert Louis Stevenson's *A Child's Garden of Verses* (1885) as a crucial reinvention of the standards of poetry for children, it is far from the only example of Scottish poets engaging with children and childhood.[81] Stevenson himself would have been very well aware of the existence of a large and active culture of nursery verse known in Scotland and far beyond, yet now almost completely forgotten.

The 'music of the nursery', like 'nursery verse', is an ambiguous phrase. It incorporates songs and rhymes that can be sung to children, and that draw on older oral traditions, but it also encompasses poems *about* children and their behaviour, which are cross-audienced, as their circulation in newspaper poetry columns for an adult readership might suggest. While a lively culture of street verse and broadsides for children flourished well into the nineteenth century, nursery verse was, unlike these nursery rhymes, assumed to be original, and was usually published by a named author.[82] Setting aside those poems commissioned for Robertson's *Songs for the Nursery*, most instances of nursery verse appeared first in newspapers or periodicals, and were then reprinted in collections by their authors. In the cases of poets William Miller, Alexander Smart, James Nicholson, James Neilson, Alexander Anderson, Robert Tennant, James Smith, and others, the popularity of their Scots

---

[78]   Robert Ford, 'Preface', *Ballads of Bairnhood* (Paisley: Alexander Gardner, 1892), n.p.

[79]   MacDiarmid, 'William Soutar', in *Selected Essays*, ed. Duncan Glen (Berkeley, CA: University of California Press, 1969), 92–104, p.98.

[80]   For a broader discussion of Scottish poetry and the child reader in the Victorian period, see Blair, 'The Scottish Nursery Muse: Scottish Poetry and the Children's Verse Tradition in Victorian Britain', in Sarah Dunnigan and Shu-Fang Lai, eds., *The Land of Storybooks: Scottish Children's Literature in the Nineteenth Century* (Glasgow: ASLS, forthcoming).

[81]   See Morag Styles, *From the Garden to the Street: Three Hundred Years of Poetry for Children* (London: Cassell, 1998), which reads A Child's Garden as 'a pivotal collection' (p.170).

[82]   On broadside culture for children, see Robert Collison, *The Story of Street Literature* (London: J. M. Dent, 1973) and Hindley, p.52 on Catnach's publications for children.

nursery verse helped to make their reputations and thus enabled the publication of these collections. Anderson, or 'Surfaceman', for instance, is widely anthologized today for his poems of labour (some of which are discussed in Chapter 4), yet he established himself as a poet of nursery life through the family oriented *People's Friend*, publishing a series of child-centred poems, mostly from a mother's perspective, which are now almost entirely forgotten.[83] After the success of *Whistle-Binkie* and *Songs for the Nursery* in the 1840s, it is not surprising that working-class authors in subsequent decades saw verse for and about children as a route into the poetry market. But it is surprising that nursery verse was strongly perceived as a uniquely *Scottish* popular genre—'We know of no other country that could have produced it', *Tait's* reviewer wrote of *Songs for the Nursery*—and it is also surprising that it was regarded as primarily a *male* genre.[84] There are British and Scottish working-class women poets who wrote nursery verse, but in Victorian Scotland, the leading practitioners of this genre were working-class men. Why is it that poems for and about children took such hold on the popular imagination in Victorian Scotland, and what was at stake in their production?

One answer to this question, from a literary perspective, is that nursery verse, particularly in Scots, emerges in the 1830s and 1840s from a renewed British interest in traditional cultures of childhood and nursery rhymes, and that it is a product of Scottish claims to superiority—whether accurate or not—in this field. Reviewing the 1842 edition of Robert Chambers' *Popular Rhymes of Scotland* (originally published in 1826) alongside James Orchard Halliwell's pioneering collection of *The Nursery Rhymes of England* (1842), for instance, *Tait's* argued that despite the substantial overlap between English and Scottish nursery rhyme, Scotland took first place: 'The lullabies of the English Nursery are very inferior in poetical spirit to a few of those from Scotland'.[85] In his 1842 preface, Chambers identified popular and nursery rhyme—like ballads and songs—as essential parts of 'the *natural literature* of my native country', noting that the impetus of his collection was to preserve the 'rhymes and legends of the old Scottish nursery' that are 'threatened with oblivion' in a period that increasingly privileged 'realism' in children's education.[86] As Katie Trumpener argues, Chambers suggests that:

> If reformers cleanse the nursery curriculum of traditional ballads and implement didactic texts in their stead, future generations will lose their literary birthright. For Chambers, the nursery is therefore the site of a crucial cultural struggle, between realism and romance, past and present.[87]

---

[83] For a few examples, see 'Oor Sis', *People's Friend*, 24 July 1872; 'The Bowgie Man', *People's Friend*, 17 December 1873; 'Dingle Doozie', *People's Friend*, 28 January 1874 and 'Cuddle Doon', *People's Friend*, 1 April 1874. This last was Anderson's best-known nursery poem. His 'Jenny' is discussed below.

[84] *Tait's Edinburgh Magazine* 11 (July 1844), p.469.

[85] 'The Nursery and Popular Rhymes and Tales of England and Scotland', *Tait's Edinburgh Magazine* 10 (1843), 114–22, 115, 118.

[86] Robert Chambers, *Popular Rhymes, Fireside Stories and Amusements of Scotland* (Edinburgh: William and Robert Chambers, 1842), pp.i, 44.

[87] Katie Trumpener, *Bardic Nationalism: The Romantic Novel and the British Empire* (Princeton, NJ: Princeton University Press, 1997), p.202.

In this light, *Songs for the Nursery* is an important response to Chambers because it finds a way to reconcile these differences. On the one hand, it is didactic and realist in setting, and Robertson's 1846 preface to the second edition approved reviews which stated that the *Songs* would 'supplant those senseless unmeaning rhymes that had hitherto held supreme sway in the nursery'—precisely the kind of rhymes Chambers supports.[88] On the other hand, *Songs from the Nursery* highly privileges Scots language and song and draws substantially on folk traditions. Chambers cites 'Wee Willie Winkie', which had just appeared in *Whistle-Binkie*, approvingly in a footnote to his 1842 edition. Nursery verse was native to Scotland, both Chambers and Robertson argued, in a way that it was not to England, and Robertson's collection and its later imitators would demonstrate that it was as relevant to the present and future as to the past.

Songs from the Nursery was also Robertson and the Whistlebinkians' most con-certed effort to promote Scots, in poetry and speech. Robertson's 1844 preface to the volume closed, defensively, with a lengthy quotation from Francis Jeffrey's 1809 essay on Burns, 'To those who object to the use of our national dialect in the nursery, as being the language of the vulgar and uneducated, we would reply in the words of Lord Jeffrey':

> The Scotch is not to be considered a provincial dialect—the vehicle only of rustic vulgarity, and rude local humour. It is the language of a whole country, long an inde-pendent kingdom, and still separate in laws, character and manners. It is by no means peculiar to the vulgar; but is the common speech of the whole nation in early life, and, with many of its most accomplished and exalted individuals, throughout their whole existence [...] the Scotch is, in reality, a highly poetical language.[89]

Robertson put considerable effort into thinking about how his preface would defend Scots, as his various manuscript drafts suggest. Before deciding to end with the unimpeachable authority of Jeffrey (also, of course, a pre-eminent example of a reforming politician), for example, he had returned to a critique of Jamieson:

> If we are successful in obtaining a reception for songs in our Nurseries, we conceive that we shall have done more to establish and transmit our language to future ages, than the most elaborate compiler of its Lexicon.[90]

In his later revised preface, he continued past the Jeffrey quotation, adding an extra paragraph:

> With such authorities as this on our side, we can listen without much discompose to those who insist on calling our language vulgar, and who anticipate, with satisfac-tion, its speedy commutation into that of the Saxon.[91]

---

[88] 'Preface', *Songs for the Nursery*, 2nd edn (Glasgow: David Robertson, 1846), p.ix. This new edition has minor differences in content and was more cheaply priced.

[89] 'Notice from the Publisher', *Songs for the Nursery* (Glasgow: David Robertson, 1844), p.6. See Jeffrey, 'Reliques of Robert Burns' (Jan 1809), in *Contributions to the Edinburgh Review, 3 vols*, 2nd edn (London: Longman, Brown, Green and Longmans, 1846), II, pp.155–6.

[90] 'Notice from the Publisher', revised draft for second (1846) edition. MS Robertson 11.

[91] 'Preface', *Songs for the Nursery* (1846), pp.viii–ix.

For Robertson, the idea that Scots was a language encountered in childhood did not infantilize it in a negative sense. Rather, introducing Scots in the nursery would ensure its early associations with familial and national identity, so that it was inextricably bound up with the powerful emotions associated with family and home. No patriotic Scotsman, he argues, could desire the 'extinction' of the language of his childhood. Hence, it is vitally important that Scottish children hear, speak, and learn to understand and use Scots. If they do not do so naturally in their familial context, they must do so artificially, through the medium of Scots poetry intended for their consumption.

'Establishing and transmitting' Scots to young children and their parents was a fraught enterprise. Robertson cut nearly twelve lines from the quotation he chose from Jeffrey which locate the Scots language firmly in a nostalgic childhood, as the 'familiar language' of that childhood, perhaps because Jeffrey's emphasis on the past contrasted with Robertson's focus on the future. He also did not reveal to readers that while Jeffrey had taken the trouble to write an effusive letter of praise in return for a copy of *Songs for the Nursery* ('I cannot resist expressing the great pleasure and <u>surprise</u> which I experienced on finding so much <u>original Genius</u> in a work ushered in under a title, and in a form so unpretending'), he was not entirely approving of its language, 'I cannot help thinking that some of your authors have a little caricatured it'.[92] Surviving letters suggest that Robertson and his advisors were very anxious to negotiate between realism and respectability, deploying Scots yet purging it of associations with vulgar working cultures. For example, James Manson, a *Songs for the Nursery* contributor whom Robertson used as an advisor on Scots, wrote to Robertson objecting to Smart's use of 'gang to' in a draft of 'Gang to Your Beds' (*Songs*, p.47):

> this is a mode of expression which has had its origin among the half Irish half Scottish population who throng outskirts of Glasgow, and may be heard frequently amongst the workers Cotton factories [sic] and other large works – the proper Scottish is 'gae to'[93]

Robertson changed 'gang' to 'gae' in Smart's stanzas. He supported colloquial Scots, but it should be 'proper', even if this meant changing the vocabulary that his contributors—presumably Scots speakers themselves—had selected.

Writing nursery verse, as the potential contributor Thomas Latto noted in declining to participate, offers particular linguistic challenges: 'As for Nursery Lyrics...It is ticklish ground as one is so apt in aiming at simplicity to degenerate into absolute silliness'.[94] Contributors themselves worried that the charge of 'mawkishness' might be justified by their attempts at nursery Scots. At their best, however, those nursery poems that focus on very young (pre-literate) children use the resources of dialect to imitate, successfully, what we now call child-directed speech. Linguistic theory has revalued this form of speech, which uses simple

---

[92] Letter to Robertson, 26 May 1844. MS Robertson 11.
[93] Letter to Robertson, undated. MS Robertson 11.
[94] Letter from Thomas Latto, 31 May 1843, MS Robertson 19/213.

vocabulary and repetition, short sentences, exaggerated intonation, exclamations, and strongly marked rhythms, as potentially vital in conveying 'information about emotion and communicative intent'.[95] Babyish or infantile language in poetry can be read as a serious effort to model ways of communicating, in dialect, with small children. A typical example of child-directed speech in nursery verse from later in the period would be Charles Nicol's 'Wee Jessie's First Step', which appeared in the *West Lothian Courier* as 'The Bairnie's First Step' in 1881:

> Take care na', dinna fa'
>   Better rest a wee,
> There ye are noo, come awa'
>   Try for dada's knee.
>
> Weel I'm sure I never
>   Saw the like o' this
> Oh! Yer awfu' clever,
>   That deserves a kiss.[96]

The metre here (trochaic trimeter, with three strong stresses in each line) is less regular in the first stanza than the second, nicely reflecting the tottering child and her progress. By representing a *father* directly speaking to his child and narrating and commenting on her actions, this poem highly values parent–child communication, not simply in terms of 'motherese' but between male parent and small child.[97] In common with a great many poems of this type, it deliberately challenges perceptions that working-class men 'became alienated and distant from their wives and children' in the Victorian period and were rarely involved in 'physically caring roles'.[98] The simple, exclamatory, and deliberately exaggerated ('Weel I'm sure I never') language, using colloquial Scots forms of grammar and pronunciation, is designed to appear naturalistic.

Linguistic researchers have suggested that caregivers are more likely to use dialect to children in the contexts of play, rather than discipline, and that parents and children can code-switch in sophisticated ways between standard and non-standard

---

[95] Anne Fernald, 'Human Maternal Vocalizations to Infants as Biologically Relevant Signals: An Evolutionary Perspective', in Paul Bloom, ed., *Language Acquisition: Core Readings* (New York: Harvester Wheatsheaf, 1993), pp.51–94, p.73. The debate over child-directed speech is complex and ongoing. See Ray Cattell, *Children's Language: Consensus and Controversy*, revised edn (New York: Continuum, 2007), pp.103–27 for a discussion of twentieth-century debates, including commentary on Fernald's work, and William O'Grady, *How Children Learn Language* (Cambridge: Cambridge University Press, 2005), pp.176–7 for a brief introduction to child-directed speech.

[96] Charles Nicol, *Poems and Songs* (Edinburgh: McLaren and Bruce, n.d.), p.20; *West Lothian Courier*, 6 August 1881, p.4. The WLC published several other examples of nursery verse by Nicol (born 1858), who was from south Glasgow, worked in factories and as a travelling salesman.

[97] 'Motherese' remained a key term for discussing child-directed speech until recently: Cattell, for example, defends his use of it as his primary term (p.103).

[98] Jane Humphries, *Childhood and Child Labour in the British Industrial Revolution* (Cambridge: Cambridge University Press, 2010), pp.126, 132 and *passim*.

English.[99] Nursery poets understood and represented this. In Rodger's dialogue poem, 'Brothers Quarrelling', for instance, the boys speak in naturalistic Scots:

> DAVIE: "Father, settle Sandy!
>   He's cryin' names to me,
>   He's aye tig, tiggin'
>   An' winna let me be;
>   But O sae sly, he hauds his tongue
>   Whene'er he kens ye're near,
>   An' sayst again below his breath,
>   That nane but me can hear."

When the father intervenes with a sententious moral about the need for siblings to value each other, however, he speaks in standard English;

> FATHER: "O learn to be loving,
>   And kindly agree,
>   At home all as happy
>   As brothers should be."   (*Songs*, p.80)

The regular rhythm, alliteration on 'learn/loving' and 'home/happy' and firm end-rhyme mark this as a constructed, performative utterance of a different nature to the boys' speech. In effect they mark it not simply as an adult moral, in the formal English that the boys will grow up to use on serious occasions, but as a typical example of didactic verse. The stanza would be entirely at home in Cecil Frances Alexander's *Hymns for Little Children* (1846), a collection which appeared contemporaneously with Robertson's and that would become one of the most influential of the period. (Alexander was Irish and worked extensively with working-class children in Ulster, but there is no trace of dialect in her poetry.) What Rodger shows us in these stanzas is that he himself can code-switch, from Scots to English nursery verse, and that this has implications for genre (religious, didactic) as well as language.

If one impetus behind nursery verse was the promotion of Scots language and literature, its rise was also strongly connected to growing debates about children and childhood in Victorian Britain. The 1840s were particularly marked by discussions and publications about child labour and education, notably the shocking Parliamentary reports into child workers in mines and factories, and the consequent agitation for more stringent laws (or any laws) on both, as a growing sense of childhood as a defined state that needed legal protection met with the realities of new forms of industry that deployed child labour.[100] Historians such as Lynn Abrams have argued that the particularly extreme pace of change in Victorian

---

[99] See, for example, William Labov, *Principles of Linguistic Change. Volume 2: Social Factors* (Oxford: Blackwell, 2001), p.437. I am grateful to Jennifer Smith for sharing her work in this field: see, for example, Jennifer Smith, Mercedes Durham and Liane Fortune, '"Man, my trousers is fa'in doon!": Community, Caregiver and Child in the Acquisition of Variation in a Scottish Dialect', *Language Variation and Change* 19 (2007), 63–99.

[100] See Humphries and Eric Hopkins, *Childhood Transformed: Working-Class Children in Nineteenth-Century England* (Manchester: Manchester University Press, 1994).

Scotland was more testing for traditional family structures than in England, suggesting that 'the Scottish family suffered more than most' in the period from the 1840s to the First World War, and that in both urban and rural parts of Scotland 'the family could frequently be described as broken, dysfunctional and fractured'.[101] Furthermore, in the 1830s, 'there was believed to be a crisis in Scottish education', exacerbated by the fracturing of the parochial school system after the division of the Church in 1843, as well as the influx of families into industrialized cities.[102] Contemporary Scottish commentators and activists, such as Thomas Guthrie, presented readers with troubling case-studies of a dangerous underclass of Scottish children 'growing up in misery' who, if left to their own devices, would 'disturb and disgrace society with their crimes'.[103]

Songs for the Nursery can therefore also be read as the cultural response to a perceived crisis in childhood. Its visions of the happy working-class nuclear family, managing to remain cheerful despite acknowledged poverty and hardship, are certainly escapist. They are also, however, a profoundly ideological response to the testing of the family unit and parent–child relationships in a period of economic uncertainty and consequent internal migration and emigration, growing child and female labour, a perceived failure in the educational system, and a shift from rural to industrial city communities. The *Dundee Courier* and other reviewers predicted that the collection would 'speedily become a great favourite with all classes', and while *Songs for the Nursery* certainly presents a reassuring vision of working-class family life to middle and upper-class readers, it clearly also operates as both a parenting manual for working men and women and a didactic work for children.[104] Scottish writer and critic John Brown, for instance, cited 'Willie Winkie' in its entirety as the ideal picture of a 'healthy and happy' child, in an 1861 article aimed at lower-class mothers, 'Children, and How to Guide Them'.[105] In the nursery verse tradition, working-class writers address their own community, while simultaneously presenting an idealized vision of 'their' lives and circumstances for the purpose of convincing middle-class readers to re-evaluate their perception of working-class children and families.

Moreover, the depiction of children and families in *Songs for the Nursery* and the succeeding nursery verse culture is, in the broadest sense, radical. As Anna Clark and others have shown, Chartists and radicals deliberately deployed the rhetoric of domesticity and happy family life in order to 'refute claims that working people were immoral, undeserving of both family life and political rights':

> [R]adicals stole the notion of domesticity from middle-class moralists and manipulated it to demand the privileges of separate spheres for working-class, as

[101] Lynn Abrams, *The Orphan Country: Children of Scotland's Broken Homes from 1845 to the Present Day* (Edinburgh: John Donald, 1998), p.2.

[102] Jane McDermid, *The Schooling of Working-Class Girls in Victorian Scotland: Gender, Education and Identity* (New York: Routledge, 2005), p.4.

[103] Thomas Guthrie, *A Second Plea for Ragged Schools, or Prevention Better Than Cure* (Edinburgh: John Elder, 1849), p.7.

[104] 'Songs from the Nursery', *Dundee Courier*, 11 June 1844, p.2.

[105] John Brown, 'Children, and How to Guide Them'. *Good Words* 2 (December 1861): 309–13, 310.

well as middle- and upper-class, men and women. Domesticity proved to be a potent rhetorical weapon – but also a double-edged sword.[106]

It was a 'double-edged sword' in gender terms because this ideology effectively also fostered more conservative views of family, and of women's role. In literary terms, this is also true. As this chapter shows, publications and genres that offered spaces for radically inclined working-class men to publish sentimental and 'domestic' verse, including nursery verse, did so at the expense of women writers, who were largely excluded from these spaces and whose voices were appropriated by men. Generically, domestic and nursery verse is also simultaneously radical and conservative, though its radicalism has been entirely occluded in subsequent literary histories. In terms of content, language, and didactic intent, for instance, this lost culture of Scottish nursery verse is innovative compared to the main current of British children's verse up until the mid-century and beyond, which, with few exceptions, tended to be overtly moral and religious, and was universally written in standard English. The poets discussed here also appear to be the only example of a cohort of working-class writers, male or female, invested in writing dialect verse for and about children.

The prime mover in creating Scottish nursery verse was William Miller, since it was the popularity of 'Wee Willie Winkie' on its first outing in the Third Series of *Whistle-Binkie* (1842) that seems to have led Robertson to consider creating a separate selection of poems for and about children. In fact, Robertson originally intended that Miller (a disabled wood-turner in Glasgow who suffered from increasingly difficult circumstances) would be the editor of the collection. That his assistance was unofficial rather than official was because the second most prominent contributor, Ballantine, objected to Miller's youth and lack of standing in the literary community in a private letter to Robertson.[107] Robertson removed Miller's name from the volume, but this did not prevent the fame of 'Wee Willie Winkie' from overshadowing all other Scottish nursery verse, with the possible exception of Ballantine's own 'Castles in the Air'. It is difficult to overestimate the popularity of Miller's most famous poem. Robert Buchanan, who famously dubbed Miller 'the laureate of the nursery', commented that 'Every corner of the earth knows "Wee Willie Winkie" ... Few poets, however prosperous, are so certain of their immortality'.[108] Miller's poem was widely republished in newspaper poetry columns and periodicals, illustrated, sculpted, set to new tunes, circulated in performance and in collections, and provided the title for a Rudyard Kipling story (and collection) in 1888. The poet himself, it is worth noting, benefited little from this: he may have become a minor Glasgow celebrity, but his excellent collection *Scottish Nursery Songs* (1863) was privately printed rather than taken up by a major press, and Buchanan's article formed part of an appeal to save him from destitution.

---

[106] Anna Clark, *The Struggle for the Breeches: Gender and the Making of the British Working Class* (Berkeley, CA: University of California Press, 1995), pp.220, 178.
[107] See MS Robertson 19/162.
[108] Robert Buchanan, 'The Laureate of the Nursery'. *Saint Paul's Magazine* 11 (July 1872): 66–73, 66.

'Wee Willie Winkie' survives today in a bowdlerized nursery rhyme version, often presented as anonymous and consisting entirely of the opening stanza without context. In Miller's original poem, however, the speaker is a tired mother who cannot get her son to sleep, and so threatens him with the bogeyman figure of 'Wee Willie Winkie' (a figure which may come from a Jacobite nickname for King William III). The third and fourth stanzas run:

> Onything but sleep, you rogue!
>   Glow'ring like the moon,
> Rattling in an airn jug
>   Wi' an airn spoon,
> Rumblin', tumblin', round about,
>   Crawing like a cock,
> Skirlin' like a kenna-what,
>   Wauk'nin' sleeping folk.
>
> Hey, Willie Winkie,
>   The wean's in a creel!
> Wamblin' aff a bodie's knee
>   Like a verra eel,
> Ruggin' at the cat's lug,
>   And ravelin' a' her thrums –
> Hey, Willie Winkie –
> See, there he comes!   (*Songs from the Nursery*, 1)

Scots in this poem activates linguistic connections and echoes. The figurative phrase 'in a creel' (in a state of confusion and madness), for instance, relates through its literal meanings—'creel' as a basket for catching fish—to its rhyme-word, 'eel'. The rhyme of 'rug' (pull) and 'lug' (ear), and the relationship of both to the unspoken but felt 'tug', or the alliteration of 'ruggin' and 'ravelin', also provide effects unavailable in anglicized versions. When this poem, and others from *Songs for the Nursery*, was translated for the North American market by Marianne Silsbee in 1859, her version renders the lines 'Ruggin' at the cat's lug,/ And ravelin' a' her thrums' as 'Pulling at the cat's ear/ While she drowsy hums'.[109] Besides losing the sound-effects, this loses another double meaning. 'Thrums' is a figurative term for a cat's purr ('three-threads-an-a-thrum', perhaps related to the sound of a loom) that is connected to 'thrums', as loose threads in weaving. So to 'ravel' (to tangle, disorder or snarl) creates a pun only possible in the Scots. Stopping the cat's purrs is like snarling up a thread, with another play on the sense of 'ravel' as 'dishevel', thinking of the cat's ruffled fur. This is cleverly constructed and sophisticated linguistic play, which a Scots speaker would recognize as referencing terms familiar from nineteenth-century labour.[110]

---

[109] M. C. D. Silsbee, ed., *Willie Winkie's Nursery Songs of Scotland* (Boston: Ticknor and Fields, 1859), p.13. Silsbee's version is also used in John Greenleaf Whittier's anthology *Child-Life* (London: James Nisbet, 1874), which includes four *Whistle-Binkie* poems. Whittier's editorial note thanks Robertson for permission to republish.
[110] Neither 'ravel' nor 'thrums' are included in Robertson's 'Glossary' to *Songs for the Nursery*, indicating that he saw them as common terms.

In Miller's poem, the unnamed toddler is mischievous, constantly in motion and upsetting to the order and peace of a domestic scene explicitly identified as lower-class, since the setting is a kitchen (with iron jug and spoon to hand) and contains a dog, cat, and hen. The focus, in this poem and others, on the mother's relationship with her child, without the intermediaries of nurse or servants, is a class marker, as of course is the parents' Scots speech. The parents in Scottish working-class nursery verse do not have nurses, nor indeed a nursery. They are hard-working, inside and out of the home, and they recognize the trials as well as pleasures of parenthood: 'Wearied is the mither/ That has a stoorie wean' ('stoorie', from 'stour', battle or strife, is first attributed in adjectival use to Miller's poem), as the speaker in Miller's poem ruefully notes.[111] In the light of its semi-comic take on the labour of parenting, a labour that was of course particularly hard for working-class women, it is interesting that on 'Wee Willie Winkie's' first outing in *Songs for the Nursery*, the given tune was a popular plantation song, 'Jim Along Josey'. The song survives on an 1841 broadside. Like all songs in this genre, it is in dialect, and it has an implicit abolitionist message in a verse comparing the 'New York nigger' to the state of affairs in the South, 'But de poor Kentuck nigger when der day gone by,/ Dey sarve dem like an old horse, kick'd out to die'.[112]

Without wishing to read too much into this choice (which disappears from later editions, once 'Wee Willie Winkie' had gained its own tune), it effectively means that the opening poem in *Songs from the Nursery* compares domestic labour and slave labour, as unpaid and unappreciated forms of work. One of the striking aspects of Scottish nursery verse is the respect that these poems accord to the hard work of childcare, as in another sleepless child poem, Fergusson's 'A Mother's Cares and Toils', which concludes, not very cheerfully:

> O! her heart had need be tender,
>   And her love had need be strang,
> Else the lade she bears wad bend her
>   Soon the dreary mools amang.[113]

Almost all the poems in this genre are authored by working men, yet most are spoken (as here) in a mother's, grandmother's, or child's voice. To some degree, male working-class poets use these perspectives to explore the position of those still more politically and economically disenfranchised than themselves—a group that includes both women whose primary work is in the household, and children. On the other hand, this male adoption of the maternal voice is an act of appropriation as well as identification: the best-known authors and prime movers in the nursery verse genre were all men.

Miller's poem inspired a further set of 'bogeyman' poems about sleepless children, capturing the mingled exhaustion, exasperation, and affection of the parental speakers. At least two well-known later examples, Anderson's 'Jenny Wi' the Airn

---

[111] *Songs for the Nursery*, p.1.

[112] NLS 'English Ballads'. Copy at http://digital.nls.uk/english-ballads/pageturner.cfm?id=74894 806&mode=transcription (consulted 26 September 2018).

[113] *Songs for the Nursery*, p.20.

Teeth' and James Nicholson's direct reworking of Anderson's poem, 'Jenny Wi' the Lang Poke', adopt a bogeyman who is the figure of a down-at-heel woman. Both poems appeared in the *People's Friend*, which marketed itself as a family magazine and in effect took up the mantle of nursery verse from its foundation in the late 1860s (as an offshoot of the popular *People's Journal*) onwards. Most of the key later examples of nursery verse first appeared in its pages. Andrew Stewart, its sub-editor, set a number of nursery poems, including Anderson's, to music, and published a now lost collection titled *Sangs for the Bairns*. It may be his taste that assisted the revival of nursery verse culture amongst the poets featured in the *Friend*. Nicholson's poem was additionally incorporated into the 1890 edition of *Whistle-Binkie*. His third stanza runs:

> Gudesake! Noo I hear her!
>   There she's on the stair,
> Sapples o' the sea-bree
>   Stickin' in her hair,
> Hushions on her bare legs,
>   Bauchels on her feet,
> Seekin' waukrife bairnies
>   Up an' doun the street![114]

'Hushions' are footless stockings or leggings used for warmth by workers, and 'bauchels' are worn-down shoes or slippers. 'Jenny' is a poor woman, coming in from the cold, and as such a threat in representing the flip side to the mother in her cosy domestic space. Anderson's Jenny is also a perversion of domesticity, with her 'beetle feet' (a beetle is a wooden tool for mashing food, or for beating laundry), and a genuinely scary figure:

> Sleep! an' let me to my work,
>   A' they claes to airn:
> Jenny wi' the airn teeth,
>   Come and tak' the bairn;
>
> Tak' him to your ain den,
>   Where the bowgie bides
> But first put baith your big teeth
>   On his wee plump sides.[115]

The rhythm becomes more pronounced as the speaker moves from casual speech ('a they claes to airn'), into an invocation, which (like many children's rhymes) uses a series of unstressed beats to create a sense of anticipation and a tripping rhythm: 'Jenny wi' the airn teeth,/ Come an tak' the bairn'. Both poems have a performative emphasis on immediacy and exclamation—'Mercy me, she's at the door!'—and both show the parents' playful imagination at work.

---

[114] James Nicholson, *Kilwuddie and Other Poems, with Life-Sketch and Portrait of the Author*, 4th edn (Glasgow: James McGeachy, 1895), p.163.
[115] Anderson, 'Jenny wi' the airn teeth', *People's Friend*, 26 November 1873.

Sleepless children were, of course, more of a problem with several in the same bed and in the same kitchen and living space as their parents. The 1861 Census showed that 34 per cent of Scottish families lived in one room, and 37 per cent in two.[116] Peter Taylor, lodging with a local family while working in Kilmarnock, recalled being fascinated by the mother's ability to sit by the fire and read the *Kilmarnock Post*, ignoring the noise the children were making in the corner: 'I soon found I could not read for a racket going on in one of the beds... Pillows were flying, and legs and arms mixing and separating like a country dance, and the noise was appalling'.[117] Nursery verse recognizes this scenario. Miller's 'Gree, Bairnies, Gree', for instance, asks quarrelling children to 'Mind how ye sleepit, cheek to cheek/ Atween me an' the wa'', while the accompanying engraving shows a mother rocking a cradle in a cluttered kitchen while two children (one barefoot) fight and another lies on the floor.[118] Nicholson's mother also puts her child to bed with his brothers in the kitchen:

> Cuddle doun fu' cosy – that's my ain wee lamb;
> Dinna spurtle wi' yer feet, or ye'll wauken Tam.[119]

'Spurtle' (a spatula for stirring porridge), is another nice use of domestic terminology to describe a child's physical behaviour. With little available physical distance between parents and children in the space of the home, it is not surprising that such poems stress the importance of emotional closeness, as in the forgiving ending of 'Wee Willie Winkie', 'But a kiss from aff his rosy lips/ Means all the world to me'.[120]

The children in bogeymen poems are, by definition, behaving badly. One of the more surprising aspects of Scottish nursery verse is the extent to which it tolerates, and even celebrates, naughtiness. Little such tolerance is evident in mainstream English nursery verse, at least prior to the 1860s and the start of the 'Golden Age' of children's literature. Perhaps still more surprising in Scottish nursery verse is the fact that bad behaviour, including physical defiance, is attributed to young girls as well as boys. There are certainly poems in the tradition that celebrate girls for their sweetness and motherly qualities, like Anderson's 'Wee Tottie', but there are an equal number that do not. In James Neilson's 'The Greeting Wean', also published in the *People's Friend*, a small girl is having a tantrum:

> Rowing, roaring on the flur,
>   Thumping wi' your feet, –
> Come, and sit on your wee chair,
>   Tak a nice bit greet.
> There's a bonnie greeting wean –
>   Oh, you're unca braw!
> Can this be our Tot again?
>   Would you hit your ma?[121]

---

[116] John McCaffrey, *Scotland in the Nineteenth Century* (Houndmills: Macmillan, 1998), p.34.
[117] Peter Taylor, *The Autobiography of Peter Taylor* (Paisley: Alexander Gardner, 1903), p.96.
[118] *Songs for the Nursery*, pp.6, 5.   [119] 'Jenny', in *Kilwuddie*, p.163.
[120] *Songs for the Nursery*, p.1.
[121] James M. Neilson, 'The Greeting Wean', in *Songs for the Bairns, and Miscellaneous Poems* (Glasgow: William Rankin, 1884), pp.22–3. *People's Friend*, 16 August 1876.

Small children *do* hit their parents in a rage, but they rarely do so in Victorian poetry. Neilson's poem is itself a reworking of Smart's 'O This is No My Ain Bairn' in *Songs for the Nursery*, in which another kicking and screaming small girl is 'A randy, roarin', cankert thing,/ That nought will do but flist and fling' (*Songs*, p.61).[122] The most famous instance in this subgenre was James Smith's 'Wee Joukydaidles':

> Wee Joukydaidles,
> > Toddlin' out an' in:
> Oh but she's a cuttie,
> > Makin' sic a din!
> Aye sae fou' o' mischief,
> > An' minds na what I say:
> My very heart gangs lowp, lowp,
> > Fifty times a-day!
>
> ***
>
> Wee Joukydaidles,
> > Paidlin' i' the shower –
> There she's at the wundy!
> > Haud her, or she's owre!
> Noo she's slippit frae my sicht:
> > Where's the wean at last?
> In the byre amang the kye,
> > Sleepin' soun' an' fast![123]

Like Nichol's 'Wee Jessie's First Step' and Neilson's 'The Greeting Wean', these poems about (and for) toddlers are written in shorter lines with two or three strong beats, in imitation of the clapping or play rhymes traditionally used with small children (Smith's second best-known poem was a clapping rhyme, 'Clap, clap handies'). 'Wee Joukydaidles' was enormously popular. It first appeared in the *Scotsman* on Saturday 20 August 1864, and by Monday 22nd it had already been reprinted by at least two other papers; by late 1864 it had been set to music and was being performed in Christmas concerts.[124] This success materially helped Smith, a journeyman printer, to publish a volume of poems and consequently move up in the world, as Chapter 1 notes, by being appointed librarian to the Mechanics' Institute in Edinburgh. In common with the other poems in this tradition, this uses exclamations and questions, half-playful and half-exasperated, to create immediacy and realism. Although it stresses the difficulty of watching small children while doing domestic chores, it also celebrates their freedom, independence, and

---

[122] Smart's title refers to the well-known song 'This is no mine ain house', which originally existed as a nursery song before being reinterpreted by Allan Ramsay, as a Jacobite song, and by Burns in 'This is no my ain lassie'. See Alexander Whitelaw, ed. *The Book of Scottish Song* (London: Blackie and Son, 1844), pp.413–14.

[123] *The Scotsman*, 20 August 1864, p. 3, stanzas 1, 6. See also James Smith, *Poems, Songs and Ballads*, 3rd edn (Edinburgh: Blackwood, 1869). The DSL translates 'joukydaidles' as 'ducky-daddles', a pet name for a child, though Smith's poem is the only instance given.

[124] The British Newspaper database contains reprints of the poem in the *Birmingham Daily Post* and *Dundee Courier* on 22 August 1864. For its performance as a song, see advert in the *Aberdeen Herald*, 28 December 1864, p.1.

enterprise: though with the sense that girls in particular, as the representation of harassed mothers shows, may never have such freedom again.

'Wee Joukydaidles' is the younger sister of Nicholson's equally well-known 'Oor Wee Kate', an important instance of a literary tomboy:

> I wish she'd been a callan, she's sic a steerin queen –   *callan – lad*
> For ribbons, dolls, an' a' sic gear, she doesna' care a preen,
> But taps an' bools, girs, ba's an' bats, she plays wi' ear' an' late;   *gir(d) – hoop*
> I'll hae to get a pair o' breeks for oor Wee Kate.
>
> Na, what do you think? The ither day, as sure as ony thing –
> I saw her fleein' dragons, wi' maist a mile o' string;   *dragons – kites*
> Yer jumpin' rapes and peveralls, she flings oot o' her fate,   *peverall – spinning top*
> But nane can fire a towgun like oor Wee Kate.[125]

Nicholson was a tailor at the Govan Poorhouse and part of a mid-Victorian Glasgow-centred circle of working-class poets; like Anderson and many of the other poets discussed in this book, he was heavily influenced by the temperance movement and belonged to the Good Templars, an association notable for its commitment to gender and class equality.[126] As noted in Chapter 1, his career as a poet was fostered by performance in temperance venues. While this poem, like the others, performs comic exasperation, the reader is expected to recognize that the speaker takes pride in their child's lively, if contentious, behaviour. Kate's decisive rejection of girlish toys in favour of sports and physical activity is a sign of character and is actively supported by her family. While the poem also praises her kindness and intelligence and implies that she will, one day, grow out of these preoccupations, it is *difference*—even defiance—rather than conventionality that Scottish nursery verse such as 'Oor Wee Kate' welcomes and praises.

'Oor Wee Kate' also notably celebrates a girl's achievements at school, 'She taks the lead in ilka class, an' many a prize she's won', as does Nicholson's 'The Auld-Farrant Wean', published in the *People's Journal* on 9 November 1872, which shows a young girl combining domestic labour with learning:

> The cradle I rock while my lessons I learn,
> I brush faither's buits an' I sing to the bairn;
> I prig doon the butcher the siller to hain,
> Is't that gars folk ca' me an auld-farrant wean?[127]

The child speaker, and indeed performer ('Wee Tibbie' also recited this poem) is comic and touching because of her innocence of the distance between her precocious adult care for her family and the usual pursuits of childhood; yet it is also this

---

[125] 'Oor Wee Kate', in *Wee Tibbie's Garland, and Other Poems* (Glasgow: James McGeachy, 1873), p.116. The poem was first published c.1863. Kate was reportedly based on Nicholson's daughter Ellen, who grew up to become a *People's Friend* poet. See Robert Ford's biography in Nicholson, *Kilwuddie and Other Poems, with Life-Sketch and Portrait of the Author*, 4th edn (Glasgow: James McGeachy, 1895), pp.184–5.

[126] On the Templars, see David Fahey, *Temperance and Racism: John Bull, Johnny Reb, and the Good Templars* (Lexington, KY: University Press of Kentucky, 1996).

[127] Nicholson, 'The Auld-Farrant Wean', reprinted in *Wee Tibbie's Garland*, p.51.

innocence that confirms her childishness. She is closely related to Dickens's 'adult' girls, such as Jenny Wren in *Our Mutual Friend* (1865), though she is much more positive—or less aware of any elements of exploitation in her position. It was 1872 when the Scottish Education Act finally inaugurated compulsory state education. Nicholson's stanza might be read both as a celebration of this, and as a recognition of the difficulty it created in households where children, daughters particularly, had to take on adult responsibilities at a young age, such as haggling with the butcher to save money. Janet Hamilton's 'Phases of Girlhood', published in the *Airdrie Advertiser* in March 1864, discusses 'daughter Maggie', who has been schooled for four years, but now has to leave 'not for the cost,/ For that is small—at home she's wanted':

> There's more to do than mother's able
> To perform, and Maggie's clever
> And now is done with school for ever,
> She now is set to washing, scrubbing
> Baking, cooking, wringing, rubbing,
> Nursing little sis or brother
> To relieve poor weary mother.[128]

Although Hamilton was highly progressive in her support for political causes, she was conservative on women's role in Victorian society, and there is no sense of regret in this poem. Maggie's fate may seem harsh, but her duty is to her family. Unlike boys, working-class Scottish girls in the mid-Victorian period had almost no access to social advancement via education, and nursery verse does, unsurprisingly, find it hard to imagine a future for them outside the bounds of family and domesticity.

In contrast, *Songs from the Nursery* and later nursery verse strongly promote boys' education as a means to social mobility and increased happiness. These poets share the common early nineteenth-century perception, identified by R. D. Anderson, that:

> [E]ducation was one of the sources of Scottish national identity and [...] its internal cohesion and distinctive features needed to be preserved if Scotland was to retain its cultural independence within a political union which was itself fully accepted.[129]

The key 'distinctive features' of Scottish education, for these writers, are its accessibility and the potential it offered for the 'lad of parts' to proceed through parish schools to university, and thus to a higher-status career. In Alex Laing's 'The A.B.C.', hard-working parents have only just managed to look beyond the provision of food and clothing:

> To win our laddie meat an' claes
> Has aye been a' our care;
> To get you made a scholar neist,
> We'll toil both late an' ear'

---

[128] Janet Hamilton, 'Phases of Girlhood', *Airdrie Advertiser*, 5 March 1864, p.1. This poem is not included in the 1885 edn of Hamilton's works.

[129] R. D. Anderson, *Education and the Scottish People, 1750–1918* (Oxford: Clarendon, 1995), p.24. See also Anderson's *Education and Opportunity in Victorian Scotland: Schools and Universities* (Oxford: Clarendon Press, 1983).

If he works hard, the poem suggests, he can access the route through university into the professions:

> Wha kens but ye may get a schule,
>   An' syne ye'll win our bread?
> Wha kens but in a pulpit yet
>   We'll see you wag your head?   (*Songs*, p.55)

In the succeeding poem in the collection, Miller's 'Ye Maun Gang to the Schule', the final verse runs:

> So ye'll gae to the schule again' summer, my bairn –
> Ye're sae gleg o' the uptak' ye soon will learn; –
> And I'm sure ere the dark nights o' winter come on,
> Ye'll can read William Wallace or Gilpin John.   (*Songs for the Nursery*, p.56)

The mother's language, especially the non-standard grammar in 'Ye'll can read', her error in naming William Cowper's poetic hero, John Gilpin, and also the potential stress on 'ye'll', may indicate her own low level of education or illiteracy. 'Again' here may be used either in the sense of going back to school in summer, or in the older colloquial sense of 'in anticipation of', given that summer is the period when country children were most likely to be needed for help with the harvest. In either case, the implication in this poem is that schooling is dependent on seasonal needs. One of the primary reasons to learn to read (or the one the parental speaker thinks most attractive, since the poem is about encouraging a reluctant schoolgoer), is in order to access exciting accounts of Scottish heroes. Hugh Miller wrote that it was reading 'a common-stall edition of Blind Harry's Wallace' that caused him to first become 'thoroughly a Scot', at the age of ten.[130] Either William Miller or Robertson, revising the poem for a new 1846 edition, strengthened the notion of literacy as an aid to national pride by changing the final lines to 'And I'm sure ere the dark nights o' winter keek ben,/ Ye'll can read William Wallace frae en' to en'!' (*Songs for the Nursery*, 1846, p.79).

Every parental speaker in nursery verse shares a personal ambition for their child's future with a patriotic ambition that their lively children will be the future of Scotland—and, indeed, of Britain and its Empire. Their support for education, in particular, adds these poems to the weight of material published in favour of retaining what was perceived as Scotland's superiority over other nations in enabling universal access to education. Such aspirations are so much part of the genre that successful poems emerged to subvert them, like John Young's 'My Big Jock', in which a mother comments on how useless her son is at all forms of achievement.[131] But aspiration is shadowed by anxiety about whether these children will make it to the future. Tumbling and kicking on the floor, slithering off a parent's knee, firing towguns, escaping out of the window, throwing a tantrum over homework and

---

[130] Hugh Miller, *My Schools and Schoolmasters, or The Story of My Education* (Edinburgh: Johnstone and Hunter, 1854), p.38.

[131] John Young, *Poems and Lyrics* (Glasgow: George Gallie, 1868), p.160. Young's collection includes several other examples of nursery verse.

always making a 'din': the lively, sensuous physicality of these children, mirrored by the language used to describe them, is significant not simply because it enables the perception of play and physicality as natural parts of childhood, but because in the context in which these verses appeared, it signals that the children are more likely to survive. In a period when 'rarely was a working man able to earn sufficient to provide for a family', and when malnutrition and disease were extremely common, 'wee plump sides' could be as much of a fantasy as any bogeyman.[132]

The rate of survival for children under five with parents working as 'operatives' across Britain was 44.6 per cent in the mid-Victorian period.[133] In 1861, 42 per cent of all deaths in Glasgow were of under-fives.[134] Taylor, for instance, who was born in 1837, recalls that his three- and one-year-old sisters died in an epidemic during the hard economic times of the 1840s, and that 'many' of his childhood friends from Paisley, left to play unsupervised while their parents worked, were drowned in the river or died in accidents: 'It was an anxious time for parents'.[135] The authors and parental speakers in these poems, which appeared in newspaper columns and poetry collections alongside elegies, obituaries, and dramatic accounts of the injury and death of children, share with their readers the knowledge that the lives of these children are highly precarious. Contemporary readers would also have recognized that poems about mischievous, happy and loved young children operate in conscious contrast to the popular genre of poems concerned with suffering, homeless, or parentless children, and with child labour. Working-class children were, indeed, most likely to feature in Victorian poetry in this guise. Elizabeth Barrett Browning's enormously influential 'The Cry of the Children' is the key example in England and inspired social-reform poems such as Ann Hawkshaw's 'The Mother to Her Starving Child' or John Critchley Prince's 'The Death of the Factory Child', both originating from industrial Manchester. Scottish poetry was far from immune to this genre. Examples that were published in *Songs for the Nursery*, with the intention of invoking pity and sympathy in the child reader, include William Thom's 'The Mitherless Bairn', James Ballantine's 'The Orphan Wanderer' and Alexander Smart's 'The Herd Laddie'. As I have examined in detail elsewhere, the abused child also features in perhaps the single most popular poem of Victorian Scotland, Paul Rookford's tragic temperance song, 'The Drunkard's Raggit Wean'.[136] Such verse serves to highlight just how unusual many of the lively, naughty child protagonists in Scots nursery verse seemed by contrast to the accepted norms of their period.

In early 1850, Rev. Robert Buchanan identified a 'mass of idle, neglected, uneducated children', of whom only a third were attending school, in the parish of Tron in Glasgow—less than five minutes' walk from Robertson's bookshop on Trongate.[137] *Songs for the Nursery* and its imitators sought to demonstrate that not all working-class Scottish children were idle, neglected, and uneducated. Nursery

[132] Abrams, p.9.

[133] Thomas E. Jordan, *Victorian Childhood: Themes and Variations* (New York: SUNY, 1987), p.84.

[134] W .W. Knox, *Industrial Nation: Work, Culture and Society in Scotland, 1800-Present* (Edinburgh: Edinburgh University Press, 1999), p.92.

[135] Taylor, p.31.   [136] 'See Blair, 'The Drunkard's Raggit Wean'.

[137] Buchanan, *The Schoolmaster in the Wynds*, 3rd edn (Glasgow: Blackie & Son, 1850), pp.11, 14.

verse is conservative in that it does not directly seek state intervention on behalf of these children: it promotes good citizenship, and it is strongly invested in the standard Victorian doctrine of self-help and in the gendered norms of the period. But it does not exist in cosy ignorance of contemporary realities, either. It seeks to show that Scottish working-class parents, mothers *and* fathers, despite the challenges supplied by the contexts in which they lived and worked, were committed to bringing up their children to be responsible, well-educated, ambitious and adventurous members of society, with an ingrained love of Scotland and the Scots language. These poems express a national pride in Scotland's heritage and in the future that she will have if all her children possess the confidence, independence, and determination of those represented in these poems.

Whistle-Binkie and nursery verse are products of 'the depressing city of Glasgow, with its foul air, its hideous slums, and its still more hideous social life', and thus of the Scottish city perceived, then and now, as exemplary of the challenges caused by rapid industrialization.[138] Robertson's bookshop on the Trongate reshaped Scottish working-class verse culture. His collections and collaborations, like his own social circle, in which literary and political discussion overlapped, are direct outcomes of the age of Reform—political, educational, and social. By encouraging working men to participate in literary and song culture, by putting their family values on display, and by offering a positive evaluation of 'vulgar' Scots, such publications created and fostered the much maligned genres of sentimental domestic verse and nursery verse, yet in doing so they strongly emphasized working-class fitness for full participation in politics and society.

---

[138] Buchanan, 'The Laureate of the Nursery', p.72.

3

Stands Scotland Where It Did?
Nostalgia, Improvement, and the Uses of the Land

In his poem 'Stands Scotland Where It Did?' of 1860, emigrant poet Hew Ainslie looked back towards the Scotland he had known in the first decades of the century, from the perspective of mid-Victorian modernity:

Hoo's dear auld mither Scotland, lads?
  Hoo's kindly Scotland noo?
Are a' her glen's as green's of yore,
  Her harebells still as blue?

I muckle dread the iron steed,
  That tears up heugh an' fell   *heugh – cliff or steep bank*
Has gien oor canny auld folk
  A sorry tale to tell.

Hae touns ta'en a' your bonnie burns,
  To cool their lowin' craigs?   *lowing – blazing, fiery; craigs – throats*
Or damm'd them up in timmer troughs   *timmer – wooden*
  To slock their yettlin naigs?   *yettling – made of cast-iron; naigs – horses*

Do Southern loons infest your touns
  Wi' mincin' cockney gab?
Hae "John and Robert" ta'en the place
  O' plain auld "Jock an' Rab"?

**

They're howkin' sae in bank an' brae,   *howking – digging*
  An' sheughin' hill an' howe,   *sheughing – digging a trench, furrowing*
I tremble for the bonnie broom
  The whin an' heather cowe.[1]   *cowe – twig or stem, usually of heather*

'Stands Scotland Where It Did?', according to the *Aberdeen Herald*, which reprinted it on 14 July 1860, first appeared in the *Chicago Church Record*. Ainslie, a law clerk in Edinburgh in the 1810s, had a long-standing poetic reputation. His *A Pilgrimage to the Land of Burns* appeared in 1822, he was a contributor to *Whistle-Binkie*, and his poems appear very widely across the Scottish newspaper press up until his

---

[1] 'Stands Scotland Where It Did?', *Aberdeen Herald*, 14 July 1860, signed 'Hew Ainslie, Chicago Church Record'. Reprinted in Hew Ainslie, *A Pilgrimage to the Land of Burns, and Poems*, with memoir by Thomas C. Latto (Paisley: Alexander Gardner, 1892), pp.333–4.

death in 1878. He published a volume in the United States in 1855, though 'Stands Scotland Where It Did?' does not appear until a posthumous 1892 collection, edited by another emigrant poet (and member of the *Whistle-Binkie* circle), Thomas C. Latto.[2] Ainslie's biographers and his own poems suggest that he emigrated (in the early 1820s) out of discontent with the British political situation. In America, he was briefly a member of Robert Owen's co-operative New Harmony community in Indiana, tried his luck in Cincinnati, and spent a period as a successful brewer in Louisville, Kentucky, settling there and eventually working with his sons in a foundry. He is a significant example of the settler poet, comparable to the 'colonial laureates' recently discussed by Jason Rudy.[3]

Ainslie's poem sets the keynote for this chapter because of its concerns with environmental and social change, caused primarily by Victorian industrial development, and with the impact that these changes might have on the language and customs of the country. By deliberately writing in a more difficult Scots dialect than that which American readers would have known from other emigrant poems (requiring, for instance, his readers to translate 'yettlin' naigs' into 'iron horses' and then 'trains', and to hear rhymes on how/now/blue and loons/towns) Ainslie signalled his uncompromising allegiance to tradition. As the poems in this chapter show, the major issues he identifies—railways, the construction work on previously wild land that they enabled, and the need to exploit Scotland's natural resources of rivers and lochs to supply the growing towns with water—were common topics in the poetry of the period. The new technologies of transport and communication that enabled Ainslie's Scots emigrant poems to circulate so widely in his native land, the new ease of emigration, and the new processes that enabled his farming, brewing, and foundry work in the United States, are precisely the developments that threaten the imagined Scotland of his youth, in a nostalgic rural vision shared by thousands of Scottish writers. In Elizabeth Helsinger's phrasing, he is one of those who can 'afford' nostalgia in changed times, as part of a generation who 'most benefit from the changes, actively contributing to them or implicitly condoning them'; she cites Robert Hewison's helpful definition of such nostalgia as a 'sweet sadness conditioned by the knowledge that the object of recall cannot—indeed, must not—be recovered'.[4]

Poems and songs in the very common 'dear auld mither Scotland' genre (gendering the nation as an older maternal figure is a repeated trope throughout the period) or the 'auld native hame' genre, where 'hame' covers both the physical home of the poet's real or imagined childhood, the community in which it is placed, and the scenery which surrounds it, constitute the largest sub-genre in

---

[2] See Ainslie, *Scottish Song, Ballads and Poems* (Redfield: New York, 1855). Latto emigrated to New York and became the first editor of the Scottish American Journal.

[3] Rudy, Imagined Homelands, chapter 5, pp.134–62.

[4] Elizabeth Helsinger, *Rural Scenes and National Representation: Britain, 1815–1850* (Princeton, NJ: Princeton University Press, 1997), p.4. Helsinger's study, though focused largely on England and Englishness, is seminal in its discussion of how 'the economic and symbolic uses of rural land' were reimagined in the early Victorian period (p.6). See also Robert Hewison, *The Heritage Industry: Britain in a Climate of Decline* (London: Methuen, 1987), p.134.

Scottish verse culture, whether in English, Scots, or Gaelic. As Derick Thomson comments, 'The commonest theme of Gaelic verse in the nineteenth century is that of "homeland"…seen primarily in a nostalgic light: a place of youthful associations, family and community warmth, a Paradise lost', an observation that holds equally true for the English and Scots poets examined here.[5] Scottish newspaper poets cut their teeth on poems lamenting (and celebrating) their lost childhood home and its rural scenery, poems longing for the freedom to wander through Scotland's mountains and glens and by her streams, poems filled with homesickness for this landscape, written from a geographical and temporal distance that could stretch from a few miles and a few years to, as in Ainslie's case, thousands of miles and several decades. The aspects of Scotland that are missed and lamented are often very specific—naming and preserving the memory of particular local places and features—yet can equally stretch to generic signifiers of 'Scotland', such as mist-covered mountains, craggy glens, waterfalls, and fields, streams, woods, and moorland filled with bluebells, hawthorn, gorse (gowans), and heather.

While these representations are profoundly influenced by the depiction of Scottish landscape in Macpherson's Ossian and Walter Scott's fiction and poetry, if one urtext were sought for this genre, it would be the second and third stanzas of Burns's 'Auld Lang Syne', which economically present nostalgia for childhood experiences of rural Scotland's environment and community, from a perspective of adult loss and distance:

> We twa hae run about the braes,
>   And pou'd the gowans fine;
> But we've wandered mony a weary fitt,
>   Sin auld lang syne.
>
> We twa hae paidl'd in the burn,
>   Frae morning sun till dine;
> But seas between us broad hae roar'd,
>   Sin auld lang syne.[6]

The first section of this chapter examines how poems which build on Burnsian pastoral can be reread as part of an activist tradition, in which the freedom to paddle in the burn, to pick wild flowers, to wander by the banks and braes, becomes part of an ongoing nineteenth-century dispute over access and rights of way. Precisely because this freedom had been so often and so influentially imagined by Scottish poets and songwriters, I argue, poetry and song played a vital part in shaping the terms of these debates. The second chapter returns to questions of 'improvement. The issue of rights of way was politically straightforward for working-class poets publishing in the liberal or radical press: lairds, landowners, and their employees were inarguably in the wrong. Land improvement, and the transformation of Scotland's rural economy, produced more ambiguous responses. Ainslie might

---

[5] Derick Thomson, *An Introduction to Gaelic Poetry* (London: Gollancz, 1977), p.223.
[6] Robert Burns, *Selected Poems and Songs*, ed. Robert P. Irvine (Oxford: Oxford University Press, 2014), p.186.

lament the coming of the railways and the new building trade, from his position outside Scotland, but railways opened up possibilities for Scottish communities— towns fought to be on the line—and workers in the new industries needed homes, amenities and, for those in major cities, refreshing access to the countryside via new forms of transport, or new public green spaces such as civic parks. Poets vacillated between elegiac laments for the lost rural Scotland, and paeans to the developments that had led to this imagined loss. Finally, the last section of the chapter returns to emigrant poets, briefly considering how emigrant or settler poets drew on aspects of 'native hame' poetry in making a case for or against emigration to their peers.

All the poems discussed in this chapter draw on the tropes of nostalgic pastoral, a genre usually linked to the 'kailyard' sensibility of the later Victorian period. There is nothing necessarily 'authentic' about such verse. In the emigrant poem genre, for instance, for every writer like Ainslie who was composing from overseas, there were many writing *as if* they had or were about to emigrate, without ever leaving Scotland. Evidence suggests that the popularity of the 'auld native hame' and the local scenery genres led to a certain cynicism about producing set-piece pastoral poems using familiar tropes, with a knowing eye to publication. Hugh Miller, for instance, trying to establish a reputation in Inverness, started by writing an ode on the beauty of the Ness and presenting it to the editor of the *Courier*.[7] It is fair to say that within Scottish studies, the consensus about the value of poems in these genres has been summed up by Gifford's description of an 'unhealthy and anachronistic movement towards evasive ruralism in literature throughout the nineteenth century', featuring:

> endless imitators of Burns, Hogg and Wilson who preferred to freeze Scotland as they liked to think it had been in their time, preserving an anachronistic discourse which suggested that they were farmer-shepherds rather than the factory workers, weavers and tradesmen of the industrial revolution.[8]

Alan Riach, in a discussion of emigrant poetry in New Zealand, associates poems in the nostalgic pastoral tradition with:

> the exaggerated emotions of yearning nostalgia for a lost homeland among exiles: or, among residents, the longing for the assurances provided by domestic stability, pastoral wisdom, and happy childhood adventures enshrined in 'kailyard' fiction and the 'Whistlebinkie' anthologies of Scottish verse.[9]

Even Nigel Leask, in his seminal and revisionary account of Robert Burns, pastoral and improvement, comments on the Victorian period that:

> Unfortunately Burns's consummate success seems to have deterred skilled followers, and poetry written in Scots was easily subsumed into the 'Kailyard', the purely nostalgic and parochial nineteenth-century version of Scottish pastoral.[10]

---

[7] Miller, *My Schools and Schoolmasters*, p.398.

[8] Gifford, 'Scottish Literature in the Victorian and Edwardian Era', p.324.

[9] Alan Riach, 'Heather and Fern: The Burns Effect in New Zealand Verse', in Tom Brooking and Jennie Coleman, eds., *The Heather and the Fern: Scottish Migration and New Zealand Settlement* (Dunedin: University of Otago Press, 2003), pp.153–71, 158.

[10] Nigel Leask, *Robert Burns and Pastoral: Poetry and Improvement in Late Eighteenth-Century Scotland* (Oxford: Oxford University Press, 2010), p.8.

Reassessments of kailyard fiction have, of course, argued that this genre is more complex than has previously been assumed, and the previous chapter makes a similar argument for *Whistle-Binkie*. This chapter seeks to revise such perceptions of Scottish Victorian pastoral as 'purely nostalgic and parochial'. It demonstrates that 'parochial' concerns invariably feed into major national debates; that when we replace nostalgic pastoral in its original reading context, the newspaper column, its specific political motivations become clear; and that working poets operating in subsets of this genre use their readers' pre-existing familiarity with its tropes to produce intelligent and revisionary versions of pastoral.

   Ainslie himself is a good example. Given its initial publication in the American newspaper press, 'Stands Scotland Where It Did?' would seem to be addressed to the emigrant community, perhaps the 'lads' who are more recent arrivals from Scotland than Ainslie himself. As such it constructs a vision of Scotland from a self-identified elderly man seeking reassurance and opposed to any improvements made since the days of his youth. It also shows, as is common in emigrant poetry, the persistence of Scottish identity amongst emigrants, especially in the use of Scots. For readers of the Scottish press, however, knowing Ainslie from his other poems, this poem operated in a context of Ainslie as a fervent supporter of emigration (as I discuss below, emigration was a major topic of discussion in mid-Victorian provincial newspaper columns.) His equally well-known poems, published in the 1855 collection, 'Harvest Home in America', 'Come Awa' to the West' and 'A Foreigner's Feelings in the Far West', again first printed in newspapers, are advertisements for the greater liberty and equality experienced by Scots in America. The latter, in a final verse nostalgically recalling Scotland, concludes:

> But the heart still will roam
> To the sweets of its own native plains,
> Tho' reason hath found it a home
> Where RIGHT and EQUALITY reigns.[11]

Nostalgia, Ainslie argues here, is dangerous because it leads poets—like himself— to forget the oppressive political conditions of Britain. A true pastoral vision, in which the rural labourer enjoys the fruits of his labour, is found in America, as 'Harvest Home in America' notes:

> But stent or tax or tythe, boys,   *stent – a limit, a set task*
>   Our girnals daurna spill;   *girnal – granary, grain - chest*
> These burdens were bought aff, boys,
>   Langsyne at Bunker's Hill.[12]

American independence enables the reconstruction of a better Scots-speaking community than that found in 'dear auld mither Scotland', particularly when the positive values of rural community associated with auld Scotland are in the process of being destroyed. The function of pastoral poetry in Ainslie is not simply to romanticize a lost past but to celebrate the present freedom, enabled by distance from Scotland, that permits such romanticization.

---

[11] Ainslie, *Scottish Song, Ballads and Poems*, p.43.   [12] Ibid., p.32.

Nostalgia, pastoral, and the uses of the land in eighteenth and nineteenth-century literature and culture have each been the subject of intense critical scrutiny in the twenty-first century. Nostalgia, Nicholas Dames argues, became central to a Victorian society 'for whom mobility and the possibility of rapid change is increasingly likely'.[13] His study, and related studies by Linda M. Austin and Tamara Wagner, amongst others, follow different lines of enquiry while strongly agreeing that 'Even in its most sentimentalized versions... nostalgia was never straightforward nor even 'necessarily' conservative or bourgeois'.[14] These critics associate nostalgia primarily with fiction, while I would argue with Aaron Santesso that the eighteenth century serves to construct the 'nostalgia poem', 'poems that take nostalgia as their central concern and represent it through set rules and tropes', extending his argument by contending that in the Victorian period also, poets:

> were doing something more ambitious than expressing unthinking nostalgia: they were teaching their audience what nostalgia was and how to feel it – with specific, often political purposes in mind.[15]

Working-class Scottish poets were very familiar with the writers Santesso discusses (including Pope, Goldsmith, and Gray), and with their versions of nostalgic English pastoral. While the influence of any other poet pales beside that of Burns, many of the poems discussed in this chapter are reminiscent of, and in some cases undoubtedly directly influenced by, the politics of pastoral in James Thomson's *The Seasons* (1726–30) and Oliver Goldsmith's *The Deserted Village* (1770), especially the latter's emphasis on how the dispossession of the poor by the greedy rich has led to the wreck of countryside and community, and ultimately to exile through emigration.

As Rachel Crawford, John Goodridge, Tim Fulford and many others have shown, eighteenth-century poetry in the pastoral and georgic modes was profoundly engaged with the uses of the land, in terms of enclosure, land improvement and the effects of sweeping agricultural change, and used its focus on the (English) countryside to examine 'the proper nature of moral and political authority for a nation whose physical and social organization was changing rapidly'.[16] Goodridge, Leask, and Bridget Keegan, in her recent *British Labouring-Class Nature Poetry*, demonstrate that labouring-class writers made a major contribution to these debates around rural space and its literary representation. As Keegan helpfully reminds us, 'Nature – variously defined – is never a socially neutral space, all

[13] Nicholas Dames, *Amnesiac Selves: Nostalgia, Forgetting and British Fiction, 1810–1870* (Oxford: Oxford University Press, 2001), p.14.

[14] Tamara S. Wagner, *Longing: Narratives of Nostalgia in the British Novel, 1740–1890* (Lewisburg: Bucknell University Press, 2004), p.13. See also Linda M. Austin, *Nostalgia in Transition, 1780–1917* (Charlottesville, VA: University of Virginia Press, 2007).

[15] Aaron Santesso, *A Careful Longing: The Poetics and Problems of Nostalgia* (Newark, DE: University of Delaware Press, 2006), pp.12, 20.

[16] Tim Fulford, *Landscape, Liberty and Authority: Poetry, Criticism and Politics from Thomson to Wordsworth* (Cambridge: Cambridge University Press, 1996), p.1. See also Rachel Crawford, *Poetry, Enclosure, and the Vernacular Landscape* (Cambridge: Cambridge University Press, 2002) and John Goodridge, *Rural Life in Eighteenth-Century English Poetry* (Cambridge: Cambridge University Press, 1995). For a further discussion of georgic, see below, pp.122–3.

the more so for the labouring poor'.[17] Both Keegan and John Barrell, in his outstanding discussion of sentimental pastoral verse in the 1790s' radical press in London, however, have noted the difficulty of finding an 'explicitly political argument' in such verse.[18] Barrell concludes that radical editors may have included nostalgic pastoral simply because they saw the 'cultivation of sentiment as an important aspect of the political education they seek to impart'.[19]

In relation to the poets featured in this chapter, many of whom moved in radical or at least reformist political circles, sentimental education was an entirely valid aim. But their poems differ from the periodical poems in Barrell's study in that they deploy the reader's assumed familiarity with the pastoral genre for political and environmental activism, usually in relation to a specific case or issue. They are able to do this through their publication in the provincial newspaper press. Every poem discussed below, though it may have been reprinted in other contexts, was initially written as a direct intervention in a local question, and engages with a local community. Can this landowner legitimately prevent us from walking through his estate? What are the advantages and disadvantages of draining this piece of land? Does our town need a railway? Would farm workers in this area be better off if they emigrated, and if so, which country offers the best prospects? One of the purposes of this chapter is to show that pastoral poetry and georgic were perceived as crucial vehicles for debating these questions, and thus are always 'explicitly political'.

Of course, such issues also raise environmental concerns, and a number of the poems discussed below could be read through the lens of ecocriticism, extending recent work by Louisa Gairn and Graeme Macdonald on twentieth- and twenty-first-century Scottish literature and its 'feeling for nature' back to the early to mid Victorian period.[20] Almost all the writers in this chapter—none of whom have attracted any significant critical attention—would be doubtful recruits to the genre of ecological writing, however, in the sense that they do not generally emphasize human accountability to the environment, and tend to prioritize human interest above all.[21] Unlike John Clare and Gerard Manley Hopkins (whose works are unlikely to have been known to these poets) or even Wordsworth, they rarely perceive intrinsic value in leaving nature to itself. Wordsworth, who is often read as a founder of late Victorian and twentieth-century environmentalism, moved

---

[17] Bridget Keegan, *British Labouring-Class Nature Poetry, 1730–1837* (Houndmills: Palgrave, 2008), p.2.

[18] Keegan, p.173. John Barrell, 'Rus in urbe', in Nigel Leask and Philip Connell, eds., *Romanticism and Popular Culture in Britain and Ireland* (Cambridge: Cambridge University Press, 2009), pp.109–27.

[19] Barrell, p.123.

[20] Louisa Gairn, *Ecology and Modern Scottish Literature* (Edinburgh: Edinburgh University Press, 2008) and Graeme Macdonald, 'Green Links: Ecosocialism and Contemporary Scottish Writing', in John Rignall and H. Gustav Klaus, eds., *Ecology and the Literature of the British Left: The Red and the Green* (Farnham: Ashgate, 2012), pp.221–35. The phrase 'feeling for nature', as used in Gairn, comes from John Veitch's *The Feeling for Nature in Scottish Poetry, 2 vols* (Edinburgh: Blackwood, 1887). Veitch briefly discusses some working-class writers, in vol II, p.314.

[21] I take the criteria for 'ecological writing' from Lawrence Buell's foundational *The Environmental Imagination: Thoreau, Nature Writing, and the Formation of American Culture* (Cambridge, MA: Harvard University Press, 1995), pp.7–8, also cited and discussed in Greg Garrard, *Ecocriticism*, 2nd edn (London: Routledge, 2012), p.58.

from early concerns about enclosure to a stance that saw the invasion of the Lake District by day-tripping workers from the industrial cities as a deeply dismaying prospect.[22] The poets in this chapter are these workers, and it is not surprising that when Wordsworth's newspaper sonnet in opposition to the Kendal and Windermere railway line ('On the Projected Kendal and Windermere Railway') was republished in the Scottish press, it met with a hostile response poem in the *Scotsman* in support of railway development, opening 'O thought unworthy of the poet sage'.[23] At points, working-class poets do argue for 'environmental justice', resisting the 'toxi-fication of local environments' and arguing for land rights for the disenfranchised, yet their nature poems can also favour, even celebrate, the exploitation of wild spaces by men.[24] For local working-class poets, Scotland's countryside is highly valued for its beauty and meaning, yet in terms of how these can be used and accessed, how the natural environment can profit the working man and woman—including through literary endeavours. As they sought to reform and improve themselves, for both personal and political ends, so they also sought to reform and improve their land.

ACTIVIST POETICS AND
THE RIGHTS OF WAY DEBATE

It would be difficult to locate a Scottish working-class poet who never wrote a poem in praise of a native river or stream. Journalist and poet Hugh MacDonald, whose 'Rambles Round Glasgow' series in the *Glasgow Citizen* helped to start a fashion for rambling clubs in Scotland, commented that:

> The Scotch have a perfect passion, indeed, for the "living waters" with which their beautiful country is everywhere so delightfully intersected. Every one of them, from the greatest even unto the least, is duly named.[25]

Every Scottish poet has a 'natal burn', MacDonald notes. His own river is the Clyde, but literature has taught him affection for Scotland's other streams:

> We love thee also, O sylvan Tweed! Although to us thou art but a name. Yarrow, albeit unvisited, is dear unto our heart, for the sake of those who have sorrowed and sung by her side. The Doon, the Lugar, and the Cart have, since our earliest days, been in name familiar as household words to our ear and our soul in the lyrics of Scotland's sweetest singers.[26]

---

[22] Dewey W. Hall, in *Romantic Naturalists, Early Environmentalists: An Ecocritical Study, 1789–1912* (Farnham: Ashgate, 2014), describes Wordsworth as 'the seminal figure joining the literary with the proto-environmental' (p.89). For a detailed discussion of Wordsworth's opposition to railways, see Hall, pp.85–104.

[23] The exchange is reprinted in the *Dundee Courier*, 5 November 1844, p.2.

[24] See Buell, *The Future of Environmental Criticism: Environmental Crisis and Literary Imagination* (Oxford: Blackwell, 2005), p.141, 114. Buell briefly suggests that nineteenth-century poets, especially William Blake, are early voices for environmental justice issues (pp.119–20).

[25] Hugh MacDonald, *Rambles Round Glasgow, Descriptive, Historical, and Traditional* (Glasgow: James Hedderwick, 1854), p.138.

[26] Macdonald, p.139.

It is literature, as Wordsworth wrote of Scott in his 'Yarrow Revisited', that transfers 'the power of Yarrow' to 'streams unknown', and creates a patriotic affection for Scotland's rivers, whether or not the reader has seen them in person: MacDonald's alteration of Wordsworth's 'revisited' to 'unvisited' deliberately highlights the power of literary investments. Commemorating one's wandering by a local stream, usually with nostalgic regret for this lost pleasure, is an essential part of developing an appropriate poetic persona, as 'Yarrow Revisited' and many other Romantic poems make explicit.[27]

David Carnegie, who worked in a power-loom factory in Arbroath and contributed to the *People's Journal* under a pseudonym, opened 'Brothock Water' with a stanza economically combining the value of the native stream in childhood and courtship:

> Flow on, little streamlet! Thou'rt dearer to me
> Than the proudest of rivers that roll to the sea;
> On thy braes, when a bairn, I aften hae played,
> On thy banks, when a lover, I aften hae strayed.[28]

As Keegan observes, Romantic-era labouring-class poets who wrote about native streams did so from a position of identification, 'for many the obscurity of the streams they depicted provided an easy figure for the poet's sense of his or her fame and lack thereof', so that affection for the 'little' streamlet slides into a defence of both the 'little' newspaper poem, as worthy of consideration as its greater rivals, and the 'little' poet.[29] The language of Carnegie's opening lines recalls a wider tradition of popular Victorian poetry celebrating rivers, notably Tennyson's well-known recitation pieces and song lyrics, 'Flow Down, Cold Rivulet' and 'The Brook'. The shift into Scots in the second couplet, however, not coincidentally at the point when he recalls his childhood, relocates Carnegie in the Burns tradition. 'Straying' (associated with the Scots 'stravaiging', or wandering) is a crucial, recurring, word in such poems because it suggests the value of leisure, of free, undirected wandering, as opposed to following a route to a destination. Amongst Macdonald's circle, to take only one further example, William Penman ('Rhyming Willie'), a blacksmith at the Star Foundry, Paisley Road until he was disabled by an accident, described his wanderings by south Glasgow's Cart:

> By Cart's clear stream nae mair I'll stray,
>   When the mune is in the cloudless sky;
> For ither climes, far, far, away,
>   Tae seek a hame I noo maun hie.[30]

Penman, as the volume in which this was published tells us, never left his local area. The poem, like those discussed below, is about the literary tropes of emigration rather than the author's literal departure. The conscious interchangeability of

---

[27] On the popularity of rivers and streams in Romantic-era writing, see Keegan, p.100.
[28] Carnegie, *Lays and Lyrics from the Factory* (Arbroath: Thomas Buncle, 1879), p.60. Carnegie's pseudonym is 'A Son of St Tammas'.
[29] Keegan, p.121.
[30] William Penman, *Echoes from the Ingleside* (Glasgow: Porteous Brothers, 1875), p.65.

such lyrics with others in the genre is shown by the intersection of Penman's title 'Farewell Sweet Netherlea', with the given tune, 'Farewell Sweet Ballochmyle'.

In the course of the Victorian period, 'straying', or attempting to stray, became a politicized act. In MacDonald's *Rambles*, for instance, he encourages readers to seek the streams and rivers hallowed by association with local poets. In one section he and a friend attempted to visit Gleniffer Braes, to walk by the ravine and water-falls associated with the Paisley weaver-poet Robert Tannahill. But although they 'knew every linn and pool' from their reading, they could not experience the loca-tion themselves, 'for my lord's game might chance to be disturbed, or haply we might fall in with some one of his lordship's surly keepers'.[31] Macdonald uses this incident and others to argue that landowners who shut out ramblers are denying access not merely to beautiful features and scenes, but to Scotland's literary heritage—a heritage that, like the countryside, should be accessible to all. Published in volume form in 1854, *Rambles Round Glasgow* coincided with the ongoing dis-pute with the Duke of Atholl over the right of way through Glen Tilt in the Highlands, the most celebrated Scottish rights of way case of the nineteenth cen-tury, which led to the foundation of the Association for the Protection of the Public Rights of Roadways and Footpaths, later the Rights of Way Society, in Edinburgh in 1847. Every local paper in this study discussed Glen Tilt, and many working-class writers, notably Miller, wrote pieces in opposition to the Duke.[32]

By 1854, however, the question of rights of way had already been a live issue in Glasgow for over thirty years. Contemporary writers, including MacDonald, were well aware that the most significant nineteenth-century Glasgow case, the dispute over access to the banks of the Clyde in 1822, had been influentially supported by the poet Alexander Rodger, encountered in the previous chapter as an editor and contributor to *Whistle-Binkie*. In the second series, *Whistle-Binkie* published a song of Rodger's from the 1820s, 'Come to the Banks of the Clyde', also published in his collected poems of 1842. The opening seems innocent enough:

> Come to the Banks of the Clyde
> Where health and joy invite us,
> Spring, now in virgin pride
> There waiteth to delight us.[33]

It is the stated air, 'March to the Battlefield' (a marching tune for pipe or flute) that indicates the political freight of the song. This was not an invitation to pastoral rambling, but to battle, against the self-made wealthy brewer Thomas Harvie and his insistence on walling off a traditional path along the Clyde in summer 1822.

[31] Macdonald, p.217.

[32] Miller, 'Glen Tilt Tabooed', in Peter Bayne, ed., *Essays, Historical and Biographical, Political, Social, Literary and Scientific*, 5th edn (Edinburgh: William P. Nimmo, 1872), pp.112–20. This essay originally appeared in the Witness. For discussions of the importance of Glen Tilt, see Robert A. Lambert, *Contested Mountains: Nature, Development and Environment in the Cairngorms Region of Scotland, 1880–1980* (Cambridge: White Horse Press, 2001), p.36 and *passim*, and Tom Stephenson, *Forbidden Land: The Struggle for Access to Moorland and Mountain* (Manchester: Manchester University Press, 1989), pp.120–3.

[33] *Whistle-Binkie* (1839), p.57. Rodger, p.172.

Villagers demolished the wall; he rebuilt it and hired armed guards, whereupon the radical young men of Glasgow, including Rodger, organized a band of 'enraged colliers' with their pick-axes, who marched to the wall singing 'Scots Wha Hae' and knocked it down.[34] The consequent arrest of twenty to thirty of the colliers incited a mass movement in Glasgow to raise funds for their defence and for a court case against Harvie, for which Rodger was active in organizing benefit concerts. Harvie lost his case in January 1826, appealed to the House of Lords, and lost again in 1828. Rodger's second 'banks of Clyde' song, 'Roll, Fair Clutha', probably celebrates one of the trials: the resounding chorus is 'Roll, fair Clutha, fair Clutha to the sea,/ And be thy banks forever free!'[35] By setting these lyrics to the stirring tune of 'Rule Britannia', Rodger linked this local dispute to wider British attitudes towards liberty as a national right, as would become a common tactic in later political debates about access. The Harvie's Dyke case is cited by historians of the access movement, such as Harvey Taylor, as 'the first effectively organized campaign to defend a right of way as a public amenity'.[36] The fact that the man who, according to the *People's Friend*, 'organized and directed' the opposition to Harvie was a radical poet shows how poetic abilities—writing protest songs amongst them—could be profitably marshalled to such causes.[37]

As Taylor suggests, from the 1820s onwards:

[T]he right of the public to walk on long-established footpaths was adopted as an urban radical cause…Local challenges to the landowners' reassertion of the exclusiveness of their domains were strongly influenced by the practical utilitarian motive of improving the physical health and morals of factory workers and their families.[38]

Taylor's focus is primarily on industrial Lancashire and the North of England, but he argues throughout that key developments in England were influenced by Scottish movements. Scotland provided 'early practical and rational motives for walking through wild landscapes [...] as part of the relatively advanced rational culture pursued by the commercial and professional social stratum', and it was Scotland that supplied 'the first really serious consideration of the question of access to open country' and the 'earliest direct origins' of the British access lobby.[39] What Scotland also supplied, however, was a very widespread and politically inclined literary tradition of Scottish pastoral that could easily be enlisted in the cause. Numerous poems were written by minor Scottish poets of all classes on the rights of way debate, and these intersect with, and feed into, better-known poetic interest in the Highland Clearances and the late-century crofters' disputes,

---

[34] Peter Mackenzie, *Reminiscences of Glasgow and the West of Scotland, 2 vols* (Glasgow: John Tweed, 1866), vol II, p.439. Mackenzie, a leading Reform journalist and editor, supplies one of the most detailed accounts of this case.

[35] Rodger, p.173.

[36] Harvey Taylor, *A Claim on the Countryside: A History of the British Outdoor Movement* (Edinburgh: Keele University Press, 1997), p.20.

[37] 'Alexander Rodger', *People's Friend*, 19 February 1873, p.124.   [38] Taylor, p.5.

[39] Ibid., pp.16, 127.

especially by Gaelic poets.[40] Charles Mackay's poems, many written during his stint as editor of the *Glasgow Argus*, are one example of the engagement of rela-tively prominent literary figures with the rights of way cause, as are John Stuart Blackie's.[41] Because of the focus on the 'health and morals' of workers in these debates, however, working-class poets could present themselves as personally invested in, and persecuted by, rights of way cases.

Vast numbers of poems from the period celebrate the escape from the industrial town to the beauty of the countryside, and in terms that explicitly link access to the countryside to increased productivity and contentment for the worker. Ebenezer Smith, an Ayr cobbler, writes, in a 'holiday' poem on 'Arran':

> We came from the crowd – from the tumult and rattle,
> The dust and the din of the great field of strife
> We came to seek rest, and grow strong for the battle,
> And hopeful and fresh for the journey of life.
>
> How gaily the sides of the grey hills we've clamber'd,
> Through blue-bells and purple heath wending our way![42]

Giving workers a holiday amidst beautiful Scottish scenery, Smith implies, will pay off in a renewed determination to work hard. David Tasker, a factory worker and newspaper poet (associated with the *Weekly News*) in Dundee, similarly paints a picture of the grim industrial workplace as opposed to the rural idyll in 'Summer Come':

> The pale-faced ones that sweat
> In the close factories – where they weave and spin –
> In idle hours seek some cool green retreat
> Far from the city's smoke, and dust, and din
> And joyous climb the breezy, ferny hills.[43]

Tasker's use of exactly the same metonymic phrases for labour, 'dust' and 'din', indicates the standard shorthand for representing industrial towns and cities versus the countryside, in which dirt, noise, heat, exhaustion and close proximity to others were contrasted with cool, fresh, peaceful scenes inspiring vigorous exercise. Gilfillan, introducing Tasker's collection, identifies Tasker's 'breathings after the country and breathings *in* the country', 'so characteristic of those children of toil who, amidst the dusty mill or in the centre of the fiery forges, sigh so sincerely for the beauties and salubrities of nature' as a hallmark of good character.[44] Workers

---

[40] Gaelic poems on the Highland Clearances and land rights are discussed and republished in Meek's *Tuath Is Tighearna*. See also Thomson, pp.233–48.

[41] See, for example, Mackay's 'Baron Braemar; or, The Lord of Glen Tilt', in *Voices from the Mountains and the Crowd* (Boston, MA: Ticknor, Reid & Fields, 1853), p.357 and Blackie's poems on Glen Tilt and the dispossession of the poor in the Highlands, 'The Lords of the Glen' and 'The Cottar's Fate', in *Lays and Lyrics of Ancient Greece, With Other Poems* (Edinburgh: Sutherland and Knox, 1857), pp.217, 223.

[42] Ebenezer Smith, 'Arran', in *Verses* (Ayr: Henry and Grant, 1871), p.63. His profession is identi-fied in Macintosh, *The Poets of Ayrshire*, p.95.

[43] David Tasker, '*Summer Come*', *Musings of Leisure Hours* (Dundee: James P. Mathew, 1865), p.21.

[44] George Gilfillan, 'Testimonial' in Tasker, p.viii.

who can gaily and joyfully climb mountains on their rare days off are not only displaying healthy, manly physical fitness, they are demonstrating a love of nature that marks them as fundamentally untainted by the presumed horrors of hard labour and the immorality of town and city life.

Love of country—in both senses—also serves as a unifying factor across classes, as in William Knight's 'Come let us tae the heather hills', in which workers 'lay the spade and hammer doun' and escape the city for a day:

> Come a' wha like, we mak nae odds
> Gif manly worth ye've got;
> The fustian jacket taks oor like,
> As weel's the braw dress coat.
> An' brithers a', we will be fain
> Tae speak, an' act, an' feel as men.[45]

In Knight's fantasy, class distinctions disappear in the fresh air of Scotland. What happens to such rural idylls of freedom and equality, however, when workmen are denied access to the countryside by landowners? As Andy Wightman observes, 'Throughout the nineteenth century 90% of Scotland continued to be held by less than 1500 landowners'.[46] Rights of way established by long-term use, and necessary to provide a route between two public places, could, in theory at least, be legally defended. Robert Lambert notes, however, that the status of mountains and wilderness as public space was ambiguous at best. As nineteenth-century owners cleared their land of people in favour of sheep, deer, or crops, or as land previously thought of as 'common' space was appropriated for the growing towns and cities and their needs, the right to stray, to wander freely without thought of destination, was threatened.[47] Opposition, as Miller noted, was couched in class terms, as rights of way became a major issue 'between the people and the exclusives among the aristocracy', with the general attitude highly 'unfavourable to the latter'.[48]

Thomas Stewart ('Rustic Rhymer'), a miner poet from Larkhall in Lanarkshire, for instance, represented the perceived landowner attitude in 'The Aristocratic Thieves', in which two landowners (unusually represented as speaking in Scots, which may be designed to undermine their pretence at being high-class) discuss their plans to circumvent the law in fencing off a path:

> We maun own we've eneuch, but the scum of Millheugh,
> And thae wannerin' weavers frae Laverickha',
> They stalk doon my glen as majestic, ye ken,
> As if that were their ain, an' my mansion an' a'[49]

---

[45] William Knight, *Auld Yule and Other Poems*, intro. George Gilfillan, ed. William Lindsay (Aberdeen: W. Lindsay, 1869), p.140. Knight obtained access to higher education, but chose to work as a shoemaker for the mobility it offered; he was involved in radical politics in Aberdeen and died young, suffering from alcoholism. See obituary, 'The Knight of the Awl', in the *People's Journal*, 11 August 1866, p.2.

[46] Andy Wightman, *Who Owns Scotland* (Edinburgh: Canongate, 1996), p.10.

[47] Lambert, p.35 and *passim*.   [48] Miller, Essays, p.124.

[49] Thomas Stewart, *Doric Rhyme, Some Hamely Lilts* (Larkhall: William Burns, 1875), p.190.

As in a number of rights of way cases (at least as represented by their advocates), the landlords have no use themselves for the disputed route, they simply want to render working-class 'scum' and their labour invisible. Again, it is 'wandering' that is the problem, exercising leisure. Although this case, and that in Stewart's other fierce right of way poem, 'The Laird's Reverie', is not named, 'The Aristocratic Thieves' most likely references the Fairholm Right of Way dispute from 1870— two Lanarkshire landowners sought to close a route through the valley of the Avon, between Millheugh and Fairholm—which led to direct action from colliers as well as a lawsuit.[50]

Scottish newspapers of a liberal or radical persuasion tended to be deeply embroiled in local rights of way cases, and the poetry columns could be key to organizing local resistance. In many cases newspaper editors and proprietors, like James Adam of the *Aberdeen Herald* or John and William Leng of the *Dundee Advertiser* and *People's Journal*, helped to found and support rights of way societies. In October 1860, for instance, the Lengs were active in establishing the Dundee Right of Way Association. The Dundee *Weekly News*, a great rival of the *Advertiser*, initially mocked the enthusiasm for access to the mountains shown by the Lengs and their supporters. In its 'Barber Shop' column, one of the barber's customers sums up the conclusion of the Rights of Way meeting of 13 October 1860 as 'the hills are eternal, therefore they belong to everybody in general, and nobody in particular...Let's go to the Hielands, Sandy'. 'But what will the laird say?' Sandy asks. 'The laird! Quote Genesis and Mr Leng till him', is the derisive response.[51] Yet the *Weekly News* writer, a week earlier, had put a trenchant defence of rights of way into the mouth of the radical weaver Treddles, who recites a composition titled 'The Right of Way', mentioning each of the key Dundee issues, including the banks of the river Tay (sold to the railway company) and the path up the Law hill (fenced off). It concludes:

> Our roads to hills and burnsides,
>   Through meadows green and gay,
> Alas! are gone, we called our own –
>   They've stopped our RIGHT OF WAY.[52]

The 'Barber Shop' column, through the Treddle character, both mocks and supports the perceived radical tendencies of working-class poets and their predilection for reciting topical poems on any possible occasion. By including the *poem* 'The Right of Way' in the newspaper debate, however, the *Weekly News* gave the issue visual prominence on the page, through spacing and capitalization, and enabled readers to gain a rapid overview of the areas under threat, all couched in the familiar and appealing language of nostalgic pastoral.

---

[50] 'The Laird's Reverie', in Stewart, *Among the Miners: Being Sketches in Prose and Verse* (Larkhall: W. Burns, 1893), pp.166–7. The Fairholm case is briefly discussed in Alan B. Campbell, *The Lanarkshire Miners: A Social History of Their Trade Unions 1775–1874* (Edinburgh: John Donald, 2003) (first published 1979), pp.229–30.

[51] 'The Barber's Shop', *Weekly News*, 20 October 1860, p.2.

[52] 'The Barber's Shop', *Weekly News*, 13 October 1860, p.2.

Every case over rights of way and access in Scotland in this period, and there were a great many, attracted poets and poems to its cause. Poems like Rodger's, which do not explicitly mention the case for which they were written, only reveal their status as activist poems when reinserted in their original context. Rodger and the Harvie's Dyke case were significant enough to be remembered in memoirs and accounts of this period of Glasgow history. This is not necessarily the case with many other local disputes, which are only recoverable through detailed study of local newspapers and other such sources, where these still exist. Elizabeth Hartley's stirring 'The Right of Way', for instance, probably references a specific case from around the 1860s and was likely published in the *Dumbarton Herald*, since the Herald Office published her collection. But the poem does not include any identifying detail:

> The wealthy have mansions, and couches of down –
>   They have lawns, they have gardens and fountains;
> While we, when released from the dust of the town,
>   Have naught but the moors and the mountains.
>
> What wonder that grief o'er our perishing rights
>   In each bosom indignantly gathers,
> As from us they wrest, by the strong hand of might,
>   The wild mountain paths of our fathers.[53]

If local readers knew, as they may well have done, that Hartley was a gardener's daughter, then the 'lawns, gardens and fountains' take on special significance through her family involvement in tending leisure spaces for those who would deprive their workers of the same rights. In Hartley's case, the poem does specify in its title and rhetoric that it is concerned with rights of access. Many newspaper poets, however, assumed that local readers knew that a seemingly innocuous pastoral poem about wandering by the banks of the Tay like 'The Shepherd's Song' by 'Factorius', when it appeared contemporaneously with editorials concerned about the sale of those banks to the railways, related to current political concerns.[54]

Nineteenth-century 'native stream' poems, in particular, frequently related to local issues about access to riverbanks, a charged concern given that rivers had use-value (fishing, washing, transport) as well as leisure value (walking, paddling, and swimming). Contemporary cases clearly show the significant role that nostalgic pastoral poetry about rivers and streams played in the Rights of Way disputes. On 9 October 1847, for instance, the *Aberdeen Herald* printed a poem by regular contributor William Anderson (a factory worker, later a policeman poet), 'My Native Streams', including the stanzas:

> Through Seaton Vale uncheck'd I've rang'd,
>   Where lav'rocks sing an' wild flowers grow;   *laverock – lark*
> But, ah! the scene is sairly chang'd
>   From what it was lang years ago.

---

[53] Elizabeth Hartley, *The Prairie Flower and Other Poems* (Dumbarton: Bennett Brothers, at the Herald Office, 1870), p.81.

[54] For a discussion of this poem see Kirstie Blair, ' "A Very Poetical Town": Newspaper Poetry and the Working-Class Poet in Victorian Dundee', *Victorian Poetry* 54 (2014), 89–109.

Through spots where we, 'mang broom an' whin,
   Hae harrit nests and howkit bykes,   *harrit – robbed (of nests); howkit*
                                         bykes – dug out bees' nests

We daurna gang and canna win
   For fences, rails, an' five-feet dykes.

The little path that we hae trod
   Sae aft, the worldlin' winna spare –
He filches e'en the ancient road
   Our fathers took to kirk an' fair.
Though the usurper be a lord,
   My hearty benisons I gie
To ilk bauld son o' Bon-Accord,
   Wha wishes still his streamlets free.[55]

The poem deploys the standard tropes of nostalgic pastoral: the recollection of innocent childhood pleasures, the larks and wild flowers of the countryside, the poet wandering by a stream, and above all the sense of change and loss from what once was. But here the loss is far from safely located in a vague past. As any reader of the *Herald* would have known, the 'Seaton Vale' reference alludes to Lord James Hay shutting off a riverside path by the Don that ran through his estate, because it had enabled workers to be seen 'strolling on the river bank, within a few yards of the drawing-room windows of Seaton House'.[56] 'My Native Streams' appeared on page 4 of the 9 October *Herald*, and on page 1, the paper advertised 'A meeting of the inhabitants of Aberdeen and Neighbourhood' in the Mechanics' Hall, 'to take into consideration the propriety of forming an Association for Protecting the Rights of the Public Against the Encroachments of Private Individuals, on Roads, Pathways, and Other Public Property'. The reason for this meeting is not given in the advertisement or anywhere else in this edition, but it *is* given in the poetry column. It is Anderson's poem that presents the case against Seaton that Adam, editor of the *Herald*, and the proposer of the motion to form such a society, wishes to make. We might note especially how Anderson's appeal to sentimental tradition, in referencing the 'ancient' road of 'our fathers' and in the reference to kirk and fair, actually makes the legal point that the path has been in use to travel between public places for over forty years. The last four lines of the poem, unlike the careful language of the advertisement, incite resistance to Hay—in the first case, by attending the advertised meeting.

The *Aberdeen Herald* reported on the Don case, and other related disputes (including the Glen Tilt case and another dispute about the banks of the Clyde), throughout 1847 and 1848, supported by at least one further poem by a close friend and poetic collaborator of Anderson's, factory worker William Cadenhead.

---

[55] W. A., 'My Native Streams', *Aberdeen Herald*, 9 October 1847, p.4.
[56] See letter from Hay's representatives, *Aberdeen Herald*, 12 February 1848, p.1. The Hay case of 1849 became a famous test case for public access to land, and its loss 'hampered the efforts of campaigners...for a century and a half'. Andrea Loux Jarman, 'Urban Commons: From Customary Use to Community Right on Scotland's Bleaching Greens', in Andrew Lewis, Paul Brand and Paul Mitchell, eds., *Law in the City: Proceedings of the Seventeenth British Legal History Conference* (Dublin: Four Courts, 2007), pp.319–45, 341.

Cadenhead's 'Right of Way to the Braes of Don', 'Inscribed to the Working Men of Aberdeen', is a plea for funds:

> Must we be penn'd to narrow paths, close lined by lofty walls
> Where the same eternal sunshine glares, or ceaseless shadow falls
> Must we be penn'd to narrow paths, where never floweret grew
> Or even a slender blade of grass inhaled the evening dew?
> Where never hath a bluebell sprung, or yellow primrose grown
> Where many a fragrant bank and brae we once could call our own!
> Must we forget the loving thoughts that speak from tinted blooms?
> Must we renounce the memories sweet that rise from bland perfumes?
> The violet and the primrose and the 'craw-flower's early bell'
> And the 'modest, crimson-tipped flower' that Burns hath sung so well!
> Must we renounce our joy in these, and in a long-loved scene
> Because a lordling hath enclosed their charms in his demesne – [57]

Cadenhead's unusually long lines for a newspaper poem (with seven beats rather than the common four or three) might exemplify the rejection of 'narrow paths' that he twice emphasizes in this extract. Enclosed couplets also speak to this sense of containment and limitation. His highly allusive poem references two works that most Scottish working-class readers would know: Tannahill's 'Gloomy Winter's Now Awa'' ('Sweet the crawflowr's early bell/Decks Gleniffer's dewy dell'), a poem that celebrates straying over the braes with a lover, and Burns's 'To a Daisy'.[58] In doing so he points out the importance of nature not simply in refreshing and purifying suffering workers, but in sustaining a working-class Scottish literary tradition. As a biography of Cadenhead observes, the Braes of Don were 'the scene of his youthful poem, and the spot where, on many a summer evening, he had charmed his admiring shopmates with a recital of its various parts then in manuscript'.[59] Such sites, this implies, are locations for poetic community and poetic composition, as well as individual inspiration.

Poems about rights of way, as Cadenhead's allusions make clear, are thus also concerned with poetic rights. One of the most common similes for the working-class poet is the poacher, invading territory that is not his (or her) own.[60] John Younger wrote in his autobiography:

> The actors in my condition of life, who feel their state, and, self-taught or inspired, attempt to describe what they feel, are neglected, or instantly borne down by the plodding reviewer of the day, who, like my lord's gamekeeper, must do his duty in strapping off the unlicensed vulgar as poachers on the assumed manor of this same classical community.[61]

---

[57] William Cadenhead, 'Right of Way to the Braes of Don', in *Flights of Fancy and Lays of Bon-Accord* (Aberdeen: A. Brown, 1853), pp.54, 55. First published in the *Aberdeen Herald*, 14 August 1847.

[58] Robert Tannahill, in *Poems and Songs, Chiefly in the Scottish Dialect*, 4th edn (London: Longman, 1817), p.193.

[59] William Walker, *The Bards of Bon-Accord, 1375–1860* (Aberdeen: Edmond & Spark, 1887), p.528.

[60] For example Philip Connell, a 'self-taught peasant', originally from Gaelic speaking Ireland, published a collection titled *Poaching on Parnassus* (Manchester: John Heywood, 1865).

[61] Younger, p.xxi.

Younger, who also wrote a book on angling, was equally concerned with the status of literal poachers, and included a bitter wish that in heaven, Scottish rivers and streams 'will not be patched and parcelled out in pools and streams amongst a very few exclusives—assumptive, selfish, gripping, and despicable'.[62] Because rivers, streams and glens are sites of poetic production, their enclosure damages the people's right to participate in an aesthetics of pastoral shaped by a proud labouring-class poetic tradition. The loss of the ability to stray through Scotland's countryside is also a loss of Scotland's cultural heritage, in removing the connections that contemporary poets and readers can make to that heritage, and in denying them the same streams and fountains of inspiration—literal as well as metaphorical—that their predecessors could access. If Burns and Tannahill had not been able to wander by the banks of Doon and down Gleniffer Braes, if they had instead been pent up in city factories, how could they have made a lasting contribution to Scotland's literature? Working-class poets were, after all, frequently urged to study nature and describe the scenery that surrounded them. The argument about rights of way, as Miller wrote, thus involves 'Not merely the rights of the poor man, but the privileges of the man of literature'.[63] In defending these privileges, poets conveyed their argument about the ownership of Scottish literature, as well as Scottish land, through generic choices, not simply through content. Just as a right of way is established by constant use, so the repeated tropes of nostalgic pastoral, its embrace of cliché at the level of both form (the ever-recurring rhyme of 'stray' and 'away', for instance) and content, should be read not as careless or poor writing, but as a deliberate effort to keep a well-trodden poetic right of way open for Victorian working-class writers.

IMPROVING THE LAND

Nostalgic pastoral by Victorian working-class writers is always conscious of the changes caused by modernity, and it operated in publishing contexts where the reading community was expected to know about the specific changes that had occurred to the local scenes described. As in the submerged allusions of pastoral poems to rights of way disputes, local allusions to the effects of population growth and industrialization are not always readily visible to the twenty-first-century reader. Carnegie's 'Brothock Water', cited above, is a good example. As is standard of native stream poems, after celebrating the pleasures he has enjoyed by this Arbroath stream in the past, he comments that these are 'joys I never maur see', that 'naught noo remains', and all is 'sadly changed'.[64] This is entirely typical of the genre, in which such phrases often indicate the poet's real or imagined departure from a childhood location to another region or country. In the case of the Brothock, though, the change mourned by the poem is not a change in the situation of the

---

[62] Ibid., p.433.   [63] Miller, *Essays*, pp.129–30.   [64] Carnegie, p.60.

poet, but in the stream itself. This is nowhere evident in Carnegie's 'Brothock Water'. It is, however, clear from another contemporary poem by an Arbroath poet, G. W. Donald (keeper of Arbroath Abbey grounds and a *People's Journal* contributor), 'Lament o' Brothock Water', which opens:

> An' ye ca' me noo a loathsome thing,
>   The source o' muckle dool,   *dool – grief, suffering*
> Whaur Death aft dips his murky wing,
>   An' hovers ower the pool.

No longer the crystal stream of celebratory pastoral, the Brothock is polluted, dirty and, in the light of a new scientific understanding of diseases spread by water, blamed for illness in its town. But this, the stream explains, is not its fault but the consequence of the perversion of its nature by man:

> But gie nae me the wyte o' this,   *wyte – blame, guilt*
>   As wyte there sure maun be
> I'm tortured till I feam an' hiss,
>   When fain I would be free.
>
> Wi' bolts o' airn ye bend my soles,
>   An' when ye let me rin,
> I'm crushed sae sair thro' your drearie holes,
>   I roar an' make a din.[65]

In the period when Donald and Carnegie were writing, Arbroath had been transformed from a small, prosperous fishing town to an industrial powerhouse. Over thirty mills, weaving shops and ropeworks drew power from the Brothock, and these brought with them new housing and a new town layout which built over parts of the stream. The suffering stream becomes a symbol for the sufferings wrought by industrial 'improvement'. By giving the stream a voice, as was a common and long-standing device in complaint poems spoken by landscapes or animals, Donald heightens the comparison between stream and poet. Men also, as the next chapter discusses more fully, are crushed, trapped, and tortured by the requirements of industry into unnatural positions. What should be a native stream poem, in the tradition of rural Scottish idylls, is transformed into an activist, even environmentalist, work. And crucially, *both* poems are contributing to this debate. That we cannot see the political resonances of Carnegie's poem as easily as those of Donald's is because of our removal from its historical and geographical reading contexts, rather than a function of the poem itself.

The tradition of lamenting changes to the British landscape in poetry and debating whether such changes constituted genuine 'improvement', was of course far from new: as noted above, critics have extensively discussed this genre in eighteenth- and nineteenth-century poetry. For Victorian Scottish poets, a key text on

---

[65] G. W. Donald, *The Muckle Skeel, and Other Poems* (Dundee: Lawson Brothers, 1870), pp.34–5. I have not examined the local Arbroath press, but it is not impossible that like the 'Muir of Alyth' poems discussed below, Carnegie and Donald's poems were directly in dialogue with each other.

industrial improvements was Thomas Campbell's 'Lines on Revisiting a Scottish River', which opens:

> And call they this Improvement? – to have changed,
> My native Clyde, thy once romantic shore,
> Where Nature's face is banish'd and estranged,
> And Heaven reflected in thy wave no more;
> Whose banks, that sweeten'd May-day's breath before,
> Lie sere and leafless now in summer's beam,
> With sooty exhalations cover'd o'er;
> And for the daisied green-sward, down thy stream
> Unsightly brick-lanes smoke, and clanking engines gleam.[66]

Many areas in Scotland were, of course, experiencing more rapid transformation into industrial regions than anywhere else in Britain. This gives a sharp edge to such environmentalist poetry set in industrial Scotland. Not only was the land-scape of Scotland being fenced off from the poor by landowners, poets argued, its beauty was in the process of being destroyed. A great many working poets follow Campbell's lead in adopting straightforward positions of dismay and regret at the destruction of pastoral scenes through modern developments. In Allan Park Paton's 'The Road Round by Kennedy's Mill':

> The steam carriage now rushes angrily o'er
> The fields, where in youth's golden hours I have rang'd;
> The streams where I tracked my flag-boats are no more,
> And the dells where I lay reading ballads are changed.[67]

Again, the pastoral landscape is associated with the reading and writing of Scottish literature. Paton's 'angrily' displaces the poet's anger at this loss to the machinery that has caused it. 'The Road Round by Kennedy's Mill' first appeared in the *Greenock Advertiser* under the pseudonym 'Heather'. No less a poet than E.B.B praised these verses 'as being of a nature far above their newspaper sphere', in her short correspondence with Paton—a Greenock librarian, and another *Whistle-Binkie* contributor—in this year.[68] In another example, Ayrshire poet Lizzie Ramsay's 'Lagg Hill Improvements', like Campbell, calls into question the discourse of 'improvement' itself:

> Dear me! What sight is this I see,
> As I look out what meets my e'e!
> A score o' men wi' picks and shools
> Howking and wheeling awa' the mools.   *mools – broken soil (mould)*
> My heart is wae when I look oot –
> There's nae improvement there, I doot.[69]

[66] Thomas Campbell, *The Poetical Works of Thomas Campbell* (London: Edward Moxon, 1837), p.212.

[67] Allan Park Paton, *Poems* (London: Saunders and Otley, 1845), p.79. Originally in the *Greenock Advertiser*, 16 May 1845 (as 'Heather').

[68] EBB to Allan Park Paton, *The Brownings' Correspondence*, ed. Philip Kelly and Ronald Hudson (Winfield, KA: Wedgestone Press, 1992), 10, pp.244–6.

[69] Elizabeth Ramsay, *A Garland of Verse, with Prose Writings*. 2nd edn, enlarged (Glasgow: Bell & Bain, 1914), p.43. Internal evidence suggests that most of Ramsay's poems appeared in the Ayrshire press from the 1870s–1890s.

By presenting herself as directly affected by changes she can witness through the window of her cottage, and by writing in a deliberately colloquial Scots, Ramsay emphasizes the affect created by a continuous history of attachment to a now-changed locality. Unlike the cosmopolitan Campbell, who is passing through Glasgow, she and other working poets directly and daily experience the consequences of improvement.

Factory worker Colin Sievwright's 'The Rocking Stones', published in the *Weekly News* in July 1868, is another fine instance of a poem that argues that not only the landscape itself, but also the (literary) history and heritage associated with it, is threatened by improvement. 'The Rocking Stones' opens as a tourist poem. The poet invites the 'gentle reader of the *Weekly News*' to take a trip by rail with him to Kirriemuir and climb the nearby hill, familiar from Sievwright's childhood and 'Once the Parnassus of your humble bard'. This is also poetic tourism in another sense—they seek the Rocking Stones, witnesses to a heroic imagined Scotland, 'When Fingal fought, and Ossian's song was heard,/Resounding through the trackless forests'. But all is changed:

> But though we find the sacred spot, alas!
>   The rocking stones are now departed thence;
> The muir that held them is a field of grass,
>   And they are built into a farmer's fence –
>
> A great improvement, we might surely own;
>   Yet relics such as these might have been spared.[70]

Sievwright's poem highlights the irony of improvement. The railway enables him to visit the key landscapes of his youth with ease, yet the broader improvement signalled by the railway means that those landscapes themselves are forever altered. For Sievwright, the fate of the stones signals Scotland's 'shame', her descent from a wild, free country filled with 'hardy sons' and 'good and fair' women, to a landscape marked by 'the *Bothy* and the *Spinning Mill*' as sites of degradation and enslavement of both countryside and people.

Sievwright's 'improvement', like Campbell's and Ramsay's, is used bitterly. For many working-class writers, however, the changes to Scottish landscapes, waterways and towns were not necessarily negative. MacDonald cites Campbell's poem critically in *Rambles Round Glasgow*, commenting, 'The splendid discoveries of a Watt, or the ingenious application of these discoveries to the propulsion of vessels by Bell, were nothing in his eyes to the preservation of a flowery bank'. In contrast, he argues, Burns was in favour of 'improvement', and 'well knew that the right onward furrow of utility was not to be interrupted by a sickly sentimentality'.[71] Those who espoused progressive politics (and it is worth noting that Sievwright, unusually, was strongly Tory in loyalty) also ought to support Scotland's progress in the vanguard of industrial nations, with no room for sentimentality about the changes this wrought in town and country. Hartley, for example, fiercely defended traditional rights of way and wild Scottish landscapes in 'The Right of Way', positioning herself against change. But in her 'The Auld Town of Dumbarton's Address

---

[70] *Weekly News*, 18 July 1868, p.4.   [71] MacDonald, pp.230, 232.

to Helenslee, Residence of P. Denny, Esq', the town reluctantly acknowledges the benefits brought by the growth of local entrepreneur Denny's shipbuilding industry:

> Tho' I'm no' just like what I was,
>   I'm maybe just as weel.
> I'd hae nae railroad noo tae boast,
>   If I'd been left the same;
> Nae printin'-press, or newspaper,
>   Tae celebrate my name,
>   Frae day tae day.[72]

In using the stanzaic form known to Victorian poets from Burns's 'Holy Fair', Hartley links her poem to the 'improving' Burns identified by MacDonald. The poem implicitly points out that its own existence, as a newspaper poem, is due to developments in the technology of printing. Industry grows towns, which creates a market for a local newspaper, which in turn creates a market for poetry.

John Palmer, an Annan poet associated with the *Dumfries and Galloway Courier*, is one of the most vehement and interesting poetic supporters of agricultural improvement; not surprisingly, since after a career as a herd laddie, factory worker, and travelling agent for a bookseller, he settled down to develop land in Annan into a nursery that became famous for its rose varieties. As an elegy in the *Annan Observer* comments:

> His skilful hand, on progress bent,
> Raised on the Moor his monument,
> Where roses, tint with heavenly dyes,
> Seem all too fair for mortal's eyes.[73]

Palmer wrote poems in praise of the wonders of 'new manure' and fertilizer— including the excellent 'The Rash Buss', a poem spoken by a clump of marsh rushes facing extermination—and of new agricultural equipment. 'Song of the Deanston Plough', for instance, celebrates the subsoil plough invented by James Smith of Deanston, author of the influential pamphlet, *Remarks on Thorough Draining and Deep Ploughing* (1831), a work Palmer undoubtedly knew. The plough advises readers of the *Courier*:

> Then drain! oh, drain! – oh, most thoroughly drain
> Every wet acre of Britain's domain!
> With team of power, then how bold and free
> I will stir the earth, *as it stirr'd should be*,
> Where air and moisture may circulate through –
> Then mark the effects of the Deanston plough![74]

---

[72] Hartley, p.34.

[73] Jane M. Cuthbertson, 'The Late Mr John Palmer', *Annan Observer* and *Annandale Advertiser*, 20 October 1870.

[74] John Palmer, Annan, 'Song of the Deanston Plough', *Dumfries and Galloway Courier*, 1 September 1845, p.2. The poem was also republished in the *Dundee Courier*, 9 September 1845, p.3.

Poems offering advice on agricultural improvements, in a georgic mode, were the inheritors of a prominent georgic tradition in eighteenth-century literature. This genre, as David Fairer notes, displays a 'fascination with mastering nature and exploiting the earth's resources for human ends' and is often characterized by 'practicality':

> Attentiveness to detail, often of the most mundane kind, is a feature of the unprepossessing quality of some georgic poetry, in which there is little that is incidental or merely atmospheric in the descriptions. It is often in that sense a working language, where words justify themselves by the practical job they do, by their exactness of reference.[75]

Palmer's poems are precisely in this mode, and his working verse additionally espouses deliberate practicality because it supplies immediately topical advice in a local newspaper aimed at a farming community. 'Song of the Deanston Plough' appeared on 1 September 1845, at the conclusion of a successful harvest season, and just over a month before Smith of Deanston was a key speaker at the Dumfries Exhibition of the Royal and Highland Agricultural Society of Scotland. Not only did the *Courier* report Smith's speech on soils and drainage word for word, it also reflected on the ploughing exhibition that 'wherever till or clay lurks at bottom, our own opinion is that the sturdy Deanston subsoiler should be used in preference to every other instrument'.[76]

Palmer's poem is an advertisement for the superiority of Scottish agricultural inventions over any others, and an advert for his own agricultural knowledge and experience—the expert knowledge that a successful nurseryman as well as farmer might require. Moreover, it is part of a clear effort by the *Courier* and its well-known liberal and reformist editor, John M'Diarmid, to promote Dumfries and environs as an improved and improving region. 'Wonders Achievable By Skilful Cultivation', one week prior to the publication of 'Song of the Deanston Plough', typically discusses how a Mr Jardine has 'revolutionized' the wild by turning a field 'of a moorish character, a stranger to the plough in the memory of man', into a productive oatfield, thus setting an example to 'the rural public at large, enterprising enough to go and do likewise'.[77] Several months earlier, at a local dinner attended by M'Diarmid, a speaker was greeted with 'repeated bursts of cheering' when he stated that:

> Of all the changes I have observed in the neighbourhood of Sanquhar, none have given me more satisfaction than the marked improvement of agriculture, and the improved condition of the tillers of the soil.[78]

---

[75] David Fairer, '"Where Fuming Trees Refresh the Thirsty Air": The World of Eco-Georgic', *Studies in Eighteenth-Century Culture* 40 (2011), 291–18, 203, 212, 205.

[76] *Dumfries and Galloway Courier*, 9 October 1845, p.2.

[77] *Dumfries and Galloway Courier*, 25 August 1845, p.4.

[78] 'Public Dinner and Presentation of Plate', *Dumfries and Galloway Courier*, 23 April 1845, p.2.

Of course, a local citizen, like Palmer, who rises from herd boy to successful businessman and eventually Provost of his town, *and* who has the culture and skill to write poems, is another example of regional improvement. Contemporaries frequently linked agricultural and mental improvement through language and imagery: a magazine produced by a group of 'mutual instruction' clubs in the north, for instance, followed its opening article on 'Self-Instruction' and the need to cultivate 'intellectual soil' with an article on 'The Advantages of Draining'.[79]

Palmer stands out from his peers because he is unequivocally in favour of the enclosure of wild land, and its transformation into productive land through drainage and cultivation. His poems consciously resist any hint of nostalgia. 'Address to Davy Drummond', in which the addressee is a tree supposedly planted 150 years ago by Drummond, defiantly praises the appropriation of common land for farmland:

> In your young days ye lookit o'er
> Nocht but a dreary barren moor –
> Nae house, nae hedge, – wild, rouch, an' poor,   *rouch – rough*
>   Wi' scarce a bound,
> Whare every body's beast micht scour
>   Ower common ground.[80]

Now, in sharp contrast, 'ye look ower a kintraside/ O' smiling fields'. The clearly regulated form of the habbie stanza here seems particularly appropriate for a poem about the value of boundaries and fences. Palmer's poems are markedly unsympathetic to the attitudes expressed elsewhere in the Scottish press opposing enclosure of common land. Most striking in his repeated championing of improvement are his three 'Lochar Moss' poems. Spoken by the Moss itself, these are pleas to invest in draining the Moss, a large area between Dumfries and the sea, for agricultural purposes, unashamedly couched in terms of profit:

> Shares in ships, canals, an' railways
>   Aft in disappointment en'
> As for me, depend I'll always
>   Gi'e a swingin' dividend.[81]

Published from 1846 to 1849, these poems repeatedly remind readers of the *Courier*, via detailed footnotes, that new techniques for draining moss land have been recently developed, citing names, dates, and the author's own experience of inspecting the newly drained land. They therefore again support the editorial stance of the *Courier*, which urged readers to take advantage of the new legislation

---

[79] The *Rural Echo*, and *Magazine of the North of Scotland Mutual Instruction Associations*. Conducted by the Lentush Club (Aberdeen: Lewis Smith; Lentush: James Robertson, 1850), 1 February 1850, pp.1, 3.

[80] John Palmer, *Poems and Songs* (n.pub, n.d [1871]), p.53.

[81] 'Complaint of Lochar Moss', *Dumfries and Galloway Courier*, 18 August 1849, p.2. *Poems and Songs*, p.115.

on drainage and repeatedly brought up the local issue of Lochar Moss, that 'disgrace to the county'.[82] As Palmer's Moss puts it:

> Must I lie a black, unsichtly,
>   Wet and wild neglected thing?
> Cultured, I wad shine fu' brichtly;
>   Gowd in gowpens I wad bring.[83]   *'gowd in gowpens' – double handfuls of gold*

One of the fascinating contexts to Palmer's poems is the knowledge that Lochar Moss *had* delivered 'gold', in another sense. Palmer must have known about the discovery of a unique Early Iron Age 'Celtic' torc and collar there a few years prior to his poem, particularly since in May 1846, three months before his first plea, they were put on display in the British Museum. Unlike Sievwright's lament for the destruction of Scotland's Celtic, druidical past, however, Palmer's poems have little interest in the value of land for its historical associations or its beauty; what matters is its use-value for the present. A Celtic torc in the British Museum does not benefit the people of Dumfries.

Palmer's 'Wet and wild neglected thing' is the diametric opposite of Hopkins at Inversnaid, and his famous cry, 'O let them be left, wildness and wet,/ Long live the weeds and the wilderness yet'; an attitude, Palmer and others' poems suggest, easier to live with as a better-off tourist.[84] Surely, the land of Scotland, if it could speak, would choose to benefit the people who live on it in material, not in aesthetic, terms? The Moss is desperate to promote its ability to become 'cultured' to developers:

> I, Lochar Moss, do humbly pray
> That engineers may me survey,
> My capabilities report
> Then men of capital exhort
>
> **
>
> Say that the rail will traverse o'er me;
> Say that the sea lies just before me;
> That lime and coal are cheap and good,
> Manures may come by land or flood;
> The best of markets I'll command
> For Liverpool is just at hand[85]

That the Moss can adopt either homely Scots for its appeal, or business English, is already a sign of its culture. Such poems also invite readers to connect the culture

---

[82] 'The Drainage Act', *Dumfries and Galloway Courier*, 28 December 1846, p.4. See also letter on 'Cultivation of Waste Lands', 12 October 1847, p.3 and 'Rural Affairs', 18 April 1848, p.4, in the same issue as Palmer's second poem.
[83] 'Second Humble Petition of Lochar Moss', *Dumfries and Galloway Courier*, 18 April 1848, p.2. *Poems and Songs*, p.112.
[84] 'Inversnaid', l.13–14, in Gerard Hopkins, *Gerard Manley Hopkins: The Major Works*, ed. Catherine Phillips (Oxford: Oxford University Press, 2009).
[85] 'The Humble Petition of Lochar Moss', *Poems and Songs*, pp.110–11.

of 'neglected' land, and the culture of the local poor, a link particularly evident in Palmer's case because he produced contemporary activist poems about the repeated failure to pass a Scottish Education Act, thus arguing for the simultaneous improvement of the land and people of Scotland.

Palmer's sequence predates the similar 'Muir of Alyth' poems, which appeared in 1858 in the newly established Dundee, Perth, and Forfar *People's Journal*, and helped to set its poetic and political tone for the coming years. These three poems, all written in Scots and in habbie stanzas, clearly relate to the division of the South Commonty of Alyth 'after eighty years of legal wrangling' in 1858, and to the permission to build a railway link connecting to Alyth, which was granted in the same year.[86] In the opening poem, signed 'The Muir', the muir, about to be drained, used as a water supply ('drawin' my water frae me there') and built upon, laments its fate:

> Nae mair wi' bonny blooms I'm drest
> > In blythesome Spring –
> For hooses noo they think I'm best,
> > Or some sic thing.
>
> Nae mair, when ends the Autumn days
> > The laddies rin to licht the blaze,
> On stane an' lime they noo maun gaze
> > Instead o'whins,
> An' ower the ance broom covered braes
> > The street noo rins.
>
> Nae mair my birns shall eldin gie   *birns – heather-stems; eldin – fuel*
> > Tae them wha haena cash tae pay
> For sticks to licht their firies wi'
> > To stand Cauld's shock;
> Nae mair my grass shall pasture gie
> > To passin' flock.[87]

Far from being valueless land, this poem argues, the moor supplies firewood and grazing to the poorest members of society, besides its importance as a place for play and for traditional community pursuits such as curling. In a response poem by 'Trebor', 'Consolation to the Muir of Alyth', published only one week later, however, the author consoles the moor by offering an alternative portrayal of an improved future:

> They'll rid ye o' yer tatter'd claes,
> Yer whin an' broom, an' bogs an' braes,
> An' dress ye up, frae tap to taes,
> > In verdure green,

---

[86] Wightman, *The Poor Had No Lawyers: Who Owns Scotland (and How They Got It)* (Edinburgh: Birlinn, 2011), p.305.

[87] 'The Muir', 'Complaint and Petition of the Muir of Alyth', *People's Journal*, 23 January 1858, p.2. I discuss these poems briefly in 'A Very Unpoetical Town', pp.103–5, and they are reprinted in *The Poets of the People's Journal* (Glasgow: ASLS, 2016), pp.3–8.

And then ye'll bless the navvies' days –
               That will be seen.
And when yer dress'd and made afield,
An' stappit fu' o' seed an' dreel'd,
Ye'll gladden mony a cozie bield   *bield – shelter*
               Wi' milk an' meal,
An' pack the wymes o mony a chield   *wyme – stomach*
               Wi' spuds an' kale![88]

Making specific reference to the economic downturn of 1857–8 and the 'ruin' it threatened, Trebor points out that not only will the regeneration of the Muir offer employment to labouring men, it will also help to feed and house the poor. Nostalgia for the past is misplaced. The Muir needs to be transformed from the persona of a shabby, 'tatter'd' vagrant into a respectable, fertile, well-dressed Victorian. (There are no explicit references to moors as feminine in any of these poems, but the gendering is arguably implicit, and there are certainly hints of sexual innuendo in Trebor's 'stappit fu' o' seed'). In the final poem, responding to Trebor, the Muir compromises. Yes, she acknowledges, the use of her land for houses for local workers is justifiable and can be supported. But there is a new risk, that the railway will enable workers from Dundee to move into the town, or well-off families to commute, and that the new-build homes will go to them:

But I had heard, an' think it's true,
A Railway's to be brought tae you;
"An', then," I says, "am thinkin' noo
               'Twill be a case,
They'll hooses big for Dundee crew,   *big – build*
               An' me disgrace!"

An', thinkin' sae, I almost grat,   *grat – wept*
But noo I houp you'll no do that;
An' when ye ha'e some hooses gat
               Upon my soil,
You'll lat the puir man's parritch pat
               In them aye boil![89]

Whether these three poems were really written by more than one author is impossible to discern, and they are certainly suspiciously similar in style. What is important is that they work through the varying positions on improvement described above, presenting an anti-improvement, pastoral Paradise Lost poem; a pro-improvement poem; and a compromise position with radical political overtones, in which the division and reworking of common land is only defensible when it benefits the local community and its needy citizens. In publishing this set of poems in the first month of its existence, the *People's Journal* also established its own agreement with a stance that put the rights and needs of working people above other considerations, as well as displaying its willingness to host debate

[88] Trebor, 'Consolation to the Muir of Alyth', *People's Journal*, 30 January 1858, p.2.
[89] 'The Muir', 'Eik to Petition of the Muir of Alyth', *People's Journal*, 27 February 1858, p.2.

between working men and to include diverse perspectives on the same issue. In other words, it marked itself as a newspaper dedicated to improvement, and as an improvement on previous papers aimed at working-class readers, through the publication of poetry that took the improvement of Scotland as its subject.

LAND, LIBERTY, AND EMIGRANT POETICS

These questions about improvement, and about the relationship of the working poor to the land of Scotland, were important far beyond Scotland itself, because of their ramifications in the debate over emigration. As Marjory Harper notes, in the long nineteenth century emigration was 'an essential part of the fabric of Scottish life, and a commonplace device for self-improvement, to a much greater extent than south of the border'.[90] In the decades around mid-century, one of the key issues in this debate—as Ainslie's poems make clear—was whether working people would find a better life in Australia, New Zealand, Canada, South Africa, and the United States because they would be able to own and work their land. The pastoral vision in which British emigrants find health and liberty farming in the backwoods of the colonies, as popularized in the happy ending of Victorian texts such as Elizabeth Gaskell's *Mary Barton* (1848) and Arthur Hugh Clough's *The Bothie of Tober-na-Vuolich* (1848), is very strong in emigrant poetics. So, however, is a counter-narrative of homesickness and struggle, in which the link with Scotland created by poetry sent back to the local press is imagined as sustaining the poet in exile.

As Rudy notes in his important new study of settler poetry, emigrant song and poetry has not been highly regarded by those few critics who assess it. It has usually been perceived as unashamedly steeped in nostalgia and in stock tropes. Edward Cowan, for example, sees the emigrant poetry tradition as 'maudlin indulgence', mostly consisting of 'lamentable and sentimental poems or songs in the Doric, often composed by people who had never set foot in Scotland, but who none the less felt compelled to eulogize the "auld hame"'.[91] The question as to *why* so many poets—including not only those who had never set foot in Scotland, but those who had never set foot *outside* Scotland—composed such poems, and why the Scottish press was so invested in them, has seldom been considered. Emigrant poems and songs in the nostalgic pastoral genre had an important role in sustaining ethnic identity in diasporic communities, perhaps particularly so in that they bridge the divide between private expressions of such identity and 'organized'

---

[90] Marjory Harper, *Adventurers and Exiles: The Great Scottish Exodus* (London: Profile, 2003), p.3.

[91] Rudy, Imagined Homelands, *passim*. Edward J. Cowan, 'From the Southern Uplands to Southern Ontario: Nineteenth-Century Emigration from the Scottish Borders', in T. M. Devine, ed., *Scottish Emigration and Scottish Society* (Edinburgh: John Donald, 1992), pp.61–83, 75. Cowan makes the same case in 'The Myth of Scotch Canada', noting the huge number of Canadian Scottish poets, but characterizing most of their works as 'dismal sentimental effusions'. In Marjory Harper and Michael E. Vance, eds., *Myth, Migration and the Making of Memory: Scotia and Nova Scotia c. 1700–1990* (Edinburgh: John Donald, 1999), pp.49–72, 63. See also Riach, 'Heather and Fern'.

expressions, such as this St Andrew's and other societies studied by Tanja Bueltmann, 'which operate, at least partially, in the public sphere'. Bueltmann's important study is concerned with recovering the 'potential instrumental value' of 'homeland culture' for migrants.[92] What I consider in this brief discussion is the instrumental value of Scotland's land, as imagined by migrants in poetry and song in the nostalgic pastoral mode.

The local press in Victorian Scotland frequently published poems apparently sent in by overseas readers, and Scottish papers circulated widely in the colonies, either via subscription or because relatives in Scotland posted their copies. Newspapers were keen to advertise that their readership was global. The *People's Journal*, for example, published, amongst others, accounts from devoted Australian readers located in a Quarry Camp in Ballarat, Victoria, and in Gundaroo, New South Wales. This last account specifically asked that the deadlines for the *People's Journal*'s famous Christmas literary competitions be set earlier so that colonial readers could enter.[93] When the *People's Journal* editorial and letters pages became preoccupied in spring and summer 1867 with an intense debate about the conditions for emigrants in New Zealand, authorities in New Zealand were so alarmed that they entered the debate themselves, publishing a letter in the *Journal* and discussing its stance in the major New Zealand papers; these discussions were then themselves reprinted in the *Journal*.[94] Poems published in the provincial Scottish press, from writers identifying themselves as located in the colonies, therefore speak to a dual community: Scots at home, and the emerging diasporic Scottish community. Many were also either first published or republished in the colonial press. John Barr's 'There's Nae Place Like Otago Yet', discussed in detail by Rudy, is a key example.[95] Whether they clearly display their intentions or not, such poems inevitably engage with the question of whether emigrants will be better off in a new land than they could ever be in 'auld mither Scotland'.

Emigrant poems are particularly invested in the nostalgic pastoral trope of wandering in Scotland's wilderness, with the loss of this freedom now symbolized by reluctant, or indeed forced, removal to another land. Gaelic emigrant poetry of the period, though outside the scope of this chapter, is of course particularly concerned with the Highland Clearances, while many if not most English and Scots poems emphasize the broader attitudes of landowners and employers towards workers and the hard economic conditions of life in modern Scotland as reasons to

---

[92] Tanja Bueltmann, *Clubbing Together: Ethnicity, Civility and Formal Sociability in the Scottish Diaspora to 1930* (Liverpool: Liverpool University Press, 2014), p.9.

[93] See 'Bodkin at the Diggings' (13 Oct 1866, p.2); 'From an Australian Correspondent' (9 June 1866, p.2); 'To Correspondents' (5 March 1870, p.2).

[94] See, for example, John Rogers, 'Advice to Intending Emigrants' (16 March 1867), p.2; Alex Rennie, 'Emigration to Otago' (6 April 1867), p.2; 'New Zealand as a Field for Emigration' (13 April 1867), p.2; 'A Friend to the Scotch Ploughman' (20 April 1867), p.2; 'New Zealand as a Field for Emigration' (Editorial, citing NZ papers, and letters) (31 August 1867), p.2; letter from 'A Cairnie Reader' (21 September 1867), p.2.

[95] See Rudy, pp.91–5.

emigrate.[96] One of the most highly influential poems and songs in this mode of loss and exile was Byron's 'Lachin Y Gair' or 'Dark Lochnagar':

> Yet, Caledonia! belov'd are thy mountains,
>   Round their white summits though elements war,
> Though cataracts foam, 'stead of smooth-flowing fountains,
>   I sigh, for the valley of dark Loch na Garr.
>
> Ah! there my young footsteps, in infancy, wander'd,
>   My cap was the bonnet, my cloak was the plaid;
> On chieftains, long perish'd, my memory ponder'd.
> As daily I strode through the pine-cover'd glade;[97]

Byron's lyrics, also widely circulated in variant versions in broadside form, describe exile to England in adulthood, setting an early example for poets of internal exile, and foster the associations between straying through Scottish scenery and the freedom of childhood, now lost in the constraints of adulthood. 'Dark Lochnagar' had many imitators. The *Aberdeen Herald*, for example, published 'Scotland – An Air of the Expatriated', to the tune 'Lochnagar', in 1849. The poem opens:

> I'm far frae my hame, in the climes of the stranger
> I'm far frae loved Scotland, the land of my birth –

But after establishing through the Scots that the speaker is a native, s/he then switches to standard English for the remainder of the poem, which concerns an imagined return to Scotland:

> I see loving faces, I hear charming voices,
>   With fond friends I wander by flower-fringed rills;
> At gay golden sunrise, my spirit rejoices
>   To gaze on thy green woods and bonnie blue hills![98]

The phrasing here, and techniques such as the almost over-the-top alliteration in line 2, are designed to fit with the very familiar 'Lochnagar' tune. As with all such lyrics, readers were expected to hear the tune in the act of reading. That the poem is signed 'A. H. – Huntly' (Huntly being a town in Aberdeenshire) again shows the extent to which authenticity can be irrelevant in the genre of the emigrant song, with the pose of missing Scotland from abroad as a recognized literary stance.

The *Herald* did also, however, publish various poems signed with overseas locations, such as 'On Receiving From Scotland a Withered "Forget-me-not"', by J. R., Sydney. Similarly, this poem laments the lost landscapes of Scotland, in very familiar terms, 'Thy mountains blue, whose lofty heads aspiring kiss the skies,/ And thy wild and deep romantic glens before me seem to rise'. Like A. H.,

---

[96] On Gaelic emigrant poetry see Margaret MacDonell, *The Emigrant Experience: Songs of Highland Emigrants in North America* (Toronto: University of Toronto Press, 1982) and Thomson pp.220–1.

[97] George Gordon Byron, *The Complete Poetical Works*, vol I, ed. Jerome J. McGann (Oxford: Clarendon Press, 1980), p.103. First published in Hours of Idleness (1806).

[98] A. H. Huntly, 'Scotland: A Song of the Expatriated (Air – Lochnagar)', *Aberdeen Herald*, 17 March 1849.

J. R. associates the loss of such scenery with the loss of community, as fond friends are scattered over the world:

> I miss them now, when wandering forth in this delightful isle
> Where the genial soft Australian sun makes every season smile;
> I miss them when my footsteps wend along the crowded street,
> Where not a friendly face appears a friendly face to greet.[99]

'On Receiving from Scotland' is more ambiguous than 'An Air of the Expatriated', because of this emphasis on the 'delightful' Australia and its beneficial climate. Although the writer gloomily concludes that emigration forces Scots to spend their lives 'midst scenes which serve to bind/ Our soaring spirits to the dust, and brutal-ize our minds', the picture painted of Australia is not unattractive. By publishing this poem, of course, the writer also indicates that *his* (or her) mind is not brutal-ized, as shown by the capacity for cultural production. Writing an emigrant poem *about* lost community is also a way of re-entering community, through the interaction of poet and readers in the newspaper column. Publishing a poem from Sydney in the Aberdeen press demonstrates, further, that the writer has retained emotional, material and cultural ties to home. 'To emigrate in the mid-Victorian period', Rudy notes, 'was to risk the loss of literary culture—which is to say the loss of British culture altogether'.[100] By placing themselves within an existing tradition of Scottish poetry and song, such poems reassure readers that this tradition is port-able property, while their appearance in the newspaper columns signals their role in 'a mass media era in which collective memory was based on imagined experience reaching across enormous territories'.[101]

These two poems typify the standard tropes of emigrant poetry and song and its focus on a sense of loss and nostalgia. Scotland's mountains and glens, visualized in the emigrant imagination, become a synecdoche for the people of Scotland. Location is unspecified: while readers of the *Herald* might be expected to picture the scenery around Aberdeen, these could be any Scottish landscapes, and the writer could be located in any distant land. Two key subgenres of emigrant poetry rework these standards, however. As in poems about improvement, one is pro-emigration, and one against; both use far more localized and seemingly genuine references to particular countries and issues in order to frame a case around agricultural opportunities for emigrants. On the anti-emigration side, poems by Will Harrow (the pseudonym of John Campbell, a radical Chartist poet from Stanley, Perth), supply a good example. In 1871, the *People's Journal* bade farewell to Harrow, a contributor to its poetry columns for over a decade, and wished him

---

[99] J. R. Sydney, 'On Receiving from Scotland a Withered "Forget-me-not"', *Aberdeen Herald*, 22 May 1841.

[100] Jason R. Rudy, 'Floating Worlds: Émigré Poetry and British Culture', *ELH* 81 (2014), 325–50, 331.

[101] Anne Rigney, *The Afterlives of Walter Scott: Memory on the Move* (Oxford: Oxford University Press, 2012), p.8. I borrow the term 'portable property' from John Plotz's study of the Victorian novel, *Portable Property: Victorian Culture on the Move* (Princeton, NJ: Princeton University Press, 2008), in which he describes portability as a mechanism 'for inserting local mementos into global circulation without detaching them from their original locale' (p.5).

'prosperity and length of days in the land of his adoption', while publishing a poem sent to the *Journal* from his ship to South Africa.[102] Distance was no barrier to Harrow's continued participation in the *People's Journal*'s poetic community, however, and during his years as an agricultural labourer in Cape Town he sent back several epistolary poems—addressed to the famous pseudonymous *Journal* contributors 'Tammas Bodkin' and 'Poute'—and letters in Scots about his negative experience of leaving Scotland. As is typical of Harrow's politically inclined poems, he emphasizes the effects of the economic problems of the 1860s on the poor. He emigrated not from choice, but from necessity:

> An' sae the wolf began to howl,
>   An' chased me far away;
> Far frae the braes o' sweet Strathmore,
>   An' flowery banks o' Tay;[103]

The memory of Scottish rivers has particular significance for Harrow because he locates himself in the African desert, 'There's no a runnin' river here/In a' this parched land'. Promises that South Africa would supply a rural idyll for the labourer have proved false:

> Frae Cape de Verd to Somali,
> Frae False Bay to Rosetta,
> There's nocht but rocks or blawin' sand;
> In course ye canna get a
> Decent rig o' corn land
> In a' that weary world o' sand;
> An' lookin' frae the heichest hill
> You'll scarcely see a trace
> Or touch o' Labour's golden hand
> Upon its ugly face.[104]

Scotland's braes and banks are not valued in this poem as wild places, but because they bear the traces of labour, including literary labour. Describing himself in a letter as 'out of society here as much as if I were in the great Sahara', Harrow's visions of a green, watery Scotland are also visions of re-entry into the poetic community he left behind, and which will help to provide the society of 'Labour' that he lacks.[105]

Readers following Harrow's career through the 1870s would have read of his return to Scotland near the end of the decade. His poems are, like many emigrant poems, laments for his absent homeland. Yet they are not the unfocused laments of J. R. from Sydney and his ilk, but specific warnings to labourers like him (he was

---

[102] '"Will Harrow" at the Cape of Good Hope', *People's Journal*, 30 September 1871, p.2. Campbell's life and works are discussed in J. Menzies Fergusson, *A Village Poet* (Paisley: Alexander Gardner, 1897).

[103] Will Harrow, Capetown, 'Epistle to Tammas Bodkin', *People's Journal*, 13 July 1872, p.2. Fergusson, p.166.

[104] 'Epistle from Will Harrow at Saat River, Capetown, to Poute, at Leven Saat Pans', *People's Journal*, 14 November 1874, p.2. Fergusson, pp.170–1.

[105] Fergusson, p.176n.

an expert with the spade) to avoid South Africa as a destination. Harrow's poems
are part of a *People's Journal* debate, carried on through poems, editorials and letters, about where and whether to emigrate. Representing emigration in far more
positive terms, for example, is 'Backwoodsman's' 'The Land That Rear'd Us A', a
Canadian emigrant poem with the subtitle 'Composed and Sung in a Backwoods
Shanty'. It opens with a picture of emigrants longing for Scotland, and then
describes in detail the hardships of labour, climate and diet in backwoods Canada:

> For there's nae heather on our hills
>   We're sax months i' the snaw:
> There's nought to see save muckle trees
>   Nor heard but "Gee! Wo! Haa!"

Halfway through (at stanza 5 out of 8), however, the poem changes tack:

> But we sit on our ain bit land
> Frae laird and factor free
>
> ***
>
> Nae sneakin' keeper spies around
>   To trap our cat or dog;
> We're everywhere as free as air
>   And happy o'er our grog.[106]

The author reminds Scottish readers that the land which reared them is not owned
by them, and that nostalgia for an imagined Scotland—as in Ainslie's poems—can
go hand in hand with satisfaction at having escaped the problems experienced by
working people in Scotland as it is. Still more striking is an epistolary address from
an Ontario emigrant, 'To the Farm Servants of Aberdeenshire' by 'An Aberdeenshire
Chiel", which directly critiques the ideology of a pious and content peasantry
promoted by Burns's revered 'The Cottar's Saturday Night':

> The picter o' a cottar's hame which Robbie Burns drew
> Is nae doot gran', but I ha'e seen few like it amang you.
> Of coorse it's doonricht heresy, or proves ye are a gowk,
> Gin ye'll nae tak' in a' he says aboot the cottar fowk.
> But for a' that, I'm unco sure that ye'll nae aften see
> Sic hame amang the cottar puir between the Don and Dee.
> Noo here ye soon may save eneuch to buy a bit o'lan',
> And then ye'll nae for ithers plough or be an orra' han.[107]   *orra – spare*

In the debates over rights of way, the literary construction and heritage of rural
Scotland was a powerful tool on the side of the people. Here, the writer implies that
this heritage is a drawback in impeding a clear-eyed view of Scotland's disadvantages.
Fantasies of peasant life cover up the truth about lack of rights to the land, a situation
that can best be remedied by rebuilding a Scots-speaking community in Canada.

---

[106] Backwoodsman, 'The Land that Rear'd Us A', *People's Journal*, 24 September 1870, p. 2.
[107] 'An Aberdeenshire Chiel', Toronto, 'To the Farm Servants of Aberdeenshire', *People's Journal*,
1 November 1871, p.2.

This poem, and those by Harrow and 'Backwoodsman', distinguish themselves from the 'Lochnagar' tradition by writing in colloquial Scots, and assume a working man's persona. Because the *Journal* only published pseudonymous poems if writers had also supplied a real name and address, the poems appeared to readers as genuine appeals from the people to the people. They are, though, also part of a concerted effort (and a lucrative industry) run by colonial administrations, emigration agents, steamship companies and other organizations to sell emigration to the Scottish people. Both pro-emigration poems appeared in the early 1870s, in years when the emigration debate (probably due to the lasting effect of the difficult economic conditions of the mid-1860s) was particularly acute. The ongoing disputes over land rights and rights of way, and related disputes about the difficult housing and working conditions of agricultural labourers, were powerful tools in convincing readers that freedom could be obtained overseas. A letter republished from the *Otago Daily Times* by a William Hay, for example, could confidently state that 'nowhere in Scotland, is the position of the working classes, in respect to independence, comfort, wages, food, clothing, and future prospects, on an equal footing with that of Otago or Australia'.[108] Andrew Orr's 'The Men of Australia', apparently sent from Ballarat to the *Airdrie Advertiser*, viewed Australia as 'leading the vanguard of freedom's battalion':

> The downtrodden slaves of the North-rolling waves
>   May boast of a freedom they never have tasted yet;
> If they saw us out here, in our manful career,
>   It would teach them the might of the power they have wasted yet.[109]

Orr's 'yet' is an awkward addition to his rollicking rhythms, but invites a stress because of his emphasis on futurity, on opportunities yet to be seized. The difference between such poems and the pro-improvement writings of Palmer and others, is that these emigrant poets argue that it is time to give up on pleading for Scotland's improvement at the hands of those in power, and become those who have the power to instigate improvements, whether in the backwoods of Canada or the wilds of New Zealand.

Pro-emigration poetry is a powerful discourse, which does not dismiss the concerns of nostalgia but points out its problems. So important was this discourse that the papers also published assorted poems mocking its assurances, for example 'Otago is a wonderous place' by 'Craigilee'. This comic poem contains seven stanzas of exaggerated praise of New Zealand and its opportunities for advancement:

> Our working-men keep carriages
>   To please their lady-loves
> Our ploughmen never go to work
>   Till they put on kid gloves.[110]

---

[108] *People's Journal*, 18 August 1866, p.2.

[109] Andrew Orr, Ballarat, 'The Men of Australia', *Airdrie Advertiser*, 20 August 1859, p.4.

[110] Untitled poem by Craigielea, dated 18 January 1871, *Tuapeka Times*, 9 February 1871, p.7. Copy available in the 'Papers Past' database: http://paperspast.natlib.govt.nz. (consulted 27 September 2018).

In concluding with a flourish that working men will be able to fish for salmon 'so large that one would think/Them very like a whale', the author implies, in a reference to Hamlet's fooling with Polonius, that this poem—and implicitly all those offering extreme praise of New Zealand—is an effort to fool readers. The poem appeared in at least one New Zealand paper, the *Tuapeka Times*, on 9 February 1871, with a headnote 'For the information of intending emigrants in England, Ireland and Scotland, more especially in that part of it called Aberdeen. "Home papers please copy."' By including this note, the author satirically signals that poems in praise of the colonies published in the colonial press always have a hidden ideological intent, since they can reasonably expect to be picked up by British papers. Their overtly intended audience is other residents of New Zealand, Australia, or (in Ainslie's case) the United States. But their implicitly intended audience is a readership of potential emigrants. In this case, the poem critiques the effort to entice emigrants to Otago with promises of 'a well-ordered Christian society...and an unambiguously Scottish culture'.[111] At least one paper in the north of Scotland, the *Invergordon Times*, did republish it.[112]

Emigrant poetry, like poems on rights of way and on improvement, is politically activist. It sets nostalgia to work. It does not unquestioningly buy into myths of a distant Scotland characterized by the rugged grandeur of its landscape and the hearty virtues of its people. Rather, it exposes, and enjoys, the literary construction of these myths, questioning their affective power and use in political debates about the future of Scotland's workers. While the poems discussed above are centred on the distant locations of Canada, South Africa, Australia, and New Zealand, many of the other poems in this chapter, in their concern with the lost 'native hame', are also migrant poems. The experience of internal migration was extremely common for those from rural areas, with 'high levels of internal mobility' and 'rural depopulation' across Scotland as people moved to the towns and cities in search of work.[113] Even for those who, like Carnegie, lament the changes to a native place where they still reside, Victorian industrialism has created the *feeling* of being a migrant, of being homeless while at home. Scott Mackenzie has recently argued, with a focus on eighteenth- and early nineteenth-century literature, that the Scottish (literary) relationship with the emerging concept of 'home' is 'very diasporic':

> Rather than approaching, the Scottish subject is always receding from her home...The Scottish subject can only look forward to the hope of founding a new home-place, but that new home must be in some sense the habitation of exiles or émigrés, even when it is within the borders of Scotland.[114]

---

[111] Harper, p.108. She notes that 80 per cent of those arriving in Otago between 1848 and 1860 were Scots-born (p.108).

[112] 'Otago', *Invergordon Times*, 17 May 1871, p.4.

[113] Devine, Scottish Nation, pp.464, 253. See also M. Anderson and D. Morse on migration and emigration statistics in 'The People', in W. Hamish Fraser and R. J. Morris, *People and Society in Scotland, vol II (1830–1914)* (Edinburgh: Economic & Social History Society of Scotland, 1990), pp.8–45, 22.

[114] Scott R. Mackenzie, *Be it Ever So Humble: Poverty, Fiction, and the Invention of the Middle-Class Home* (Charlottesville, VA: University of Virginia Press, 2013), pp.38, 176.

I would add that even when they are located not merely within the borders of Scotland, but at home, in the sense of being embedded in the surroundings in which they grew up, Scottish working-class writers still often present themselves as exiles because their home has changed so dramatically, for better or worse.

Nostalgic pastoral is a genre that is highly self-conscious about its dual relationship with a lost past and with modernity, signalled by its publication in the new cheap popular press. It looks like one of the least political of all poetic genres in this period, but its naïvety is a front. As the poems in this chapter show, *no* pastoral poem by a working-class writer, no matter how clichéd, can be assumed to be apolitical. Every lament for a lost home, for the mist-covered mountains of Scotland, for its sparkling rivers and waterfalls; every discussion of local landscapes and what is being, or should be, done with and to them, is a charged intervention in the debate over where Scotland's people stood in relation to the land in which, and on which, they lived, played, and worked.

4

The Measure of Industry

One of the most abiding perceptions of Victorian Scottish literature is that, at a point when Scotland underwent unprecedented industrialization, Scottish writers blithely or wilfully ignored this in favour of the pastoral literature of the kailyard. As Olive and Sydney Checkland put it, in the literature of this period:

> The great entrepreneurs, the projectors and swindlers, the hard-faced rejectors of organized labour, together with the working classes, indeed the new realities of the age, are all passed over. Glasgow could not itself repair the omission, for it was too much involved in projects, toil and bustle to produce literature... Thus it was possible for Scottish literature either to live largely in a previous pre-industrial age, or to indulge in an unrealistic idyll as with the Kailyard school... In Scottish Victorian literature industrialization and the Enlightenment are both missing. One would scarcely know from it what was happening to the majority of Scots.[1]

As we saw in the previous chapters, Victorian Glasgow made a very substantive contribution to popular verse cultures, and pastoral poetry from Victorian Scotland is neither pre-industrial nor does it consist of 'unrealistic idylls'. Although the decades since the publication of the Checklands' study have seen some revisionary moves, similar views, as the Introduction shows, continue to be expressed, by both historians and literary critics, and the argument that 'industrial change had to wait until the Renaissance to be fully explored in literature' remains pervasive.[2] Such assertions, I argue here, are largely inaccurate, especially in relation to the working poets who were themselves key participants in burgeoning industrial culture.

To critique working-class poets for failing to deal adequately with Victorian industry applies an anachronistic twentieth-century understanding of the function of verse in culture and society to a historical culture that, as we have seen, viewed the purpose of poetry in a different light. In addition, to assume that poets *could* have written of the horrors of industry in a realist mode, even had they wished to, is questionable when applied to those writers who were actually engaged in industrial labour and dependent on it for their income. Even when publication venues open to a working-class poet accepted verse that presented a bleak or graphic vision of industrialism, rather than more favoured genres, publishing such verse was a risky strategy. Anonymous or pseudonymous publication was not a reliable protection. Readers gossiped, and especially so if they felt indignant about an author's

---

[1] Olive and Sydney Checkland, *Industry and Ethos: Scotland 1832–1914*, 2nd edn (Edinburgh University Press, 1989), pp. 139–40.

[2] Gifford and Riach, *Scotlands: Poets and the Nation* (Manchester: Carcanet, 2004), p.xxv.

treatment of their own profession or workplace (as in the example of 'Davie's' newspaper poem on a wife-beating collier, cited below). Anything that openly treated a particular workplace culture or its owners and managers negatively risked being read by them; and they were unlikely to be pleased. That the excellent poet James Young Geddes is one of few who did write openly critical and experimental poetry about factories and industry undoubtedly shows his efforts to challenge social and poetic conventions. But the likelihood that he would have written and published 'Glendale & Co', a radical poem that also serves as a critique of the factory system, if he worked for the imagined Glendale & Co (Geddes was a draper in Dundee and then in Alyth) is extremely slim.[3] More probably, he would have produced verse akin to Ellen Johnston's celebratory 'Lines to Mr James Dorward, Power-Loom Foreman, Chapelshade Works, Dundee', her employer, 'I'm happy as a queen, Jamie, in the bonnie Chapelshade,/And whilst you're pleased to keep me there, wi' you I'll earn my bread'.[4]

Johnston's poem may or may not reflect the lived conditions and social relations of factory work as she perceived them, but it clearly reflects on the relationship between poetry and the factory. It is far from true that industrialization is absent from Scottish poetry of the period. On the contrary, Scotland's industrial development is the context that shapes the verse culture of the period. Even irrespective of content, every time a poet signs their poems with a pseudonym such as 'The Factory Girl' or with information about their workplace ('Colin Sievwright, Don's Factory, Forfar'[5]), the poem enters into a debate about how industrialization and literary efforts intersect. Indeed, simply signing a published poem with a location known to readers as a hub of industry (like the Lanarkshire towns discussed below) is enough to signal its relation to industrial production. Scotland's emergence at the forefront of technological and industrial development in the early to mid Victorian period, and its emergence at the forefront of working-class verse cultures and their dissemination, were not two separate and unrelated enterprises. They were both, contemporaries strongly argued, signs of the hard-working mentality, enterprise, and ambition of the Scottish working classes and of Scotland itself.

Much industrial verse—Johnston's 'Lines' are a good example—implicitly or explicitly plays on the varied meanings of 'industry'; verse celebrating industry also celebrates the industrious poet, working hard at her profession *and* at the work of verse. Emma Griffin's recent study, which analyzes attitudes towards the industrial revolution in working-class autobiography, suggests that too much emphasis has been placed on middle-class writers' wholly negative view of industrialization, and that a study of working-class writing questions standard attitudes about the negative impact of Victorian industrialism on workers' lives. She argues that the 'dismal litany of industrialisation's failure to adequately recompense working men must be tempered by an appreciation of their own sense of empowerment' and that 'these writers viewed themselves not as downtrodden losers but as men and women in

---

[3] Geddes, *In the Valhalla* (Dundee: John Leng, 1898), pp.122–35.
[4] Johnston, Autobiography, *Poems and Songs* (Glasgow: William Love, 1867), pp.86–7, 87.
[5] Sievwright, 'Colin's Reply to "J.G." Arbroath', *Weekly News*, 6 April 1867, p.4.

control of their destiny'.[6] This is equally true of most industrial poets, though their writings are more equivocal about whether or not industry offers 'empowerment' than Griffin's analysis might suggest. Many poems, notably in the genres of miners' and railway workers' verse discussed in the second and third sections of this chapter, are highly critical of the working conditions that enabled Scotland's progress, and use poetry to expose those conditions as much as to signal their own ability to transcend them. Poems that deal with engineering, railway work, and other forms of labour that engage directly with machinery, featured in the third section, are particularly ambivalent, responding to anxieties such as those famously expressed by Carlyle, in 'Signs of the Times' (1829), about men's spiritual and mental state in an 'Age of Machinery', 'Their whole efforts, attachments, opinions, turn on mechanism, and are of a mechanical character'.[7] Engine and railway poets, in defiance of writers like Carlyle, value and celebrate machines, even as they query where power lies in the relationship between man and the new machinery, and hence consider issues of control, fate, and fatality tied to the relentlessness of the mechanical.

While industrial verse does strongly relate to the issues raised in Chapters 2 and 3 (and, of course, poets working in industrial occupations were major contributors to the genres of nursery verse, verse on domestic life, and nostalgic pastoral), the poems discussed in this chapter are different in that they have a greater concern with the invention of a new tradition. Scottish pastoral poets, as shown above, are well aware that they are working in an established mode familiar to their readers and with a long-established reputation in Scottish literature, as are nursery verse poets in their association with traditional rhyme and song for children. In contrast, although poetry about industrial landscapes and labour does date back to the eighteenth century, the rapidly changing conditions of Victorian Scottish industry meant that poets were discussing aspects of these landscapes and labour that felt new. No one prior to the 1830s and 1840s had ever seen a spectacle like the blast furnaces of Lanarkshire, or experienced working in the deeper, larger and more mechanized coal mines of the area, or driven a train at full speed. There is a far greater concern in these poems, then, on *how* to represent the sights, sounds and experience of industry and industrial labour, and on how to insert these into literary culture. This was, of course, a question that concerned a great many Victorian writers, yet relatively little has been written about the way in which workers in industry and working-class inhabitants of industrial regions answered it. All the poets discussed below explicitly or implicitly question why—and whether—poetry might be fit for the representation of industry. Though some amongst them reached a wider audience, they primarily set out to represent the experience of industrial labour and landscapes to their own working communities, by publishing their poems in the local press and with local publishers.

<hr />

[6] Griffin, *Liberty's Dawn: A People's History of the Industrial Revolution* (New Haven, CT: Yale University Press, 2013), pp.19, 20.

[7] 'Signs of the Times', *Edinburgh Review* (1829), reprinted G. B. Tennyson, ed. *A Carlyle Reader* (Cambridge: Cambridge University Press, 1984), pp.31–55, 34.

I focus first on regional identity and the industrial poet, by assessing poems and poetic culture from Lanarkshire, the region that includes and surrounds Glasgow and was known for its iron towns, collieries, gasworks, and furnaces. The first section discusses how writers from this area engaged with literary culture, in defiance of perceptions of industrial Lanarkshire as dangerously uncivilized and devoid of beauty and natural inspiration. The second and third sections of the chapter turn to professional identities, first concentrating on miner or collier-poets from Lanarkshire and central Scotland and their productions, and finally moving beyond Lanarkshire to the engine and railway poets of Scotland, briefly examining poetic form as well as content in considering how poetry written about engines and railways incorporated the 'beat' of industrial labour. While the chapter as a whole only examines a tiny percentage of Scottish poets who wrote on industrial landscapes and labour (leaving out, for instance, the factory workers, such as Johnston, Effie Williamson of Galashiels, David Carnegie of Arbroath, and many others) it seeks to show that verse was embedded in industrial cultures in myriad and complex ways, and to a substantial extent, operated as a product as well as interpreter of these cultures.

SINGING THE IRON TOWNS

Nowhere was the rise of Scotland to one of the world's great industrial powers more evident than in Lanarkshire, Scotland's largest county by population from 1801. Glasgow's claim to be the second city of the British Empire, Michael Fry comments, 'might have had almost a modest ring' in an 'industrial sense', given how dominant the city, Lanarkshire and the central belt were in the production of coal, iron, shipbuilding, railway engines, and other products and machinery of all kinds.[8] While Glasgow itself was transformed, the changes were still more dramatic in the small towns and villages, within thirty miles of the city, which emerged as major producers of coal and ironstone. Coatbridge and Airdrie, the focus of my discussion in this section, became central to debates over the impact of industry in Scotland and beyond, as they expanded at an unprecedented rate and absorbed surrounding villages. Their long-term residents had witnessed first-hand the transformation of relatively rural towns and villages by an influx of new industrial workers, and the destruction of parts of the countryside by mining operations, works, and new housing for these workers. By the 1840s, Coatbridge and Airdrie had a reputation as 'frontier towns', noted, as Christopher Whatley describes, for poor living conditions, 'inadequate water supplies, over-crowding, disease and levels of drunkenness and petty but savage crime which in Airdrie in 1848 may have surpassed those of Glasgow'.[9] 'Lanarkshire's industrial frontier',

---

    [8] Fry, p.48.
    [9] Christopher A. Whatley, *The Industrial Revolution in Scotland* (Cambridge: Cambridge University Press, 1997), p.85. See also McCaffrey, p.30, on the iron and coal boom, 'The whole thing had something of a frontier-like atmosphere about it'.

Alan Campbell comments, created a 'rootless and heterogeneous population', where the rapidly growing presence of immigrant Irish workers (and, towards the end of the century, a smaller population of Polish miners) brought about 'ethnic and religious fragmentation' and led to political and sectarian tensions.[10] Tom Millar's comic prose recitation about the fear of sectarian riots in Coatbridge, for example, in his *Readings and Rhymes from a Reeky Region*, has the narrator casually observe, 'In yae street they'll knock the puddins oot o' ye if ye're no a disciple o' Dan [Daniel O'Connell]; an' in anither, if ye're no a follower o' Billy [King William of Orange], ye've every chance to share a similar fate'.[11]

Coatbridge, Airdrie, and the mining settlements that surrounded them, were from one perspective the chief beneficiaries, and from another the primary sufferers, of the effects of Victorian Scotland's industrial might. The contemporary literary culture of these 'iron towns' has never been investigated. Yet this tension between local pride in Lanarkshire's global significance and industrial modernity, and anxiety about the effects of this on the land and people; and the desire to participate in verse culture combined with a recognition that industrial regions were perceived as 'unpoetic', produced significant poems and critical commentary that set out, defiantly, to show that culture and industry are not incompatible. Readers and writers in Airdrie and Coatbridge, and the nearby districts, were well aware that their region had a reputation as perhaps the least poetical in Britain. 'Few places could be more unfavourable for the cultivation of the poetic faculty than the smoky region in which the rapidly growing town of Coatbridge is situated, with its flaming furnaces and great mounds of slag', wrote Alexander Wallace in a preface to Janet Hamilton's poems (Hamilton came from a hamlet, Langloan, that became a suburb of Coatbridge), adding that 'the very idea of Coatbridge being the haunt of the muses' seemed to contradict notions of poetic inspiration.[12] 'One would naturally think that this bare region of coal and iron is not the place we should expect to find the companions of Apollo', as 'A.S.'s preface to David Morrison's poems (Morrison was a miner for fifteen years and then moved to a paper mill and to Caldervale Printfield, South Lanarkshire) agreed.[13]

When the *Airdrie and Coatbridge Advertiser* began in July 1855, then, it deliberately took up the challenge of contesting such opinions, stating in an editorial that developing 'native talent' in verse was 'one of the chief objects we have ever had in mind in the publication of the *Advertiser*', and promising to 'gratify our readers with native productions' and thereby 'promote a literary spirit among the working classes'.[14] In its early years, it published several extensive selections by local writers,

---

[10] Campbell, p.2.

[11] Tom Millar, 'In the Blues', *Readings and Rhymes from a Reeky Region* (Coatbridge, printed for the author by William Craig, 1887), p.73. Millar was a tailor in Coatbridge.

[12] Alexander Wallace, 'Janet Hamilton At Her 'Ain Fireside', *Poems, Sketches and Essays by Janet Hamilton* (Glasgow: James Maclehose, 1885), pp.14–23, 14. The essay is dated 1868.

[13] David H. Morrison (Caldervale by Airdrie), *Poems and Songs* (Airdrie: Baird and Hamilton, Advertiser Office, 1870), p.v. See brief discussion of Morrison in chapter 1.

[14] 'Local Poetry', *Airdrie Advertiser*, 12 January 1856, p.2.

showing 'the latest poetic fire of our district'.[15] 'The cold and barren soil of a mineral district may at first seem uncongenial for the growth and development of that divine afflatus which fills the soul with *"thoughts that breathe, and words that burn"*', writes the editor in 'Our Local Poets' in September 1855, echoing standard assumptions about the region, yet 'Tell it in Gath, or publish it in the streets of Askelon if you will, but of a truth there are poets amongst us'.[16] 'Poetic fire', 'divine afflatus' and 'words that burn' (from a famous quotation from Thomas Gray) consciously pun on the fire, hot blasts, and gases more usually associated with Lanarkshire industry. On 6 September 1856, the *Advertiser* published one and a half pages of poems, divided by the name of the poet's town, after another discussion of 'Local Poetry':

> The following rhymes are by no means of equal merit, nor are they intended as chosen pieces by which the poetic quality of the several places may be determined. They are rather, in the present instance, to be regarded as indications of the literary and rhyming character of the iron district.[17]

The towns or villages of Airdrie, Bathgate, Coatbridge, Hillend, New Mains, Torphichen, Bellshill, and Whitburn were all represented by a sample poem; their authors included Janet Hamilton, the only poet from this region who is known to scholarship today, David Thomson ('D. T.') of Hillend (briefly discussed in Chapter 1), and Robert Tennant of Airdrie, a well-known 'postman poet' and part of a family of newspaper poets—his brother George Tennant was included in the paper's earlier 1855 selections.[18] None of the poems presented in the *Advertiser*'s selection are *about* the 'iron district': what they intend to show of its 'character' is that it supports at least as many, if not more, aspiring and hard-working poets as other regions of Scotland. Poetry is another product of local industry in which readers can take pride. By the early twentieth century, James Knox, the compiler of *Airdrie Bards, Past and Present*, was able to claim that 'if there should be a competition as to which town can produce the best local anthology Airdrie would have a fair chance of again securing first honours'.[19] Many of the poets he discusses were known because the *Airdrie Advertiser* office, Baird & Hamilton's, had assisted them to publish a volume. Poetry, Knox argues, was an essential part of Victorian Airdrie's 'progressive character', and he highlights the vitality of its literary scene, its dynamic associational and print cultures, from the 1830s to the 1930s. Similarly, in his 1864 *The Rise and Progress of Coatbridge*, local historian Andrew Miller, in analyzing Coatbridge's industrial progress, chose to include an extensive section on poetic celebrities as part of his vision of the progressive character of Victorian Lanarkshire, as evident in the enterprise of its poets as its industrialists.[20]

---

[15] *Airdrie Advertiser*, 20 October 1855, p.2.

[16] 'Our Local Poets', *Airdrie Advertiser*, 22 September 1855, p.2.

[17] 'Local Poetry', *Airdrie Advertiser*, 6 September 1856, p.2.

[18] On Thomson, The Tennant scrapbook is discussed in chapter 1, p.48.

[19] James Knox, *Airdrie Bards, Past and Present* (Airdrie: Baird and Hamilton, 1930), p.8.

[20] Andrew Miller, *Dundyvan Iron Works, The Rise and Progress of Coatbridge and Surrounding Neighbourhood* (Glasgow: David Robertson, 1864), pp.147–66.

While many of the poems produced by Coatbridge and Lanarkshire poets are indistinguishable from any other Scottish poetry of the period—this, of course, was the point—a number of poets do take on the challenge of writing about, as well as from, the 'bare region of coal and iron', in defiance of the notion that their region is equally bare of inspiration. In this they join a tradition of British poetic engagement with the industrial and technological sublime, the awe and terror inspired by man-made structures and landscapes, that stretches back to the eighteenth century, but which has been more associated with middle-class observers than with labouring-class verse.[21] Coalbrookdale, a Shropshire location which developed as a hub of iron ore smelting in the 1790s, attracted numerous artists and poets, including Anna Seward, whose sonnet 'To Colebrooke Dale' is both horrified by and admiring of the

> columns large
> Of black sulphureous smoke, that spread their veils
> Like funeral crape upon the sylvan robe
> And stain thy glassy floods.[22]

Such hellish depictions of a polluted landscape were already well established by the late eighteenth century, and like all such poems, are heavily indebted to Milton's depiction of Hell in *Paradise Lost*, Book I, in which Milton takes the opportunity to rebuke Satan and his devils for their industrial mining activities.[23] In the nineteenth century, as Rosalind Williams notes, 'associations between industry and hell grew even stronger', as popular travel writing and fiction incorporated descriptions of satanic mills and polluted industrial regions.[24] Dickens's terrifying portrayal of the Black Country landscape through which Little Nell and her grandfather travel in *The Old Curiosity Shop* (1841) is a particularly famous example, in which the horrors of industry and the fear of radical Chartism led by a savage workforce are notably blended.[25] Scottish poets would have remembered Burns's comparison of

[21] For a general and still seminal account, see Francis Klingender's *Art and the Industrial Revolution*, ed. and revised by Arthur Elton (London: Paladin, 1972, first published 1947), especially pp.16–36 on eighteenth-century poets and industry. On the industrial sublime, see Rosalind Williams, *Notes on the Underground: An Essay on Technology, Society and the Imagination* (Cambridge MA: MIT Press, 1990), pp.84–8 and *passim*. David E. Nye's exploration of the *American Technological Sublime* (Cambridge, MA: MIT Press, 1994), though its comparisons with England are brief, also discusses the emergence of new attitudes towards the Romantic sublime.

[22] *The Collected Poems of Anna Seward, vol I*, ed. Lisa L. Moore (New York: Routledge, 2016), p.208. On Seward's Coalbrookdale poems see Timothy Webb, 'Listing the Busy Sounds: Anna Seward, Mary Robinson and the Poetic Challenge of the City', in Lilla Maria Crisafulli and Cecilia Pietropoli, eds., *Romantic Women Poets: Genre and Gender* (Amsterdam: Rodopi, 2007), pp.79–112, 83–9, and Martin A. Danahay on Coalbrookdale in 'The Aesthetics of Coal: Representing Soot, Dust and Smoke in Nineteenth-Century Britain', in William B. Thesing, ed., *Caverns of Night: Coal Mines in Art, Literature and Film* (Columbia, SC: University of South Carolina Press, 2000), pp.3–18, 5–9. Klingender additionally discusses the significance of Coalbrookdale for artists and writers (pp.75–80).

[23] John Milton, *Paradise Lost*, ed. Alistair Fowler, 2nd edn (Harlow: Longman, 1998), Book I, lines 670–92.

[24] Williams, p.66.

[25] Charles Dickens, *The Old Curiosity Shop*, ed. Angus Easson (Harmondsworth: Penguin, 1985), chapters 44 and 45, especially p.424.

Ayrshire's Carron Ironworks to hell in a poem he engraved on a window there, and many would also have encountered Wordsworth's lament for the effect of 'potent enginery' on landscape and communities in *The Excursion*:

> Meanwhile, at social Industry's command,
> How quick, how vast an increase! From the germ
> Of some poor Hamlet, rapidly produced
> Here a huge Town, continuous and compact,
> Hiding the face of earth for leagues – and there,
> Where not a Habitation stood before,
> The Abodes of men irregularly massed
> Like trees in forests – spread through spacious tracts,
> O'er which the smoke of unremitting fires
> Hangs permanent, and plentiful as wreaths
> Of vapour glittering in the morning sun.[26]

Unlike Wordsworth's traveller, Dickens's characters, Seward, or indeed most commentators on the industrial sublime (including Campbell on the Clyde, cited in Chapter 3), however, Lanarkshire working-class poets are not passing through or visiting these transformed landscapes as outsiders, but rather consciously present themselves as commentators on the lived experience of such transformation, and as stakeholders in the industry it fostered.

Some local poets followed these standard tropes and adopted straightforward positions of lament and elegy for the lost rural scenes of their region. John Liddell Kelly, for instance, a journalist who began his career at the *Airdrie Advertiser* before moving to New Zealand in 1881, wrote three linked poems, 'Airdrie', 'Dreams of Airdrie', and 'Airdrie Revisited', which serve to commemorate the distance between the 'verdant braes' of his youth and the reality of 1870s Airdrie:

> Dark mounds of earth deface the sward;
> 'Mid whirr of wheels and hammer's clank
> The grimy workers, rank on rank,
> Sweat at the furnace or the forge;
> Great bridges span each beauteous gorge
> Loud engines shriek; and over all
> Thick smoke lies like a funeral pall.[27]

Kelly does not perceive sublimity in either landscape or machinery. The bridges are 'great' merely in terms of size, and it is the natural gorge, not the man-made bridge, that is beautiful. 'Dreams of Airdrie' and 'Airdrie Revisited', both written from New Zealand (and possibly published in the New Zealand press) highlight the particular distance between an emigrant's dreams of his childhood home, and the reality of returning to find childhood scenes lost and destroyed, and thus form part

---

[26] Wordsworth, *The Excursion*, ed. Sally Bushell, James A. Butler and Michael C. Jaye (Ithaca, NY: Cornell University Press, 2007), Book VIII: 118–27. See also Klingender, pp.101–4.

[27] John Liddell Kelly, 'Airdrie', *Heather and Fern: Songs of Scotland and Maoriland* (Wellington: New Zealand Times Company, 1908), p.145.

of the nostalgic pastoral genre discussed in the previous chapter.[28] By implicitly celebrating the emigrant's new, happier, community overseas these poems are an important part of Kelly's reinvention as a New Zealand poet. They are also not entirely typical, in that many poems from the region celebrated the iron towns for their busy and noisy modernity.

'Monkland''s poem on Coatbridge, in the *Airdrie Advertiser*, for instance, opens:

> My muse on Zion Hill has droop'd her wing,
> Coatbridge to survey and her praise to sing.
> In looking over all the land around,
> Pits either spoil or ornament the ground;
> The thick and murky smoke is rolling high
> From rows of chimneys gaping to the sky;
> The whole air fill'd is with a leaden load,
> Like a dun canopy both wide and broad:
> Mix'd with a brazen tinge of fire, this crown,
> Of sulphury hue, floats ever o'er the town.[29]

The 'drooping' wing may signify dismay at the task that faces the poetic muse, confronted with this landscape. Imagery of fire, sulphur and smoke recalls Milton and Wordsworth's wreaths of smoke, while the heroic couplet looks back to eighteenth-century prospect verse. The 'crown' seems sardonic, as Coatbridge has effectively elected to reign in hell; she is brazen in a double sense, unashamed of her appearance. 'Either spoil or ornament' introduces an important distinction, not between the differing appearances of the pits, but in the perspective of the observer, and so acknowledges from the outset that adopting a negative poetic attitude towards this vision of industry as a poet with local loyalties (Monkland is the local parish, and the poem's full signature is 'Monkland, Coatbridge') is difficult. The poem continues by switching from sight to sound and motion:

> All sorts of sounds discordant ever ring
> That strong machinery and men can bring
> From tongues unpolish'd and from hard, rough hands,
> Mingled with whirr of wheels that never stand;
> While everywhere steam hissing to get vent,
> Is seething, snorting, till the air is rent.
> And heavy beams, with dull and grinding sound,
> Make all things shake and vibrate round and round.
> The railway whistle, ever far or near,
> With harsh and grating sound still pains the ear;
> Ceaseless and tireless, working night and day,
> The engine runs, the long trains whirr away.[30]

---

[28] 'Dreams of Airdrie' and 'Airdrie Revisited', reprinted in Knox, pp.152–5.

[29] Monkland, Coatbridge, 'Coatbridge', *Airdrie Advertiser*, 7 May 1864, p.2. This poet had several other poems in the *Advertiser* in this period, but has not been identified.

[30] Ibid., p.2.

Language—'tongues unpolish'd' may suggest dialect as well as impolite speech—is melded with the noise of machinery, so that workers' speech is simply another part of the general discordance of the scene. 'Monkland' takes the perspective usual in poems on the industrial sublime, that of an observer surveying the region from above. As David E. Nye comments, in literary accounts factory and industrial districts were 'typically viewed from a high place or from a moving train':

> The industrial sublime combined the abstraction of a man-made landscape with the dynamism of moving machinery and powerful forces....It threatened the individual with its sheer scale, its noise, its complexity, and the superhuman power of the forces at work.[31]

Yet the usual threat of such scenes is complicated when the poet defines himself (or herself) as a local speaking to local readers, and as someone who is invested in the rise and progress of Coatbridge and the improvement of its workforce, because he or she may be presumed to be one of them. In the conclusion, 'Monkland' reminds the reader that 'Both far and near, in the world's business eye/Coatbridge commercially is rising high', and affectionately ends, 'Farewell, thou upstart, enterprising place,/ Thy heart beats right though sooty is thy face'.[32] Nye suggests that while outsiders might view a factory as 'a form embodying certain abstract ideas', labourers themselves 'usually saw the factory not as a landscape but as a process' and as 'a place of action'.[33] What 'Monkland''s poem presents is precisely a descent from detached observation to engaged process, linguistically registered through present participles (hissing, seething, snorting, grinding, grating, working) and the present continuous, in which Coatbridge 'is rising high'. This is the language of energy and movement, which references the energy, from coal and gas, that Lanarkshire's activities produce and market. 'Coatbridge' is itself an 'unpolished' poem, and one that might 'pain the ear' of a sensitive critic: the roughness of the workers and forces described, and the roughness of the verse, are akin. The poem's heart is in the right place, even if it is not the smoothest or most polished verse.

Similar energies run through Hamilton's poems on Coatbridge and surroundings, for instance 'Our Local Scenery':

Smoorin' wi' reek an' blackened wi' soot,	*smoor – to choke*
Lowin' like Etna and Hecla to boot,	*lowing – flaming*
Ought o' our malleables want ye to learn? –	
There's chappin' an' clippin' an' sawin' o' airn;	
Burnin' an' sotterin', reengin' an' knockin';	*sotter – to boil, to sputter*
Scores o' puir mortals roastin' and chokin'.[34]	

Hamilton's list of activities creates the same effect of continuous noise and motion as Monkland's. 'Malleables' is a key term, standing out amid Hamilton's otherwise colloquial Scots. In relation to Coatbridge's industry, it refers to steel and iron

---

[31] Nye, p.126.   [32] *Airdrie Advertiser*, 7 May 1864, p.2.   [33] Ibid., p.116.
[34] Hamilton, *Poems, Sketches and Essays*, p.157.

working and the shaping of the heated metal. The 'scenery' in Hamilton's poem, however, also includes the stifled workers in the furnaces, whose hard labour makes them as malleable as the metals they shape, in that they are easily swayed towards hard drink. All Hamilton's poems on the state of Coatbridge, including the more famous 'Oor Location' ('A hunner funnels bleezin', reekin'/Coal an' ironstane, charrin', smeekin")[35], are also temperance poems, in which the fires of industry and of alcohol both require, as a political, religious and social necessity, a supply of fresh drinking water.

As a figure who had lived through the changes in Coatbridge and surroundings, had overcome difficult circumstances and hardship, and was still politically and poetically active into old age, Hamilton herself seemed to embody the adaptability and force that poets celebrated in their location. In Tom Millar's 1880s poem 'Coatbridge: What It Has, and What It Has Not', the second claim to fame that Coatbridge has after its industrial might is 'Janet'. Hamilton's poems, though, rarely celebrate the changes brought by industry; their stance tends towards rueful acceptance. For other poets, the industries of Coatbridge, and particularly the effects created by the seemingly hellish flames of the furnaces, which famously lit up the landscape by night and day, were welcomed as (literal) bringers of light rather than darkness, symbols of modernity and progress. William Miller, well known in the area as a radical reformer who had been arrested several times in the agitations of the 1820s, and who also ran various literary enterprises in Airdrie, produced an early poem for an 1838 'social meeting' at the Calder Iron Works, marvelling at the novelty of constant light:

> Oh brightly glows Gartsherrie Works,
> And bright's the low's about Dundyvan;
> And Summerlee, tho' bright thy be,
> Nae better trade than us they're drivin' –
>   Braw, braw lichts.
> Braw, braw lichts on Calder braes,
> How brightly on yon sky they're glancing,
> And, lighting up ilk knowe and glen,
> Gars ilka tree and bush seem dancing –
>   Braw, braw lichts.[36]

The moonlight of standard Scots verse is replaced with the beautiful lights from the works. The brighter they shine, the greater the triumph of that particular work-place. Miller's poem is, of course, written for a specific audience who wish their labour to be complimented, as is arguably true of all the poems here, given their appearance in the Lanarkshire press. But Miller chose to act as the laureate of Calder Iron Works on this occasion, and he used it as an opportunity to play with

---

[35] Ibid., p.59.
[36] 'Calder Braes', reprinted in Andrew Miller, *The Rise and Progress of Coatbridge*, p.159. Andrew is William Miller's son. William Miller's works were never collected.

poetic standards. James Stewart, a later poet, made a similar move to Miller in 'Sweet Bell O' Summerlee' (Summerlee was a major ironworks in Coatbridge):

> I love the ruddy furnace glare,
>   Which glints the Luggie Burn;
> I like to watch the flash and flare
>   Reflected at each turn.
> There gently winds, frae oot the west,
>   Blaw saftly o'er the lea,
> Where lives the lassie I lo'e best –
>   Sweet Bell o' Summerlee.[37]

Half sardonically, and half seriously, Stewart adapts the highly familiar tropes of pastoral love-poetry to a setting in which industry and nature meet, where the glow of sunset reflected in a Scottish stream (the Luggie Burn was also itself used to power industry) is replaced by the flashier lights of the blast furnaces. Although perhaps not deliberately, both poems recall the common argument, in Victorian scientific and popular discourse, that coal was a product of sunlight and therefore its fires are also natural; industrial and natural process are thus intertwined rather than separate.

Stewart and his contemporary Millar, in the 1880s, wrote two of the most striking 'Coatbridge' poems, 'The Iron Village', and 'The Song of the Iron Town'. In 'The Iron Village', Stewart opens:

> Some poets sing of a sunny glade,
>   With lovers among the trees,
> Of singing birds, and the leafy shade,
>   And the sighing summer breeze,
> But to Coatbridge, of world-wide fame,
>   I will sing a cheery sang,
> Of its flash and flare, and tongues of flame,
>   And its busy clank and clang.
> *Chorus* – Then let us drink to its flash and flare,
>   Its clatter, jingle and clang,
>   Its rolling mills, and the fiery glare,
>   And the hammer's thumping bang.[38]

The tropes of pastoral are here outdated, drowned out by the brash noise of modernity. 'Flash and flare', clearly key words for Stewart, signify the unabashed (and perhaps slightly vulgar) flair with which Coatbridge conducts its affairs. Rather than lamenting that Coatbridge is an unpoetical district and an unpoetical subject, Stewart deliberately questions the readers' sense of fit topics for poetry. Although the noise and smoke may 'mar' life's pleasures, he concludes, still 'The people are flocking from afar/ The iron race to win'. Whether Stewart's poem appeared in the newspaper press is unclear, but Millar noted that his own 'The Song

---

[37] James Stewart, *The Twa Elders, and Other Poems* (Airdrie: Baird & Hamilton, 1886), p.21.
[38] Stewart, *Twa Elders*, p.50.

of the Iron Town' had 'appeared in the *Coatbridge Express* exactly twelve months before Mr Stewart's book was published'. This is an implicit accusation of imitation, since Millar's poem similarly opens:

> Sings our proud Scotland in her raptured lays,
> Of her matchless mountains, and her flowery braes,
> But we tune our praises to her great renown,
> In the humble carol of an Iron Town.
> > *Chorus*
> Where the mighty furnace spreads its fiery gleam,
> And the curling smoke kisses the rising steam;
> While each wild work screaming with a dismal frown,
> Sends a dinsome echo thro' the Iron Town.
>
> There's a whole world's market in the grand discharge
> Of the fire's huge fortress, and the frantic forge,
> For our town, unrivalled in her funeral shade,
> Is the great Scotch centre of the iron trade.[39]

Again, the language emphasizes noise and speed. As the *Coatbridge Express* only began in 1885, this would have been one of its early poems, with the probable intent of assisting the newspaper's mission to increase pride in the locality, and perhaps also to rival nearby Airdrie as a centre for poetic enterprise and a cultured press. Neither song gives a suggested tune. Their designation as songs, however, marks them as a product that can be collectively used, rather than intended for private reading. The effect of Millar's headnote about Stewart's comparable poem is also to suggest that 'we' is a genuine collective of industrial poets, determined that Scotland's poetic output should celebrate industrial might as well as 'matchless' natural beauty. The 'funeral shade' that is described in elegiac poems about industry is still present, but now the 'unrivalled' smoky darkness is a source of immense pride. As Millar wrote in 'Coatbridge: What It Has, and What It Has Not':

> Long may her blackening smoke arise,
> To hide the beauty of the skies!
> What though it is not her's to view
> The firmament in all its blue;
> Is it not better far to see
> Smoke, indicating industry?[40]

'Though Coatbridge is a most interesting seat of industry', David Bremner wrote, in his widely circulated newspaper articles on *The Industries of Scotland* (1869), 'it is anything but beautiful'.[41] Why, these poets ask, does beauty have to be the primary criteria of value? This is a question that applies to the verse culture of the region, as well as to the region itself. Though the poets of Coatbridge may not write the most

---

[39] Millar, p.9.   [40] Millar, p.5.
[41] David Bremner, *The Industries of Scotland: Their Rise, Progress and Present Condition*, intro. by John Butt and Ian L. Donnachie (Newton Abbott: David and Charles, 1969), pp.35–6. These essays first appeared as articles in the Scotsman in 1868.

beautiful verse, by the aesthetic standards of the day, they are highly industrious, and they take the business of promoting their town seriously.

Within the genre of working verse, these writers highlight the functions of energy. When Andrew Miller—employed in an ironworks—writes that 'there are few districts in Scotland in which the results of individual energy are so fully exemplified as in Coatbridge' he knowingly takes on the conflicted double meanings of energy in the mid-Victorian period.[42] As Allen MacDuffie has recently discussed in detail, the 'thermodynamic definition of "energy"—a measurable quantity of motive power, or work—was in wide circulation in the British periodical press by the 1860s', yet this definition was 'still in competition with the longstanding, non-technical use of the word, which could signify a personal *quality* of autonomy, diligence or activity'.[43] 'Energy' was an important keyword in Romantic poetry, as Barri Gold has shown, but Gold and MacDuffie both argue that the new meanings the term takes on by the mid-Victorian period open up 'a darker connotation: people defined as fuel within a system of production'.[44] The iron town poets are aware of this, just as they are also aware, at least by the time that Stewart and Millar are writing, that coal resources are finite and that the smoke of industrial processes is polluting and dangerous. In one sense they perpetuate a cover-up about the forces that drive Scottish industry. But in another, they take on discourses of 'thermopoetics' and energy and rework them, to give agency to working poets and working readers, and to make the themes of Victorian popular poetics malleable enough to incorporate the business of industry.

DARK SCENES OF LABOUR: THE LANARKSHIRE MINER POETS

In his 1875 collection, *Sparks from a Miner's Lamp*, Francis Barnard opened with a sonnet on 'An Evening in Spring':

> How sweet, how beautiful, how mild and still,
> Now that young Spring has shown her infant face.
> The sun has set behind the western hill,
> And gold-tinged clouds swim thro' the vaulted space,
> Like golden fishes in a crystal vase.
> Pleasant the murmur of the purling rill,
> Mix'd with the little songsters of the grove,
> All sweetly caroling their lays of love.[45]

---

[42] Miller, Rise and Progress, 'Preface'.

[43] Allen MacDuffie, *Victorian Literature, Energy, and the Ecological Imagination* (Cambridge: Cambridge University Press, 2014), p.115. Barri J. Gold, *Thermopoetics: Energy in Victorian Literature and Science* (Cambridge, MA: MIT Press, 2010).

[44] MacDuffie, p.118; Gold, pp.49–52 and *passim*. MacDuffie notes the importance of Catherine Gallagher's 'bioeconomics' in relation to this question: see *The Body Economic: Life, Death and Sensation in the Victorian Novel* (Princeton, NJ: Princeton University Press, 2006).

[45] Francis Barnard, *Sparks from a Miner's Lamp* (Airdrie: Baird and Hamilton, 1875), p.1.

The final couplet concludes, addressing the birds, 'O! I could dwell among the woods with thee,/ To listen to thy strains of richest melody'. Barnard was a newspaper poet, whose works tended to appear as 'F. B., Woodend' in the *Airdrie Advertiser*, the *West Lothian Courier* and other local papers: 'An Evening in Spring' first appeared in the former on 5 April 1862.[46] Hundreds of poems on spring, of course, appeared in the newspaper and periodical press every April, and in subject matter and indeed in form, Barnard's is entirely unexceptional. What makes it significant, however, is the way in which the poet's stated location—Woodend is a colliery village—constitutes the poem as the production of a local miner. Barnard spent twenty-five years working at Woodend Colliery in Armadale, Lanarkshire, for the Coltness Iron Company, and identifies himself as writing from the mines in the preface to *Sparks from a Miner's Lamp*.[47] Behind 'An Evening in Spring' is the understanding that the poet spends his days (in his own words, though published under a pseudonym), 'Toiling hard all day in the dark recesses of the perilous mine', deprived 'of the pleasures and enjoyments that fall to the lot of the wealthy; nay, even of many of the sights and sounds which his fellow-toilers in the open sunlight enjoy'.[48]

In 'An Evening in Spring', the sensuous enjoyment of such 'sights and sounds'—which can *only* be experienced in the evening, on the miner's walk home after work—is evident in the murmur of the rill, the emphasis on birdsong, and the beauty and clarity of the evening sky, undimmed by smoke. Barnard's somewhat whimsical simile for the clouds tinged by the setting sun, 'Like golden fishes in a crystal vase', describes luxury possessions (both crystal and attractive goldfish) which a miner is unlikely to possess and may not have seen. In its evocation of crystal and water as transparent, beautiful, clean, and expensive, however, it consciously recalls the opposing characteristics associated with mines in the Victorian popular imagination: dirt, darkness, pollution, and poverty. Likewise, Barnard's repeated celebrations of birds and birdsong, here and throughout the volume, works in counterpoint to the noise pollution linked to mining, the 'sound of the pit wheels, the stertorous breathings of the engine, the clangour of the signals to hoist or lower, the cries of the banksmen, and the rumbling of the wagons'.[49] In opening his collection with a sonnet, Barnard also implicitly comments on a widespread understanding of colliers as semi-literate and ignorant, by displaying in contrast his ability to handle a canonical form. Readers are expected to understand that the closing couplet is deeply melancholy, since Barnard will never be able to linger in nature as he might wish. A sensitive and intelligent writer, alert to and in love with nature, is shut out from its pleasures, yet he should be commended for the ability to rise 'above all his disadvantages' in producing poetry.[50]

---

[46] 'F. B., Woodend, 'An Evening in Spring', *Airdrie Advertiser*, 5 April 1862, p.1.

[47] See also biography in Edwards, 9, p.290.

[48] Barnard, *Poetry of the Dell, Being Sketches of the Poets and Poetry of the District of Woodend, Torphichen* (Bathgate: Laurence Gilbertson, 1887), p.16. This series on local poets first appeared pseudonymously in the local press.

[49] 'My Colliery Experiences', *Once a Week*, 3.53 (5 Jan 1867), 8–13, p.8.

[50] *Poetry of the Dell*, p.16.

Nature poetry by Lanarkshire miner poets—including the three most successful identified poets, Barnard, David Wingate, and Thomas Stewart (already encountered in Chapter 3 for his right of way poems)—always makes similar points. Its depiction of clear rippling streams, green leaves and birdsong, in particular, is designed to show that despite the poet being deprived 'during a great part of life, of the humanizing influence exerted by the sights and sounds of nature', as one periodical article on 'The Collier at Home' put it, and thus being subject to 'a more than ordinary temptation to break the monotony of life with sensual indulgence', he remains keenly aware of nature's beauties.[51] This sensitivity designedly heightens the reader's sense of the horrors of pit life. Stewart's miner, on a beautiful autumn day filled with birdsong, goes mournful and 'mute tae his toil',

> Though Phoebus is beamin' her bonniest smile,
> As she peeps frae her rosy, red robe o' a cloud,
> Wi' its border o' beauty, like glitterin' gowd;
> An' deem ye he heeds nae their love-breathin' notes,
> Or sees nae the saul-blessin' beauty that beams
> Frae the lift, o'er the laun, in sae glorious gleams.
> Yes, he lo'es sic a scene wi' the saul o' a bard [52]

The glittering gold of the sunrise, like Barnard's 'golden fishes', reminds the reader of the wealth and beauty that the miner cannot have. 'Lift', in Scots, is the sky or heavens, but its English meaning also comes into play in the sense of the soul uplifted by beauty, before it must descend into the pit. In another of Barnard's poems on nature and the miner, he asks readers of the *Airdrie Advertiser* not to censure miners for missing church on Sunday:

> One day a week, O let him breathe the pure and wholesome air,
> In Nature's temple while he treads, think, wish and pray that he
> May read the love and care of God in bird, flow'r, herb, and tree.[53]

'Pure and wholesome' air reminds us that for the remainder of the week, miners, as Stewart put it, will be 'smeekit daily, in the deep', breathing 'filthy air/The British collier's greatest curse'.[54] Both Stewart and Barnard distance themselves from the miner they describe, speaking *for* the miner (who, in Stewart, is 'mute'). But since their volumes identify them by profession, it is understood that their poems display the privileged insight into their fellow workers that only another sympathetic collier can have.

Since these three writers were always identified not simply as collier-poets, but as *Lanarkshire* collier-poets, their paeans to the beauty of their local landscape, and the emphasis in their poems on emerging from the pit directly into contact with rural scenes, also contradicted both general and regional perceptions of mining and

---

[51] 'The Collier at Home', *Household Words* 15 (28 March 1857), 289–92, p.290.

[52] Stewart, 'The Miner', in *Doric Rhyme*, p.111.

[53] F. B., Woodend, October 1866, 'The Miner's Song', *Airdrie Advertiser*, 3 November 1866. Reprinted in *Sparks from a Miner's Lamp*, pp.34–7.

[54] Stewart, 'To My Brother', in *Doric Rhyme*, p.152.

industrial landscapes. As an 1860 *Chambers*'s article, 'A Peep at the Mining Districts' informed readers:

> We have in our mind's eye, as we write, a grimy hole in the side of a hill... Out of it oozes a dirty, red-brown fluid, which mingles with, and moistens and soaks the black smudge around and in front, and flows down over the adjoining turnpike, to the horror of the pedestrian, a stream of liquid coal-dust. Rank leaves grow in its neighbourhood, and the atmosphere is raw and unhealthy.[55]

Similarly, the author of 'The Newcastle Collier' in *Good Words* describes a typical mining village in which 'the dirty ducks are washing in vain in a dirty stream beneath a dirty bridge; the church and its tombstones are both streaked with smoke instead of lichen, and the grass and the trees look as if their pores were clogged with coal-dust', while 'My Colliery Experiences' in *Once a Week* describes a stream near a colliery as a 'villainous compound of peaty ooze and the mineral water that had been pumped into it from the collieries along the line of its course'.[56] This imagery of degraded and polluted landscapes, and especially depictions of the environmental damage to water sources, are the rationale for the strong presence of celebratory stream and river poems in miners' poetic collections, such as Barnard's 'To the Level', 'Clear, sparkling, halesome, bonnie spring'. 'O 'tis a gladsome sicht to see/ Thee gush sae pure, sae fresh, yet free', he comments, again invoking, in 'yet free', both the confinement of streams to serve industry and the cost of bringing clean, fresh water to the inhabitants of the industrial regions—clean drinking water was a major local political issue in Lanarkshire, as in other coal-producing regions.[57] These poems also want to emphasize that Lanarkshire, despite 'seething with lurid coal-pits, iron furnaces flaring night and day, railroads innumerable, canals, crowds of ships', as one writer described it in reviewing Wingate's poems, had not entirely lost its connection to nature and to Scottish pastoral scenes.[58]

Degraded landscapes and soundscapes were intimately associated, by contemporary writers, with the degradation of the mining population. Mining was 'at the hub of Victorian industrial enterprise', with coal production more than doubling between 1855 and 1875, and doubling again between 1875 and 1910.[59] John Benson notes that in the second half of the nineteenth century in Britain 'more than one person in twenty looked directly to the coal industry for his livelihood'.[60]

---

[55] 'A Peep at the Mining Districts', *Chambers's Journal* 324 (17 March 1860), 174–6, 174.

[56] 'Our Working People and How They Live: The Newcastle Collier', *Good Words* (11 Jan 1870), 53–60, p.55; 'My Colliery Experiences', p.8.

[57] Barnard, 'To the Level', in Sparks, pp.82–5, 82. John Benson discusses the recurring issue of water supply in mining areas in *British Coalminers in the Nineteenth Century* (Aldershot: Gregg, 1993, first published 1980): 'Even when not polluted, the age-old sources of water often broke down in mining districts under the pressure of growing demand' (p.98).

[58] 'David Wingate's Poems', *London Review* 4 (31 May 1862), 506–8, 507. The author of this review (perhaps Charles Mackay) notes the unusual intertwining of industry and untouched nature in the Clyde valley.

[59] Michael Pollard, *The Hardest Work Under Heaven: The Life and Death of the British Coal Miner* (London: Hutchinson, 1984), p.1.

[60] Benson, p.27.

In Scotland, the number of miners grew from 50,000 to 130,000.[61] Yet miners, though figures of fascination, were frequently perceived as a race apart, 'confined...to areas where decent folk need not penetrate'.[62] Periodicals and newspapers from the eighteenth century to the end of the Victorian period were filled with 'day in the pit' accounts of tourist visits to mines and miners' homes, and with the 'real-life' experiences of middle-class writers living near or amongst the miners. To appreciate what it meant to be a Victorian collier or pitman-poet, it is crucial to understand that miners were widely presented in such accounts as 'proverbial for their ignorance' and as unprepared to remedy it; to the extent that the common and disastrous pit accidents of the period were frequently attributed to the miners' illiteracy (they could not read the regulations) or stupidity (they did not understand the need to obey them).[63] 'The miner holds an humble position in the industrial ranks', Bremner wrote. 'His occupation does not require much skill, nor has it any tendency to incite him to intellectual pursuits'.[64] In 'My Colliery Experiences', the author recounts how he tried to set up mutual improvement classes and a reading room, but the miners were uninterested. 'As a general rule, there is no book or periodical to be seen' in a miner's home, wrote the author of 'A Peep at the Mining Districts', while J. R. Leifchild, government inspector, in a *Good Words* article on 'Colliers at Home and at Work', commented that 'as for the literature of the mass of these mining labourers it is just what might be expected, common, cheap, entertaining, harrowing, and sometimes unholy'.[65]

Miners were additionally perceived as liable to drink, fight, and engage in loose interpretations of the marriage bond; a perception assisted by their appearance as comic figures in widely circulated broadsides, such as 'Jolly Joe, the Collier's Son'.[66] Their poor housing was discussed as both cause and symptom of their lack of interest in domesticity and family bonds. Their language was unintelligible and coarse. 'I was anxious to converse with these men', wrote another *Chambers* author, 'having heard of their remarkable and peculiar character; but their uncouth language, marked, it seemed to me, by an absence of all firm articulation, proved fatal to my wishes'.[67] And, as Pollard and others have noted, the exploration tropes frequently used in descriptions of mines and the miners' black appearance, as 'dusky and hideous-looking figures' meant that racial (and imperialist) metaphors were common: 'Innumerable observers...recorded their view of colliers as little more, and in some cases less, than savages'.[68] In the case of Lanarkshire and Scotland, these discourses were especially marked because the miners were only one or two

---

[61] Michael Fry, *A New Race of Men: Scotland 1815–1914* (Edinburgh: Birlinn, 2013), pp.29, 30.

[62] Pollard, p.18.

[63] 'Weavers and Miners at Airdrie', *Chambers's Journal* 335 (1 June 1850,) 339–40, 340. On accidents as caused by miners, see also 'The Perils of Industry', *Tait's Edinburgh Magazine* (December 1854), 705–12, p.706.

[64] Bremner, p.19.

[65] 'My Colliery Experiences', p.9; 'A Peep at the Mining Districts', p.174; J. R. Leifchild, 'Colliers in their Homes and At Their Work', *Good Words* 3 (December 1862), 213–20, 214.

[66] For this and a selection of collier songs, see 'Broadside Ballads Online', Bodleian Library, http://ballads.bodleian.ox.ac.uk (consulted 27 September 2018).

[67] 'A Visit to the Monkwearmouth Pit', *Chambers's Edinburgh Journal* 49 (7 Dec 1844), 355–7, p.356.

[68] Ibid., p.355. Pollard, p.14. See also Danahay, p.8.

generations removed from actual slavery to their owners. The 'burden of arrears' this had created, the *Falkirk Journal* suggested, meant that by the 1860s Scottish miners were only starting to cast behind them their long-term reputation for being 'most brutal, illiterate and godless' and to join the culture of improvement.[69]

Most importantly, miners were more politically (and economically) suspect than other workers because they were liable to form unions and to strike. Even though it proved difficult to form stable national miners' unions in this period, smaller-scale union activity was widespread. The young David Wingate, in his memoirs, recalled the excitement of attending meetings in 1837 'to hear harangues about the terrible injustices we, in common with our collier brethren, had been suffering'; he joined in the strike but then had to return to work to support his mother, widowed by his father's death in the mine, and was persecuted for this to the extent that he ran away.[70] Recalling this in 1884 for a magazine run by the Church of Scotland, he unsurprisingly condemns strikes and unions and attributes them to the miners' failure to understand the system. There was very little sympathy from the mainstream Scottish press, or indeed even from the provincial press with its definite Liberal principles, for miners' strikes, which were a regular feature of the industry. In part this was because miners were regarded as being better paid and possessing shorter working hours than other labourers. As the *Airdrie Advertiser* editor commented during a period of dull trade coinciding with a major miners' strike in the early 1860s: 'The public can scarcely be expected to sympathize with an effort for further advance of wages by a class of workmen who are making four shillings per day, while half a million of their fellow men are suffering from starvation for want of employment'. He openly recommended that starving weavers take the places of the striking miners in the district.[71] This lack of sympathy was also due to familiarity, as miners' strikes became seen as commonplace. A letter to the *Glasgow Herald* in 1861 on 'Miners and their Grievances Again' asked:

> Why is it that this question is everlastingly before the public? Is it because the miners are stupid, ignorant and contumacious, or are they really aggrieved so much as to prevent them working quietly much over three consecutive months at a time?[72]

In a common move, the author, 'A Coalmaster', concludes that while miners do have some legitimate cause for complaint, constant strikes and demands are not the best way to persuade their employers to adopt better systems. It is this additional perception of the miners as aggrieved and politically agitated which highlights why soothing nature poems like 'An Evening in Spring' seemed important to miner-poets: they help to cast the collier in a remarkably new light.

Coal mines were one of the most investigated sites of the period, yet they were invariably represented as an unimaginably awful place of darkness, 'viewed by commentators as a negation of the aesthetic or beautiful', and had little place in

---

[69] 'Our Coal-Pits and Colliers', *Stirling Observer*, 20 April 1865, reprinted from Falkirk Journal, p.2.

[70] David Wingate, '*Mining Memories No IV – Strikes and Runaways*', *Life and Work (1884)*, cited in Guy A. S. Wingate, *A Century of Scottish Coalmining Ancestry 1778–1878: The History of the Wingate Family* (Stockton-upon-Tees, Cleveland: Petunia Publishing Company, 1994), p.42.

[71] Editorial, 'The Miners and the Unemployed Weavers', *Airdrie Advertiser*, 6 December 1862, p.2.

[72] A Coalmaster, 'Miners and Their Grievances', *Glasgow Herald*, 31 June 1861.

art, while miners themselves were frequently depicted as a political and social problem, in part admired for their heroic and manly qualities (as shown in many accounts of pit rescues), but more often perceived as degraded specimens of industrial humanity, to be pitied and feared.[73] Yet poetic mineworkers were not uncommon within Britain. Goodridge and Keegan have identified approximately forty-five poets associated with the mining industry, and have discussed the lives and work of English mineworker poets, as have Martha Vicinus, H. Gustav Klaus, and most recently Gordon Tait.[74] It was the standard rejection of any connection between mining and high culture that made these poets notable in their time, and which provides a reason for the preservation of their lives and poems.

In Scotland, whose mineworker poets have been little discussed, the complex self-positioning required by writers in this profession is most notable in the case of Wingate, one of few poets studied in this book to gain a reputation beyond the local. Barnard, who dedicated his volume to Wingate as 'the father of the Mining Muse', wrote in the preface:

> In my earlier days, I could not discover, from what I had read, that, in these isles, anything in a literary point of view, and more especially in the art of poesy, had been produced by the mining population. The counting-house, the workshop, the factory, the pasture lands, and even the 'mighty deep,' had all contributed to the poetical literature of the country; but nothing, so far as I knew, had, as yet, emanated from the mine. So, having a knack for rhyming, I thought I might, at least, make an attempt, and, by dint of perseverance, might possibly, at some time or another, produce something which would reflect a little credit on that class of the community to which I belong, viz., the miners.[75]

But then, as he ruefully acknowledges, Wingate appeared. In Barnard's metaphor and explanation for his volume's title, *Sparks from a Miner's Lamp*, Wingate is the lamp that illuminated the innovative concept of the cultured and poetic miner, leaving Barnard with only some modest sparks of light to contribute. Wingate's newspaper pseudonym, 'Davie', enables an implicit play here on the Davy lamp, the invention that had largely enabled the expansion of Victorian mining; Wingate's poems, Barnard suggests, are similarly a sign of nineteenth-century progress and innovation.

That Wingate possessed this authority was entirely due to his unusual adoption by *Blackwood's Edinburgh Magazine*, which published fourteen pages of Wingate's poems in March 1862 with the headnote 'The following are Preface and some specimens from a forthcoming volume containing Poems and Songs which have been sent to us from Lanarkshire'. 'From *Lanarkshire*', here, told the reader that

---

[73] Danahay, p.3.

[74] John Goodridge and Bridget Keegan, 'Modes and Methods in Three Nineteenth-Century Mineworker Poets', *Philological Quarterly* 92 (2013), 225–50 and Keegan, ' "Incessant toil and hands innumerable": Mining and Poetry in the Northeast of England', *Victoriographies* 1 (2011), 177–201. See also Vicinus, Industrial Muse, pp.60–93; Klaus, *The Literature of Labour: Two Hundred Years of Working-Class Writing* (Brighton: Harvester, 1985), pp.62–88; and Gordon Tait, Coal, Correspondence and Nineteenth-Century Poetry: Joseph Skipsey and the Problems of Social Class. PhD thesis, University of Hull, 2018.

[75] Barnard, 'Preface', *Sparks from a Miner's Lamp*.

the author was an industrial worker even before they read Wingate's Preface. *Blackwood's* followed this up in July, after publishing Wingate's *Poems and Songs*, with a lengthy review of his life and works commissioned from novelist and journalist Margaret Oliphant, introducing him as 'a new poet', who, in an extensive set of analogies drawing on Wingate's profession, had burst his way to the surface:

> The light that is in him is underground and has somehow to make its own individual way to the surface. Safety shafts and openings which have served once will not answer a second time – a separate outgate must be burst through the earth for every new illumination.[76]

While disavowing the fact that it is Wingate's background—he worked in the mines almost continuously from the age of nine—which makes him interesting as a poet, such language repeatedly draws attention to it, and Oliphant is implicitly as much concerned with celebrating Wingate as a new type of collier, as celebrating him for his poetic skill:

> We will not, accordingly, attempt to prove that Wingate is wonderful because he is a collier. He has borne his collier burden like a man – which is far higher praise – and vindicated his higher nature and office by steadfastly and courageously holding up, high above the damps and darkness of his surroundings, the gentle lamp of genius which God has confided to his hands. It is not to the credit of his poetry that he was born and bred and has toiled all his life in the Lanarkshire mines; but it is to the credit of his manhood that, being a collier, with hard work enough, Heaven knows, to keep life afloat in that dusky world, he has braced his heart and faculties with voluntary toil of another kind, and disclosed a delicate vein of verse in those dark places where nothing lovely was to be looked for.[77]

Wingate's poetry, here, is equivalent to the minerals he delves for; something valuable obtained from the depths of the 'dusky world'.

Not surprisingly, such praise from *Blackwood's* brought Wingate's verse a level of attention far beyond that usually accorded to working-class poets. Between March and June 1862, other newspapers and periodicals reprinted his poems from *Blackwood's*, and when *Poems and Songs* came out it was widely and favourably reviewed, invariably contrasting Wingate's position as 'a worker in a Lanarkshire coal-pit' and his supposed physical disadvantages, 'the poor Lanarkshire collier, with his grimy features and toil-hardened limbs', with the surprising 'delicacy' or 'delicacy and grace' of his poetic productions.[78] Local newspapers, in which Wingate had been publishing for a number of years, were quick to lay claim to him, sometimes with a note of scepticism about *Blackwood's* emphasis on having 'found' a new poet. The *Hamilton Advertiser*, which had published 'Davie''s poems and critiqued them

---

[76] 'David Wingate', *Blackwood's Edinburgh Magazine* 92 (July 1862), 48–61, 48. On this review, see Joanne Shattock, ed., 'Margaret Oliphant and the Blackwood "Brand"', in *Journalism and the Periodical Press in Nineteenth-Century Britain* (Cambridge: Cambridge University Press, 2017), pp.341–52.

[77] Ibid., pp.50–1.

[78] 'David Wingate', *London Review*, p.506, John Plummer, 'Our Wayside Poets', *National Magazine* 14 (July 1863), 141–4, 141

regularly from the summer of 1857 (a year after its foundation), anticipated his volume favourably in February 1862, appealing to 'readers of the *Advertiser*, who have so often been delighted with the singer', to buy his book and thereby 'lift him out of the pit'.[79] After *Blackwood's* July piece, however, which translated Wingate from a subject of local interest to national, the *Advertiser* fell silent on Wingate's merits until June 1863, when the author of an 'Our New Poets' series noted that 'Hundreds read Wingate's poems in our columns without thinking them above mediocrity. *Blackwood's* published them and praised them, and the same persons then saw at once the great merit they possessed'.[80]

Wingate had in fact been 'discovered', even before he began to publish in the Hamilton press, by Hugh MacDonald and the *Glasgow Citizen* in the 1850s, and then by the Glasgow *Commonwealth* (a newspaper operated on reformist and temperance principles) in its 1856 autobiography competition. Although the *Commonwealth* rated its set of 2-guinea prizewinners equally, Wingate's name was first on the winners' list and his was the first autobiography published in the paper, giving the impression that it was the best of nearly eighty entries received. In advertising the competition, the editor justified the need for the competition and the donations of prize money received for it through another metaphor of mining the working classes for talent:

> Our friends believe that deep down among the masses are unwrought seams, rich in manifold human experiences, that it were well for all the world to be better acquainted with. They have determined that something shall be done to dig up these treasures, and so set up at home a kind of opposition to California or Australia.[81]

Inviting the submission of working-class autobiographies is equivalent to sinking 'their first shaft'. As in *Blackwood's* language and imagery, Wingate himself becomes a treasure disinterred from the dark regions inhabited by the working classes and put on display for the benefit of a cross-class readership. Scottish wealth, the gold-mining comparison suggests, is vested in her working people, whose experiences will directly profit readers. Wingate's 'Narrative of a Miner' in the *Commonwealth* also advertises him as a poet, and includes in full his bitter adaptation of Thomas Hood's 1843 'The Song of the Shirt', 'A Song of King Coal':

> Dig – dig – dig
> Till the labouring bosom heaves
> As each clogg'd lung expands in pain
> With the poison it receives.
> Hole, and tumble, and draw,
> Crawl, and sweat, and gasp,
> Till the pick becomes an unwieldy weight
> In the toil-enfeebled grasp.[82]

---

[79] *Hamilton Advertiser*, 22 February 1862, p.2.   [80] Ibid., 6 June 1863, p.1.

[81] 'Popular Autobiographies. Twenty Prizes for Working Men', *The Commonwealth*, 9 February 1856, p.4.

[82] 'Narrative of a Miner', *The Commonwealth*, 25 October 1856, p.4.

Following Hood's 'Stitch – stitch – stitch', the refrain in the first line of the stanza mimics the repetition of the same manual task. Wingate's wordplay on 'labouring' serves to highlight the physical suffering of the miner. In a context in which the *Commonwealth*, like all other Glasgow papers in these years, frequently debated the rights and wrongs of miners' strikes and discussed their social and moral condition, it is this poem rather than the prose autobiography around it (which is largely written in a tone of humorous resignation despite its emphasis on poverty, illness, and times of despair) that most strongly expresses Wingate's anger and agitation for better working conditions.

When *Blackwood's* adopted Wingate and his volume, the politicized bent of his mining verse became far less evident. His appeal to *Blackwood's* at this precise time was probably less due to his unrecognized merit as an extraordinarily good working-class poet—his preface and autobiography do stand out in their bluntness and lack of apology, his poems, as more sceptical reviewers commented, are less original—and more due to the particular valence that a marketable collier poet had in the spring of 1862. Between 16 and 22 January 1862, 204 men died in the Hartley Colliery disaster in Northumberland, Britain's worst up to that date, when the shaft was blocked by the collapse of the pumping machinery above it. The nation was gripped by extensive newspaper accounts of the rescue attempts for a week, and then by the tragic stories of the recovery of the bodies. Subsequently, the inquest concluded that the tragedy would have been averted if the pit had had a second shaft, and by August, after considerable agitation, legislation had been introduced to this effect. The Hartley disaster spurred movements towards a national miners' union, culminating in a national conference in Leeds in autumn 1863, and it also roused indignation and sympathy for miners and their exploitation by owners—sympathy that had been damaged by the strikes and agitation of the early 1860s, which were ongoing throughout 1862 and 1863. Wingate's poems, and his designation by *Blackwood's* as an eminently worthy and manly Christian poet, modest and dedicated to self-improvement rather than to dangerously radical ideas, could only assist in re-evaluating the miner as a sympathetic figure reassuringly attuned to middle-class sentiment, and in offering an imagined alternative to the menacing, striking collier. As the *Airdrie Advertiser* wrote in reviewing Wingate's *Blackwood's* collection:

> [W]e believe these poems will have an elevating and purifying tendency among the class from whom the singer has sprung, and that this book will gain for them a consideration from other classes which has hitherto been withheld. It will be impossible to pass a miner after this without feeling that he is a man.[83]

One of Wingate's most popular and most frequently reprinted works, the opening poem of his collection and the first printed beneath the preface in *Blackwood's* in March 1862 (though it had appeared in the *Hamilton Advertiser* four years earlier), was 'A Miner's Morning Song'. In entirety, it runs:

> Awake, brother miner! The stars have grown dim,
> 'Tis time to be stirring the sleep-strengthened limb;

---

[83] *Airdrie Advertiser*, 20 May 1866, p.2.

The lark is saluting the regions of love,
And soon will the sun flash the grey mists above:
Prepare thee to sink, though the fancy should soar;
We must to the dark scenes of labour once more.

Come! rise, brother, rise! and from grumbling refrain;
He who murmurs in idleness, murmurs in vain:
A sweet slumber hangs on thy little one's brows,
A love-hallowed prayer's in the heart of thy spouse:
She pleads where thou knowst she has pled well before,
That angels may guard thee to safety once more.

Arise! brother miner! 'Twas only a dream,
That hum of green woodlands, that stroll by the stream;
Some joy-loving fairy, in portraiture gay,
Hath shown thee by night what thou seest not by day.
Yet, brother, despair not; the hours will pass o'er:
We'll rise, as the day wanes, to gladness once more.

Suppress those deep sighs, brother, though it may be
The fate of thy kinsman is waiting for thee:
O'er sorrows untasted 'tis folly to brood;
We must, like that kinsman, brave danger for good.
Then up and be stirring; like serf-men of yore,
We'll rest when we've plodded our portion once more.

Be cheerful, poor brother! I've heard of a land
Where no over-labour e'er blisters the hand –
A land where no fetters of slavery are seen.
Where the grindstone of tyranny never hath been.
Perhaps we'll go there when our ploddings are o'er,
And then we'll be weary-boned miners no more.[84]

The 'delicacy' in 'A Miner's Morning Song' lies in its careful negotiation of cheer-
fulness and suffering, conservatism and radicalism, as Wingate manages to evoke
the harsh conditions of the miner's lot and the need for change while overtly
espousing a position of duty, piety, and the dignity of labour. His repetition of
'plodding' consciously recalls the opening stanza of Gray's 'Elegy in a Country
Churchyard' ('The ploughman homeward plods his weary way'), a key intertext for
working-class writers, and its musings on the unsung heroes and poets of the
labouring classes.[85] Rather than watching the exhausted labourer, as in Gray, the
poet himself is the plodding and wearied worker. The poem's theme, represented in
its literal scenario of the miner urging his companion out of bed, is the miner's
rise to higher things, in which he must struggle to prevent an internal 'sinking' that
will mirror his actual daily descent into the pit, and instead elevate his thoughts

[84] Davie, 'A Miner's Morning Song', *Hamilton Advertiser*, 10 July 1858, p.1. Reprinted Wingate,
Poems and Songs (Edinburgh: William Blackwood, 1862), pp.1–3. The Glasgow Herald stated that it
had printed this poem 'some time ago' in its review of *Poems and Songs*, 'Literature', 26 April 1862.
[85] Wingate cited a stanza from Gray's 'Elegy' as the epigraph to 'Narrative of a Miner', *The
Commonwealth*, 25 October 1856, p.4.

and feelings, following Wingate's successful example as the composer of this poem. What the poem also tells us, however, is that mining is extremely dangerous, since the 'fate of thy kinsman' presumably indicates death or serious injury and the same fate may well await him; that miners are overworked and subject to 'the grindstone of tyranny'; that the abolition of serfdom in Scotland's mines means little, since miners are still treated like slaves; and that they are physically exhausted and despairing, weary to the bone.

Wingate's language of brotherhood, tyranny, and slavery is akin to the pro-trade union and radical mining poems published, for example, in *The Miner and Workman's Advocate* (a trades journal coinciding with the period when Wingate was best-known) in the run-up to the Leeds mineworkers conference of 1863: 'A law for our freedom soon, soon will be passed/And tyrants will have to be milder at last', or 'The collier's time is coming, when he no slave will be/ But he his birthright will obtain—sweet blessed liberty'.[86] Several such poems also evoke, as does Wingate's, the painfully early awakening of miners (whose shifts, as in 'A Miner's Morning Song', often began before sunrise):

> I've known my tender mother sigh
> When my early time to toil grew nigh
> And I myself would sob and cry:
> > Then she would weep
> When she let me out, dark, wet or dry
> > Three parts asleep.[87]

The author, James Anderson, then calls for all miners to 'unite in brotherly love' to end such hardships. For miners to 'up and be stirring', in this poetic culture, will not lead to Christian hopes of redemption in heaven but to direct action.

Wingate's poem was originally written for the local press rather than a national high-status periodical, and in this location its affinity with more radical verse by and about miners was far clearer. 'Davie's' oppositional stance to the rich coal-owners and his sometimes hard-hitting social problem verse, as in 'There's Aye Something Better Before Us', in which 'Labour' tells the wealthy, 'I warn ye, defiant we look on ye still,/And free as the lark soar aboon ye', are more apparent in the *Hamilton Advertiser*, as is his broader position in collier verse culture.[88] Although the Lanarkshire press was less radically inclined than a periodical like *The Miner*, it also published many other anonymous and pseudonymous poems by self-identified miners, expressing anger and outrage. Willoughby, for instance, in the powerful 'A Miner's Song', in the *Hamilton Advertiser* (dated July 1862), evoked the miners' descent down the shaft in his first stanza:

> Down from pure air and light,
> Far from pleasure and health,

---

[86] George Cooke, 'A New Song for the Leeds Conference', *The Miner and Workman's Advocate*, 7 November 1863, p.7 and W. Hartley, 'The Collier', ibid., 9 January 1864, p.5.

[87] James Anderson, 'To the Miners', *The Miner and Workman's Advocate*, 7 November 1863, p.7.

[88] *Poems and Songs*, p.128.

> To toil for others' wealth, my boys –
> To bring up hidden wealth.

Implicitly recalling Hartley Colliery, this poem ends by picturing the miners' death from gas and their weeping widows.[89] To take only one further example, the later poem 'The Miner's Lot' by 'Equality', for Bathgate's *West Lothian Courier*, argues for the miners' rights in an ongoing strike:

> We only claim a right to live,
> 　　A portion of our masters' wealth,
> Who says his profits cannot give
> 　　The shilling asked – their secret stealth.
>
> What flesh and blood could stand and bear, –
> 　　The men of coals their souls belie, –
> For wealth they make the miner here
> 　　A slave to torture, and to die.[90]

As 'Davie', Wingate was part of this established culture of newspaper poems by and about Scottish miners.

Stewart, whose *Among the Miners* was serialized in the *Hamilton Advertiser* in 1879, recalled indignant discussions amongst miners in his colliery about Davie's 'A Ballad (Seeking an Air)', a poem in which a woman marries her collier sweetheart only to find herself a victim of his drunken violence, published in the *Hamilton Advertiser* on 21 January 1860. As the title suggests, it is a satirical take on the popular songs about colliers' weddings and courtships. Stewart tells us that he knew Wingate and read his early newspaper pieces:

> It was at this time I first met with a 'live poet', and where? Among the miners? Aye, among the miners, although I know there are still those who will use such an expression as – 'Can any good thing come out of Nazareth?' Among the miners, and working in a wild-looking hole, that some of our mines at the present day are palaces in comparison with.[91]

He relates how:

> [T]here had appeared in the newspaper a poem of [Davie's] in illustration of some of the characters and scenes he had witnessed among the miners … It is over twenty years since that poem appeared, but it is as clear to me as an event of yesterday, the storm of bitter epithets, such as 'slanderous renegade,' etc., which two young miners, who were working beside me, poured against 'Davie'.[92]

One of the miners claimed he would answer the poem in the following week's paper, though Stewart asserts that he never did, and instead the *Hamilton Advertiser* followed 'A Ballad' with a letter on 6 February denigrating colliers' behaviour,

---

[89] Willoughby, 'A Miner's Song', *Hamilton Advertiser*, 30 August 1862, p.1.
[90] Equality, 'The Miner's Lot', *West Lothian Courier*, 28 May 1881, p.4.
[91] Thomas Stewart, *Among the Miners: Being Sketches in Prose and Verse* (Larkhall: W. Burns, 1893), p.28. This chapter appears on the front page of the *Hamilton Advertiser*, 16 August 1879.
[92] Stewart, *Among the Miners*, p.28.

and advising them to 'Go more frequently to the reading-room, and less to the dram-shop'.[93]

As Stewart's anecdote shows, many miners *were* apparently going to the reading room, if only to read the local press. He reports it to show that miners were literate and took note of what they read, to demonstrate that he knew Wingate before he was famous, and also to suggest that Wingate was not even the only poet in one specific mine. Far from Wingate being a rare and extraordinary artefact, Lanarkshire miners, like their counterparts in Wales, Cornwall, and the North of England, were substantially involved in the production and performance of verse and song and were often keen participants in literary culture. Stewart's one published poetry collection, which includes pieces recited at meetings for Larkhall natives in Glasgow (Larkhall was his native Lanarkshire town), at Burns Clubs and at Masonic meetings, particularly emphasizes the role of associational culture in promoting literary endeavours, and includes an 'Essay on Social Intercourse' in verse, seemingly read at Larkhall's literary society.[94] Of course, such societies were frequently founded and supported by employers and religious institutions: colliers and ironworkers, who often lived in housing built by the coalmasters and were far more dependent on the masters than in other industries, were particularly likely to owe the existence of night schools, reading rooms, libraries, institutes, and societies to their employers' perception that these would induce positive habits of sobriety and hard work. But colliers and workers in related industries did also set up their own collaborative means of self-improvement, and not always with a view to becoming resigned to their limited position in life. Robert Smillie, born 1857, a miner at Summerlee, Coatbridge, in his teens and later a Labour M.P., wrote that as soon as he accepted a position as a union organizer, he felt the need to embark on a course of literary education using books from Larkhall subscription library; he read and memorized Shakespeare and other writers and, 'must not forget my treasured copy of the *Fifth Standard Royal Reader*, in which I made my first acquaintance with Gray's *Elegy* and Goldsmith's *Deserted Village*, and in which I first saw the name of Oliver Goldsmith'.[95] His autobiography proudly states that 'To-day the walls of my sitting-room are not only lined with books, but hung with portraits of Carlyle, Ruskin, Russell Lowell, Longfellow, Walt Whitman, Burns and Scott'.[96] Acquiring an understanding of poetry could only help with politics. Even Labour leader Keir Hardie wrote occasional verse for the miners' cause.[97]

'[H]ere the human degradation of the industrial revolution reached its nadir', Fry writes of Scottish miners in the nineteenth century. This is a view that is in many ways difficult to dispute. The collier-poets of the period, however, did want to dispute it, not because they disagreed that their working conditions were appalling and urgently required rethought legislation and reform, but because they

---

[93] 'Our Neighbours the Colliers', *Hamilton Advertiser*, 4 February 1860.
[94] Stewart, 'Essay on Social Intercourse', *Doric Rhyme*, p.33.
[95] Robert Smillie, MP, *My Life for Labour*, foreword by J. Ramsay Macdonald (London: Mills & Boon, 1924), pp.50, 52.
[96] Ibid., p.53.
[97] See verses in letter on 'Miners' Union', *Hamilton Advertiser*, 29 May 1880, p.2.

did not wish to perceive themselves as degraded. Wingate's self-depiction as a rare sensitive miner, crushed and deformed by circumstances, as in 'To a Spriglet' (addressing a 'tiny white spray' that springs from the 'trees' supporting the roof of the mine), is strategic:

> Puir, sickly spriglet, pale and clear,
> This sunless cavern, dark and drear,
> Was never meant the life to cheer
>   O' plants like thee –
> I sairly doubt thou'lt flourish here
>   Nae mair than me.[98]

In the atmosphere of the mine, a truly inorganic environment, both nature and poetry struggle. Wingate's implicit suggestion, that he needs to be rescued from the mine to allow his poetic gift to flourish, paid off. He earned enough from his poems to study at the Andersonian Institute at Glasgow and qualify himself as a mining overseer, and was eventually awarded a Civil List pension for his literary labours. Yet in being lionized by *Blackwood's* and other middle-class periodicals as unique, his significance as a representative example of miners' literary culture, rather than the *only* example of it, was obscured, and the rich strand of working verse by Scottish miners has remained uninvestigated.

MAN AND THE ENGINE: BEATING INDUSTRY

After decades working in the pit, Francis Barnard was injured and had to take an above-ground position in the colliery as an engine-keeper. He thus moved from being a miner-poet, as the title of his first volume indicated, to an engine-poet, as his second volume's title, *Chirps Frae the Engine-Lum* (1887), signified. The key poem in this collection is 'To My Engine', subtitled 'While the steam is being raised for commencing the week's work, and the steam beginning to hiss through the cylinder'. Barnard's engine, perhaps surprisingly in the context of this poetic genre, is female:

> Hae patience lass – jist bide a wee –
> Ye're gettin' fidgety, I see;
> Ye're no as young as ye wad be
>   When first I kent ye;
> E'er the week's dune, 'tween you an' me,
>   Ye'll jist get plenty.
>
> **
>
> Ye mind me' o' my winsome Nell,
> To me a credit an' yoursel';
> An' hear me, tho' I say't mysel'.
>   But for that lung, an'

---

[98] Wingate, *Poems and Songs*, p.177.

> That nasty croich, ye look as well   *croich – cough*
>   As ony young ane.[99]

Barnard's habbie stanza would have reminded readers of the common use of this stanza, post-Burns, either in epistolary poems or to sympathize with animal suffering (following 'To a Mouse') and link it to the sufferings of the labouring classes, so that form here serves to humanize the machine. The failure of the masters to take proper care of their hard-working engine (which ventilates the mine), to 'feed' her the right materials, means that her lungs are 'stiff an' wheezie', and her days are numbered, 'Little I can, but what I may,/ I'll dae't tae ease ye'. Barnard's care for the engine, his desire to see her clean and working well, stands in implicit opposition to the owners' lack of interest. He would have assumed that his readers knew how many pit accidents were associated with machinery failure above ground (at Hartley, for instance, machinery collapsed into the shaft and blocked it), which in turn was linked to the carelessness of human operators. The injured worker and the suffering engine—suffering, moreover, from the wheeziness and lung damage so characteristic of miners, and associated with the polluted air both below and above ground—are akin. Both are industrial tools that in old age, worn out by labour, will be discarded.

Barnard's poem, explicitly concerned with disability, is a quiet rejoinder to the masculinist discourse of strong-armed, muscled workers characteristic of many songs of labour. Such discourse was perhaps most influentially formulated in Glasgow engineer Alexander G. Murdoch's 'The Breeks o' Hodden Grey', inscribed 'with manly respect, to my compeers in toil, the engineers of the Clyde':

> God! What impassioned power is this, that, blotch'd with fire and grime,
> Beats down the hills of labour, and contests the flight of Time?
> And who are they who shape its course, through rock-embattled shires,
> Who bind and build its ribs of steel, and feed its throbbing fires,
> Who loose its panting lungs of steam, and urge and guide its way?
> Who, but the rough-spun men who wear the breeks o' hodden grey.[100]

Tamara Ketabgian has argued that in the Victorian 'industrial imaginary', machines 'were not simply soulless, lifeless, predictable, and unidimensional; not simply opposed to organic feeling and vitality; and not simply reductive material objects— if objects are ever so'; rather, they were frequently depicted using the language and metaphors of organicism and vitality.[101] Scottish writers, including George Wilson, Edinburgh professor of technology, and Andrew Ure, who taught working men's scientific classes at the Andersonian Institute in Glasgow in the 1820s, were arguably particularly influential in their writing on this topic.[102] Ketabgian does not

---

[99] Barnard, *Chirps Frae the Engine Lum* (Bathgate: L. Gilbertson, 1889), p.147.

[100] Murdoch, *The Laird's Lykewake and Other Poems* (Edinburgh and Glasgow: John Menzies, 1877; printed by John Leng, Advertiser Office, Dundee), p.167.

[101] Tamara Ketabgian, *The Lives of Machines: The Industrial Imaginary in Victorian Literature and Culture* (Ann Arbor, MI: University of Michigan Press, 2011), p.2.

[102] See George Wilson, 'On the Physical Sciences', *Edinburgh New Philosophical Journal*, 5 (1857), 64–101 and Andrew Ure, *The Philosophy of Manufactures, or, An Exposition of the Scientific, Moral and*

discuss poetry, but her argument is especially pertinent to this genre: a great many poems, like Barnard and Murdoch's, conflate the relationship between man and machine so that their bodies become indistinguishable.

This relationship between man and the engine was vital to working-class verse culture because, more than any other genre discussed in this volume, it enabled the integration of form and content. The engine or machine poem is a discrete genre in this period. Although some poets did define themselves through their profession as engineers, most notably the highly successful William Allan, who wrote several volumes of Scots verse from his position in Sunderland, an 'engine-poet' in this definition is not necessarily an engineer as such, but someone, like Barnard, who represents their labour and that of others as intimately dependent on forms of machinery. Barnard's choice of form is important, but it is not imitative of the motions of the engine he addresses. Many other poems, however, did consider how metrical verse might render the beats of industry, the repetitive sounds and motions of labour: Murdoch's lines are one example of how poets typically sought to represent the force of machinery through long lines and insistent driving rhythms. Poetry can engage with machines in ways that prose cannot, both because of its rhythmic force, and because of its increasingly vexed associations with mechanical repetition in an age of industry. Jason Hall has recently studied how theories of metre in this period are intimately connected to new technologies, arguing that 'meter participated fully in the machine culture of the nineteenth century' and hence 'many of the signal theories, instantiations, and institutions of meter' in this period were 'shot through with traces of contemporary technologies'.[103] As Max Cavitch perceptively comments, in a suggestive consideration of American poetry of slavery, 'in an age of rapid industrialization and depersonalization of the labouring subject', the 'literal mechanization of poetic creation...was a very worrisome prospect'. To counter this, he suggests that poetry may have acted as 'the assertion of rhythmic complexity and forms of dissonance against the mechanistic regularity of repetitive coerced labour'.[104] Engine poets, I argue here, offer us a sophisticated account of how rhythm might simultaneously collude with and celebrate the inhuman forces of industry, and oppose them.

The single Scottish poem which reflects on mechanical and poetic rhythm most vividly, is Geddes' 'The Man and the Engine', published in his 1886 collection *The Spectre Clock of Alyth*. Valentina Bold and Gioia Angeletti both briefly discuss this poem and suggest that the engine works as a 'metaphor for working class misery:

Commercial Economy of the Factory System of Great Britain, 3rd edn, cont. by P. L. Simmonds (London: H. G. Bohn, 1861). David F. Channell discusses Wilson and notes that Karl Marx, in his famous chapter on machines in Das Kapital, cites Ure. See *The Vital Machine: A Study of Technology and Organic Life* (Oxford: Oxford University Press, 1991), pp.81–7.

[103] Jason David Hall, *Nineteenth-Century Verse and Technology: Machines of Meter* (London: Palgrave, 2017), pp.2, 7.

[104] Max Cavitch, 'Slavery and its Metrics', in Kerri Larson, ed., *The Cambridge Companion to Nineteenth-Century American Poetry* (Cambridge: Cambridge University Press, 2011), pp.94–112, 99, 100.

the masses exploited by their masters and goaded to the point of rebellion'.[105] Unlike most of the poets in this book, Geddes was well read in contemporary experimental verse. He was particularly influenced by Walt Whitman, whose paeans to the American industrial sublime often lie behind Geddes' more sceptical verse, though 'The Man and the Engine' is more intimately linked to Tennyson's *Maud* (1855) in its formal debt to the dramatic monologue, its possibly insane speaker and his fatalistic despair, and its varied rhythms. Geddes' speaker opens by disclaiming any status as a poet 'Nothing know I of the tricks of verse', linking this to his distance from natural inspiration in the city, where he has 'become as a part/Of the mill machinery'. Yet, he continues:

> I think I could find a poem here,
> Were I only blessed with a little wit,
> And my engine should be the theme of it.
> Perhaps for you it has not charms,
> Though it magnetises me;
> Yet in my room I only see
> The ponderous beam and its ponderous arms
> Toiling on continually.
>
> And there answers back to its throb and beat
> A throbbing in my brain,
> Which feels like a weight and a pain,
> And I carry it everywhere;
> There! it is always there.
> My very thoughts move to and fro,
> And rhyme themselves to its swing and throw;
> And its wearisome refrain
> Seems welded or woven in
> With the texture of my brain.[106]

'Magnetises', another semi-scientific term, carries the sense of hypnotism, falling under a spell, so that 'charms' becomes a more loaded word, whereas 'welded or woven in', given that the imagined speaker is probably in a Dundee textile factory, show him incorporating and incorporated by his work. Geddes' longer lines here stand out as those in which the motions of the engine are pictured and felt, and tend to use two unstressed beats ('to its swing') to drive these lines onward. But there is no stable rhythm in these stanzas, as though the worker resists or moves in and out of alignment to machine regularity. Nor is there a stable rhyme-scheme: the stanzas run abbcddcd, abbccddbeb, so are not identical, and the rhymes again speed up and slow down the movement of the verse according to whether they form couplets, or whether the reader has to look back several lines for a rhyme. The speaker imagines the engine mocking the man's pretence of superiority, as it is given a voice to point out not simply that this particular worker is trapped in the same

[105] Bold, p.291. Her study also contains a short assessment of Wingate as a poet (pp.272–5). Gioia Angeletti, *Eccentric Scotland: Three Victorian Poets* (Bologna: CLUEB (Cooperativa Libraria Universitaria Editrice Bologna), 2004), pp.262–7.
[106] Geddes, *The Spectre Clock of Alyth* (Alyth: Thomas McMurray, 1886), pp.58–9.

mechanical rhythms as the machine, but that humans are God's machines and thus free-will is a delusion, 'The crank may be hid, but the crank is there,/ And He turns it on, and He turns it off'. Geddes' disturbing rhythms are at one with his aim to unsettle the reader's firmly held religious convictions. The insistent and triumphalist beat of 'The Breeks O' Hodden Gray' becomes a swaying or swinging motion that is repetitive without steadiness, leaving nowhere to rest. Taking into account Matthew Campbell's argument that Victorian poets use rhythm to represent the will, Murdoch's poem is about the forward march of the unconquerable will in an age of mechanical progress, whereas Geddes' is about the unwanted surrender of will to the monstrous and unpredictable force of machinery.[107] In 'The Man and the Engine', humanizing the engine corresponds to the dehumanization of men.

Neither Murdoch's nor Geddes' attitudes were unusual in Victorian perceptions of machinery. Geddes, who knew Carlyle's writings very well, is again looking back to 'Signs of the Times' and its comments on machinery, emotion, and spirituality: 'Not the external and physical alone is now managed by machinery, but the internal and spiritual also', and 'Our true Deity is mechanism'.[108] Murdoch, in contrast, follows Ure in arguing for the benefits of machinery and the 'benignant power of steam' in adding its superior energies to those of man.[109] The sophistication with which working-class poets engaged with these conflicting attitudes has rarely been recognized. For the remainder of this chapter, I turn to railway poets—like miner-poets, a relatively discrete grouping—since the railways offer, as Wolfgang Schivelbusch argues, the most trenchant example of how 'mechanical regularity triumphed over natural irregularity' in terms of time, space, and the bodily habits of the Victorian labourer.[110] Railways differ from mines, or from the factories and blast furnaces of industrial Lanarkshire, in that the safety and quality of their construction and their good management had an immediate impact on the middle classes. Trains were known through the personal experience of travellers in a way that coal mines were not, and hence poems about the accidents and damage caused by the exploitation of railway workers were arguably more immediately relevant (and threatening) to a wider readership than were poems on the poor conditions of other industries.

Britain had a very substantial number of poetry-writing railway workers, in all the different grades and types of the profession. In Scotland, however, by far the most famous was Alexander Anderson, or 'Surfaceman', author of *Songs of the Rail* (1878). Anderson, discussed in Chapter 2 as a nursery verse author, was a friend of Murdoch's, and of many other contributors to the 'songs of labour' subgenre popular in the Scottish press. He was perceived as especially remarkable as an example of a navvy poet, since navvies, like miners, were often regarded as:

> Rough alike in morals and in manners...displaying an unbending vigour and an
> independent bearing...with all the strong propensities of an untaught, undisciplined

[107] Matthew Campbell, *Rhythm and Will in Victorian Poetry* (Cambridge: Cambridge University Press, 1999).

[108] Carlyle, 'Signs of the Times', pp.35, 46.   [109] Ure, p.18.

[110] Wolfgang Schivelbusch, *The Railway Journey: The Industrialization of Time and Space in the 19th Century* (Berg: Hamburg, 1986, first published 1977), p.23.

nature; unable to read and unwilling to be taught; impetuous, impulsive and brute-like; regarded as the pariahs of private life; herding together like beasts of the field; owing no moral law and feeling no social tie.[111]

John Taylor, a navvy poet briefly discussed in Chapter 1, told his readers in one of his first published efforts, 'Compassion and loyalty beat in our breast,/ And surely poor navvies are men like the rest', evidently fearing that they did not perceive this to be true.[112] But a marketable navvy poet, like a marketable miner-poet, was a strong proposition. While *Songs of the Rail*, like Anderson's other collections, highlighted his wide reading and his self-taught familiarity with European literature, this came after a frontispiece of Anderson leaning on his spade and dressed in his work clothes; a portrait that (minus the woman) effectively portrays the myth of the 'extraordinarily potent navvy man . . . a fine muscled animal, standing with legs braced apart, grasping in one hand a pick by the shaft and in the other a woman'.[113]

Anderson's 'A Song of Labour', reprinted immediately after the dedicatory poem in *Songs of the Rail*, rejoices in the potency of machinery and of the men who tend it, adopting a 'virile and evangelical persona', in Bold's terms.[114] He writes on the steam train, in driving couplets:

> Arm to arm, and lay the metals, glowing but with one desire—
> To do honour to the mightiest of the worshippers of fire.
> All the great in early fable, mighty-pulsing Anakim,
> All the thew'd and swarthy Cyclops are as nothing unto him.[115]

Here and elsewhere, Anderson repeatedly compares engines to monstrous creatures of myth and legend, and the men who build them to Mary Shelley's Frankenstein, potentially overmastered by their creation. Workers are in awe of the giant railway engines they serve, but are also always threatened by their monstrosity and relentlessness. *Songs of the Rail* and later volumes of railway verse, notably William 'Inspector' Aitken's *Lays of the Line* (1883), are remarkable for their emphasis on human flesh and blood 'Tossed among the ruthless wagons,/ Mangled by the gory wheel', and counterpoint the 'iron pulses' of the rails with the fragile and easily damaged rhythms of the human body.[116] Their focus on horrific accidents serves as a trenchant comment on the impossibility of expecting human physiology to withstand the stress and strain of relentless industrial rhythm. (Simon Bradley reminds us that the rhythm of Victorian trains was 'closer to an incessant thumping and banging' than we might think from twentieth-century experience.)[117]

---

[111] John Francis, A History of the English Railway (1851), p.ii, 67–9, cited in J. E. Handley, *The Navvy in Scotland* (Cork: Cork University Press, 1970), p.32.

[112] Taylor, p.31. See also Taylor's 'The Navvies' in *Poets of the People's Journal*, p.58.

[113] Terry Coleman, *The Railway Navvies* (London: Pimlico, 2000, first published 1965), p.187.

[114] Bold, p.278. Her broader critical consideration of Anderson (pp.275–84) connects him strongly to Geddes.

[115] 'A Song of Labour', *Songs of the Rail* (London: Simpkin, Marshall, 1878), p.29.

[116] Inspector Aitken, St Enoch Station, Glasgow, 'William Morton', *Lays of the Line* (Edinburgh and Glasgow: John Menzies, 1883), p.82.

[117] Simon Bradley, *The Railways: Nation, Network and People* (London: Profile, 2015), p.258.

For Anderson, the suffering of railway workers through contact with machinery may have been a particularly topical theme, since *Songs of the Rail* appeared in the year that the Railway Returns (Continuous Brakes) Act, which required railway companies to report on their braking systems for the first time, was passed.[118] Eleven out of thirty-four poems in *Songs of the Rail* involve accident or death, while *Lays of the Line* was explicitly written, Aitken notes in his preface, to show that 'of all other occupations either on land or sea, that of the ordinary railway employee is by far the most hazardous'. While there is a strong element of sensationalism in railway accident poems, many of which are dramatic monologues spoken by railway employees who caused, or failed to prevent, terrible losses of life, they are not necessarily inaccurate representations. As P. W. Kingsford's study of Victorian railwaymen notes, this *was* one of the most dangerous professions: in 1871 the Casualty Fund of the Railway Benevolent Association estimated that the risk of injury or death for railwaymen was 1 in 37.[119] Unquestionably, however, these poets capitalize on public interest in tales of heroism and disaster on the rails. Nicholas Daly's influential article on railway rescues in melodrama argues that this interest can be attributed to 'a popular perception of something qualitatively different in all industrial-technology accidents, they occur in "machine time", not human time'.[120] What railway poets can do, more easily than fiction writers, is showcase this 'machine time' versus 'human time' through their rhythms. Anderson's and Aitken's poems are deeply self-conscious about 'the voiceless measure ranging through our toiling day' and its relationship to metrical composition.[121] This is poetry that uses form to represent how, in the creation and running of railways, human physiology is tested by the unremitting beat of the machine.

'Iron pulses', is a phrase from Anderson's 'On the Engine by Night':

> On the engine in the night-time, with the darkness all around,
> And below the iron pulses beating on with mighty sound.[122]

This uses the rapid beat of three unstressed syllables followed by a stressed syllable, in a long fifteen syllable line, to recreate an approximation of the train's rhythm. What Victorian readers would also hear, however, was the beat of Tennyson's 'Locksley Hall', 'Let the great world spin for ever down the ringing grooves of change' (l.182). Nearly one in four poems in *Songs of the Rail* follow this metre, as do a substantial number in *Lays of the Line*:

> Down he dropped among the wagons, scarcely time to think and feel,
> Onward came the grinding engine, o'er him passed the crushing wheel.[123]

---

[118] For a contemporary discussion, see Tatlow, *Fifty Years of Railway Life*, p.87. Tatlow knew Anderson in the 1870s.

[119] P. W. Kingsford, *Victorian Railwaymen: The Emergence and Growth of Railway Labour, 1840–1870* (Routledge: London, 2006, first published 1970), p.47

[120] Nicholas Daly, 'Blood on the Tracks: Sensation Drama, the Railway, and the Dark Face of Modernity', *Victorian Studies* 42 (1998), 47–76, p.60.

[121] 'A Song of Labour', *Songs of the Rail*, p.30.   [122] Ibid., p.79.

[123] Aitken, 'Convict Jim', *Lays of the Line*, p.3.

Such lines signal homage to Tennyson, but Anderson and Aitken's poems also point out to the reader that Tennyson—like other Victorian poets who wrote railway-carriage poems—was a relatively ignorant spectator. Aitken and Anderson are not at a safe remove from the rhythms they describe, but caught up in their diurnal round; they seek to imagine what it is like to *work* to the beat of unstoppable machines, and repeatedly emphasize that their verse is inspired by direct contact. Anderson notes in his dedicatory poem, 'To My Readers':

> What marvel then, that seeing, day by day,
>   The engine rush along,
> That I send you, from out the 'four-feet way'
>   This book of railway song.[124]

Labouring as a navvy meant serving the trains, and also often being in dangerous proximity to them as they travelled at speed. Anderson's reference is to the standard width of British track, but he is undoubtedly aware of the metrical pun ('To My Readers' *is* out of the 'four-feet way' in its use of pentameter and trimeter lines). In both collections, trochaics and anapaests are used in conjunction with strong end-rhymes to drive long lines forwards: these, interspersed with more standard tetrameter, are the metrical foundation of *Songs of the Rail* and *Lays of the Line*.

Aitken uses these long lines, in 'Convict Jim' and elsewhere, specifically to emphasize that the relentless rhythms of railway labour are impossible for flesh and blood to sustain. In 'Widow Morgan', an only son, a signalman, is forced to work day and night because he needs the money to repay an unjust fine from the railway company:

> Backward promptly in the morning to his signal work again,
> Wearied out, and dull and heavy with the long continued strain,
> Now and then a drowsy numbness creeping o'er his eye and brain.
>
> Up against the dreamy monster all day long he bravely bore,
> Never in his whole experience had he felt so press'd before,
> Till he could no longer battle, down he sat and toppled o'er.
>
> Scarce a minute had he slumbered, when the shrieking whistle blew,
> Up he sprung in dreamy blindness, pulled a lever ere he knew.[125]

Unsurprisingly, he has pulled the wrong lever, causing a fatal accident. The poem ends with the son in prison and the mother dying in the workhouse. Similarly, in 'The Maniac's Story', the speaker was in charge of a repair crew on the line:

> Then 'twas march with pick and shovel, all the same by day and night,
> Scarcely time a crust to swallow till the place again was right.[126]

In a state of exhaustion, he also blunders, leading directly to the hideous death of the stoker on the oncoming train, who, in Aitken's standard coincidence, is his son; the speaker consequently goes insane. These poems are striking indictments of the railway companies for assuming that human workers can keep pace with

---

[124] *Songs of the Rail*, p.12.   [125] *Lays of the Line*, p.10.   [126] Ibid., p.13.

machines, disregarding the natural rhythms of night and day and the body's need for sleep and sustenance. They might also, using Henri Lefebvre's comments on the 'dispossession of the body' caused by workers being 'rhythmed', be read as a wider indictment of the forces of industrialism or modern capitalism, which 'constructs and erects itself on a contempt for life and from this foundation: the body, the time of living'.[127] Aitken's metre in 'Widow Morgan' deliberately does not embody the Keatsian 'drowsy numbness' of the signalman; it indicates the force that he must strive to obey as opposed to the fatigue of his human body and mind. The mechanics of these poems set a beat that the labourers within them cannot sustain.

Many of Anderson's poems also follow this pattern, though he tends to leave more scope for man to triumph. In 'Nottman', the men attempt to halt a train on seeing a body ahead on the line:

> The great wheels stagger'd and span with the strain,
> While the spray from the steam fell around us like rain,
> But we slacken'd our speed, till we saw with a wild
> Throb at the heart, right before us, – a child![128]

Anderson uses the double stress on 'great wheels' to slow the start of the line, mimicking the attempt to slow down. Repeated anapaests indicate the failure of this attempt, in the second and third lines, and alliteration nicely signifies the hiss of steam as the driver tries to slow the train. At the close of the third line, the rhythm starts to stagger: the enjambement and absence of punctuation, the stress on 'Throb' and pauses and uneven stresses on 'right before', suggest human rhythm interrupting the potentially fatal beat of the train. In this case, human ingenuity saves the child. Unable to stop the train, Nottman dangles precariously from it and pushes the toddler away from the rails. The child is, it emerges, his son. The repeated emphases on railway workers who kill or almost kill members of their own family, in these poems, further operates as a metaphor for the threat to domestic ties created by the brutal requirements of railway work, which alienate working men from wives and children.

Anderson is more celebratory than Aitken, and his poetry lacks Aitken's gloomy fatalism; he usually images labour as part of a mutual relationship between man and machine, in which the worker checks the monster he has created: 'Yet I glory to think that I help to keep/ His footsteps a little in place'.[129] Anderson's train is also interchangeable with, and consistently personified as, the male working-class poet—'each throb that shook his being found a ready voice in mine'.[130] (Indeed, if Barnard imagines his engine as a wife, Anderson's powerfully masculine and sexualized identification between man and engine, consistently figured in physiological terms, invites a homoerotic reading.) *Songs of the Rail* continually questions where

---

[127] Henri Lefebvre, *Rhythmanalysis: Space, Time and Everyday Life*, trans. Stuart Edlend and Gerald Moore (London: Continuum, 2004), pp.75, 51. On workers' time and capitalism, see also Rancière, *Proletarian Nights*, p.xi and *passim*.

[128] *Songs of the Rail*, p.112.

[129] 'The Engine', *Songs of the Rail*, p.44. First published in the *People's Friend*, 8 March 1871, p.151.

[130] *Songs of the Rail*, p.82.

control lies: with the machine creating the beat, or the man who created and operates the machine? Anderson, Aitken, and the other railway and engine poets trace a complicated relationship between poet and machinery, poetic metre and the rhythms of industry. Like the Coatbridge poets, they are inclined to celebrate the sublimity of industry, the awe and terror it inspires, and the need to sacrifice aspects of usual human life, indeed human lives themselves, to its relentless progress. But like the miner-poets, they also use the resources of poetry to draw attention to particular, contemporary issues in professions that they know from the inside, in order to make a case for change.

5

Humour, Satire, and the Rise
of the Bad Poet

As previous chapters have shown, the firm belief in Scotland's remarkable track record in producing 'peasant' poets was highly promoted, both in Scotland and further afield. In 1863, for instance, W. H. Wills' play *The Man o' Airlie* opened in London with striking success, eventually transferring to New York in 1871. The eponymous hero is Jamie Harebell, a lowly Scottish poet; the American advertisement for the play described him thus:

> JAMES HAREBELL is simple in mind; pure in heart; delicate and sensitive in temperament; chaste in conduct; generous as the noonday sun; sympathetic with all innocent joys and real griefs; fond of all natural beauties; kind to everybody; a true husband; an affectionate father; a considerate neighbor; a manly, cheerful creature, living on terms of loving intimacy with grass, and flowers, and birds; diffusing happiness around him, by word and deed, wherever and whenever he can; writing simple songs that the poor people love; – and so leading a life that blesses by goodness and teaches by example.[1]

Naturally, being a model poet and thus entirely unworldly, Harebell is conned out of his money and his book, his wife dies in poverty, and he is presumed dead until he shows up, a raving beggar, in time to die poetically at the feet of his own statue, erected as a belated recognition of his genius. The *People's Friend* reviewer was impressed with the play, describing it in detail and commenting on Harebell's first scene that:

> The hill-bred genius clad in hodden gray enters the room at that moment; over his shoulders he wears a homely plaid. He is the type of those poetic sons which only Scotland seems to produce, as if there was something in the mountain breezes and heather of that romantic land which made her indeed a fit nurse for a poetic child.

The reviewer praises Wills' Harebell as a 'true perception of the Scottish type': the type of the noble peasant poet.[2]

One week after this review, however, the *Friend* published a comic tale as a first person account from would-be newspaper poet Willie Grahame, who shows up

---

[1] The Man o' Airlie; A Drama of the Affections. The Dramatic Sensation of London in 1863, and acted with equal success in America, where it was first produced in June, 1871, by Mr Lawrence Barrett, at Booth's Theatre, New York. (Philadelphia, PA: Ledger Steam-Power Printing Office, 1871), p.8.

[2] 'The Man o' Airlie', *People's Friend*, 2 August 1876.

with his manuscript to give it to an editorial friend, is admitted to the editor's sanctum to wait for his friend's return, and finds the following note on his desk:

> These poets! We feel utterly overwhelmed – distracted. For four mortal hours have we sat here opening envelope after envelope till we have completed our fourth hundred – and nothing but poetry! Three hundred "first attempts," ninety-nine pieces of sheer doggerel from those we have snubbed before, and one, with four lines, passable! And the cry is, still they come! We have given them up. In perfect frenzy we have plucked the hair from our head, and are off, uncertain whether to commit suicide or join a temperance society. *Vale*![3]

Grahame then gives some examples of the bad poems he found amongst the editor's papers, before deciding, chastened, that the pursuit of poetry is not for him. On the one hand, then, the *People's Friend* argues that only Scotland can produce natural poetic genius from the ranks of the people. On the other, Scotland's contemporary 'people's poets', increasingly unlikely to have been nursed by mountain breezes and heather in the new modern nation, produce 399 bad poems for every good poem and specialize in 'doggerel'.

The standard editorial stance, in every newspaper and periodical examined in this study, was to exalt the significance of poetry (the *Friend* also specialized in publishing inspirational biographies of working-class poets, such as James Stewart, the 'Poet of Dunkeld', Janet Hamilton, the 'Poetess of the West', and Gerald Massey) while expressing exasperation and despair about the hordes of bad poets in Scotland, who had been encouraged to believe they should endeavour to write poetry by seeing their peers in the press.[4] 'We believe that six people, out of every dozen, some time during the course of their life, have imagined that they could write poetry', the *Friend* editor noted to one rejected poet in February 1870, following this up in March with a longer critique:

> The more we read the effusions of the bards who daily indundate us with their wares the more we are impressed with the conviction that rhyming is inherent in Scotchmen... This conviction is forced upon us by the fact that in no other branch of literature that falls under our notice does there occur so many instances of bad spelling and bad grammar, or so many indications of youthful and immature attempts to appear in public... rhyming is a terribly infectious disease, among the young more especially.[5]

The association of poetry with the 'youthful and immature' is picked up again and again, here and elsewhere in the Scottish press; with the editor's sardonic comments especially directed towards 'our young poets howling over the death of some imaginary fair one' and 'our young aspirants towards poetical laurels' who 'often think that when they can string a number of lines together with the necessary

---

[3] Willie Grahame, 'Among the Poets: A Singular Adventure', *People's Friend*, 9 August 1876, pp.500–1.

[4] Nisbet Noble, 'James Stewart, the Poet of Dunkeld', *People's Friend*, 27 July 1870, pp.470–1; 'Janet Hamilton, the Poetess of the West' (unsigned), 3 August 1870, pp.48–5; 'The Poetry of Gerald Massey' (unsigned), 22 November 1871, pp.741–2.

[5] 'To Correspondents', *People's Friend*, 9 February 1870, 23 March 1870.

amount of syllables in each that it is all right, and they are then poets'.[6] This constructed image of the foolish adolescent poet and their 'first attempt'—which is indebted in part to real-life Scottish authors like David Gray and his self-presentation as tormented young genius—was also picked up in comic prose accounts, for example Alexander Whamond's very popular fictional autobiography of Jamie Tacket, draper's assistant. Tacket titled one chapter 'I Become Poetical', ruefully commenting: 'Almost every young man between the ages of fourteen and twenty takes to writing verses; and so long as he is content to enjoy them in the privacy of his own chamber, or in the domestic circle, they do no harm'.[7] The implication, of course, is that it *is* harmful to the cause of Scottish poetry if such verses make it into print.

As the previous chapters amply show, poets, readers, and editors took the work of poetry seriously. Becoming a published poet was laudable, a signal of self-improvement, intelligence, and industry, and a demonstration of fitness to participate in politics and society. Yet alongside a publication culture that highly encouraged and valued the practice of poetry stood this parallel and overlapping culture that mocked would-be poets, lamented and laughed at their attempts to produce poems that would pass muster, and worried that the hordes of would-be poets were doing nothing for Scotland's literary reputation. Whether Scotland was producing more Willie Grahames than Jamie Harebells was a question frequently, albeit satirically, discussed by critics and editors. In newspaper poetry columns in the new popular press, these editors saw an unprecedented opportunity not simply to promote poetry, but simultaneously to discourage would-be authors and entertain their readership by satirizing the verse they received which was 'Not Up to Our Standard', in the rueful title of one newspaper poem about a would-be poet.[8]

The Scottish press built on and developed readers' pre-existing enjoyment of bad verse, their pleasure in encountering poetry that attempted to follow the standard norms of the period yet consistently failed to live up to these. This culture of bad verse as it operated in Victorian Scottish popular literature—and beyond, though my focus is solely on Scotland—is highly complex and has never been examined. As I note in the Introduction, critical judgements about the aesthetic quality and value of particular kinds of verse are problematic and historically specific. Many poems highly admired and widely circulated in the popular Victorian press are not, in the twenty-first century, accorded much if any value as 'good' poems by literary critics and readers. There is a definite consistency between Victorian readers and twenty-first-century readers, however, about what constitutes 'doggerel' or bad verse as opposed to 'good': such verse is usually grammatically inaccurate, poorly spelled or lacking in punctuation, its rhymes are inharmonious, its language is inappropriate to its theme, its metre and line-lengths are awkwardly uneven, and it lacks the qualities of smoothness and regularity so beloved by Victorian critics and editors.

---

[6] 'To Correspondents', *People's Friend*, 13 July 1870, p.433; 22 March 1871, p.192.

[7] Alexander Whamond, *James Tacket: A Humorous Tale of Scottish Life*, 3rd edn (Edinburgh: Seton and Mackenzie, 1877), p.150. This first appeared in the newspapers, including the *People's Journal* and the *Hamilton Advertiser*. The latter published this chapter on 8 October 1859.

[8] A. W. C., Addiewell, 'Not Up to Our Standard', *West Lothian Courier*, 28 January 1882, p.4.

It has generally been assumed that although there are 'good bad' poets whose work continues to make readers laugh, like William McGonagall or the poets featured in the well-known 1930 anthology *The Stuffed Owl*, such poetry is the product of a failure of intelligence or skill on the part of the authors.[9] Its humour is often unintentional. Indeed, the reason it is funny is because the poet intended it to be taken seriously.

While the overt attitude of newspaper editors involved disparaging bad verse and discouraging doggerel poets, newspapers in fact did a great deal to encourage them. Moreover, the Scottish popular press from the mid nineteenth-century onwards rapidly developed a culture of *deliberate* bad verse, with transatlantic links to American comic writing and, as I suggest below, a strong relationship to ongoing debates over the future of written English. The self-conscious bad verse discussed in this chapter emerged in Britain in roughly the same period as nonsense verse in England—the early 1860s onwards—but it is in a different category. The best-known practitioners of nonsense verse were highly educated members of the intellectual elite, like Edward Lear, Lewis Carroll, and Christina Rossetti, as opposed to the self-taught working-class poets discussed here; nonsense was usually directed more towards child readers than adults; and its humour generally rests on the dichotomy between knowing obedience to complex verse forms and grammatical structures, contrasted with non-standard and invented language, wordplay, and comedic scenarios. There is no mention of nonsense verse or its authors in any contemporary commentary on humorous verse culture in Scotland, in contrast to multiple references to the, now largely forgotten, American comic writers Artemus Ward and Josh Billings.

For readers who encountered a bad poem in their local paper in the 1860s or 1870s, the decades when the culture of presenting poorly written poems to readers was most prevalent, part of the pleasure lay in guessing whether, given that bad verse was becoming a highly publishable subgenre, the author was writing strategically as opposed to ignorantly. The poem was entertaining in either case, but additional satisfaction could be had from any ambiguity, especially if it seemed that the all-powerful editorial figure responsible for sending poorly written poems to the 'Balaam Box' (for rejected manuscripts) had been taken in by a poet cleverer than they might seem. The central figure here is Poute of the *People's Journal*, whose writings I have already examined in brief elsewhere.[10] Poute (the pseudonym of Alexander Burgess, dancing-master and musician from Fife) is the leading example of a writer who developed a successful alter ego as a bad poet. Although he enjoyed a stellar career as part of the *People's Journal* coterie of authors, and gave rise to a host of imitators, only Donaldson has commented on his significance, situating him in relation to the 'vernacular revival'.[11] The second section of this chapter

---

[9] D. B. Wyndham-Lewis and Charles Lee, eds., *The Stuffed Owl: An Anthology of Bad Verse* (London: J. M. Dent, 1930).

[10] 'McGonagall, Poute and the Bad Poet in Victorian Scotland', *The Bottle-Imp* 14 (2013), https://www.thebottleimp.org.uk/2013/11/mcgonagall-poute-and-the-bad-poets-of-victorian-dundee/ (consulted 14 September 2018).

[11] See Donaldson, pp.59–60.

examines his works in detail, placing them in the context of the wider culture of publishing bad verse in the newspaper press.

No study of Scottish Victorian poetry can ignore the looming influence of William McGonagall, and the third section of this chapter takes McGonagall seriously. Hugh MacDiarmid wrote, in his essay on 'The Great McGonagall':

> Contrary to the general opinion...William McGonagall was not a bad poet; still less a good bad poet. He was not a poet at all, and that he has become synonymous with bad poetry in Scotland is only a natural consequence of Scottish insensitivity to the qualities alike of good poetry and of bad. There is so much of bad in all the poetry that Scots people know and admire that it is not surprising that for their pet example of a good bad poet they should have had to go outside the range of poetry, good, bad, or indifferent, altogether. McGonagall is in a very special category, and has it entirely to himself.[12]

This is, of course, part of MacDiarmid's general disparagement of Victorian Scottish verse cultures and depends on a number of assumptions about what might constitute 'poetry'. There is little meaningful distinction between McGonagall's style and content and that of a hawker of street verse in 1830s or 1860s Scotland, like those discussed elsewhere in this study, other than McGonagall's far greater reputation and longevity. As I will argue here, McGonagall's success, if it can be called such, rests not on distinctiveness but on *familiarity*. His poems, printed in the newspapers, were clearly participating in a pre-existing genre of bad verse—deliberate or otherwise—in the popular press. Yet because they were also published as broadsides and designed for performance, McGonagall's poems, unlike much of the bad verse in newspapers, lean heavily in their rhythms and topics on the particular forms of broadside verse and oral performance culture. As Gord Bambrick has argued most trenchantly, McGonagall 'made his living in the working-class genres of broadside balladry and music-hall entertainment', and replacing him in these genres, alongside more detailed study of the culture of newspaper verse that surrounds him, makes it all the more likely that his verse is knowingly, rather than accidentally, bad.[13]

The purpose of studying 'bad' poetry in Scotland is to demonstrate that, far from being 'insensitive' to the qualities of verse to the point that they could not distinguish between 'good, bad, or indifferent', Scottish readers of the popular press had a very clear sense of the poetic standards assumed and accepted in their day, and were well aware of the differences between poetry that met these standards, and poetry that flouted them, either deliberately or not. Their enjoyment of poems in the second category rested on an understanding of the first. McGonagall, Poute, and the coteries of bad newspaper poets and performers, rely heavily on

---

[12] MacDiarmid, 'The Great McGonagall', *Scottish Eccentrics*, pp.57–75, 57.

[13] Bambrick, 'The Heroic Warrior: Sir William Topaz McGonagall, Poet and Tragedian, Knight of the White Elephant, Burmah' (Masters thesis, University of Guelph, 1992), archived online at http://www.oocities.org/williamtopazmcgonagall/thesis.htm (consulted 14 September 2018). See also Gord Bambrick, 'The Real McGonagall', 'McGonagall Online', http://www.mcgonagall-online.org.uk/articles/the-real-mcgonagall (consulted 14 September 2018).

their audience's understanding of what local poetry is meant to do and how a local bard might represent him or herself. Whether they seek to produce a serious effect or write satirically, these local poets are more self-aware and conscious of their engagement with generic norms than we might expect, and as such they have a tendency to satirize or question the 'standard' that working-class poets were expected to live up to. Given that these standards are set by the literary and cultural establishment, flouting them can be, to some extent, an act of subversion. The remarkable work done by these neglected subcultures of bad verse, and their influence on verse culture more broadly, is the focus of this chapter.

'VERDICT, RUBBISH': CORRESPONDENCE COLUMNS AND THE MAKING OF THE BAD POET

Victorian newspapers and periodicals, as several historians and literary critics have examined, frequently included 'correspondence' columns, in which editorial staff would respond to questions on a wide variety of topics submitted by readers, offering an 'unprecedented opportunity' for readers to receive advice and communications from their favoured media outlet.[14] Andrew King notes, in his case study of *The London Journal*, that reader interaction via these columns became 'a characteristic that defined newspapers and low-status periodicals'.[15] As Berridge comments on the burgeoning weekend press:

> In their enormously popular correspondence columns...the Sunday papers acted as advisers on a whole range of concerns...Newspapers at this stage were not writing for a passive audience. There was still an expectation that the relationship would be a lively one.[16]

Few newspaper historians comment, however, on the tendency of the provincial press to use these columns as a venue for sardonic and serious commentary on readers' poetic submission. This was not unique to Scotland: Mike Sanders' work on the *Northern Star* shows that it sometimes included comments on readers' poems, as did other English and international papers, but it does seem to have become especially popular in the provincial Scottish press from the 1860s onwards. As I examine elsewhere, by the mid-1860s, in newspapers such as the *People's Journal*,

---

[14] Claire Furlong, 'Health Advice in Popular Periodicals: Reynolds's Miscellany, the Family Herald, and Their Correspondents', *Victorian Periodicals Review* 49 (2016), 28–48, 31.

[15] Andrew King, *The London Journal, 1845–83: Periodicals, Production and Gender* (Aldershot: Ashgate, 2004), p.55.

[16] Berridge, p.252. Correspondence columns have attracted considerable attention from critics, particularly in relation to gender issues. See, for example, Barbara Green, 'Complaints of Everyday Life: Feminist Periodical Culture and Correspondence Columns in The Woman Worker, Women Folk and The Freewoman', *Modernism/Modernity* 19 (2012), 461–85; Cynthia Ellen Patton, '"Not a limitless possession": Health Advice and Readers' Agency in The Girls' Own Paper, 1880–1890', *Victorian Periodicals Review* 45 (2012), 111–33 and Lynn Warren, '"Women in Conference": Reading the Correspondence Columns in Woman 1890–1910', in Laurel Brake, Bill Bell and David Finkelstein, eds., *Nineteenth-Century Media and the Construction of Identities* (Houndmills: Palgrave, 2000), pp.122–34.

the *Weekly News* and the *Penny Post*, more poetry appeared in the correspondence columns than in the section of the paper devoted to 'Original Poetry'.[17] Most importantly for the concerns of this chapter, these columns also demonstrated how editors pursued their goal of helping working-class readers to improve by deploying the comic potential of badly written verse, and the (supposed) deterrent of withering editorial scorn.

Correspondence columns commented on all aspects of submitted poems, including poor presentation and handwriting, spelling and grammar, style, content, and form. J. K. from Kirkcaldy was warned, for example, that:

> in addition to the bad writing, the quantity of dirt collected on the sheet had nearly obliterated the ink marks... If you should ever be so indiscreet again as to court the Muses, don't carry the manuscripts about in your pocket for a week before you forward them here.[18]

The dirty pocket as well as poor handwriting suggests the writer's status as uneducated or working-class. In a reversed comment, J. B. M. was told by the *People's Friend* that 'Your verses won't do, but your handwriting is fair, and might pass muster in a merchant's office'.[19] One instance from the *Weekly News* includes three typical criticisms:

> MILTON – Your lines are not nearly so bad as your spelling. Do buy a shilling dictionary.
> SANDY – Very passable poetry, but hardly up to our mark.
> JM – Your lines have the right stuff in them, and it gives us great pleasure to smooth off any little blemishes.[20]

Editors had no hesitation in altering poems before publication—smoothing off the blemishes—or in recommending revisions or inserting editorial notes to bring poems into line with contemporary morality. 'Make the lass walk beside you in the last verse but one, instead of following you through the snow, and we will insert your verses', D.J. from Glasgow was told in the *Hamilton Advertiser*, presumably because the stanza in question was impolite to the 'lass' of the poem; while one of hundreds of elegies for children was printed with the disapproving note, 'The only defect in the foregoing is the absence in the maternal musings of all allusions to the heavenly life which the departed babe now spends'.[21]

The difference between such comments and those discussed in Chapter 2, as part of the similar editorial practice of the *Whistle-Binkie* editors, is of course that these criticisms and revisions appear in a public space. They arouse curiosity about the poems themselves (what were the poet and his lass doing in the snow?) and about the hapless poets who submitted them. They advertise the function of the

---

[17] Blair, 'Let the Nightingales Alone', *passim.*   [18] *Weekly News*, 6 January 1874, p.3.
[19] 'Friends in Council', *People's Friend*, 1 September 1869. 'Friends in Council' was the original title of the PF correspondence column.
[20] *Weekly News*, 7 April 1860, p.6.
[21] *Hamilton Advertiser*, 1 February 1862, p.2; 'Baby's Shoes', 2 May 1857, p.4.

newspaper as a venue for poetry publication and highlight editors' direct engagement with their reading community and their willingness to spend time and effort working with would-be writers to improve their submissions. That this engagement was often dismissive, condescending and unkind was beside the point. Correspondents' columns were, above all, designed to be witty and entertaining in their critical commentary. The *Fife News* of 1870, for example, produced perhaps the best example of the constant wordplay on poems' titles in these columns when it responded to a request to publish a poem titled 'Brevity' with 'No'.[22] The *People's Friend* published the most painful critique, when it informed 'Macleod' that 'The poem you have been ten years upon we have disposed of in as many minutes – verdict, rubbish'.[23] Readers seemingly loved this. The 'Stra'ven Callan', an emigrant who contributed a regular 'American Letter' to the *Hamilton Advertiser*, wrote of himself and fellow Scots abroad, 'We relish profoundly the compilation of the *Advertiser*. You seem to give some unmerciful cuffs to your poetic characters'. He then offers a poem, hoping that 'distance...will dull the edge of your pruning-blade'.[24] Evidently the 'unmerciful cuffs' were part of the relish. 'It always affords me (as well as thousands more, I reckon) a great pleasure to glance over your column "To Correspondents", though, it strikes me, your *soothing* comments are not always appreciated by some of your contributors', one reader of the *People's Journal* wrote, ruefully acknowledging that he had 'been intending for some months past to send you a few verses for dissection', but 'never got beyond the first or second line'.[25] J.F. from Meldrum even suggested that 'There is assuredly no single column in the paper that is more anxiously scanned by weekly readers than that to Correspondents; and moreover, there is no single column more truly valuable as a literary school'.[26] Although such letters are obviously highly mediated sources, these correspondence columns did mean that would-be poets were not simply scanning the newspaper to see if they were included, but to see if they had been subjected to critique; whereas casual readers could enjoy the scathing comments and speculate on the identity of criticized poets from their local area.

J. F.'s suggestion that the correspondents' columns are 'truly valuable' rests on the assumption that it was important for working-class readers to be educated in the correct standards for literary production. These columns perform the ideological function of imposing middle-class standards on a group of writers who were predominantly self-educated. Editors had a very clear and consistent sense of the kind of poem that would be considered satisfactory. It should be well presented (not always easy for poets with limited access to paper, pens, and a desk), use correct spelling and grammar, and deploy steady rhythms, firm end-rhymes ('The exact number of feet in each line is not very well preserved, and the rhymes are, in some cases, faulty') and a recognizable and familiar form, usually four-line stanzas.[27] It should also possess the hard to define quality of 'smoothness', in both form and

---

[22] *Fife News*, 23 April 1870, p.2.   [23] *People's Friend*, 17 March 1875.
[24] 'Stra'ven Callan', 'American Letter', *Hamilton Advertiser*, 14 January 1865, p.1.
[25] 'The Benefits of Newspapers to the Working-Classes', *People's Journal*, 17 January 1863, p.2.
[26] 'Literary Culture', *People's Journal*, 22 July 1865, p.2.
[27] 'To Correspondents', *People's Journal*, 11 February 1860, p.2.

content. Although editors rarely explain this term, it tends to imply that the poem looks and sounds familiar and expresses unexceptionable sentiments, which all readers might be presumed to share. Experiment and innovation are discouraged. The ideal model, mentioned again and again in the correspondence columns, was Longfellow's inspirational lyric verse. The judges of the *People's Journal* poetry competition in 1875 were amongst many authorities to note how common it was for aspiring poets to plagiarize Longfellow, perhaps unintentionally, given how popular his poems were.[28]

Correspondence columns did not simply put editorial standards on display and strongly incentivize poets to follow them. They also set out to train readers in these standards. Correspondents and would-be poets were not only *told* which aspects of poetic production they should work on, they were *shown* examples of faulty poetry in the column, and expected to be able to identify the faults, laugh (or despair) with the editor over them, and learn from example:

> The author of the 'Elegy on My Brother' is indignant that we should have had the audacity to call his production 'nonsense'. We shall, in reply to his strictures, simply quote the first verse, and ask our readers to say if the term 'nonsense' was inapplicable: –
>
> > How oft have poets, by poetry's fill,
> > Sung the echoes of the dead
> > How oft have they, by soft touch'd thrill,
> > Melted a soul though hard as lead.
> > So here I too would sing and weep,
> > And, till, in anguish, sob and sigh.[29]

This is a particularly interesting instance because while grammar, spelling, and prosody are unexceptional, readers are being asked to identify that the lines do not make sense (why 'poetry's fill'? 'Till' what?) and perhaps more importantly, that they are unintentionally comic because they are a compendium of exaggerated, shopworn clichés. Similarly, the *Friend* editor wrote:

> D. M. S. Glasgow – As you wish us in 'briefest words' to criticize your poem, we will comply – rubbish. Prove it? Here you are: –
>
> > Here in this city of death
> > How numerous the sleep
> > How hushed every breath
> > That once heaved deep
> >
> > And with throbs of life
> > In a different scene lived
> > Here memory only is rife
> > All life long since delved.[30]

---

[28] 'To Correspondents', *People's Journal*, 18 December 1875, p.2.
[29] 'To Correspondents', *People's Journal*, 7 March 1863, p.2.
[30] *People's Friend*, 18 March 1874, p.32.

Again, this looks and sounds almost like a conventional poem, but close examination indicates that the metrics are awkward, the grammar is poor ('sleep' cannot be numerous) and the meaning is confused. Editors assume an imagined audience of readers who are also poetry fans, and so will be able to identify why this poem is 'rubbish' for themselves.

The deployment of poorly written verse in a newspaper demonstrates that paper's adoption of critical and cultural standards, and its adherence to doctrines of self-improvement. Unlike the forms of verse that circulated in broadsides and songsters, tracts and pamphlets, in shop-windows, posters and on the back of pound notes, bad verse in the newspaper press was openly critiqued. It also constitutes a distinctive culture because newspaper editors, from at least mid-century onwards, realized that they could create comic effects by preserving the errors made by the poet in their manuscript submission. What this fosters is a *visual* culture of bad verse, frequently (unlike the poems cited above) in Scots, where the humour lies primarily in seeing how words are written and presented in the newspaper column, and in the contrast between this bad verse and the norms of spelling, punctuation, and layout adopted by newspaper copyeditors and printers. Unlike street verse, which is presumed to be hastily printed, and in which inaccuracies could be attributed to the printer, mistakes in 'bad' newspaper verse are assumed to be the fault of the author. William Tennant's scrapbook, discussed in Chapter 1, contains a good example: a carefully preserved newspaper poem, clipped from an unidentified local paper, on the phenomenon of a 'moving bog' at Slamannan:

> tam
> youl maby ha'e hard tell
> oh this great moving bog
> that has stoped all the traffack
> upon the slammanan road
>
> wher scors were flocking to
> and driving in cars
> to see the great bog
> that has drifted so far
>
> but think a' man tam
> that it was a fearfu like Job
> to see the braw lasses
> as they sunk in the bog
>
> wa'e their hoops an white cots
> they looked sae fine
> and clay an inch thick
> around them did twine
>
> but loach man tam
> had they been a tent their
> they woud selt mair drink
> than they woud at the fair [31]

---

[31] Untitled verses, stanzas 1–5, William Tennant's Book, p.8.

At twelve stanzas long in total, this poem is complete, meaning that it was published in entirety for readers rather than as an extract selected for criticism in the correspondents' section. It epitomizes the chief characteristics of popular bad verse from the local press. It commemorates a local incident that resists commemoration because of its lack of grandeur or broader interest, and which is in itself humorous, since it involves locals getting stuck in the bog, and it uses the same off-kilter rhymes that are often evident in broadside verse ('Job' and 'bog', for instance). 'Job' and 'bog' are also amusing because of the bathetic contrast between the Biblical Job's sufferings and the scene described, and because of the incongruity of the reference, suggesting that the author does not have an intelligent understanding of the Bible. But other aspects of this poem are more typical of newspaper verse, such as its epistle form, which presents the writer as a fairly uneducated local writing to another member of his community in informal language and tone. His comments on drink and how much money could be made from it, as well as his perhaps lascivious interest in the trapped girls, mark him as crude. Although the verses indicate a rudimentary sense of what a poem should look like—four short three- or four-beat lines in a stanza, rhyming abab—the writer also cannot use punctuation or capital letters. Most importantly, the phonetic spelling indicates a lack of knowledge of either standard English or Scots spelling: 'oh' in line 2, for instance, should be 'o'' (of), rather than the exclamatory 'Oh'', and 'loach' is an exclamation that Scots writers usually render as 'Losh'.

In the 1860s and 1870s, this kind of poetry became relatively common in the press. In the *Hamilton Advertiser* for 1860, for example, 'J. H., Kirkfieldbank', suffered the editor's scorn:

> We suspect that you never have had the pleasure of seeing yourself in print before, nor in all human probability ever will again – so to gratify you and those of our readers who admire the sublime and the beautiful, we give the following elegant extract from your song: –

> This dayweek when you cam hame
> Ey said to me ey had got nane
> its soon as I your face did see
> I knew you hade been on the spree
> Jenny you are an unco lass
> I see theres naught you will let pass[32]

'Elegant Extracts' was the title of a long-running and improving series of anthologies (originally compiled by Vicesimus Knox) which started in the late eighteenth century and would have been familiar, and clichéd, for Victorian readers. 'Sublime', 'beautiful' and 'elegant', along with words such as 'precious' or 'exquisite', are adjectives that came to be associated with editorial sarcasm and were almost invariably used in a satirical sense in poetic correspondence columns. The extract concludes with the poet and Jenny happily drunk in the pub, 'I thought that I was greatly blesst/While Jennys roseay cheeks I kisst'. The editorial commentary signals that

---

[32] 'Notices to Correspondents', *Hamilton Advertiser*, 8 September 1860, p.2.

the topic is, again, unfit for poetry. Neither the subject matter, especially in its depiction of a drunk woman, nor the language have any pretensions to elegance or beauty. The poem might not be far removed from traditional drinking songs or bawdy ballads, but it shows a misunderstanding of the generic norms for newspaper verse; J. H.'s belief that these lines might deserve publication is ridiculous.

Bad poetry of this kind is ostensibly published purely so that the reader can mock it, but it often has licence to be more politically and sexually subversive than 'good' poetry. By printing it, editors highlighted the existence of working-class verse that did not espouse the principles of morality, temperance, sentimentality, and upward mobility usually seen in the poetry columns. In a politicized example, one of the few poems published on the 1867 Reform Act by the *Hamilton Advertiser* appeared in 'Notices to Correspondents' on 3 November 1866, with a note to its author, 'Liberty':

> Your poem is not remarkable for poetic beauty or grammatical accuracy, but perhaps you think learning is as little needed for the writing of poetry as you think it is for exercising the franchise.

The first ten lines run:

> I tell you, sir, there's many a man
> As well as you on Nature's plan,
> Which have no education got,
> And yet deserves to have a vote.
> Some have wise thoughts within their head
> Although they have not learned to read,
> It needs not to have learned to write,
> To see the wisdom of John Bright;
> Thousands could vote for men like *he*
> Who could not work the Rule of Three.[33]

John Bright, radical MP, was a leading supporter of Reform. The poem continues by supporting John Stuart Mill's call for universal franchise (including women's suffrage), but rejecting Mill's suggestion (discussed in the Introduction) that only those who could read, write and do basic arithmetic should be allowed to vote, 'I hold in detestation/ His notions about education'. That this poem is so obviously 'uneducated' (particularly in the line 'Which have no education got') invites the question of whether it is parody rather than the genuine product of an author with little formal education; it stages itself deliberately in opposition to the principles held by both Mill and the editor, who had largely agreed with Mill's stance in the paper's editorials on Reform. Here, 'Liberty's' badness is part of his (or her) political intent, designed to make a point.

Staying with the *Hamilton Advertiser*, in 1860 it also published an extract from a bad poem on the local Rifle Volunteers, with the comment 'We have received several effusions of late...on the volunteer movement, most of which we have

---

[33] *Hamilton Advertiser*, 3 November 1866, p.2. I discuss this poem in a blog post, 'Poetry, Education and the Franchise in the Local Press', http://thepeoplesvoice.glasgow.ac.uk/poetry-education-and-the-franchise-in-the-local-press/ (consulted 14 September 2018).

rejected for their feeble and common-place character'. In the extract, however, 'there is such an air of originality with such a total disregard of rhyme, reason or logic' that readers must be 'treated' to it:

> O! the brave Volenteers of Hamilton clan
>   They stand up in uniform
> Aye, just to a man
>   With their Belts and Broadswords
> So gallant and gay
> They would make yaur eyes dazzle
>   As they march all away.[34]

The *Advertiser*, like the rest of the Scottish press, strongly approved of the Volunteer movement, and indeed rejected a poem on it by 'Davie' (Wingate) because it was 'not up to our standard of loyalty'.[35] The *People's Journal* was similarly enthusiastic about the Volunteers, yet had also published a bad poem on them, 'Poem on the Forfar Volunteers':

> We ill go and Join the volunteers
> For we are sworn to Perteck victoria our queen
> Annd all the rest of her Peers
> And who would not serve where glory to be seen
> Along with the Brave volunteers
> For now we are threatened abroad and at home
> But britain is ready so let them come on[36]

Like the Hamilton poem, the Forfar poem (an 'effusion in every way so precious that we grieve to cut it down', in the editor's words) threatens to induce mockery not simply of the poet, but of the movement he seeks to promote. If the authors, as the Forfar poem implies, are part of the Rifle Volunteer movement, then the ignorance shown in their verse might justify some alarm about the intelligence of the men being entrusted with the defence of Britain. The patriotic discourse surrounding the Volunteers, bolstered by a number of exhortatory poems by Tennyson and other writers, lent itself to parody, particularly when the threat from France failed to cohere, and although these poems are *not* presented as parodic, their effect is to undermine both the seriousness of patriotic discourse on the Rifle Brigades, and the seriousness of editorial discourse on self-improvement via the writing of poetry.

POUTERY IN THE PRESS

In late 1859, the *People's Journal* editor noted the receipt of an angry letter from Mr Burgess of Baintown (a small Fife village), complaining that his local community had assumed that he was the author of an anonymous 'Baintown' poem selected

---

[34] 'Notices to Correspondents', *Hamilton Advertiser*, 31 March 1860, p.2.
[35] 'Notices to Correspondents', *Hamilton Advertiser*, 8 September 1860, p.2.
[36] *People's Journal*, 3 August 1861, p.2, reprinted in Blair, *Poets of the People's Journal*, p.22.

for critique and that his reputation was being damaged.[37] Editor and readers did not know this at the time, but this was most likely an early—and perhaps satirical—engagement with the *Journal* by a writer who would shortly become one of its biggest stars, Alexander Burgess, dancing-master, violinist, and, as 'Poute', a poet. As the 1860s progressed, there was a remarkable shift in newspaper columns towards a highly ambiguous and self-conscious culture of bad verse, verse deliberately written to appear bad for comic effect. While this culture has connections to earlier comic phonetic writing and to contemporary American humour, as discussed below, its spread across the Scottish press is quite possibly linked to the rise of Poute. A month after publishing the Forfar Volunteers poem, the *Journal* editor received the poorly written 'Lines addressed to a Water Lily', and apparently took it at face value:

> We have received 'Original Poetry' being 'Lines addressed to a Water Lily'. Whether it be 'poetry' or not, it is unquestionably highly 'original;' and the author has more of it, 'a great deal of manuscripts in a book', which he would sell us to print, should we wish to buy them. He sends us his right name, but…'I do not want you to print my own name but Just poute and when I send you any more poems i will Just keep the name of poute.' He tells us, moreover, that he is a self-taught man, and does not know where to put in the 'comies' and the points, and asks us as a favour to do that duty for him […] Well, now for the original 'poetry.' It is such a gem in its way that we would have liked to have given it entire as it dropped from the author's hand, with, of course, the addition of the 'comies'. We are obliged to curtail it, however, but here goes a 'blad' from the exordium: –

> > Inspire me, o thou heavenly muse,
> > When I do try my Own powers to use,
> > To sing the Praise of a sweet Flower,
> > Which grew in a running stream and not in a lady's bower;
> > But Bloomed in Modest Beauty bright,
> > Its leafs were green But its blades was splendid white;[38]

This is an unusually long editorial note about a poorly written poem, and the editor goes on to cite another sixteen lines with sardonic commentary. 'Lines to a Water Lily' is similar to the extracts quoted above in its misspellings and poor grammar ('leafs', 'was splendid'), use of over-long lines, metrical awkwardness, and its tendency to insert random capital letters on inappropriate words, either as a fault in orthography or a seeming imitation of eighteenth-century verse. Given the editor's sardonic promise to add the commas on the poet's behalf, it is hard to tell whether these extracts are altered—the poem as presented for publication in Poute's volume at a later date is far more unorthodox in spelling and capitalization than this extract indicates.[39] What makes 'Lines to a Water Lily' particularly amusing, in contrast to examples like the 'moving bog' poem, is its relationship to established verse culture, signalled initially by the invocation to a 'heavenly muse'. Poems

---

[37] *People's Journal*, 24 December 1859, p.2.
[38] 'To Correspondents', *People's Journal*, 7 September 1861, p.2.
[39] See *Poute! Being Poetry, Poutery and Prose* (Coupar-Fife: A. Westwood, n.d.), pp.1–2.

contrasting the beauty of modest wild flowers to hothouse blooms or cut flowers were extremely common in the Victorian periodical and newspaper press. Although this subgenre was associated with women's poetry, the neglected wildflower was also an image repeatedly used by male working-class poets to signal their modesty and obscurity (following, of course, Thomas Gray's 'Full many a flower is born to blush unseen'). 'Lines to a Water Lily' therefore seemingly indicates an author's misguided attempt to insert his work into an existing subgenre of respectable verse, one current in the *Journal* and elsewhere.

As with other bad poems published in the press, these extracts and the editorial commentary can seem like cruelly tinged mockery of a writer's lack of formal education—the flip side of the *Journal's* oft-expressed support and encouragement for working-class poets. Whatever the editor may or may not have known from 'poute's' letter, there was no particular reason for readers to suspect that the author knew what he was doing; they could simply enjoy this (and respond to it in print) as an entertainingly bad poem characterized by aspiration falling flat. As 'Poute' submitted more material to the *People's Journal*, however, it became increasingly evident that his productions were not so much genuinely bad poetry as satirical takes on the kind of bad poetry likely to be produced by the persona of an ignorant, provincial young worker employed in the salt pans in Leven, Fife, convinced of his own poetic genius. In October 1861, one month after the success of 'Lines on a Water Lily', the *Journal* published an untitled epistle poem signed 'Poute':

> Sir.
> Youve surly gotin your stamik cleen.
> For you have lately spewed much spleen.
> your korispondints all Rank and file.
> Are like yourself Mighty Spittirs of Bile.
> its them and you has much to ansir.
> for me. i am above ether your praise or sencir.
> I sore aloft in regons high.
> beyond the reach of all you small fry.
> I say yet I am self taught. a natures poet.
> and well does your poor meen critiks know it.
> But tho ive got small edication.
> ive raised your Journals circulation.
> My lily made your Reedars all to wonder.
> and caused you to print thirty three thousand hunder.
>
> But like all poets sprung from the ranks.
> From you ive only got the divil for my thanks.[40]

Indignation, whether rueful or outraged, about the insulting comments made in 'To Correspondents' was in itself a standard pose. In representing himself as a 'natures poet', 'beyond the reach' of the hostile community of unappreciative editor and readers, Poute deliberately evokes the 'Jamie Harebell' figure of the naturally gifted Scottish peasant poet persecuted by his betters. But the immediate turn to

---

[40] 5 October 1861, reprinted in Blair, *Poets of the People's Journal*, p.26.

financial considerations rather than aesthetic in assessing the worth of verse, 'ive raised your Journals circulation', slyly undercuts this. Poute's repeated claims to have single-handedly increased the *People's Journal*'s readership (circulation figures were prominently cited on the top left hand corner of the second page, the home of poems and 'To Correspondents') are entertaining because they are ridiculous, yet they have a grain of truth. His poem *did* make readers wonder—in part because of the question mark over its authenticity as a bad poem—and also because of the value to editors of bad as well as good verse.

As Poute's career as a newspaper poet progressed, his popularity became such that poems by him were often trailed several weeks in advance of publication, and numerous contributors wrote in to comment on his works. It does not seem that his reputation reached far beyond Scotland, but an unpublished letter states that his *The Book of Netter-Caps*, heavily promoted in the *People's Journal*, sold out in an edition of 1000 copies, a substantial number for a working-class poet: we might compare the difficulty that the *Penny Post* had in attracting subscriptions for Ellen Johnston's collection.[41] His regular complaints about the lack of recompense for poets 'sprung from the ranks' ('P.S. If i got a peny a line the Above would come to 20 pense') are satirical not simply because Poute's cynical financial valuation of poetry shows that he rejects the accepted ideological stance that poetry composition is a valuable end in itself, but because they threaten to expose this ideology as highly exploitative of the working-class poet.[42] Bad poets, in particular, materially benefited local newspapers without generally receiving anything other than abuse.

As befits a 'natures poet', one of the key topics for Poute's poetry was nature, and his poems constitute another, highly satirical, take on the pastoral tradition and its marketability in the press. When he writes on a traditional subject for poetry, in 'Apostroffe to the Rainbow', he begins by discussing (inaccurately) the Christian message of the rainbow ('You are there im Told for A Sign when it Is rainy'), but then immediately turns to speculation about how much money a painting of this rainbow might fetch, followed by a critique of the rainbow for not looking quite good enough:

> Im pretty sure you would been beter had the cloud been white
> Im sure some of the coullers would have come out mor bright
> Them that use majeklantrns hing up a white shroud
> But it mabey wudna be very easy to Make it White cloud
> But I shal Drop the subjek For varios resins
> If any wishes Mor he can go to tamsons seasons[43]

Poute's vision of a rainbow is triply mediated: by the art he has encountered, by the visual technologies of the period and how their techniques could enhance the

---

[41] Undated letter, inserted in author's own copy of *Poute!*

[42] 'Apostroffe to the Rainbow', *People's Journal*, 30 January 1864, p.2. Reprinted in Blair, *Poets of the People's Journal*, pp.46–7.

[43] Ibid., p.47.

natural, and by his reading of a canonical work by a Scottish poet, James Thomson's *The Seasons* (1730). Thomson's famous passage on the rainbow occurs in 'Spring':

> Meantime, refracted from yon eastern cloud,
> Bestriding earth, the grand ethereal bow
> Shoots up immense; and every hue unfolds,
> In fair proportion running from the red,
> To where the violet fades into the sky.[44]

Poute's conversational and colloquial phrasing, in comments like 'Im pretty sure' and the Scots 'wudna be very easy' form an intentional contrast with the grandeur of Thomson's blank verse, as does his own line on the colours of the rainbow, 'Blue red and green and gud kens how Many'. While Poute knows that a rainbow is an ideal poetic topic, he cannot muster the concentration to stay with it, 'I shal Drop the subjek', and his rainbow resists idealization by being stubbornly rooted in the local 'One of your ends is at the bass and one right over largy law' (Bass Rock and the Law hill are landmarks, known to Dundee readers). 'Apostroffe' directly questions the widespread critical view that self-taught poets had an unmediated relationship with nature and could represent it in a realist, 'natural', manner, as influentially expressed by George Gilfillan:

> The self-taught have usually greater freshness of feeling in beholding Nature... Having read fewer descriptions, they look at the thing described more exactly as it is. Many see not Nature's thunderstorm, but Thomson's or Byron's; not Bruar-water itself, but Burns's picture of it; Scott's Trossachs, not the beautiful place itself... The self-taught simply record the contact between their own genius and Nature's works.[45]

As all the nature poetry cited in previous chapters demonstrates, these claims are highly doubtful. Poute certainly knew Gilfillan's views, though this particular passage was published four years after his 'Apostroffe', and his poem takes great delight in satirizing and directly countering them.

Unlike many other, and presumably less intentional, bad poets, Poute consistently links his work to the accepted canon of poetry in his period, usually as a means of demonstrating the pretentiousness of writers who reference established poets while lacking any of their talent. In his 'Odd to a Krokis', he opens:

> selestial apoley which Didest inspire.
> the souls of burns and pop with sackred fir.
> kast thy Mantil over me When i shal sing.
> the praiz Of A sweat flower who grows in spring.[46]

High-flown allusions to Apollo, Burns, and Pope are undercut by misspelling, lack of capitals and misuse of full stops (part of the recurring joke about Poute's inability to 'dot' his poems correctly), while the misspelling of 'sweet' as 'sweat' is a reference

---

[44] Thomson, lines 202–6.

[45] George Gilfillan, 'Janet Hamilton: Her Life and Poetical Character', in Hamilton, *Poems, Sketches and Essays*, pp.1–13, 3.

[46] 'Original Poutery', *People's Journal*, 22 March 1862, p.2.

to the vagaries of English spelling and pronunciation (compare 'eat'), while also linking two incongruous concepts. As in many of his poems, Poute plays on the felt need for nature poems to carry a moral message, in this case, that the crocus, like some poets, has appeared too early to survive the harsh weather, 'alas. alas. theres Men which tries to rime./who have like you kome out befor there time'. Poute presents himself as superior to such immature poets, though this may also imply that he himself is an instance of the stereotypically fragile and beautiful poet, whose hostile environment is not ready to receive his genius.

Locality is an essential part of Poute's character as a poet, and the aspect of his comic verse that makes him most distinctive as a *Scottish* poet. A crucial aspect of Poute's poetic identity was this status as a provincial 'peasant' poet. Taking on board the Wordsworthian imperative to live, like the imagined Harebell, 'on terms of loving intimacy with grass, and flowers, and birds', Poute's poems interpret this as a ground-level focus on his kailyard and an intimate attention to the vegetable patch and the insects that plague it. His best-known poems were concerned with 'Kail Wurms' (the caterpillars that eat his kail), 'Nettercaps' (spiders) and, repeatedly, with praise of his enormous vegetables, as in 'My' 67 Leeks. A Pome':

> Salubrious Sovren leeks Al Hail
> you teste sublime Among My kail
> i hop nae *hary-wurm* nor Snail
>   wull bite yer ruits
> My wife wud kil them wi' a Flail
>   The Ugly bruits.[47]

One of the recurring jokes in Poute's poetry is that his wife is endowed with epic heroic skill in killing pests; another joke lies in the frequent descent from Miltonic openings to colloquial Scots. The bathos of the poet's concentrated focus on his vegetable garden makes the point that for a working man, nature is most beautiful when it supplies a vital source of food; from this perspective, of course a leek is more salubrious and sovereign than a rose. The natural world of Poute's poems is usually resolutely down to earth, concerned entirely with production, consumption, and the recycling of waste materials; his poems include, for instance, a brilliant panegyric to an Irish manure company.[48] They are closely related to the georgic poems of agricultural improvement discussed in Chapter 2, and to the emphasis in the provincial press on country shows, vegetable competitions, and the advantages of new technology and materials in growing foodstuff. In Poute's case, however, there is a sharp edge of parody to his engagement with this discourse.

Poute's local bounds of cottage and kailyard, and the traditional provincial life that his creator imagined for him, are constantly infringed on by modernity, quite literally so in one poem about a mechanical threshing mill that almost knocks down his house. He consistently reads the natural world through metaphors of labour and industry that reflect upon the increasing industrialization of rural

---

[47] *Poute!*, p.46.
[48] 'Gouldings Manur', reprinted in Blair, *Poets of the People's Journal*, p.101.

Scotland. The nettercap (spider), for example, reminds him of a 'Sooter' (souter, a tailor), and his primary interest lies in how it manages to spin:

> Yer netts & Girns – ye spin them a' Yersel'.
> qweer, whaur ye get The lint – to Mak' yer girns . !
> Is yer inside a' Stappit Fu' o' pirns ?
> If so; unlike the wheel o' Mistress Moyce,
> Yer wheels, an' faktry Bobbins Mak Nae noice[49]

'Pirn' is a weaver's spool, and 'girn' a net or snare. The spider moves from being like an individual weaver or tailor, to being like a miniature net factory. Indeed, the mention of factory bobbins may have specific local reference to the net factory started in 1867 in Largo, Fife, close to Poute's stated location. Though his hyper-local dialect and pose of astonishment at the wonders of machinery (in one poem, he describes a disastrous brief stint as a factory worker) might seem to situate Poute as a stereotypical rustic, his given location, Leven, as his poems note, is a site of industry as well as rurality. His version of a traditional song, 'The Merry Ploughboys', ignores pastoral pleasures to describe the 'Grate commotion' of Poute's locality:

> Wi' taaty Warks – & Foondry foke – and dirty ingine fylers –
> ane canny hear Their Neebir Speak for "Cairney" Klinkin' Boilers
> The Rattlin o' the Hammer-Smiths – 4. by the Bakir's Vans. –
> They mak' A noyce lyke beddlum – In Leven at The pans[50]

This combination of traditional song title and form with modern content high-lights the overall impetus of Poute's poems, which have a tongue-in-cheek take on the themes, language and form of canonical Scots and English verse. They slyly undermine, yet simultaneously promote, the high valuation of local verse and the local bard in the verse culture of the period.

As is evident from the examples above, the humour of Poute's verse relies on print, and specifically on its transgression of *newspaper* print conventions, for its effects. Poute's poems regularly include self-satisfied comments about his new-found ability to obey such conventions, such as 'I have written this on one side of the papir' (texts sent in for publication should not be double-sided) and instruc-tions to the printer, such as 'dont dot it'. The effect is to display the extent to which original poetry in the press is mediated and altered, deliberately on the part of the editor, and sometimes accidentally by the typesetter. Poute's commentary brings the process of this editorial mediation to the forefront. It also shows that humour lies not simply in content but in strikingly variant presentation, particularly in relation to unorthodox spacing. 'to Mak' yer girns . !', for instance, cited above, uses two punctuation marks and places extra spaces between each. The effort which typesetters are presumed to expend to preserve, exactly as presented in the hand-written manuscripts, the unconventional spelling and layout of Poute's poems is another part of the joke about both bad and mock-bad newspaper poetry for readers.

---

[49] 'The Netter Cap. In Two Parts', *Poute!*, p.15.   [50] 'The Merry Ploughboys', *Poute!*, p.17.

The printer has put considerable manual labour, more than might be required for standard verse, into making poetry this bad.

Many aspects of Poute's language and style reminded readers of contemporary American humourists Artemus Ward and Josh Billings, so much so that D. H. Edwards felt obliged to assure readers that Poute was not an imitator, because he had 'adopted a quaint and original style of spelling, before the name of Josh Billings or Artemus Ward was heard of in this country'.[51] Donaldson suggests that Poute may be the leading example of the popularity of 'American speech-based prose' in the Scottish popular press.[52] Artemus Ward, pseudonym of Charles Browne, a newspaper editor, was a supposed Indiana waxworks and menagerie showman whose best-known pieces were published in *Artemus Ward. His Book* in 1862 (not republished in Britain until 1865), and who performed at London's Egyptian Hall in 1866–7 (he died in England in March of that year). Ward's comic prose pieces describe his travels around America and meetings with different sects and celebrities. They are most akin to Poute in Ward's comments on his animal menagerie, particularly his 'snaiks' or 'snaix' (Poute's poem 'Snaix' is a direct homage), and in his dealings with local newspaper editors. As Ward writes to one editor:

> I shall hav my hanbills dun at your offiss. Depend upon it. I want you should git my hanbills up in flaming stile. Also git up a tremenjus excitemunt in yr. paper 'bowt my onparaleld Show. We must fetch the public sumhow. We must wurk on their feeling. Cum the moral on 'em strong.[53]

Ward's supposed arrogance and ignorance, combined with a shrewd knowledge about what the public wants, are echoed by Poute, and his occasional instructions to the printer, '(Notiss to the Printer: Put some stars here.)', are taken up to a higher degree in Poute's poems.[54] Ward developed immense popularity in Scotland at precisely the time when Poute's status was growing. In an advertisement for 'A NEW POEM BY POUTE', the *Journal* stated that 'Of the numerous contributors to the *Journal* one of the most quaint and original is our friend Poute, who is for Scotland what Artemus Ward is for America – the oddest of writers'.[55] The *Journal* published at least one piece by Ward in the period in which Poute was a contributor, and the *People's Friend* published articles and poems by and about Ward, including a poem celebrating him by 'Surfaceman'—Anderson was one of his biggest fans and reportedly had 'a fondness that amounts almost to a craze' for his writings.[56] Andrew Lang wrote that Ward's 'secret' lay in his 'trick of almost idiotic naivete...covering real shrewdness', while recent critics also trace his appeal to traditions of self-referential humour and parody and to his performance of 'ironic

---

[51] Edwards, *One Hundred Modern Scottish Poets*, p.271.   [52] Donaldson, p.59.
[53] C. F. Browne, *Artemus Ward: His Book* (New York: Carleton, 1865), p.18.
[54] Ibid., p.72.   [55] *People's Journal*, 14 October 1865, p.2.
[56] *People's Journal*, 19 June 1869, p.4, 'Reminiscences of a Visit to the Homes of Two Scottish Poets', *People's Friend*, 20 July 1881, p.452. In the *Friend*, see also Surfaceman, 'Artemus Ward' and James Parton, 'Artemus Ward', both 1 March 1871; Artemus Ward, 'The Cruise of the Polly Ann', 7 February 1872 and 'Artemus Ward' (unsigned), 14 October 1874.

mock-primitivism', very similar to Poute's mock-provinciality and rusticity.[57] In contrast, however, Ward is far more engaged with wider American politics and society than Poute, and he is also far more obviously a mouthpiece or persona for his author's views than either Poute or his Scots prose equivalents.

Josh Billings' comic prose pieces also appeared in the *Journal* in the late 1860s and 1870s, in very close proximity to Poute's poems.[58] The creation of Henry Wheeler Shaw, a journalist and writer in Poughkeepsie, Billings is perhaps closer to the Scots tradition than Ward, because he has a more provincial and rural persona. Like Poute, Billings satirizes the sentimentalized language of nature in Victorian discourse by undercutting it with practicalities, as in 'Spring – May 1868', where he comments on violets:

> I luv to prokure a violet as soon as i can, each year; there is such a mild impediment in their butiful fases thay put me in mind ov an orfan child, that has strayed oph into a dell and sot down tew cri.

But the rest of the article is concerned with the prices of spring vegetables, 'Dandelion greens has riz; i bought a bushel yesterday, and pade 4 dollars fur it. i wanted a mess, and mi wife sed it was just like me, bought 6 times tew much'.[59] Billings also presented a number of 'Billings Replize Teu Correspondents' articles, satirizing the editorial voice of correspondents' columns, and including the occasional comment on poetry.[60]

Ward, Billings, and Poute all rest their humour on the representation of 'provincial' speech and on their code-switching between dialect and standard English. This is far from new in humorous verse or prose, and occurs with some regularity in the popular English dialect poetry of the mid-Victorian period, by poets such as Edwin Waugh or Ben Brierley. The phonetic representation of the spoken word, however, did have particular resonance in the mid-Victorian period, because of the invention of phonetic shorthand and an ongoing contemporary debate about whether English spelling conventions should be 'reformed' into something more practical. One poem praising contributors to the *Journal* comments:

> Here 'Poute' in all his glory dazzling shines,
>   But ruthlessly he kills orthography,
> And dims the brilliant lustre of his lines –
>   Ah! pardon, "Poute," you write Phonography.
> Like Pitman, Poet "Poute" can spell by sound,[61]

[57] Andrew Lang, 'American Humor', reprinted in *Lost Leaders* (London: Kegan Paul, Trench, 1889), p.75. Simon Featherstone, 'Artemus Ward and the Egyptian Hall', in Martin Hewitt, ed. *Platform Pulpit Rhetoric* (Trinity and All Saints, Leeds: Leeds Working Papers in Victorian Studies, vol III, 2000), pp.37–49, 41.

[58] See, for example, 'Josh Billings On Milk', 6 January 1869, p.4.

[59] Henry Wheeler Shaw, *Josh Billings on Ice, and Other Things* (New York: Carleton, 1870), pp.126–7.

[60] Ibid., p.140.

[61] 'Lines on Receiving a People's Journal', by J. S. M., Oldham. *People's Journal*, 30 May 1868.

Initially criticizing Poute, the author then semi-seriously suggests that his unorthodox spelling is part of the respected rise of phonography. Isaac Pitman, of Bath, had created a famous shorthand system based on a phonetic alphabet in 1837, and supported a publishing company, correspondence courses and journals devoted both to phonography (in which 'the very sound of every word is made visible') and to the related cause of reforming English spelling.[62] As Donaldson notes, in his discussion of the influence of Pitman and his friend and colleague Alexander John Ellis on Scots prose, phonography and shorthand became so popular that 'many compositors could set directly from phonetic shorthand manuscript from the 1840s onwards'.[63]

In the decades in which Poute, Ward, Billings, and other similar writers became known, this cause of reformed spelling was gathering momentum, culminating in the 1876 foundation of the English Spelling Reform Association (Tennyson was a vice-president, Dickens also supported it) and the American Spelling Reform Association. Spelling reform, its advocates argued, was particularly essential for the progress of the working classes and universal education, and was vital if English were to remain a leading world language, given that the difficulties and irregularities of English spelling and pronunciation were off-putting for learners. Samuel Bengough was not exaggerating the movement's belief when he claimed in one talk that 'a rational system of spelling' was the '"Open Secret" of Social Progress, of National Prosperity, and Success in Military Effort'.[64] When Victorian readers saw a poem that substituted 'k' for 'c' ('kast') and 'z' for 'se' ('praiz'), contained jokes about varying pronunciation, and represented words phonetically, they would immediately have thought of reformed spelling. Practitioners of Pitman's system made a point of publishing journals, speeches, and other works in phonetic spelling: a Pitman tract in this mode opens, for example, by describing shorthand as an art 'pekiuliarli the produkt ov Inglish soil and ov the Inglish meind. Ei merely bring before you a gud, and ei kan nou add a popiular, sistem'.[65] Pitman and his supporters also deliberately translated poems and other canonical works of English literature into phonetic spelling, to show that it was viable for literature. Poute certainly knew about these efforts, and indeed wrote a poem about spelling reform that enjoys the contradictions of English spelling and pronunciation, rhyming 'Carlisle/crocodisle/misle' and 'enough/stough/hough/snough', following models such as the earlier and fairly widely circulated poem and celebrated 'Lebtor' by William Gregory, Edinburgh Professor of Chemistry, which rhymed, for example, 'expleign/rane' and 'fluds/woulds'.[66]

---

[62] Isaac Pitman, *The Phonographic Teacher*, 11th edn (London: F. Pitman, 1863), p.4.

[63] Donaldson, p.54.

[64] Samuel Edmund Bengough, *The 'Open Secret' of Social Progress, of National Prosperity, and Success in Military Effort* (Phonetic Society/English Spelling Reform Association, n.d.), p.1.

[65] Pitman, *Spelling Reform: Address by Mr Isaac Pitman to the Young Men's Christian Association, St James's Square, Bristol, 8 November, 1880* (Bath: Isaac Pitman, 1880), p.1.

[66] 'Original Poutery. An Ocular Proof that the "Spelling Reform" is Becoming an Imperative Necessity', *Poute!*, p.59. William Gregory, *An Epistle on English Orthography*. Reprinted from the Phonetic Journal, 1 May 1850 (Bath: Isaac Pitman, n.d.), p.3. The introduction states that over 20,000 copies of Gregory's 'Lebtor' were circulated and dates its composition to 1838. It is republished

What is crucial in Poute, however, as it is not in Gregory or in the efforts of Pitman and contemporaries, is the tension between Scots and English. Advocates of the reform of spelling and orthography, and of phonography, tended to celebrate the fact that the changes they championed would create a world English that erased local difficulties in comprehension caused by dialect, accent, and pronunciation. One anonymous and undated 'Song on Phonography' suggests that a key benefit is shorthand's ability to render 'The jabber of Taffy, the splutter of Pat' into clear and comprehensible English.[67] Ellis wrote that phonetic writing had the advantage of enabling all to see how the 'more educated classes' pronounced a word:

> We may expect that in a few generations after the introduction of such a system of spelling, varieties of pronunciation will practically terminate, and the same language, not only in theory, but in reality, will be spoken throughout the kingdom. Nay, we might even hope to overcome, in some respects, the peculiarities of the Scotch, Welsh, and Irish. There is no hope of overcoming them by other means. Not that we would extirpate the Scotch dialect, which has received a literary character from the pens of Burns and Scott; we would rather fix it, and make it intelligible to their southern neighbours, which, in its present dress, it certainly is not.[68]

Efforts to 'fix' Scots included the translation of 'Tam O'Shanter' into phonetic English in the *Fonetic Jurnal* of 1848.[69] Ellis's massive investigation *On Early English Pronunciation*, in its fourth volume of 1874, devotes considerable space to the difficulties of recording Irish and English dialects phonetically. While he argues that this is a vital task, both for understanding the history of the English language and because 'We know nothing of the actual relations of the thoughts of a people ... until we know how the illiterate express themselves', he regards dialects as a 'fossil' form of English. '[F]or the advance of our people, dialects must be extinguished – as Carthage for the advance of Rome', he states firmly, in a nicely imperialist simile pointing towards the global domination of English.[70]

Donaldson rightly observes that while Scots 'responded positively' to Pitman and Ellis, their response was 'not in favour of uniformity with England, and still less in favour of standardisation of the vernacular within Scotland': 'They began instead to experiment with the orthography of written Scots, making it more responsive to the regional diversity of contemporary speech'.[71] Poute's phonetic writing, like that of the American humourists, preserves 'provincial' pronunciation and language, as in 'stamik' for 'stomach' or 'hunder' for 'hundred', but it also uses Scots to create visual and sound effects not possible in English, as in the assonance in 'gump doon the lum' (crawl down the chimney) in 'Kale-Wurms', or the rhyme of 'girn' and 'pirn' in 'The Nettercap'. Reading Poute's Scots poems involves two

---

in Alexander John Ellis, *A Plea for Phonetic Spelling*, 2nd edn (London: Fred Pitman, 1848), pp.43–6.

[67] 'Song on Phonography'. Undated, author unknown. NLS Special Collections Wn68.

[68] Ellis, p.81.

[69] *The Fonetic Jurnal*, ed. Alecsander Jon Elis (Lundun: Fred Pitman, 1848), pp.145–52.

[70] Ellis, *On Early English Pronunciation, with Especial Reference to Shakspere and Chaucer, Part IV* (London: Philological Society, 1874), pp.1247–8.

[71] Donaldson, p.54.

acts of translation for the English-speaking reader, from his phonetic versions into a recognizable Scots word, and then from Scots to English. A word such as 'klekk' in 'Kale-Wurms', for example (butterflies in Poute's garden 'klekk their Skore and Mulyins of kale wurms') is a phonetic rendering of the Scots 'claik', to hatch.[72] Phonetic spelling of regional Scots, far from 'fixing' the language and making it more intelligible, renders it still more unintelligible. Through the pose of a semi-educated worker expressing himself in dialect, misspelt because he has never properly learned either standard written English or Scots, Poute implicitly mocks the earnest efforts of Ellis and his contemporaries to 'overcome' the peculiarities of dialect and to use the speech of the poor and uneducated as insights into 'the thoughts of a people'. He highlights in addition the problem of teaching any form of spelling, reformed or unreformed, to those who have not learned to spell consistently. The vitality of his Scots poems and his clever use of code-switching were key to Poute's success, and served to show that Scots in poetry was adaptable and infinitely various. Poute's take on phonetics is a substantive contribution to the *People's Journal*'s commitment to Scots, and his knowing, self-aware depiction of working-class stereotypes in terms of content, form, and language is less engaged in upholding the image of the ignorant provincial, than in supporting the *Journal*'s ongoing questioning of those stereotypes in its agitation for working-class self-improvement and reform.

Poute's success meant that a culture of publishing bad verse by ignorant authors, and a culture of publishing comic verse designed to look ignorant, collided in the poetry columns, in such a way as to cast doubt on whether any bad verse was deliberate. Many poets used their pseudonym to signal that they were comic bad poets writing phonetic verse, including Moses Dalite in the *People's Journal*, Job Sprott, Apollo B. Blode, Sawmule Slyde and Admiral Dont in the *Weekly News*. But others did not. In a selection of local verse published as a Christmas supplement in 1863, for instance, the *Hamilton Advertiser* included several 'bad' poems alongside and in the same context as the local verse it was recommending. 'To an Onion' opens 'Round bulbus thing that springest from the erth/ From out whose busum thou at first had'st birth', while 'To a Snowdrop' begins, 'Thou lovly snodrop That lifts Up thy hed/ abuve the sno and dos thy petals spred'.[73] The placement in the paper and lack of editorial comment (other than 'Verbatim and literatim' as an epigraph to 'To a Snowdrop', which might be attributable to poet or editor), suggests either that the editor believes these are deliberately comic bad poems, or that he is not sure. Given the similarity to Poute, the former is more likely but by no means certain. To take only one other example, D. M.'s 'Sonnet to My Mallet', in the correspondents' column of the *People's Friend*, contains lines such as:

> Then may I long be able for
> To handl my mall and guid my chisel
> For as long as there is stones to hew
> I care for no man not a diddle.[74]

---

[72] Reprinted in *Poets of the People's Journal*, pp.52–3.
[73] 'Poetical Supplement', *Hamilton Advertiser*, 26 December 1863, p.2.
[74] 'To Correspondents', *People's Friend*, 2 November 1870.

Is this the production of a foolish stonemason fancying himself as a poet, or is it faked? For contemporary readers, the pleasure lay in this tension, in the knowledge that a working-class writer who seemed a butt for editorial scorn might be secretly mocking the editor.

Poute differed from other bad comic poets of the period in two major ways: firstly, in his entire reliance on the visual impact of his verse in private reading rather than its effect as song or recitation performance, and secondly, in operating solely under a pseudonym. In his decades of association with the *People's Journal*, Poute never stepped out of character, and editor and readers kept up the pretence alongside him. Even in a private letter, Burgess writes of 'Poute's book' rather than 'my book'. In fact, Poute was not Burgess's only pseudonym, nor his only appearance in the press. He won a *People's Journal* essay competition, for the best essay on the properties of a model wife, as himself, and he wrote some poems and dialogues, both comic and serious, outwith the Poute persona. He also authored a comic Scots fictional autobiography, 'The History of Geordie Droner', for the *Fife News* in the early 1870s, in which Geordie is another type of the youthful, credulous, and at times idiotic rustic, reporting in garrulous detail on the minutiae of his relationships with his family and community and on his efforts to make a living and court his sweetheart, Lizzie Pinkie.[75] Readers enjoyed Droner, as a column in the *Fife News* containing 'Addresses to Geordie Droner' shows.[76] The *News* makes no link between Droner and Poute—although Poute in 1871 was a major attraction of Scotland's best-known popular weekly—and, indeed, seemingly does not mention Poute at all, even as Poute made capital from his Fife identity. Nor do the *Fife News* and *Fife Herald* mention Burgess's alter ego in their reports on his activities as dancing-master and respected local worthy in Baintown.[77] Poute's identity was hardly a well-kept secret even in the 1870s, and Edwards identifies him as Burgess in *One Hundred Modern Scottish Poets* (1880), probably with his permission. But the Fife press, either due to an embarrassment about how Poute represented their county, or due to respect for Burgess's wishes, did not link him to Poute and Droner other than in the obituaries that followed his suicide by drowning in 1886. Perhaps due to this separation of identities, and in sharp contrast to McGonagall, Poute's works entirely disappeared from critical or popular purview in the twentieth century, and so did the culture they had helped to foster.

LOCATING MCGONAGALL

Poute and McGonagall's letters and poems appeared on the same pages and in the same papers. The likelihood that McGonagall was *not* aware of the existence of a

[75] Droner's first appearance is 'The History of Geordie Droner, by Himself', *Fife News*, 25 February 1871, p.2.

[76] *Fife News*, 8 April 1871, p.2. This column also includes the Poute-like poem, 'Snales. A Nod'.

[77] For example, in the 'Baintown' news for 6 July 1871, the *Fife Herald* reported a local celebration 'for the purpose of presenting Mr and Mrs Burgess with tokens of regard for their good friendship as worthy and much-respected residenters' (p.3).

popular newspaper culture of fake bad verse is virtually non-existent. McGonagall is Scotland's best bad poet, however, because he managed to combine his participation in this newspaper culture with a career as a broadside poet and music-hall performer, meaning that, unlike Poute, he also operated in person, as himself. McGonagall was also intriguing—and remains so—because, to a far greater extent than the other poets discussed in this chapter, the question of his self-awareness about his verse remains unanswerable. Norman Watson, McGonagall's biographer and the most trenchant commentator on his life and works, acknowledges that 'it is not beyond the bounds of possibility that, rather than being an unconscious humorist, he was the master of intentional mistakes and crafted buffoonery', and suggests that:

> McGonagall's poetic ineptitude probably began as an innocent conceit. In time it became a deliberately conceived and craftily pursued funding tool, where he accepted the irony of an audience ovation or the ridiculing reviewer for what they were, a part of his act.[78]

Gord Bambrick agrees, using fine readings of McGonagall's style to back up his argument.[79] As Chris Hunt notes, though, the 'satirist argument' is 'difficult to sustain' in relation to the apparent consistency in McGonagall's persona, in print and in performance, in public and in private: 'If he was putting on an act, it was one of the most impressive feats of acting of all time'.[80] Yet, in reassessing McGonagall's works in the light of the verse discussed above, it seems equally unbelievable that he was ignorant of the market into which he entered as a would-be poet. Preserving a high level of ambiguity about his motives, and about the question of his self-awareness in producing bad poetry, was in itself highly marketable and attractive to audiences for written and spoken verse in 1870s Dundee, familiar with the trend for publishing bad verse in the newspapers they read.

McGonagall's involvement with the *Weekly News* poetry and correspondents' columns began with a note recording a contribution by 'W. Shakspeare' which had been 'dropped mysteriously into our letter box':

> The effusion is in celebration of a local tragedian, whose talents are celebrated in the following lofty strain: – All ye who are disciples of Shakespeare, I hope you'll pay attention, unto a few incidents regarding Mr McGonagall, which is worthy of being made mention – he is a gentleman of great abilities and few can him excel o' I wonder how McFarland doesn't tender him an engagement, with him he would do well o'[81]

This is, in effect, an advertising jingle, as the 'O' on the end of lines indicates, and it opens with the standard broadside invocation to particular onlookers. The humour lies in the fact that readers know who McGonagall is and that he is puffing himself, as well as in the over-running metre of the lines and their failure to

---

[78] Norman Watson, *Poet McGonagall* (Edinburgh: Birlinn, 2010), pp.260–1.

[79] Gord Bambrick, 'The Heroic Warrior: Sir William Topaz McGonagall, Poet and Tragedian, Knight of the White Elephant, Burmah'. Masters thesis, University of Guelph, 1992.

[80] William McGonagall: *Collected Poems*, ed. Chris Hunt (Edinburgh: Birlinn, 2006), pp.xiii, xv.

[81] *Weekly News*, 9 June 1877, p.6.

present themselves in the correct layout for poetry. Four weeks later, 'Notices to Correspondents' recorded:

'W.M. G.' Dundee, who modestly seeks to hide his light under a bushel, has surreptitiously dropped into our letter-box an 'Address to the Rev. George Gilfillan' Here is a sample of this worthy's powers of versification: –

> Rev. George Gilfillan, of Dundee.
> There is none you can excel;
> You have boldly rejected the Confession of Faith,
> And defended your cause right well.
>
> The first time I heard him speak,
> 'Twas in the Kinnaird Hall,
> Lecturing on the Garibaldi movement
> As loud as he could bawl.[82]

Gilfillan had provided a somewhat lukewarm reference for McGonagall earlier in his career, when he was attempting to supplement his income by public readings and recitations.[83] The poem deals with a topic of contemporary interest, since the *Weekly News* reported extensively on Gilfillan's commentary on the Confession. The deflation in 'bawl' of Gilfillan's passionate—and much admired—speech on the Risorgimento, a cause particularly dear to the hearts of Dundee people and their Liberal press, is hardly complimentary. It does, however, fit with the tendency of working-class Dundee poets to comment on Gilfillan's activism and patronage in slyly disparaging ways through the medium of the press, especially when they were *not* amongst those who needed his patronage. Poute, for instance, discusses his desire to dedicate his collection to Gilfillan, 'the frend & admirer of every tru born pote', in his preface, but then refrains because 'I was afrade he michtna tak the thing weel oot', a commentary on Gilfillan's likely disapproval of Poute's satire.[84] Moses Dalite of Kats Klos, Dundee, a Poute imitator, concludes his ode to Dundee's Old Steeple with a vision of it collapsing on the heads of the congregation of School Wynd Kirk, Gilfillan's church, 'Whair grate filgillan lifts his voyse on high':

> But I du hop that time is far away
> And that I wont be in the kirk on that disastris day.[85]

This again deploys an over-long rhyming final line to comic deflationary effect. Gilfillan was devoted to helping artisan poets, but he had relatively conservative views about what kind of poetry they should be writing. The comic scenario in Dalite, Poute, *and* McGonagall is that these admirers of Gilfillan are producing a kind of ignorant, poorly written, mock-adulatory poetry that would fill him with dismay. Such poems then act as a potential critique of middle-class patronage, by

---

[82] *Weekly News*, 7 July 1877, p.6.   [83] See Watson, p.51.   [84] *Poute!*, p.5.
[85] Moses Dalite, 'A Nod Tew the Old Steepil', *People's Journal*, 18 November 1865, p.2. Dalite was one of the pseudonyms of factory poet David Tasker, suggesting how common it may have been for serious poets to enjoy an alternative comic persona. The identification was not explicitly stated until Tasker's *Readings, Recitations and Sketches* (Dundee: John Pellow, 1907).

highlighting the sycophancy involved in courting it, and implicitly signal the poet's ability to do without it.

Throughout the autumn of 1877, McGonagall began to build a reputation as a local bad poet in the Dundee press, primarily through his submissions to the *Weekly News*. Editors responded to him as an aspiring yet not very talented poet who might on occasion produce a 'straight' poem for the columns, but had to be discouraged from sending in reams of doggerel ('we are afraid our readers are beginning to think they have had enough of McGonagall for some time').[86] But they also placed him in close conjunction to Poute. In September 1877, the *People's Journal* published McGonagall's 'An Address to Thee Tay Bridge', a month after it had featured in the *Weekly News* (as a three-stanza untitled poem), noting that 'We feel that by the publication of this exquisite poem we are conferring an inestimable boon upon the literature of the nineteenth century'.[87] McGonagall's poem, now with four stanzas, appeared in the same column as, and immediately beneath, a poem by Poute. Like Poute, in this version it contains significant visual jokes about typesetting, layout, punctuation and bad spelling. The final stanza runs:

> 6 – Beautiful ! railway bridge of the Silvery Tay!
> I hope, that God ! – will protect all passengers,
> by night, and by day .... .
> and no accident befal them while crossing,
> The bridge of the Silvery Tay – for that
> Would be most awful ! to be seen –
> Near by Dundee. – and the Magdalen Green – [88]

This closing verse on railway accidents, prescient though it now seems, would at the time have seemed a comically injudicious way to conclude a celebratory poem about a new civic feature, showing the poet's slide towards a different and incompatible genre of occasional verse, that on disasters. Labelling stanzas with numbers is a convention of some bad poems in the press, probably stemming from songbooks or hymnbooks, and thus preserved by editors to show that the author does not understand the different conventions of the published poetry stanza. There were plenty of bad poems about the opening of the Tay Bridge, a heavily celebrated event. H. W.'s ode to the Tay Bridge, extracted in the 'Correspondence' column of the *Weekly News* on 17 August 1878, opened:

> It was on the first of June, Eighteen Hundred and Seventy-eight:
> A splendid feat of engineering I am going to relate,
> It is about the nobill Bridge that Spanes the river tay,
> It was opened for passenger traffic just upon that very day[89]

This is a poem that clearly has broadside rhythms and spoken conventions in mind, however, whereas McGonagall's *People's Journal* poem, in its liberal overuse

[86] 'To Correspondents', *Weekly News*, 4 May 1878, p.6.
[87] *People's Journal*, 15 September 1877, p.2. Reprinted in *Poets of the People's Journal*, p.138. For more detail on McGonagall's relationship with the *People's Journal*, see the headnote to this poem. *The Weekly News* published McGonagall's first Tay Bridge poem on 11 August 1877, p.3.
[88] *Poets of the People's Journal*, p.138.   [89] *Weekly News*, 17 August 1878, p.3.

of random exclamation points and full stops, and its lines that drift off into oddly spaced ellipses, looks like Poute. McGonagall's surviving manuscripts are far less irregular in spelling and layout than 'An Address to Thee Tay Bridge', though they notably feature scatterings of definite black dots throughout lines of poetry, unidentifiable as either commas or full stops and misplaced as either—recalling Poute's problems with punctuation.[90] In the case of the two newspaper versions of 'An Address', either the editor of the *Weekly News* regularized the spelling, punctuation, and layout of McGonagall's stanzas, to make them more intelligible, and the *People's Journal* did not, or the *Journal* got hold of a particular version of this McGonagall poem which the *News* had not seen (a rough draft, perhaps), and decided to publish it for its humour even though the *News* had already printed extracts from a different version. That the *Journal* published it at all, despite McGonagall's usual engagement with a rival paper, shows the paper's particular interest in the comic potential of verse that was visually deviant from the norm.

The *Weekly News* continued to publish occasional McGonagall poems throughout late 1877 and 1878, besides commenting on rejected poems sent in by him. By 1878, however, McGonagall was moving away from the position of newspaper bad poet (a role unlikely to bring in any income), and into the realm of the bad poet as hawker and performer. This situated him in a different, and an older, tradition. Street performers like Glasgow's Hawkie, briefly mentioned in Chapter 2, or door-to-door poetry sellers like Susannah Hawkins, a famous 'bad' poet of the 1820s to 1840s whose publications were supported by the *Dumfries and Galloway Courier*, were part of a long-standing tradition of entrepreneurial self-marketing by writers. Rarely noted as part of this tradition, however, is a long-standing tendency for Scottish local communities to support a poet, by buying their poems and indeed paying them to perform, not because they were worthy but because they were entertainingly bad.

On his 'Rambles Round Glasgow', which sometimes serves as a guide to the number of eccentric poetic characters who live within walking distance of Glasgow, MacDonald encountered one such writer as a feature of the village of Balmore near the Campsie Fells, Thomas Hamilton Dickson. Dickson, at this point in the 1850s, had published poems, fiction, and a brief autobiography in chapbook form. MacDonald is skeptical and facetious about the 'inspired pages' of Dickson's writings, which 'sink below the level of Lindley Murray' (author of the well-known *English Grammar* of 1795, a book often recommended to aspiring self-educated writers). He suggests that Dickson's autobiography is fiction and that his verses' lack of originality shades into plagiarism. His only good poem, MacDonald notes, was lifted wholesale from Geraldine Jewsbury:

> There is a considerable amount of originality, however, in the subjects of his muse, as will be admitted when we mention the titles of two of his pieces. They are as follows: – 'Verses on a young lady refusing to accept a ticket to a ball with the author;' and 'Lines on a young lady refusing to dance' with the same illustrious individual. These are both,

---

[90] See, for example, the manuscripts of 'The Wreck of the Thomas Dryden' or 'Little Popeet, the Lost Child' in the NLS (LC Folio 71 MS 6620).

as may be easily supposed, deeply tinged with the pathetic. The second, however, concludes with the following spirited lines: –

> 'By fury! mock me not again,
>> So ruthless at your will;
> Must I endure your proud disdain?
>> Yes, no! by Jove, sit still!'[91]

Dickson goes most awry when he attempts to imitate a flowery, silver-fork style but cannot pull it off, as also in the bathetic lines he tells us he wished to place on his beloved's gravestone, 'Beneath this stone lies a beauteous form/ That seldom is by sinful mortals worn'.[92] Nonetheless, as the *Stirling Observer* noted in an obituary, Dickson managed to make some kind of living from advertising himself as 'poet, novelist and occasional lecturer':

> If Thomas was not a poet, he was at least a rhymer, for he produced a considerable amount of doggerel which he got printed at the 'Poet's Box' and hawked through the parish. Tam had many friends in the district, and his productions generally met with a ready sale – being done up in the ballad style, and the price 'only a penny'. His own estimate of his poetical talent was pretty lofty, for he considered himself the Shakespeare of the nineteenth century, and the Homer of modern times...His harangues were generally given in a barn to a number of rustics bent on amusement – Tam on these occasions being invariably the subject of some practical though harmless jokes.[93]

The local community were well aware that Dickson's poetry was entertainingly poor, and indeed, what they apparently enjoyed was the contrast between Dickson's self-belief as a poet and his terrible performances (which they paid to attend in the form of a collection). That this obituary appeared next to a new *Stirling Observer* column on 'Our Classic Poets', starting with Burns, nicely highlighted the fact that both good *and* bad poets were of interest to newspaper readers.

Dickson, most of whose works seem to be lost without trace, is a clear forerunner of McGonagall, and it is equally difficult to tell whether he was self-deluded about his talent or not. In April 1878, the *News* noted that McGonagall had published a twopenny pamphlet of his verse, and remarked on his skill in self-advertisement and enterprise as a performer. 'The human midriff may hold out against McGonagall as a poet, or McGonagall as a reader', the editor comments, 'but McGonagall as both poet and reader is a combination which, we are afraid would have doubled up even Nestor'.[94] Suffering from straitened circumstances, McGonagall evidently realized the potential to combine his interests in performance and in poetry and give local audiences a show: fifteen shillings a night for performances at the Royal Circus in Dundee was a decent income. As part of a later generation than broadside sellers like Hawkie and Milne or poet-performers like Dickson, he could draw

---

[91] MacDonald, *Rambles Round Glasgow*, pp.324–5.
[92] See Thomas Hamilton Dickson, *Life, Memoirs and Pedigree of Thomas Hamilton Dickson* (Glasgow: Printed for the Author, 1841), p.36. No surviving copy of Dickson's poems has been traced.
[93] 'Death of a Modern "Thomas the Rhymer"', *Stirling Observer*, 18 March 1875, p.2.
[94] 'To Correspondents', *Weekly News*, 27 April 1878, p.3.

on the development of music-hall and Scotch comedy to find performance spaces and audiences: Maloney describes how professional music-hall coexisted with regular amateur nights, where poor performers were treated mercilessly by the audience, and with the continued survival of many cheap theatres and other performance venues, of the kind McGonagall frequented.[95] It seems probable that the same working-class audiences who enjoyed deliberately bad poetry in the papers they read, would have enjoyed deliberately bad verse recitations and songs, and that the same tension between conscious and accidental badness may have coexisted in these performance venues. Scotch comedians, as Maloney notes, often started as part-time amateurs who gained traction by performing for societies, benefits, and special occasions, and who published their verses in the press and as broadsides. Houston, the Glasgow engineer and later professional performer discussed in Chapter 1, is a good example. McGonagall also sought to follow this route. Most of his poems were printed in broadside format, and, like both broadsides and newspaper verse, they report upon current affairs both local and national. His 'The Battle of Tel-El-Kebir', dated 1882, opens with the traditional invocation to the audience:

> Ye sons of Great Britain, come join with me,
> And sing in praise of Sir Garnet Wolseley
> Twas on the 13th of September, in the year of 1882,
> Which Arabi and his rebel horde long will rue.[96]

Specifying the date and the leading characters attracts listeners' attention, promising a newsworthy story (in this case, of the success of the British and the Highland Brigade in the conflict in Egypt, commemorated in many other newspaper poems in this year). McGonagall marketed these broadside verses not in the manner of older anonymous broadsides, but with his name and imagined title as 'Sir William McGonagall' prominently attached, alongside testimonials and statements on 'Copyright' and 'All Rights Reserved'. While these may have been genuinely meant rather than tongue-in-cheek, they make the broadside more marketable by giving it a striking and innovative appearance, and add to the overall comic effect given the contrast between 'Sir' McGonagall and the awkward grammar and phrasing of lines such as 'Arabi's army were about 70,000 in all,/ And virtually speaking, it wasn't very small'. One of the versions of McGonagall's autobiography states that he recited this poem on his return trip from New York where—emulating music-hall stars and singers on their transatlantic tours—he had gone to attempt to make his fortune. The autobiography tells us that his shipboard recitation received 'applause' and 'high compliments' and was greeted with warmth; though whether this was due to its patriotic or comic effect is unclear.[97] Once he achieved success in a genre, McGonagall, like all broadside authors, would recycle and repeat the same lines and material, hence his nineteen poems on battles, which market historical battles

---

[95] Maloney, pp.98–100. [96] 'The Battle of Tel-el-Kebir'. Broadside in NLS.
[97] *The Autobiography of Sir William Topaz McGonagall, Poet and Tragedian, Knight of the White Elephant, Burma* (n.pub, 1901), p.12.

whenever no contemporary one was available. His poems, like many which moved between newspaper, broadside, and volume, are also not stable texts. 'The Battle of Tel-El-Kebir' in his later *Poetic Gems*, for instance, replaces the final two lines above with 'Sound drums and trumpets cheerfully,/ For he has acted most heroically'.[98]

The characteristics of McGonagall's verse are not distinct from the known attributes of other bad poets of the period. What McGonagall managed to do, and they did not, was to marry newspaper, broadside, and performance in character at a point when late nineteenth-century media could ensure widespread reportage and distribution of his verse. Compared to the success of Houston, or of the rising music-hall stars of his period such as W. F. Frame or Harry Lauder, McGonagall's career was a disaster. But if we accept his chosen self-description as 'William McGonagall, *poet*', not a comedian or performer, and not a broadside seller or songwriter, then out of all the many bad poets printed in Victorian Scotland, he was the only one who managed to give up his day job and survive. McGonagall's autobiographies (at least one, like Dickson's, sold in chapbook format at 6d) consistently represent a moment of quasi-religious poetic inspiration, linked to the writing of his first poem on Gilfillan:

> I seemed to feel as it were a strange kind of feeling stealing over me, and remained so for about five minutes. A flame, as Lord Byron has said, seemed to kindle up my entire frame, along with a strong desire to write poetry, and I felt so happy, so happy, that I was inclined to dance, then I began to pace backwards and forwards in the room, trying to shake off all thought of writing poetry; but the more I tried, the more strong the sensation became. It was so strong, I imagined that a pen was in my right hand, and a voice crying, "write! write!"[99]

Given the hundreds of comic poems and prose accounts satirizing precisely such moments of vocational poetic impulse, it is extremely difficult to believe that McGonagall intends this to be taken seriously. As Poute's preface to his first volume stated 'i only rote on the Spur of the Momint – and as The Spirrit moved me…i resolvid to give to the world my gloing centymints, in thochts that Brethe & wuds that burn'.[100] As an ignorant young labourer in the Fife salt pans or an elderly weaver from Dundee, Poute and McGonagall's distance from the kind of passionate poet invoked by the references to Byron and Gray could not be more marked. Whatever McGonagall's intentions, his poetry is part of a notable tradition of satirical working-class poetic engagement with conceptions of poetry and poetic ambition, in a form of satire that manages to emphasize just how important and prevalent the practice of poetry was in Victorian Scotland, for good and bad poets alike.

---

[98] *Collected Poems*, p.42.

[99] *The Authentic Autobiography of the Poet McGonagall, Written by Himself* (Dundee: Luke, Mackie, n.d.), p.5.

[100] *Poute!*, p.v.

Afterword

From around the 1880s to the 1920s, local authors and historians in Scotland performed a remarkable act of canon formation. A small sample of the regional anthologies of Scottish poetry in English and Scots produced in this period includes Francis Barnard, *Poetry of the Dell* (1887); James Beveridge, *The Poets of Clackmannanshire* (1885); Alexander M. Bissett, *The Poets and Poetry of Linlithgowshire* (1896); George Eyre-Todd, *The Glasgow Poets, Their Lives and Poems* (1903); Andrew L. Fenton, *Forfar Poets* (1879); Robert Ford, *The Harp of Perthshire* (1893); Malcolm McL. Harper, *The Bards of Galloway* (1889); William Harvey, *The Harp of Stirlingshire* (1897); George Hay, *Round about the Round O with its Poets* (1883); James Knox, *Airdrie Bards* (1930); J. McBain, *Arbroath Poets* (1883); Frank Miller, *The Poets of Dumfriesshire* (1910); John Macintosh, *The Poets of Ayrshire* (1910); Alan Reid, *The Bards of Angus and the Mearns* (1897), and William Walker, *The Bards of Bon-Accord* (1887). There are also the broader anthologies, from Alexander Murdoch's *The Scottish Poets, Recent and Living* (1883) to James Grant Wilson's four volumes on *The Poets and Poetry of Scotland* (1876–1884) in which the last volume in the 1884 edition covers 1802–1884, and finally, the crowning achievement, Edwards' *Modern Scottish Poets* (14 vols plus index, 1880–1897). Many of these anthologies are compiled from columns published in local newspapers, and each of them takes their narrative about a region's poetic past up to the present day, celebrating living poets within their communities. They are deliberately engaged in recording the life stories of these poets, who usually published anonymously or pseudonymously, while this is still possible. The anthologists influenced (and competed with) each other, and they drew inspiration from a longer tradition of anthologizing and memorializing Scotland's poetic and musical history, dating from the mid to late eighteenth century and still very current in the song compilations produced throughout the nineteenth century. Scottish associational culture similarly thrived on efforts to revive and preserve poetic tradition, in the late nineteenth-century rise of societies like the Glasgow Ballad Club or the Border Bards Association. These collections and societies also contributed to the broader folklore revival, the interest in preserving dialect speech, and the passion for local antiquarianism, which were important aspects of late Victorian culture.

In relation to the narratives about working-class poetry highlighted in this book, this anthologizing effort seems, in hindsight, both backward and forward-looking. On the one hand, it is a last-ditch effort to preserve a vision of small-town and rural Scotland as filled with village poets, bent on self-improvement, in the face of changing social conditions and the rise of modernism and modernity. After the

First World War, poetry columns gradually began to disappear from the newspapers, and though popular poetry survived, its status and significance heavily declined. On the other hand, these anthologies form part of the emergence of cultural nationalism, chiming with renewed calls for a recognition of Scotland's cultural—and political—autonomy as the twentieth century developed, whether as part of the United Kingdom or not. Though they make little reference to what would be known as the Celtic Revival, or, in the early twentieth century, the Scottish Renaissance, their effort to display Scotland as a nation of poets ties into this broader political and cultural movement.

In her introduction to a collection of key documents on the Scottish Renaissance, Margery Palmer McCulloch suggests that the Renaissance was 'unusual in the context of the modernist period generally' because 'those involved believed that there could be no regeneration of the nation's artistic culture which did not also involve the regeneration of the social, economic and political life of the nation'.[1] But whether or not this is unusual in relation to broader developments in 'modernism', it is not at all a new position for Scottish writers at the start of the twentieth century (albeit that 'nation' was not always identified solely with 'Scotland' for many Victorian poets). The extent to which writers who would come to define themselves, or be defined, as part of a 'Scottish Renaissance' performed a conscious forgetting of their popular Victorian predecessors should not be overlooked. As scholars of Victorian poetics, notably Anne Jamison and Meredith Martin, have recently argued, perceptions of a break or rupture between 'Victorian' and 'modernist' poetics are increasingly difficult to defend.[2] Borrowing the terms of a seminal essay by Paula Bennett on late nineteenth-century women's periodical poetics, Victorian Scotland's popular poetry supplied a foundation on which later poets would 'build their own careers as risk-taking, stylistically experimental writers', and the 'erasure of this poetry from cultural memory' has thus been a 'thoroughly disruptive' event, because it made a 'flowering' of new forms of poetry in the early twentieth century seem 'a far more autonomous and self-contained event than it actually was'.[3] Bennett's description of the silencing of Victorian women's voices in this rewriting of literary history is one that I would suggest

---

[1] Margery Palmer McCulloch, ed. Modernism and Nationalism: Literature and Society in Scotland, 1918–1939 (Glasgow: ASLS, 2004), p.xiii. The term 'Scottish Renaissance' was first used in 1922. Maurice Lindsay's Modern Scottish Poetry: An Anthology of the Scottish Renaissance, 3rd edn (Manchester: Carcanet, 1976) begins with 1925. Several of the poets in his seminal anthology were born in the 1860s and 1870s: he suggests that they bridge an 'old' and 'new' movement, while also arguing that most nineteenth-century poets in Scots 'simply sank deeper into a mire of imitative sentimentality' (pp.19, 17).

[2] Meredith Martin, The Rise and Fall of Meter: Poetry and English National Culture, 1860–1930 (Princeton, NJ: Princeton University Press, 2012) and Anne Jamison, Poetics En Passant: Redefining the Relationship Between Victorian and Modern Poetry (Houndmills: Palgrave, 2009). Both studies also interrogate the role of poetry in 'national' cultures.

[3] Paula Bennett, 'Not Just Filler and Not Just Sentimental: Women's Poetry in American Victorian Periodicals, 1860–1900', in Kenneth M. Price and Susan Belasco Smith, eds., Periodical Literature in Nineteenth-Century America (Charlottesville, VA: University Press of Virginia, 1995), pp.202–19, 203, 204.

equally applies to the silencing of Victorian working-class voices, in critical narratives about twentieth-century Scottish literary history.

Caroline Levine, in an influential 2013 article, argues that it is 'urgent' for Victorian studies to 'refuse the nation's restrictive and naturalizing models of belonging', rejecting the 'logic of autochthony'. Hers is an overtly political argument, premised on the anxiety that literary criticism's presumption of 'an attachment between a land and its culture' adopts 'the starting point that most suits political nationalists'.[4] The assumption is that literary scholars—Victorianists—are unlikely to wish to aid and abet the rise of political nationalism in the twenty-first century. This is, however, a position which is a great deal more complicated for historians and literary critics working on Scotland, to use Scotland as only one example of the rise of European nationalism. I agree with Levine's broader argument about the issues involved in identifying culture and 'nation', and with her suggestion that we need to rethink categories of birth and temporal location in relation to literary alignments. I also agree with an aspect of her argument that is unspoken, in that the suggestion that Victorianists might think more closely about 'Britishness' should necessarily involve a 'four nations' approach to 'British' Victorian literature. But this does not mean that we should not explore what issues of birth and belonging meant to Victorian writers, the ways in which they identified themselves with national cultures that were not always British, and helped to shape ideas about what such cultures might be and do. Much of the work of verse in Victorian Scotland supported, deliberately or not, a sense of a peculiarly Scottish separateness and distinctiveness. It would be disingenuous to deny that the process of disinterring this host of forgotten Scottish working-class poets, who frequently and repeatedly express their love of home and country, can be interpreted as bolstering twenty-first century Scottish cultural nationalism, even as I argue that these lost poets are instead a missing link in the *construction* of Scottish cultural nationalism. The 'people's poets' of Victorian Scotland became an imagined community that fostered a resolutely local sense of Scottishness on a global scale, and made working-class verse cultures into a central, and lasting, constituent of Scotland's international cultural identity.

---

[4] Caroline Levine, 'From Nation to Network', Victorian Studies 55 (2013), pp.647–66, 654, 649, 654.

Bibliography

NEWSPAPERS PRIMARILY CONSULTED

Aberdeen Herald
Airdrie Advertiser
Annan Observer
Ardrossan and Saltcoats Herald
Ayr Advertiser
The Commonwealth (Glasgow)
Dumfries and Galloway Courier
Dundee Advertiser
Dundee Courier
Fife Herald
Fife News
Glasgow Citizen
Glasgow Herald
Glasgow Weekly Mail
Greenock Advertiser
Elgin Courant
Elgin Courier
Hamilton Advertiser
The Highlander
Invergordon Times
Inverness Courier
The Miner and Workman's Advocate
Oban Times
Paisley Herald and Renfrewshire Advertiser
Penny Post (Glasgow)
People's Friend
People's Journal
The Scotsman
Stirling Observer
Weekly News (Dundee)
West Lothian Courier (Bathgate)

MANUSCRIPT SOURCES AND EPHEMERA

A. C. Lamb Collection, Dundee Central Library.
James Maidment's Scrap Book. NLS S. 276.
William McGonagall MS poems. NLS LC Folio 71 MS 6620
D. S. Robertson Manuscripts (MS Robertson). University of Glasgow Special Collections.
'Song on Phonography'. NLS Wn68.
William Tennant's Book. Local History Centre, Airdrie Library.
David Willox, *Memories of Parkhead*. Mitchell Library, Glasgow.

PRIMARY

'A Peep at the Mining Districts', *Chamber's Journal* 324 (17 March 1860), 174–6

A Visit to the Monkwearmouth Pit', *Chambers's Edinburgh Journal* 49 (7 Dec 1844), 355–7

Ainslie, Hew, *Scottish Song, Ballads and Poems* (New York: Redfield, 1855)

Ainslie, Hew, *A Pilgrimage to the Land of Burns, and Poems*, with memoir by Thomas C. Latto (Paisley: Alexander Gardner, 1892)

Aitken, William, *Lays of the Line* (Edinburgh and Glasgow: John Menzies, 1883)

Anderson, Alexander, *Songs of the Rail* (London: Simpkin, Marshall, 1878)

Arnold, Matthew, *Culture and Anarchy*, ed. Jane Garnett (Oxford: Oxford University Press, 2006)

Barnard, Francis, *Sparks from a Miner's Lamp* (Airdrie: Baird and Hamilton, 1875)

Barnard, Francis, *Chirps Frae the Engine Lum* (Bathgate: L. Gilbertson, 1889)

Barnard, Francis, *Poetry of the Dell, Being Sketches of the Poets and Poetry of the District of Woodend, Torphichen* (Bathgate: Laurence Gilbertson, 1887)

Bengough, Samuel Edmund, *The 'Open Secret' of Social Progress, of National Prosperity, and Success in Military Effort* (Phonetic Society/English Spelling Reform Association, n.d.)

Bernstein, Marion, *A Song of Glasgow Town: The Collected Poems of Marion Bernstein*, ed. Edward H. Cohen, Anne R. Fertig and Linda Fleming (Glasgow: ASLS, 2013)

Beveridge, James, ed., *The Poets of Clackmannanshire* (Glasgow: John S. Wilson, 1885)

Bissett, Alexander M., ed., *The Poets and Poetry of Linlithgowshire* (Paisley: J. and R. Parlane, 1896)

Blackie, John, *Lays and Lyrics of Ancient Greece, With Other Poems* (Edinburgh: Sutherland and Knox, 1857)

Bremner, David, *The Industries of Scotland: Their Rise, Progress and Present Condition*, intro. by John Butt and Ian L. Donnachie (Newton Abbott: David and Charles, 1969)

Brown, John, 'Children, and How to Guide Them', *Good Words* 2 (December 1861), 309–13

Browne, C. F., *Artemus Ward: His Book* (New York: Carleton, 1865)

Browning, Robert and Elizabeth Barrett Browning, *The Brownings' Correspondence*, ed. Philip Kelly and Ronald Hudson (Winfield, KA: Wedgestone Press, 1992), vol X

Buchanan, Robert, *The Schoolmaster in the Wynds*, 3rd edn (Glasgow: Blackie & Son, 1850)

Buchanan, Robert, 'The Laureate of the Nursery', *Saint Paul's Magazine* 11 (July 1872), 66–73

Burgess, Alexander, *Poute! Being Poetry, Poutery and Prose* (Coupar-Fife: A. Westwood, n.d.)

Burns, Robert, *Selected Poems and Songs*, ed. Robert P. Irvine (Oxford: Oxford University Press, 2014)

Byron, George Gordon, *The Complete Poetical Works*, vol I, ed. Jerome J. McGann (Oxford: Clarendon Press, 1980)

Cadenhead, William, *Flights of Fancy and Lays of Bon-Accord* (Aberdeen: A. Brown, 1853)

Campbell, Thomas, *The Poetical Works of Thomas Campbell* (London: Edward Moxon, 1837)

Carnegie, David, *Lays and Lyrics from the Factory* (Arbroath: Thomas Buncle, 1879)

'Castles in the Air' (Melbourne: McCulloch and Stewart, 1859–1861)

Chambers, Robert, *Popular Rhymes, Fireside Stories and Amusements of Scotland* (Edinburgh: William and Robert Chambers, 1842)

Connell, Philip, *Poaching on Parnassus* (Manchester: John Heywood, 1865)

'David Wingate', *Blackwood's Edinburgh Magazine* 92 (July 1862), 48–61

'David Wingate's Poems', *London Review* 4 (31 May 1862), 506–8

Denham, Thomas, *Poems and Snatches of Prose* (London: Smith, Elder, 1845)

Dickens, Charles, *The Old Curiosity Shop*, ed. Angus Easson (Harmondsworth: Penguin, 1985)

Dickson, Thomas Hamilton, *Life, Memoirs and Pedigree of Thomas Hamilton Dickson* (Glasgow: Printed for the Author, 1841)

Donald, G. W., *The Muckle Skeel, and Other Poems* (Dundee: Lawson Brothers, 1870)

Donaldson, William, *The Queen Martyr, and Other Poems* (Elgin: J. McGillivray and Son, 1867)

Easson, James, *Select Miscellany of Poetical Pieces* (Dundee: Park, Sinclair & Co, 1856)

Edwards, D. H., *The Poetry of Scottish Rural Life or A Sketch of the Life and Writings of Alexander Laing* (Brechin: D. H. Edwards, 1874)

Edwards, D. H., ed., *One Hundred Modern Scottish Poets* (Brechin: D. H. Edwards, 1880)

Edwards, D. H., ed., *Modern Scottish Poets*, 15 vols (Brechin: D. H. Edwards, 1881–1893)

Ellis, Alexander John, *A Plea for Phonetic Spelling*, 2nd edn (London: Fred Pitman, 1848)

Ellis, Alexander John, *On Early English Pronunciation, with Especial Reference to Shakspere and Chaucer*, Part IV (London: Philological Society, 1874)

Eyre-Todd, George, 'A Cobbler-Artist', *The National Review* 16 (September 1890), 105–12

Eyre-Todd, George, ed., *The Glasgow Poets, Their Lives and Poems* (Glasgow: William Hodge, 1903)

Fenton, Andrew L., ed., *Forfar Poets* (Forfar: Heath & Co., 1879)

Fergusson, J. Menzies, *A Village Poet* (Paisley: Alexander Gardner, 1897)

Fisher, Robert, *Poetical Sparks* (Dumfries: Robert Fisher, 1881)

Ford, Robert, ed., *Ballads of Bairnhood* (Paisley: Alexander Gardner, 1892)

Ford, Robert, ed., *The Harp of Perthshire* (Paisley: Alexander Gardner, 1893)

Forrest, Isabella, *Islaside Musings* (Banff: Banffshire Journal, 1926)

Forsyth, William, *Selections from the Writings of the Late William Forsyth, with Memoir and Notes* (Aberdeen: L. Smith and Son, 1882)

Freer, Walter, *My Life and Memories* (Glasgow: Civic Press, 1929)

Fullerton, John, *Poems* (Peterhead: P. Scrogie, 1905)

Geddes, James Young, *The New Jerusalem and Other Verses* (Dundee: James P. Mathew, 1879)

Geddes, James Young, *The Spectre Clock of Alyth* (Alyth: Thomas McMurray, 1886)

Geddes, James Young, *In the Valhalla* (Dundee: John Leng, 1898)

Gilfillan, George [Apollodorus], 'The Modern Scottish Minstrel', *The Critic* 16 (2 March 1857), 101–4

Gregory, William, *An Epistle on English Orthography*. Reprinted from the *Phonetic Journal*, 1 May 1850 (Bath: Isaac Pitman, n.d.)

Guthrie, Thomas, *A Second Plea for Ragged Schools, or Prevention Better Than Cure* (Edinburgh: John Elder, 1849)

Hamilton, Janet, *Poems, Sketches and Essays* (Glasgow: James Maclehose, 1885)

Harper, Malcolm, McL., ed., *The Bards of Galloway: A Collection of Poems, Songs, Ballads, &c, by Natives of Galloway* (Thomas Fraser: Dalbeattie, 1889)

Hartley, Elizabeth, *The Prairie Flower and Other Poems* (Dumbarton: Bennett Brothers, at the Herald Office, 1870)

Harvey, William, ed., *The Harp of Stirlingshire* (Paisley: J. and R. Parlane, 1897)

Hawkins, Susannah, *The Poems and Songs of Susanna Hawkins*, vol V (Dumfries: J. McDiarmid, 1841)

Hay, George, ed., *Round about the Round O with its Poets* (Arbroath: Thomas Buncle, 1883)

Hedderwick, James, *Backward Glances or Some Personal Recollections* (Edinburgh and London: William Blackwood & Sons, 1891)

Hindley, Charles, *The Life and Times of James Catnach, Late of Seven Dials, Ballad Monger* (London: Seven Dials Press, 1970 (first published 1878))

The History of a Village Shopkeeper (Edinburgh: John Menzies, 1876)

Hopkins, Gerard, *Gerard Manley Hopkins: The Major Works*, ed. Catherine Phillips (Oxford: Oxford University Press, 2009)

Houston, James, *Autobiography of Mr James Houston, Scotch Comedian* (Glasgow and Edinburgh: John Menzies, 1889)

Jamieson, John, *An Etymological Dictionary of the Scottish Language*, 2 vols (Edinburgh: Edinburgh University Press, 1808)

Jeffrey, Francis, *Contributions to the Edinburgh Review*, 3 vols, 2nd ed (London: Longman, Brown, Green and Longmans, 1846)

Johnston, Ellen, *Autobiography, Poems and Songs* (Glasgow: William Love, 1867)

Jolly, William, *The Life of John Duncan, Scotch Weaver and Botanist* (London: Kegan Paul, 1883)

Kelly, John Liddell, *Heather and Fern: Songs of Scotland and Maoriland* (Wellington: New Zealand Times Company, 1908)

Kilpatrick, James A., *Literary Landmarks of Glasgow* (Glasgow: Saint Mungo Press, 1893)

Knight, William, *Auld Yule and Other Poems*, intro. George Gilfillan, ed. William Lindsay (Aberdeen: W. Lindsay, 1869)

Lang, Andrew, *Lost Leaders* (London: Kegan Paul, Trench, 1889)

Leifchild, J. M., 'Colliers in their Homes and At Their Work', *Good Words* 3 (December 1862), 213–20

Lindsay, William, *Some Notes: Personal and Public* (Aberdeen: W. W. Lindsay, 1898)

'Lives of the Poetasters', *Scots Observer* 3 (8 February 1890), 332–3

Lyric Gems of Scotland, with Music (Glasgow: David Jack, 1856)

MacDonald, Hugh, *Rambles Round Glasgow, Descriptive, Historical, and Traditional* (Glasgow: James Hedderwick, 1854)

Macfarlan, James, *The Poetical Works of James Macfarlan*, intro. and memoir Colin Rae-Brown (Glasgow: Robert Forrester, 1882)

Macintosh, John, ed., *The Poets of Ayrshire* (Dumfries: Thomas Hunter, 1910)

Mackay, Charles, *Voices from the Mountains and the Crowd* (Boston, MA: Ticknor, Reid & Fields, 1853)

Mackay, Charles, 'Minor Poetry', *The London Review* 17 (17 October 1868), 457–9

Mackenzie, Peter, *Reminiscences of Glasgow and the West of Scotland*, 2 vols (Glasgow: John Tweed, 1866)

Macpherson, Colin, *The Farmer's Friend: The Errors in the Present Method of Rearing and Breeding Cattle Exposed* (n.p.: published for the author, 1878)

McBain, J., *Arbroath Poets and Their Songs* (Arbroath: T. Buncle, n.d. [1883])

McDowall, William, *The Man of the Woods, and Other Poems* (Dumfries: J. McKinnell, 1844)

McGonagall, William, *The Autobiography of Sir William Topaz McGonagall, Poet and Tragedian, Knight of the White Elephant, Burma* (n.pub, 1901)

McGonagall, William, *William McGonagall: Collected Poems*, ed. Chris Hunt (Edinburgh: Birlinn, 2006)

McGonagall, William, *The Authentic Autobiography of the Poet McGonagall, Written by Himself* (Dundee: Luke, Mackie, n.d.)

McHutchison, William, *Poems* (npub: nd [Airdrie, 1868])

Mill, John Stuart, 'Considerations on Representative Government', in Mark Philip and Frederick Rosen, eds., *On Liberty, Utilitarianism and Other Essays* (Oxford: Oxford University Press, 2015)

Millar, Tom, *Readings and Rhymes from a Reeky Region* (Coatbridge, printed for the author by William Craig, 1887)

Miller, Andrew, *The Rise and Progress of Coatbridge and Surrounding Neighbourhood* (Glasgow: David Robertson, 1864)

Miller, Frank, ed., *The Poets of Dumfriesshire* (Glasgow: James Maclehose, 1910)

Miller, Hugh, *My Schools and Schoolmasters, or The Story of My Education* (Edinburgh: Johnstone and Hunter, 1854)

Miller, Hugh, *Essays, Historical and Biographical, Political, Social, Literary and Scientific*, ed. Peter Bayne (Edinburgh: William P. Nimmo, 1872)

Milne, John, *Selections from the Songs and Poems of the Late John Milne, Glenlivat* (Aberdeen: Free Press Office, 1871)

Milton, John, *Paradise Lost*, ed. Alistair Fowler, 2nd edn (Harlow: Longman, 1998)

Mitchell, Alexander, *Political and Social Movements in Dalkeith, from 1831–1882* (Printed for private circulation, 1882)

Mitchell, John, *Poems, Radical Rhymes, Tales etc* (Aberdeen: Published by the Author, 1840)

'Modern Scottish Poetry', *Golden Hours* (August 1884), 510–12

Morrison, David H., *Poems and Songs* (Airdrie: Baird and Hamilton, 1870)

Murdoch, Alexander, *The Laird's Lykewake and Other Poems* (Edinburgh and Glasgow: John Menzies, 1877)

Murdoch, Alexander, *Rhymes and Lyrics* (Kilmarnock: James McKie, 1879)

Murdoch, Alexander, *The Scottish Poets, Recent and Living* (Glasgow: T. D. Morison, 1883)

'My Colliery Experiences', *Once a Week*, 3.53 (5 Jan 1867), 8–13

[Myles, James], *Chapters in the Life of a Dundee Factory Boy* (Dundee: James Myles, 1850)

Neilson, James M., *Songs for the Bairns, and Miscellaneous Poems* (Glasgow: William Rankin, 1884)

Nicol, Charles, *Poems and Songs* (Edinburgh: McLaren and Bruce, n.d.)

Nicholson, James, *Kilwuddie and Other Poems*, intro. Alexander Macleod (Glasgow: Scottish Temperance League, 1863)

Nicholson, James, *Wee Tibbie's Garland, and Other Poems* (Glasgow: James McGeachy, 1873)

Nicholson, James, *Kilwuddie and Other Poems, with Life-Sketch and Portrait of the Author*, 4th edn (Glasgow: James McGeachy, 1895)

'On the Poetical Character of the Scottish Peasantry', *British Minstrel* 1 (January 1843), 290–1

'Our Working People and How They Live: The Newcastle Collier', *Good Words* (11 Jan 1870), 53–60

Palmer, John, *Poems and Songs* (n.pub, n.d [1871])

Paton, Allan Park, *Poems* (London: Saunders and Otley, 1845)

Penman, William, *Echoes from the Ingleside* (Glasgow: Porteous Brothers, 1875)

Pitman, Isaac, *The Phonographic Teacher*, 11th edn (London: F. Pitman, 1863)

Pitman, Isaac, *Spelling Reform: Address by Mr Isaac Pitman to the Young Men's Christian Association, St James's Square, Bristol, 8 November, 1880* (Bath: Isaac Pitman, 1880)

Plummer, John, 'Our Wayside Poets', *National Magazine* 14 (July 1863), 141–4

Porteous, Mitchelson, *Odd Time: A Selection of Original Varieties* (Maybole: printed for the author, 1842)

Porteous, Mitchelson, *Carrickiana* (Maybole: printed for the author, n.d.)

Prince, John Critchley, *Hours With the Muses* (Manchester, 1841)

'Rambles Round Glasgow', *Blackwood's Edinburgh Magazine* 83 (10 April 1858), 467–83

Ramsay, Elizabeth, *A Garland of Verse, with Prose Writings*, 2nd edn, enlarged (Glasgow: Bell & Bain, 1914)

Reid, Alan, ed., *The Bards of Angus and the Mearns* (Paisley: J. & R. Parlane, 1897)

Reid, H. Gilzean, 'Unaccredited Heroes', *Gentleman's Magazine* 269 (October 1890), 384–96

Robertson, David, *Songs for the Nursery* (Glasgow, 1844)

Robertson, David, *Songs for the Nursery*, 2nd edn (Glasgow, 1846)

Rodger, Alexander, *Stray Leaves from the Portfolios of Alisander the Seer, Andrew Whaup and Humphrey Henpeckle* (Glasgow: Charles Rattray, 1842)

Rogers, Charles, *A Century of Scottish Life* (Edinburgh: William P. Nimmo, 1871)

Sanderson, Robert, *Poems and Songs* (Edinburgh: Colston & Son, 1865)

Seward, Anna, *The Collected Poems of Anna Seward*, vol I, ed. Lisa L. Moore (New York: Routledge, 2016)

Shanks, Henry, *The Peasant Poets of Scotland and Musings Under the Beeches*, with memoir and portrait of the author (Bathgate: Laurence Gilbertson, 1881)

Shaw, Henry Wheeler, *Josh Billings on Ice, and Other Things* (New York: Carleton, 1870)

Silsbee, M. C. D., ed., *Willie Winkie's Nursery Songs of Scotland* (Boston, MA: Ticknor and Fields, 1859)

Smiles, Samuel, 'The Story of Robert Nicoll's Life', *Good Words* 16 (December 1875), 313–18

Smillie, Robert, *My Life for Labour*, foreword by J. Ramsay Macdonald (London: Mills & Boon, 1924)

Smith, Ebenezer, *Verses* (Ayr: Henry and Grant, 1871)

Smith, James, *Poems, Songs and Ballads*, 3rd edn (Edinburgh: Blackwood, 1869)

'Songs for the Nursery', *Tait's Edinburgh Magazine* 11 (July 1844), 469

Stevenson, Robert Louis, 'The Poets and Poetry of Scotland', *The Academy*, 197 (February 1876), 138–9

Stewart, James, *The Twa Elders, and Other Poems* (Airdrie: Baird & Hamilton, 1886)

Stewart, Thomas, *Doric Rhyme, Some Hamely Lilts* (Larkhall: William Burns, 1875)

Stewart, Thomas, *Among the Miners: Being Sketches in Prose and Verse* (Larkhall: W. Burns, 1893)

Still, Peter, *The Cottar's Sunday, and Other Poems, Chiefly in the Scottish Dialect* (Aberdeen: George and Robert King, 1845)

Strang, John, *Glasgow and its Clubs* (Glasgow: John Tweed, 1864)

Strathesk, John, ed., *Hawkie: The Autobiography of a Gangrel* (Glasgow: David Robertson, 1888)

'Tam O'Shanter', *The Fonetic Jurnal*, ed. Alecsander Jon Elis (Lundun: Fred Pitman, 1848), 145–52

Tannahill, Robert, *Poems and Songs, Chiefly in the Scottish Dialect*, 4th edn (London: Longman, 1817)

Tasker, David, *Musings of Leisure Hours* (Dundee: James P. Mathew, 1865)

Tasker, David, *Readings, Recitations and Sketches* (Dundee: John Pellow, 1907)

Tatlow, Joseph, *Fifty Years of Railway Life* (London: The Railway Gazette, 1920)

Taylor, John, *Poems, Chiefly on Themes of Scottish Interest*, intro. by W. Lindsay Alexander (Edinburgh: Andrew Stevenson, 1875)

Taylor, Peter, *The Autobiography of Peter Taylor* (Paisley: Alexander Gardner, 1903)

'The Collier at Home', *Household Words* 15 (28 March 1857), 289–92

The Man o' Airlie; A Drama of the Affections. The Dramatic Sensation of London in 1863, and acted with equal success in America, where it was first produced in June, 1871, by Mr Lawrence Barrett, at Booth's Theatre, New York (Philadelphia, PA: Ledger Steam-Power Printing Office, 1871)

'The Nursery and Popular Rhymes and Tales of England and Scotland', *Tait's Edinburgh Magazine* 10 (1843), 114–22

'The Perils of Industry', *Tait's Edinburgh Magazine* (December 1854), 705–12

The Rural Echo, and Magazine of the North of Scotland Mutual Instruction Associations. Conducted by the Lentush Club (Aberdeen: Lewis Smith; Lentush: James Robertson, 1850)

Thom, William, *Rhymes and Recollections of a Handloom Weaver*, ed. W. Skinner (Paisley: Alexander Gardner, 1880)

Twain, Mark, *The Adventures of Huckleberry Finn*, ed. John Seelye and Guy Cardwell (Harmondsworth: Penguin, 2009)

Ure, Andrew, *The Philosophy of Manufactures, or, An Exposition of the Scientific, Moral and Commercial Economy of the Factory System of Great Britain*, 3rd edn, cont. by P. L. Simmonds (London: H. G. Bohn, 1861)

Veitch, John, *The Feeling for Nature in Scottish Poetry*, 2 vols (Edinburgh: Blackwood, 1887)

Walker, William, ed., *The Bards of Bon-Accord, 1375–1860* (Aberdeen: Edmond & Spark, 1887)

Watson, Thomas, *A Collection of Poems* (Edinburgh: Printed for the Author, 1835)

Watson, Thomas, *The Rhymer's Family* (Arbroath: Kennedy & Ramsay, 1851)

Watson, Walter, *Poems and Songs, Chiefly in the Scottish Dialect* (Glasgow: David Robertson, 1853)

'Weavers and Miners at Airdrie', *Chambers's Journal* 335 (1 June 1850) 339–40

Whamond, Alexander, *James Tacket: A Humorous Tale of Scottish Life* (Edinburgh: Seton and Mackenzie, 1877)

'Whistle-Binkie', *Tait's Edinburgh Magazine*, 2 (October 1832), 125

Whistle-Binkie: A Collection of Comic and Sentimental Songs (Glasgow: David Robertson, 1832)

Whistle-Binkie; or, the Piper of the Party, Being a Collection of Songs for the Social Circle, Chiefly Original, 2nd series (Glasgow: David Robertson, 1842)

Whistle-Binkie, Third Series (Glasgow: David Robertson, 1842)

Whistle-Binkie, Fourth Series, with Supplement (Glasgow: David Robertson, 1842)

Whistle-Binkie, Fifth Series (Glasgow: David Robertson, 1843)

Whitelaw, Alexander, ed., *The Book of Scottish Song* (London: Blackie and Son, 1844)

Whittier, John Greenleaf, ed., *Child-Life* (London: James Nisbet, 1874)

Wilson, George, 'On the Physical Sciences', *Edinburgh New Philosophical Journal*, 5 (1857), 64–101

Wilson, James Grant, *The Poets and Poetry of Scotland: From the Earliest to the Present Time*, 4 vols (London: Blackie & Son, n.d.)

Wilson, John et al., *Noctes Ambrosianae*, with memoirs and notes by R. Shelton Mackenzie, vol 1: 1819–1824 (New York: Redfield, 1859)

Wilson, John, *Samples of Common Sense in Verse* by A Forfarshire Farmer (Brechin: Black & Johnston, 1875)

Wingate, David, *Poems and Songs* (Edinburgh: William Blackwood, 1862)

Wordsworth, William, *The Excursion*, ed. Sally Bushell, James A. Butler and Michael C. Jaye (Ithaca, NY: Cornell University Press, 2007)

Young, John, *Poems and Lyrics* (Glasgow: George Gallie, 1868)

Younger, John, *Autobiography of John Younger, Shoemaker, St Boswell's* (Kelson: J. and J. H. Rutherford, 1881)

SECONDARY

Abel, E. L., *Confederate Sheet Music* (Jefferson, NC: McFarland, 2004)

Abrams, Lynn, *The Orphan Country: Children of Scotland's Broken Homes from 1845 to the Present Day* (Edinburgh: John Donald, 1998)

Agathocleous, Tanya and Jason R. Rudy, eds., 'Victorian Cosmopolitanisms', *Victorian Literature and Culture* 38 (2010)

Anderson, Benedict, *Imagined Communities: Reflections on the Origins and Spread of Nationalism*, rev. edn (London: Verso, 2006 (first published 1983))

Anderson, R. D., *Education and Opportunity in Victorian Scotland: Schools and Universities* (Oxford: Clarendon Press, 1983)

Anderson, R. D., *Education and the Scottish People, 1750–1918* (Oxford: Clarendon Press, 1995)

Andrew Hobbs, *Reading the Local Paper: Social and Cultural Functions of the Press in Preston, Lancashire, 1855–1900*. Unpublished PhD thesis, University of Central Lancashire, 2010

Angeletti, Gioia, *Eccentric Scotland: Three Victorian Poets* (Bologna: CLUEB (Cooperativa Libraria Universitaria Editrice Bologna), 2004)

Armstrong, Isobel, *Victorian Poetry: Poetry, Poetics, Politics* (Oxford: Blackwell, 1999)

Atkinson, David and Steve Roud, eds., *Street Ballads in Nineteenth-Century Britain, Ireland and North America: The Interface Between Print and Oral Traditions* (Farnham: Ashgate, 2014)

Austin, Linda M., *Nostalgia in Transition, 1780–1917* (Charlottesville, VA: University of Virginia Press, 2007)

Bambrick, Gord, 'The Real McGonagall', 'McGonagall Online', http://www.mcgonagall-online.org.uk/articles/the-real-mcgonagall (consulted 14 September 2016)

Bambrick, Gord, 'The Heroic Warrior: Sir William Topaz McGonagall, Poet and Tragedian, Knight of the White Elephant, Burmah' (Masters thesis, University of Guelph, 1992) archived online at http://www.oocities.org/williamtopazmcgonagall/thesis.htm (Consulted 14 September 2018)

Barrell, John, '*Rus in urbe*', in Nigel Leask and Philip Connell, eds., *Romanticism and Popular Culture in Britain and Ireland* (Cambridge: Cambridge University Press, 2009), pp.109–27

Bennett, Paula, 'Not Just Filler and Not Just Sentimental: Women's Poetry in American Victorian Periodicals, 1860–1900', in Kenneth M. Price and Susan Belasco Smith, eds., *Periodical Literature in Nineteenth-Century America* (Charlottesville, VA: University Press of Virginia, 1995), pp.202–19

Benson, John, *British Coalminers in the Nineteenth Century* (Aldershot: Gregg, 1993, first published 1980)

Berridge, Virginia, 'Popular Sunday Papers and Mid-Victorian Society', in George Boyce, James Curran and Pauline Wingate, eds., *Newspaper History, from the Seventeenth Century to the Present Day* (London: Constable, 1978), pp.247–64

Biagini, Eugenio F., *Liberty, Retrenchment and Reform: Popular Liberalism in the Age of Gladstone, 1860–1880* (Cambridge: Cambridge University Press, 1992)

Black, Aileen, *Gilfillan of Dundee 1813–1878: Interpreting Religion and Culture in Victorian Scotland* (Dundee: Dundee University Press, 2006)

Blair, Kirstie, '"He Sings Alone": Hybrid Forms and the Victorian Working-Class Poet', *Victorian Literature and Culture* 37 (2009), 523–41

Blair, Kirstie, ed., *The Poets of the People's Journal: Newspaper Poetry in Victorian Scotland* (Glasgow: ASLS, 2016)

Blair, Kirstie, 'The Newspaper Press and the Victorian Working-Class Poet', in John Goodridge and Bridget Keegan, eds., *A History of British Working-Class Literature* (Cambridge: Cambridge University Press, 2017), pp.264–80

Blair, Kirstie, '"Let the Nightingales Alone": Correspondence Columns, the Scottish Press, and the Making of the Working-Class Poet', *Victorian Periodicals Review* 47 (2014), 188–207

Blair, Kirstie, '"A Very Poetical Town": Newspaper Poetry and the Working-Class Poet in Victorian Dundee', *Victorian Poetry* 54 (2014), 89–109

Blair, Kirstie, '"The Drunkard's Raggit Wean": Broadside Culture and the Politics of Temperance Verse', *Cahiers Victoriens et Édouardiens* 84 (Autumn 2016), 20 paras

Blair, Kirstie and Mina Gorji, eds., *Class and the Canon: Constructing Labouring-Class Poetry and Poetics, 1750–1900* (Houndmills: Palgrave Macmillan, 2013)

Blair, Kirstie, 'Dialect, Region, Class, Work', in Linda Hughes, ed., *The Cambridge Companion to Victorian Women's Poetry* (Cambridge: Cambridge University Press, 2019), pp.129–44

Bloom, Paul, ed., *Language Acquisition: Core Readings* (New York: Harvester Wheatsheaf, 1993)

Bold, Valentina, *James Hogg: A Bard of Nature's Making* (Bern: Peter Lang, 2007)

Boos, Florence, 'The "Queen" of the "Far-Famed Penny Post": The "Factory Girl Poet" and Her Audience', *Women's Writing* 10 (2003): 503–26

Boos, Florence, ed., *Working-Class Women Poets in Victorian Britain: An Anthology* (Peterborough, ON: Broadview, 2008)

Boos, Florence, 'Janet Hamilton: Working-Class Memoirist and Commentator', in Glenda Norquay, ed., *The Edinburgh Companion to Scottish Women's Writing* (Edinburgh: Edinburgh University Press, 2012), pp.63–74

Boos, Florence, '"Nurs'd up among the scenes I have describ'd": Poetry of Working-Class Victorian Women', in Christine Krueger, ed., *The Functions of Victorian Culture at the Present Time* (Athens, OH: Ohio University Press, 2002), pp.137–56

Bourdieu, Pierre, *The Field of Cultural Production*, ed. and intro by Randal Johnson (Cambridge: Polity Press, 1993)

Boyce, George, James Curran and Pauline Wingate, eds., *Newspaper History, from the Seventeenth Century to the Present Day* (London: Constable, 1978)

Bradley, Simon, *The Railways: Nation, Network and People* (London: Profile, 2015)

Brake, Laurel, Bill Bell and David Finkelstein, eds., *Nineteenth-Century Media and the Construction of Identities* (Houndmills: Palgrave, 2000)

Brooking, Tom and Jennie Coleman, eds., *The Heather and the Fern: Scottish Migration and New Zealand Settlement* (Dunedin: University of Otago Press, 2003)

Brown, Dauvit, R. J. Finlay and Michael Lynch, eds., *Image and Identity: The Making and Re-Making of Scotland Through the Ages* (Edinburgh: John Donald, 1998)

Buell, Lawrence, *The Environmental Imagination: Thoreau, Nature Writing, and the Formation of American Culture* (Cambridge, MA: Harvard University Press, 1995)

Buell, Lawrence, *The Future of Environmental Criticism: Environmental Crisis and Literary Imagination* (Oxford: Blackwell, 2005)

Bueltmann, Tanja, *Clubbing Together: Ethnicity, Civility and Formal Sociability in the Scottish Diaspora to 1930* (Liverpool: Liverpool University Press, 2014)

Cage, R. A., ed., *The Working Class in Glasgow, 1750–1914* (London: Croom Helm, 1987)

Cameron, Alisdair and Adrienne Scullion, eds., *Scottish Popular Theatre and Entertainment* (Glasgow: Glasgow University Library Studies, 1996)

Campbell, Alan B., *The Lanarkshire Miners: A Social History of Their Trade Unions 1775–1874* (Edinburgh: John Donald, 2003 (first published 1979))

Campbell, Matthew, *Rhythm and Will in Victorian Poetry* (Cambridge: Cambridge University Press, 1999)

Carruthers, Gerard, *Scottish Literature* (Edinburgh: Edinburgh University Press, 2009)

Carruthers, Gerard, David Goldie and Alastair Renfrew, eds., *Scotland and the 19th Century World* (Amsterdam: Brill, 2012)

Cattell, Ray, *Children's Language: Consensus and Controversy*, rev. edn (New York: Continuum, 2007)

Cavitch, Max, 'Slavery and its Metrics', in Kerri Larson, ed., *The Cambridge Companion to Nineteenth-Century American Poetry* (Cambridge: Cambridge University Press, 2011), pp.94–112

Channell, David F., *The Vital Machine: A Study of Technology and Organic Life* (Oxford: Oxford University Press, 1991)

Chapman, Alison, *Networking the Nation: British and American Women's Poetry and Italy, 1840–1870* (Oxford: Oxford University Press, 2015)

Checkland, Olive and Sydney Checkland, *Industry and Ethos: Scotland 1832–1914*, 2nd edn (Edinburgh: Edinburgh University Press, 1989)

Clark, Anna, *The Struggle for the Breeches: Gender and the Making of the British Working Class* (Berkeley, CA: University of California Press, 1995)

Cohen, Edward H. and Anne R. Fertig, 'Marion Bernstein and the *Glasgow Weekly Mail* in the 1870s', *Victorian Periodicals Review* 49 (2016), 9–27

Cohen, Michael C., *The Social Lives of Poems in Nineteenth-Century America* (Philadelphia, PA: University of Pennsylvania Press, 2015)

Colclough, Stephen, *Consuming Texts: Readers and Reading Communities, 1695–1870* (Houndsmills: Palgrave, 2007)

Collison, Robert, *The Story of Street Literature* (London: J. M. Dent, 1973)

Coleman, Terry, *The Railway Navvies* (London: Pimlico, 2000, first published 1965)

Cowan, Edward J., 'From the Southern Uplands to Southern Ontario: Nineteenth-Century Emigration from the Scottish Borders', in T. M. Devine, ed., *Scottish Emigration and Scottish Society* (Edinburgh: John Donald, 1992), pp.61–83

Cowan, Edward J., 'The Myth of Scotch Canada', in Marjory Harper and Michael E. Vance, eds., *Myth, Migration and the Making of Memory: Scotia and Nova Scotia c. 1700–1990* (Edinburgh: John Donald, 1999), pp.49–72

Cowan, R. M. W., *The Newspaper in Scotland: A Study of its First Expansion, 1815–1860* (Glasgow: George Outram, 1946)

Crawford, Rachel, *Poetry, Enclosure, and the Vernacular Landscape* (Cambridge: Cambridge University Press, 2002)

Crisafulli, Lilla Maria and Cecilia Pietropoli, eds., *Romantic Women Poets: Genre and Gender* (Amsterdam: Rodopi, 2007)

Cronin, Richard, *Romantic Victorians: English Literature 1824–1840* (Houndsmills: Palgrave, 2002)

Daly, Nicholas, 'Blood on the Tracks: Sensation Drama, the Railway, and the Dark Face of Modernity', *Victorian Studies* 42 (1998), 47–76

Dames, Nicholas, *Amnesiac Selves: Nostalgia, Forgetting and British Fiction, 1810–1870* (Oxford: Oxford University Press, 2001)

Danahay, Martin A., 'The Aesthetics of Coal: Representing Soot, Dust and Smoke in Nineteenth-Century Britain', in William B. Thesing, ed., *Caverns of Night: Coal Mines in Art, Literature and Film* (Columbia, SC: University of South Carolina Press, 2000), pp.3–18

Day, Graham, *Community and Everyday Life* (London: Routledge, 2006)

De Certeau, Michel, 'Reading as Poaching', in Shafquat Towheed, Rosalind Crone and Katie Halsey, eds., *The History of Reading* (New York: Routledge, 2011), pp.130–9

Devine, T. M., ed., *Scottish Emigration and Scottish Society* (Edinburgh: John Donald, 1992)

Devine, T. M., *The Scottish Nation, 1700–2000* (London: Allen Lane, 1999)

Donaldson, William, *Popular Literature in Victorian Scotland: Language, Fiction and the Press* (Aberdeen: Aberdeen University Press, 1986)

Dunnigan, Sarah and Shu-Fang Lai, eds., *The Land of Storybooks: Scottish Children's Literature in the Nineteenth Century* (Glasgow: ASLS, forthcoming)

Fahey, David, *Temperance and Racism: John Bull, Johnny Reb, and the Good Templars* (Lexington, KY: University Press of Kentucky, 1996)

Fairer, David, ' "Where Fuming Trees Refresh the Thirsty Air": The World of Eco-Georgic', *Studies in Eighteenth-Century Culture* 40 (2011), 201–218

Featherstone, Simon, 'Artemus Ward and the Egyptian Hall', in Martin Hewitt, ed., *Platform Pulpit Rhetoric* (Trinity and All Saints, Leeds: Leeds Working Papers in Victorian Studies, 2000), pp.37–49

Fernald, Anne, 'Human Maternal Vocalizations to Infants as Biologically Relevant Signals: An Evolutionary Perspective', in Paul Bloom, ed., *Language Acquisition: Core Readings* (New York: Harvester Wheatsheaf, 1993), pp.51–94

Findlay, Bill, 'Scots Language and Popular Entertainment in Victorian Scotland: The Case of James Houston', in Alisdair Cameron and Adrienne Scullion, eds., *Scottish Popular Theatre and Entertainment* (Glasgow: Glasgow University Library Studies, 1996), pp.15–38

Findlay, William, 'Reclaiming Local Literature: William Thom and Janet Hamilton', in Douglas Gifford, ed., *The History of Scottish Literature, vol 3: Nineteenth Century* (Aberdeen: Aberdeen University Press, 1988), pp.353–73

Finkelstein, David, *Movable Types: Roving Creative Printers of the Victorian World* (Oxford: Oxford University Press, 2018)

Fraser, W. Hamish and R. J. Morris, *People and Society in Scotland*, vol II (1830–1914) (Edinburgh: Economic & Social History Society of Scotland, 1990)

Fry, Michael, *A New Race of Men: Scotland 1815–1914* (Edinburgh: Birlinn, 2013)

Fulford, Tim, *Landscape, Liberty and Authority: Poetry, Criticism and Politics from Thomson to Wordsworth* (Cambridge: Cambridge University Press, 1996)

Furlong, Claire, 'Health Advice in Popular Periodicals: *Reynolds's Miscellany*, the *Family Herald*, and Their Correspondents', *Victorian Periodicals Review* 49 (2016), 28–48

Gairn, Louisa, *Ecology and Modern Scottish Literature* (Edinburgh: Edinburgh University Press, 2008)

Gallagher, Catherine, *The Body Economic: Life, Death and Sensation in the Victorian Novel* (Princeton, NJ: Princeton University Press, 2006)

Garrard, Greg, *Ecocriticism*, 2nd edn (London: Routledge, 2012)

Gibson, Mary Ellis, *Indian Angles: English Verse in Colonial India from Jones to Tagore* (Athens, OH: Ohio University Press, 2011)

Gifford, Douglas, ed., *The History of Scottish Literature, vol 3: Nineteenth Century* (Aberdeen: Aberdeen University Press, 1988)

Gifford, Douglas, 'Scottish Literature in the Victorian and Edwardian Era', in Douglas Gifford, Sarah Dunnigan and Alan MacGillivray, *Scottish Literature in English and Scots* (Edinburgh: Edinburgh University Press, 2002), pp.321–32

Gifford, Douglas and Alan Riach, *Scotlands: Poets and the Nation* (Manchester: Carcanet, 2004)

Gifford, Douglas and Hazel Hynd, 'James Young Geddes, John Davidson and Scottish Poetry', in Douglas Gifford, Sarah Dunnigan and Alan MacGillivray, *Scottish Literature in English and Scots* (Edinburgh: Edinburgh University Press, 2002), pp.349–78

Gifford, Douglas, Sarah Dunnigan and Alan MacGillivray, eds., *Scottish Literature in English and Scots* (Edinburgh: Edinburgh University Press, 2002)

Glen, Duncan, *The Poetry of the Scots: An Introduction and Bibliographical Guide to Poetry in Gaelic, Scots, Latin and English* (Edinburgh: Edinburgh University Press, 1991)

Gold, Barri J., *Thermopoetics: Energy in Victorian Literature and Science* (Cambridge, MA: MIT Press, 2010)

Goodridge, John, *Rural Life in Eighteenth-Century English Poetry* (Cambridge: Cambridge University Press, 1995)

Goodridge, John and Bridget Keegan, eds., *A History of British Working-Class Literature* (Cambridge: Cambridge University Press, 2017)

Goodridge, John and Bridget Keegan, 'Modes and Methods in Three Nineteenth-Century Mineworker Poets', *Philological Quarterly* 92 (2013), 225–50

Gray, F. E., *Christian and Lyric Tradition in Victorian Women's Poetry* (London: Routledge, 2010)

Gray, F. E., 'Journalism and Poetry in the Nineteenth Century', *Journalism Studies* 18 (2017), 807–25

Green, Barbara, 'Complaints of Everyday Life: Feminist Periodical Culture and Correspondence Columns in *The Woman Worker*, *Women Folk* and *The Freewoman*', *Modernism/Modernity* 19 (2012), 461–85

Griffin, Emma, *Liberty's Dawn: A People's History of the Industrial Revolution* (New Haven, CT: Yale University Press, 2013)

Hall, Dewey W., *Romantic Naturalists, Early Environmentalists: An Ecocritical Study, 1789–1912* (Farnham: Ashgate, 2014)

Hall, Jason David, *Nineteenth-Century Verse and Technology: Machines of Meter* (London: Palgrave, 2017)

Hall, Stuart, 'Notes on Deconstructing "the Popular"', in Raphael Samuel, ed., *People's History and Socialist Theory* (London: Routledge, 1981), pp.227–41

Handley, J. E., *The Navvy in Scotland* (Cork: Cork University Press, 1970)

Harper, Marjory and Michael E. Vance, eds., *Myth, Migration and the Making of Memory: Scotia and Nova Scotia c. 1700–1990* (Edinburgh: John Donald, 1999)

Harper, Marjory, *Adventurers and Exiles: The Great Scottish Exodus* (London: Profile, 2003)

Harris, Kirsten, *Walt Whitman and British Socialism: The Love of Comrades* (New York: Routledge, 2016)

Harvie, Christopher, 'John Buchan and *The Northern Muse*: The Politics of an Anthology', in Barbara Korte, Ralf Schneider and Stefanie Lethbridge, eds., *Anthologies of British Poetry: Critical Perspectives from Literary and Cultural Studies* (Amsterdam: Rodopi, 2000), 211–22

Helsinger, Elizabeth, *Rural Scenes and National Representation: Britain, 1815–1850* (Princeton, NJ: Princeton University Press, 1997)

Hewison, Robert, *The Heritage Industry: Britain in a Climate of Decline* (London: Methuen, 1987)

Hewitt, Martin, ed., *Platform Pulpit Rhetoric* (Trinity and All Saints, Leeds: Leeds Working Papers in Victorian Studies, 2000)

Hewitt, Martin, *The Dawn of the Cheap Press in Victorian Britain: The End of the 'Taxes on Knowledge', 1849–1869* (London: Bloomsbury, 2014)

Hobbs, Andrew, *A Fleet Street in Every Town: The Provincial Press in England, 1855–1900* (Open Books Publishing, 2018)

Hobbs, Andrew. 'Five Million Poems, or the Local Press as Poetry Publisher, 1800-1900', *Victorian Periodicals Review* 45 (2012), 488–92

Hobbs, Andrew, *Reading the Local Paper: Social and Cultural Functions of the Press in Preston, Lancashire, 1855-1900*. PhD thesis, University of Central Lancashire, 2010

Hobbs, Andrew, and Clare Januszewski, 'How Local Papers Came to Dominate Victorian Poetry Publishing', *Victorian Poetry* 52 (2014), 65–87

Holman, A. C. and R. B. Kristofferson, eds., *More of a Man: Diaries of a Scottish Craftsman in Mid Nineteenth-Century North America* (Toronto: University of Toronto Press, 2013)

Hopkins, Eric, *Childhood Transformed: Working-Class Children in Nineteenth-Century England* (Manchester: Manchester University Press, 1994)

Houston, Natalie, 'Newspaper Poems: Material Texts in the Public Sphere', *Victorian Studies* 50 (2008), 233–42

Hughes. Linda K., 'Periodical Poetry, Editorial Policy, and W. E. Henley's *Scots* and *National Observer*', *Victorian Periodicals Review* 49 (2016), 202–27

Hughes. Linda K., 'Poetry', in Andrew King, Alexis Easley and John Morton, eds., *The Routledge Handbook to Nineteenth-Century British Periodicals and Newspapers* (London: Routledge, 2016), pp.124–37

Humphries, Jane, *Childhood and Child Labour in the British Industrial Revolution* (Cambridge: Cambridge University Press, 2010)

Hutchison, I. G. C., 'Glasgow Working-Class Politics', in R. A. Cage, ed. *The Working Class in Glasgow, 1750–1914* (London: Croom Helm, 1987)

Jamison, Anne, *Poetics En Passant: Redefining the Relationship Between Victorian and Modern Poetry* (Houndmills: Palgrave, 2009)

Jarman, Andrea Loux, 'Urban Commons: From Customary Use to Community Right on Scotland's Bleaching Greens', in Andrew Lewis, Paul Brand and Paul Mitchell, eds., *Law in the City: Proceedings of the Seventeenth British Legal History Conference* (Dublin: Four Courts, 2007), pp.319–45

Jauss, Hans Robert, 'Literary History as a Challenge to Literary Theory', trans. Elizabeth Benzinger, *New Literary History* 2.1 (1970), 7–37

Jordan, Thomas E., *Victorian Childhood: Themes and Variations* (New York: SUNY, 1987)

Keegan, Bridget, *British Labouring-Class Nature Poetry, 1730–1837* (Houndmills: Palgrave, 2008)

Keegan, Bridget, '"Incessant toil and hands innumerable": Mining and Poetry in the Northeast of England', *Victoriographies* 1 (2011), 177–201

Kerrigan, Catherine, ed., *An Anthology of Scottish Women Poets* (Edinburgh: Edinburgh University Press, 1991)

Ketabgian, Tamara, *The Lives of Machines: The Industrial Imaginary in Victorian Literature and Culture* (Ann Arbor, MI: University of Michigan Press, 2011)

King, Andrew, *The London Journal, 1845–83: Periodicals, Production and Gender* (Aldershot: Ashgate, 2004)

King, Andrew, Alexis Easley and John Morton, eds., *The Routledge Handbook to Nineteenth-Century British Periodicals and Newspapers* (London: Routledge, 2016)

Kingsford, P. W., *Victorian Railwaymen: The Emergence and Growth of Railway Labour, 1840–1870* (Routledge: London, 2006, first published 1970)

Klaus, H. Gustav, *Factory Girl: Ellen Johnston and Working-Class Poetry in Victorian Scotland* (Peter Lang: Frankfurt, 1998)

Klaus, H. Gustav, *The Literature of Labour: Two Hundred Years of Working-Class Writing* (Brighton: Harvester, 1985)

Klingender, Francis, *Art and the Industrial Revolution*, ed. and revised by Arthur Elton (London: Paladin, 1972, first published 1947)

Knox, James, *Airdrie Bards, Past and Present* (Airdrie: Baird and Hamilton, 1930)

Knox, W. W., *Industrial Nation: Work, Culture and Society in Scotland, 1800-Present* (Edinburgh: Edinburgh University Press, 1999)

Korte, Ralf Schneider and Stefanie Lethbridge, eds., *Anthologies of British Poetry: Critical Perspectives from Literary and Cultural Studies* (Amsterdam: Rodopi, 2000)

Kossick, Kaye, ' "And aft Thy Dear Doric aside I Hae Flung, to Busk oot My Sang wi' the Prood Southron Tongue": The Antiphonal Muse in Janet Hamilton's Poetics', in John Goodridge and Bridget Keegan, eds., *A History of British Working-Class Literature* (Cambridge: Cambridge University Press, 2017), pp.208–25

Krueger, Christine, ed., *The Functions of Victorian Culture at the Present Time* (Athens, OH: Ohio University Press, 2002)

Labov, William, *Principles of Linguistic Change. Volume 2: Social Factors* (Oxford: Blackwell, 2001)

Lambert, Robert A., *Contested Mountains: Nature, Development and Environment in the Cairngorms Region of Scotland, 1880–1980* (Cambridge: White Horse Press, 2001)

Larson, Kerri, ed., *The Cambridge Companion to Nineteenth-Century American Poetry* (Cambridge: Cambridge University Press, 2011)

Leask, Nigel, *Robert Burns and Pastoral: Poetry and Improvement in Late Eighteenth-Century Scotland* (Oxford: Oxford University Press, 2010)

Leask, Nigel and Philip Connell, eds., *Romanticism and Popular Culture in Britain and Ireland* (Cambridge: Cambridge University Press, 2009)

Ledbetter, Kathryn, *British Victorian Women's Periodicals: Beauty, Civilization and Poetry* (Houndmills: Palgrave, 2009)

Lefebvre, Henri, *Rhythmanalysis: Space, Time and Everyday Life*, trans. Stuart Edlend and Gerald Moore (London: Continuum, 2004)

Leonard, Tom, ed., *Radical Renfrew* (Edinburgh: Polygon, 1990)

Lewis, Andrew, Paul Brand and Paul Mitchell, eds., *Law in the City: Proceedings of the Seventeenth British Legal History Conference* (Dublin: Four Courts, 2007)

Levine, Caroline, 'From Nation to Network', *Victorian Studies* 55 (2013), 647–66

Lindsay, Maurice, ed., *Modern Scottish Poetry: An Anthology of the Scottish Renaissance*, 3rd edn (Manchester: Carcanet, 1976)

Lownie, Ralph, ed., *Auld Reekie: An Edinburgh Anthology* (Edinburgh: Mainstream, 2004)

McCaffrey, John, *Scotland in the Nineteenth Century* (Houndmills: Macmillan, 1998)

McClure, J. Derrick, *Language, Poetry and Nationhood: Scots As a Poetic Language from 1878 to the Present* (East Linton: Tuckwell Press, 2000)

McCulloch, Margery Palmer, ed., *Modernism and Nationalism: Literature and Society in Scotland, 1918–1939* (Glasgow: ASLS, 2004)

McDermid, Jane, *The Schooling of Working-Class Girls in Victorian Scotland: Gender, Education and Identity* (New York: Routledge, 2005)

MacDiarmid, Hugh, *Selected Essays*, ed. Duncan Glen (Berkeley, CA: University of California Press, 1969)

MacDiarmid, Hugh, *Scottish Eccentrics*, ed. Alan Riach (Manchester: Carcanet, 1993)

MacDiarmid, Hugh, *Contemporary Scottish Studies*, ed. Alan Riach (Manchester: Carcanet, 2005)

Macdonald, Catriona M. M., 'The Vanduaria of Ptolemy: Place and the Past', in Dauvit Brown, R. J. Finlay and Michael Lynch, eds., *Image and Identity: The Making and Re-Making of Scotland Through the Ages* (Edinburgh: John Donald, 1998), pp.177–94

Macdonald, Graeme, 'Green Links: Ecosocialism and Contemporary Scottish Writing', in John Rignall and H. Gustav Klaus, eds., *Ecology and the Literature of the British Left: The Red and the Green* (Farnham: Ashgate, 2012), pp.221–35

MacDonell, Margaret, *The Emigrant Experience: Songs of Highland Emigrants in North America* (Toronto: University of Toronto, 1982)

MacDuffie, Allen, *Victorian Literature, Energy, and the Ecological Imagination* (Cambridge: Cambridge University Press, 2014)

McGill, Meredith, *American Literature and the Culture of Reprinting, 1834–1853* (Philadephia, PA: University of Pennsylvania Press, 2003)

Mackenzie, Scott R., *Be it Ever So Humble: Poverty, Fiction, and the Invention of the Middle-Class Home* (Charlottesville, VA: University of Virginia Press, 2013)

Maidment, Brian, *The Poorhouse Fugitives: Self-Taught Poets and Poetry in Victorian Britain* (Manchester: Carcanet, 1987)

Maloney, Paul, *Scotland and the Music Hall, 1850–1914* (Manchester: Manchester University Press, 2003)

Martin, Meredith, *The Rise and Fall of Meter: Poetry and English National Culture, 1860–1930* (Princeton, NJ: Princeton University Press, 2012)

Meek, Donald E., *Tuath Is Tighearna/Tenants and Landlords: An Anthology of Gaelic Poetry of Social and Political Protest from the Clearances to the Land Agitation (1800–1890)* (Edinburgh: Scottish Gaelic Texts Society, 1995)

Miller, Frank, ed., *The Poets of Dumfriesshire* (Glasgow: James Maclehose, 1910)

Miskell, Louise, Christopher A. Whatley and Bob Harris, eds., *Victorian Dundee: Images and Realities* (East Linton: Tuckwell Press, 2000)

Moine, Fabienne, *Women Poets in the Victorian Era: Cultural Practices and Nature Poetry* (London: Routledge, 2015)

Morgan, Edwin, 'Scottish Poetry in the Nineteenth Century', in Douglas Gifford, ed., *The History of Scottish Literature, vol 3: Nineteenth Century* (Aberdeen: Aberdeen University Press, 1988), pp.337–52

Morton, Graeme, *Unionist Nationalism: Governing Urban Scotland, 1830–1860* (East Linton: Tuckwell Press, 1999)

Nash, Andrew, *Kailyard and Literature* (Amsterdam: Rodopi, 2007)

Norquay, Glenda, ed., *The Edinburgh Companion to Scottish Women's Writing* (Edinburgh: Edinburgh University Press, 2012)

Nye, David E., *American Technological Sublime* (Cambridge, MA: MIT Press, 1994)

O'Grady, William, *How Children Learn Language* (Cambridge: Cambridge University Press, 2005)

Olson, Ian A., 'Bothy Ballads and Song', in John Beech, Owen Hand, Fiona MacDonald, Mark A. Mulhern and Jeremy Weston, eds., *Oral Literature and Performance Culture*; vol X of *Scottish Life and Society: A Compendium of Scottish Ethnology*, 14 vols (Edinburgh: John Donald, 2007), pp.322–59, 340n

Patton, Cynthia Ellen, ' "Not a limitless possession": Health Advice and Readers' Agency in *The Girls' Own Paper*, 1880–1890', *Victorian Periodicals Review* 45 (2012), 111–33

Plotz, John, *Portable Property: Victorian Culture on the Move* (Princeton, NJ: Princeton University Press, 2008)

Pollard, Michael, *The Hardest Work Under Heaven: The Life and Death of the British Coal Miner* (London: Hutchinson, 1984)

Price, Kenneth M. and Susan Belasco Smith, eds., *Periodical Literature in Nineteenth-Century America* (Charlottesville, VA: University Press of Virginia, 1995)

Rancière, Jacques, *Proletarian Nights: The Workers' Dream in Nineteenth-Century France*, trans. John Drury, intro. Donald Reid (London: Verso, 2012 (first published 1989))

Riach, Allan, 'Heather and Fern: The Burns Effect in New Zealand Verse', in Tom Brooking and Jennie Coleman, eds., *The Heather and the Fern: Scottish Migration and New Zealand Settlement* (Dunedin: University of Otago Press, 2003), pp.153–71

Rignall, John and H. Gustav Klaus, eds., *Ecology and the Literature of the British Left: The Red and the Green* (Farnham: Ashgate, 2012)

Rigney, Anne, *The Afterlives of Walter Scott: Memory on the Move* (Oxford: Oxford University Press, 2012)

Rooney, Paul Raphael and Anna Gasperini, eds., *Media and Print Culture Consumption in Nineteenth-Century Britain: The Victorian Reading Experience* (Basingstoke: Palgrave Macmillan, 2016)

Rose, Jonathan, *The Intellectual Life of the British Working Classes*, 2nd edn (New Haven, CT: Yale University Press, 2010)

Rosen, Judith, 'Class and Poetic Communities: The Works of Ellen Johnston, the "Factory Girl" ', *Victorian Poetry* 39 (2001), 207–227

Royle, Trevor, *The Mainstream Companion to Scottish Literature* (London: Random House, 2012)

Rubery, Matthew, *The Novelty of Newspapers: Victorian Fiction After the Invention of the News* (Oxford: Oxford University Press, 2009)

Rudy, Jason R., 'Floating Worlds: Émigré Poetry and British Culture', *ELH* 81 (2014), 325–50

Rudy, Jason R., *Imagined Homelands: British Poetry in the Colonies* (Baltimore, MD: Johns Hopkins University Press, 2018)

Ruwe, Donelle, *British Children's Poetry in the Romantic Era* (Houndmills: Palgrave, 2014)

Samuel, Raphael, ed., *People's History and Socialist Theory* (London: Routledge, 1981)

Sanders, Michael, *The Poetry of Chartism* (Cambridge: Cambridge University Press, 2009)

Sanders, Michael, ' "God is our guide! Our cause is just!": The National Chartist Hymn Book and Chartist Hymnody', *Victorian Studies* 54 (2012), 679–705

Sanders, Michael, 'Courtly Lays or Democratic Songs? The Politics of Poetic Citation in Chartist Literary Criticism', in Kirstie Blair and Mina Gorji, eds., *Class and the Canon: Constructing Labouring-Class Poetry and Poetics, 1750–1900* (Houndmills: Palgrave Macmillan, 2013), pp.156–73

Santesso, Aaron, *A Careful Longing: The Poetics and Problems of Nostalgia* (Newark, DE: University of Delaware Press, 2006)

Schivelbusch, Wolfgang, *The Railway Journey: The Industrialization of Time and Space in the 19th Century* (Berg: Hamburg, 1986, first published 1977)

Shattock, Joanne, 'Margaret Oliphant and the Blackwood "Brand" ', in Joanne Shattock, ed. *Journalism and the Periodical Press in Nineteenth-Century Britain* (Cambridge: Cambridge University Press, 2017), pp.341–52

Shattock, Joanne, ed., *Journalism and the Periodical Press in Nineteenth-Century Britain* (Cambridge: Cambridge University Press, 2017)

Shaw, Michael, 'Transculturation and Historicisation: New Directions for the Study of Scottish Literature c.1840-1914', *Literature Compass* 13 (2016), 501–10

Shaw, Michael, *The Fin-de-Siècle Scottish Revival: Romance, Decadence and Celtic Identity* (Edinburgh: Edinburgh University Press, 2020)

Smith, Jennifer, Mercedes Durham and Liane Fortune, ' "Man, my trousers is fa'in doon!": Community, Caregiver and Child in the Acquisition of Variation in a Scottish Dialect', *Language Variation and Change* 19 (2007), 63–99

Stafford, Fiona, *Local Attachments: The Province of Poetry* (Oxford: Oxford University Press, 2010)

Stephenson, Tom, *Forbidden Land: The Struggle for Access to Moorland and Mountain* (Manchester: Manchester University Press, 1989)

Styles, Morag, *From the Garden to the Street: Three Hundred Years of Poetry for Children* (London: Cassell, 1998)

Tait, Gordon, *Coal, Correspondence and Nineteenth-Century Poetry: Joseph Skipsey and the Problems of Social Class*. PhD thesis, University of Hull, 2018

Taylor, Harvey, *A Claim on the Countryside: A History of the British Outdoor Movement* (Edinburgh: Keele University Press, 1997)

Tennyson, G. B., ed., *A Carlyle Reader* (Cambridge: Cambridge University Press, 1984)

Thesing, William B., ed., *Caverns of Night: Coal Mines in Art, Literature and Film* (Columbia, SC: University of South Carolina Press, 2000)

Thomson, Derick, *An Introduction to Gaelic Poetry* (London: Gollancz, 1977)

Towheed, Shafquat, Rosalind Crone and Katie Halsey, eds., *The History of Reading* (New York: Routledge, 2011)

Trumpener, Katie, *Bardic Nationalism: The Romantic Novel and the British Empire* (Princeton, NJ: Princeton University Press, 1997)

Vicinus, Martha, *The Industrial Muse: A Study of Nineteenth-Century British Working-Class Literature* (London: Croom Helm, 1974)

Vicinus, Martha, *Broadsides of the Industrial North* (Newcastle upon Tyne: Frank Graham, 1975)

Vincent, David, *Bread, Knowledge and Freedom: A Study of Nineteenth-Century Working-Class Autobiography* (London: Methuen, 1981)

Vincent, David, *Literacy and Popular Culture: England 1750–1914* (Cambridge: Cambridge University Press, 1989), p.214

Wagner, Tamara S., *Longing: Narratives of Nostalgia in the British Novel, 1740–1890* (Lewisburg, PA: Bucknell University Press, 2004)

Warren, Lynn, ' "Women in Conference": Reading the Correspondence Columns in *Woman* 1890–1910', in Laurel Brake, Bill Bell and David Finkelstein, eds., *Nineteenth-Century Media and the Construction of Identities* (Houndmills: Palgrave, 2000), pp.122–34

Watson, Norman, *Poet McGonagall* (Edinburgh: Birlinn, 2010)

Watson, Roderick, *The Literature of Scotland: The Middle Ages to the Nineteenth Century*, 2nd edn (Houndmills: Palgrave, 2007)

Watt, Julia Muir, *Dumfries and Galloway: A Literary Guide* (Dumfries: Dumfries and Galloway Libraries, Information and Archives, 2000)

Webb, Timothy, 'Listing the Busy Sounds: Anna Seward, Mary Robinson and the Poetic Challenge of the City', in Lilla Maria Crisafulli and Cecilia Pietropoli, eds., *Romantic Women Poets: Genre and Gender* (Amsterdam: Rodopi, 2007), pp.79–112

Weinstein, Mark A. *W. E. Aytoun and the Spasmodic Controversy* (New Haven, CT: Yale University Press, 1968)

Weiss, Lauren, 'The Manuscript Magazines of the Wellpark Free Church Young Men's Literary Society, Glasgow: A Case Study', in Paul Raphael Rooney and Anna Gasperini, eds., *Media and Print Culture Consumption in Nineteenth-Century Britain: The Victorian Reading Experience* (Basingstoke: Palgrave Macmillan, 2016), pp.53–73

Weiss, Lauren, *The Literary Clubs and Societies of Glasgow in the Long Nineteenth Century.* Unpublished PhD thesis, University of Stirling, 2017

Whatley, Christopher A., *The Industrial Revolution in Scotland* (Cambridge: Cambridge University Press, 1997)

Whatley, Christopher A.,'Altering images of the industrial city: the case of James Myles, the "Factory Boy" and mid-Victorian Dundee', in Louise Miskell, Christopher A. Whatley and Bob Harris, eds., *Victorian Dundee: Images and Realities* (East Linton: Tuckwell Press, 2000), pp.70–95

Wightman, Andy, *Who Owns Scotland* (Edinburgh: Canongate, 1996)

Wightman, Andy, *The Poor Had No Lawyers: Who Owns Scotland (and How They Got It)* (Edinburgh: Birlinn, 2011)

Williams, Rosalind, *Notes on the Underground: An Essay on Technology, Society and the Imagination* (Cambridge, MA: MIT Press, 1990)

Wingate, Guy A. S., *A Century of Scottish Coalmining Ancestry 1778–1878: The History of the Wingate Family* (Stockton-upon-Tees, Cleveland: Petunia Publishing Company, 1994)

Wyndham-Lewis, D. B. and Charles Lee, eds., *The Stuffed Owl: An Anthology of Bad Verse* (London: J. M. Dent, 1930)

Index

.